I0021362

Serverless Architectures with Kubernetes

Create production-ready Kubernetes clusters and run serverless applications on them

Onur Yılmaz

Sathsara Sarathchandra

Serverless Architectures with Kubernetes

Copyright © 2019 Packt Publishing

All rights reserved. No part of this book may be reproduced, stored in a retrieval system, or transmitted in any form or by any means, without the prior written permission of the publisher, except in the case of brief quotations embedded in critical articles or reviews.

Every effort has been made in the preparation of this book to ensure the accuracy of the information presented. However, the information contained in this book is sold without warranty, either express or implied. Neither the authors, nor Packt Publishing, and its dealers and distributors will be held liable for any damages caused or alleged to be caused directly or indirectly by this book.

Packt Publishing has endeavored to provide trademark information about all of the companies and products mentioned in this book by the appropriate use of capitals. However, Packt Publishing cannot guarantee the accuracy of this information.

Authors: Onur Yılmaz and Sathsara Sarathchandra

Managing Editor: Snehal Tambe

Acquisitions Editor: Aditya Date

Production Editor: Samita Warang

Editorial Board: Shubhopriya Banerjee, Bharat Botle, Ewan Buckingham, Megan Carlisle, Mahesh Dhyani, Manasa Kumar, Alex Mazonowicz, Bridget Neale, Dominic Pereira, Shiny Poojary, Abhisekh Rane, Erol Staveley, Ankita Thakur, Nitesh Thakur, and Jonathan Wray.

First Published: November 2019

Production Reference: 1281119

ISBN: 978-1-83898-327-7

Published by Packt Publishing Ltd.

Livery Place, 35 Livery Street

Birmingham B3 2PB, UK

Table of Contents

Chapter 3: Introduction to Serverless Frameworks   75

Chapter 4: Kubernetes Deep Dive   111

Preface

About

This section briefly introduces the authors, the coverage of this book, the technical skills you'll need to get started, and the hardware and software requirements required to complete all of the included activities and exercises.

About the Book

Kubernetes has established itself as the standard platform for container management, orchestration, and deployment. By learning Kubernetes, you'll be able to design your own serverless architecture by implementing the **Function-as-a-service (FaaS)** model.

After an accelerated, hands-on overview of the serverless architecture and various Kubernetes concepts, you'll cover a wide range of real-world development challenges faced by real-world developers and explore various techniques to overcome them. You'll learn how to create production-ready Kubernetes clusters and run serverless applications on them. You'll see how Kubernetes platforms and serverless frameworks such as Kubeless, Apache OpenWhisk, and OpenFaaS provide the tooling you need to develop serverless applications on Kubernetes. You'll also learn how to select the appropriate framework for your upcoming project.

By the end of this book, you'll have the skills and confidence to design your own serverless applications using the power and flexibility of Kubernetes.

About the Author

Onur Yılmaz is a senior software engineer at a multinational enterprise software company. He is a Certified Kubernetes Administrator (CKA) and works on Kubernetes and cloud management systems. He is a keen supporter of cutting-edge technologies including Docker, Kubernetes, and cloud-native applications. He has one master's and two bachelor's degrees in the engineering field.

Sathsara Sarathchandra is a DevOps engineer and has experience in building and managing Kubernetes based production deployments both in the cloud and on-premises. He has over 8 years of experience, having worked for several companies ranging from small start-ups to enterprises. He is a Certified Kubernetes Administrator (CKA) and a Certified Kubernetes Application Developer (CKAD). He holds a master's degree in business administration and a bachelor's degree in computer science.

Learning Objectives

By the end of this book, you will be able to:

- Deploy a Kubernetes cluster locally with Minikube

- Use AWS Lambda and Google Cloud Functions

- Create, build, and deploy a web page generated by the serverless functions in the cloud

- Create a Kubernetes cluster running on the virtual kubelet hardware abstraction
- Create, test, troubleshoot, and delete an OpenFass function
- Create a sample Slackbot with Apache OpenWhisk actions

Audience

This book is for software developers and DevOps engineers who have basic or intermediate knowledge about Kubernetes and want to learn how to create serverless applications that run on Kubernetes. Those who want to design and create serverless applications running on the cloud, or on-premise Kubernetes clusters, will also find this book useful.

Approach

This book provides examples of engaging projects that have a direct correlation to how serverless developers work in the real world with Kubernetes clusters. You'll build example applications and tackle programming challenges that'll prepare you for large, complex engineering problems. Each component is designed to engage and stimulate you so that you can retain and apply what you learn in a practical context with the maximum impact. By completing the book, you'll walk away feeling capable of tackling real-world serverless Kubernetes applications development.

Hardware Requirements

For the optimal student experience, we recommend the following hardware configuration:

- Processor: Intel Core i5 or equivalent
- Memory: 8 GB RAM (16 GB preferred)
- Hard disk: 10 GB available space
- Internet connection

Software Requirements

We also recommend that you have the following software installed in advance:

- Sublime Text (latest version), Atom IDE (latest version), or another similar text editor application
- Git

Additional Requirements

- Azure account

- Google cloud account

- AWS account

- Docker Hub account

- Slack account

Conventions

Code words in the text, database table names, folder names, filenames, file extensions, pathnames, dummy URLs, user input, and Twitter handles are shown as follows:

"Write **hello-from-lambda** as the function name and **Python 3.7** as the runtime."

New terms and important words are shown in bold. Words that you see on the screen, for example, in menus or dialog boxes, appear in the text like this: "Open the AWS Management Console, write **Lambda** in the **Find Services** search box, and click **Lambda - Run Code without Thinking about Servers**."

A block of code is set as follows:

```
import json


def lambda_handler(event, context):
    return {
        'statusCode': '200',
        'body': json.dumps({"message": "hello", "platform": "lambda"}),
        'headers': {
            'Content-Type': 'application/json',
        }
    }
```

Installation and Setup

Before we can do awesome things with data, we need to be prepared with the most productive environment. In this short section, we will see how to do that. Following are the requisites that need to be fulfilled:

- Docker (17.10.0-ce or later)

- Hypervisor like Virtualbox, Parallels, VMWareFusion, Hyperkit or VMWare. Refer this link for more information: https://kubernetes.io/docs/tasks/tools/install-minikube/#install-a-hypervisor

Additional Resources

The code bundle for this book is also hosted on GitHub at https://github.com/TrainingByPackt/Serverless-Architectures-with-Kubernetes. We also have other code bundles from our rich catalog of books and videos available at https://github.com/PacktPublishing/. Check them out!

Introduction to Serverless

Learning Objectives

By the end of this chapter, you will be able to:

- Identify the benefits of serverless architectures
- Create and invoke simple functions on a serverless platform
- Create a cloud-native serverless function and package it as a container using Kubernetes
- Create a Twitter Bot Backend application and package it in a Docker container

In this chapter, we will explain the serverless architecture, then create our first serverless function and package it as a container.

Introduction to Serverless

Cloud technology right now is in a state of constant transformation to create scalable, reliable, and robust environments. In order to create such an environment, every improvement in cloud technology aims to increase both the end user experience and the developer experience. End users demand fast and robust applications that are reachable from everywhere in the world. At the same time, developers demand a better development environment to design, deploy, and maintain their applications in. In the last decade, the journey of cloud technology has started with cloud computing, where servers are provisioned in cloud data centers and applications are deployed on the servers. The transition to cloud data centers decreased costs and removed the need for responsibility for data centers. However, as billions of people are accessing the internet and demanding more services, scalability has become a necessity. In order to scale applications, developers have created smaller microservices that can scale independently of each other. Microservices are packaged into containers as building blocks of software architectures to better both the developer and end user experience. Microservices enhance the developer experience by providing better maintainability while offering high scalability to end users. However, the flexibility and scalability of microservices cannot keep up with the enormous user demand. Today, for instance, millions of banking transactions take place daily, and millions of business-to-business requests are made to backend systems.

Finally, serverless started gaining attention for creating *future-proof* and *ad hoc-scalable* applications. Serverless designs focus on creating even smaller services than microservices and they are designed to last much longer into the future. These *nanoservices*, or functions, help developers to create more flexible and easier-to-maintain applications. On the other hand, serverless designs are ad hoc-scalable, which means if you adopt a serverless design, your services are naturally scaled up or down with the user requests. These characteristics of serverless have made it the latest big trend in the industry, and it is now shaping the cloud technology landscape. In this section, an introduction to serverless technology will be presented, looking at serverless's evolution, origin, and use cases.

Before diving deeper into serverless design, let's understand the evolution of cloud technology. In bygone days, the expected process of deploying applications started with the procurement and deployment of hardware, namely servers. Following that, operating systems were installed on the servers, and then application packages were deployed. Finally, the actual code in application packages was executed to implement business requirements. These four steps are shown in *Figure 1.1*:

Figure 1.1: Traditional software development

Organizations started to outsource their data center operations to cloud providers to improve the scalability and utilization of servers. For instance, if you were developing an online shopping application, you first needed to buy some servers, wait for their installation, and operate them daily and deal with their potential problems, caused by electricity, networking, and misconfiguration. It was difficult to predict the usage level of servers and not feasible to make huge investments in servers to run applications. Therefore, both start-ups and large enterprises started to outsource data center operations to cloud providers. This cleared away the problems related to the first step of hardware deployment, as shown in *Figure 1.2*:

Figure 1.2: Software development with cloud computing

With the start of virtualization in cloud computing, operating systems became virtualized so that multiple virtual machines (VMs) could run on the same bare-metal machine. This transition removed the second step, and service providers provision VMs as shown in *Fig 1.3*. With multiple VMs running on the same hardware, the costs of running servers decreases and the flexibility of operations increases. In other words, the low-level concerns of software developers are cleared since both the hardware and the operating system are now someone else's problem:

Figure 1.3: Software development with virtualization

VMs enable the running of multiple instances on the same hardware. However, using VMs requires installing a complete operating system for every application. Even for a basic frontend application, you need to install an operating system, which results in an overhead of operating system management, leading to limited scalability. Application developers and the high-level usage of modern applications requires faster and simpler solutions with better isolation than creating and managing VMs. Containerization technology solves this issue by running multiple instances of "containerized" applications on the same operating system. With this level of abstraction, problems related to operating systems are also removed, and containers are delivered as application packages, as illustrated in *Figure 1.4*. Containerization technology enables a microservices architecture where software is designed as small and scalable services that interact with each other.

This architectural approach makes it possible to run modern applications such as collaborative spreadsheets in Google Drive, live streams of sports events on YouTube, video conferences on Skype, and many more:

Figure 1.4: Software development with containerization

The next architectural phenomena, serverless, removes the burden of managing containers and focuses on running the actual code itself. The essential characteristic of serverless architecture is ad hoc scalability. Applications in serverless architecture are ad hoc-scalable, which means they are scaled up or down automatically when they are needed. They could also be scaled down to zero, which means no hardware, network, or operation costs. With serverless applications, all low-level concerns are outsourced and managed, and the focus is on the last step – **Run the code** – as shown in *Figure* 1.5. With the serverless design, the focus is on the last step of traditional software development. In the following section, we will focus on the origin and manifesto of serverless for a more in-depth introduction:

Figure 1.5: Software development with serverless

Serverless Origin and Manifesto

Serverless is a confusing term since there are various definitions used in conferences, books, and blogs. Although it theoretically means not having any servers, it practically means leaving the responsibility of servers to third-party organizations. In other words, it means not getting rid of servers but server operations. When you run serverless, someone else handles the procurement, shipping, and installation of your server operations. This decreases your costs because you do not need to operate servers or even data centers; furthermore, it lets you focus on the application logic, which implements your core business function.

The first uses of serverless were seen in articles related to continuous integration around 2010. When it was first discussed, serverless was considered for building and packaging applications on the servers of cloud providers. The dramatic increase in popularity came with the **Amazon Web Services** (**AWS**) **Lambda** launch in 2014. Furthermore, in 2015, AWS presented **API Gateway** for the management and triggering of Lambda functions as it's a single entry point for multiple functions. Therefore, serverless functions gained traction in 2014 and it became possible to create serverless architecture applications by using **AWS API Gateway** in 2015.

However, the most definitive and complete explanation of serverless was presented in 2016, at the AWS developer conference, as the *Serverless Compute Manifesto*. It consists of eight strict rules that define the core ideas behind serverless architecture:

> **Note**
>
> Although it was discussed in various talks at the AWS Summit 2016 conference, the Serverless Compute Manifesto has no official website or documentation. A complete list of what the manifesto details can be seen in a presentation by Dr. Tim Wagner: https://www.slideshare.net/AmazonWebServices/getting-started-with-aws-lambda-and-the-serverless-cloud.

- **Functions as the building blocks**: In serverless architecture, the building blocks of development, deployment, and scaling should be the functions. Each function should be deployed and scaled in isolation, independently of other functions.

- **No servers, VMs, or containers**: The service provider should operate all computation abstractions for serverless functions, including servers, VMs, and containers. Users of serverless architecture should not need any further information about the underlying infrastructure.

- **No storage**: Serverless applications should be designed as ephemeral workloads that have a fresh environment for every request. If they need to persist some data, they should use a remote service such as a **Database as a Service (DbaaS)**.

- **Implicitly fault-tolerant functions**: Both the serverless infrastructure and the deployed applications should be fault-tolerant in order to create a robust, scalable, and reliable application environment.

- **Scalability with the request**: The underlying infrastructure, including the computation and network resources, should enable a high level of scalability. In other words, it is not an option for a serverless environment to fail to scale up when requests are rising.

- **No cost for idle time**: Serverless providers should only incur costs when serverless workloads are running. If your function has not received an HTTP request for a long period, you should not pay any money for the idleness.

- **Bring Your Own Code (BYOC)**: Serverless architectures should enable the running of any code developed and packaged by end users. If you are a Node.Js should appear together or Go developer, it should be possible for you to deploy your function within your preferred language to the serverless infrastructure.

- **Instrumentation**: Logs of the functions and the metrics collected over the function calls should be available to the developers. This makes it possible to debug and solve problems related to functions. Since they are already running on remote servers, instrumentation should not create any further burden in terms of analyzing potential problems.

The original manifesto introduced some best practices and limitations; however, as cloud technology evolves, the world of serverless applications evolves. This evolution will make some rules from the manifesto obsolete and will add new rules. In the following section, use cases of serverless applications are discussed to explain how serverless is adopted in the industry.

Serverless Use Cases

Serverless applications and designs seem to be avant-garde technologies; however, they are highly adopted in the industry for reliable, robust, and scalable applications. Any traditional application that is running on VMs, Docker containers, or Kubernetes can be designed to run serverless if you want the benefits of serverless designs. Some of the well-known use cases of serverless architectures are listed here:

- **Data processing**: Interpreting, analyzing, cleansing, and formatting data are essential steps in big data applications. With the scalability of serverless architectures, you can quickly filter millions of photos and count the number of people in them, for instance, without buying any pricey servers. According to a case report (https://azure.microsoft.com/en-in/blog/a-fast-serverless-big-data-pipeline-powered-by-a-single-azure-function/), it is possible to create a serverless application to detect fraudulent transitions from multiple sources with Azure Functions. To handle 8 million data processing requests, serverless platforms would be the appropriate choice, with their ad hoc scalability.

- **Webhooks**: Webhooks are HTTP API calls to third-party services to deliver real-time data. Instead of having servers up and running for webhook backends, serverless infrastructures can be utilized with lower costs and less maintenance.

- **Check-out and payment**: It is possible to create shopping systems as serverless applications where each core functionality is designed as an isolated component. For instance, you can integrate the Stripe API as a remote payment service and use the Shopify service for cart management in your serverless backend.

- **Real-time chat applications**: Real-time chat applications integrated into Facebook Messenger, Telegram, or Slack, for instance, are very popular for handling customer operations, distributing news, tracking sports results, or just for entertainment. It is possible to create ephemeral serverless functions to respond to messages or take actions based on message content. The main advantage of serverless for real-time chat is that it can scale when many people are using it. It could also scale to zero and cost no money when there is no one using the chat application.

These use cases illustrate that serverless architectures can be used to design any modern application. It is also possible to move some parts of monolithic applications and convert them into serverless functions. If your current online shop is a single Java web application packaged as a JAR file, you can separate its business functions and convert them into serverless components. The dissolution of giant monoliths into small serverless functions helps to solve multiple problems at once. First of all, scalability will never be an issue for the serverless components of your application. For instance, if you cannot handle a high amount of payments during holidays, a serverless platform will automatically scale up the payment functions with the usage levels. Secondly, you do not need to limit yourself to the programming language of the monolith; you can develop your functions in any programming language. For instance, if your database clients are better implemented with Node.js, you can code the database operations of your online shop in Node.js.

Finally, you can reuse the logic implemented in your monolith since now it is a shared serverless service. For instance, if you separate the payment operations of your online shop and create serverless payment functions, you can reuse these payment functions in your next project. All these benefits make it appealing for start-ups as well as large enterprises to adopt serverless architectures. In the following section, serverless architectures will be discussed in more depth, looking specifically at some implementations.

Possible answers:

- Applications with high latency
- When observability and metrics are critical for business
- When vendor lock-in and ecosystem dependencies are an issue

Serverless Architecture and Function as a Service (FaaS)

Serverless is a cloud computing design where cloud providers handle the provisioning of servers. In the previous section, we discussed how operational concerns are layered and handed over. In this section, we will focus on serverless architectures and application design using serverless architecture.

In traditional software architecture, all of the components of an application are installed on servers. For instance, let's assume that you are developing an e-commerce website in Java and your product information is stored in **MySQL**. In this case, the frontend, backend, and database are installed on the same server. End users are expected to reach the shopping website with the IP address of the server, and thus an application server such as **Apache Tomcat** should be running on the server. In addition, user information and security components are also included in the package, which is installed on the server. A monolithic e-commerce application is shown in Figure 1.6, with all four parts, namely the frontend, backend, security, and database:

Figure 1.6: Traditional software architecture

Microservices architecture focuses on creating a loosely coupled and independently deployable collection of services. For the same e-commerce system, you would still have frontend, backend, database, and security components, but they would be isolated units. Furthermore, these components would be packaged as containers and would be managed by a container orchestrator such as Kubernetes. This enables the installing and scaling of components independently since they are distributed over multiple servers. In Figure 1.7, the same four components are installed on the servers and communicating with each other via Kubernetes networking:

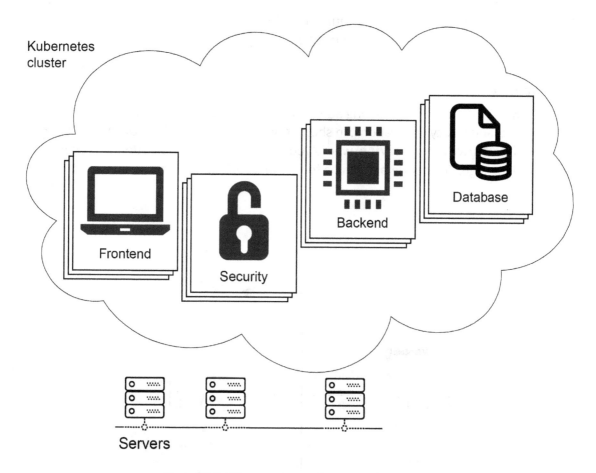

Figure 1.7: Microservices software architecture

Microservices are deployed to the servers, which are still managed by the operations teams. With the serverless architecture, the components are converted into third-party services or functions. For instance, the security of the e-commerce website could be handled by an Authentication-as-a-Service offering such as **Auth0**. **AWS Relational Database Service (RDS)** can be used as the database of the system. The best option for the backend logic is to convert it into functions and deploy them into a serverless platform such as **AWS Lambda** or **Google Cloud Functions**. Finally, the frontend could be served by storage services such as **AWS Simple Storage Service (S3)** or **Google Cloud Storage**.

With a serverless design, it is only required to define these services for you to have scalable, robust, and managed applications running in harmony, as shown in Figure 1.8:

> **Note**
>
> **Auth0** is a platform for providing authentication and authorization for web, mobile, and legacy applications. In short, it provides **authentication and authorization as a service**, where you can connect any application written in any language. Further details can be found on its official website: https://auth0.com.

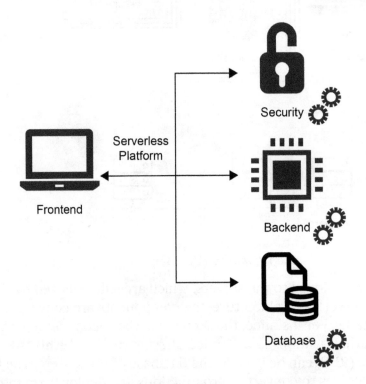

Figure 1.8: Serverless software architecture

Starting from a monolith architecture and first dissolving it into microservice, and then serverless components is beneficial for multiple reasons:

- **Cost**: Serverless architecture helps to decrease costs in two critical ways. The first is that the management of the servers is outsourced, and the second is that it only costs money when the serverless applications are in use.

- **Scalability**: If an application is expected to grow, the current best choice is to design it as a serverless application since that removes the scalability constraints related to the infrastructure.

- **Flexibility**: When the scope of deployable units is decreased, serverless provides more flexibility to innovate, choose better programming languages, and manage with smaller teams.

These dimensions and how they vary between software architectures is visualized in *Figure 1.9*:

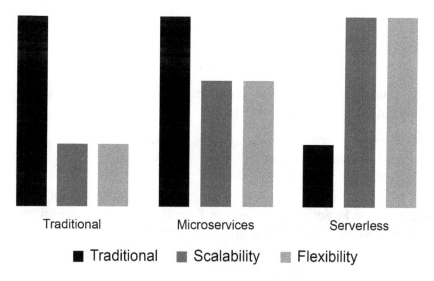

Figure 1.9: Benefits of the transition from cost to serverless

When you start with a traditional software development architecture, the transition to microservices increases scalability and flexibility. However, it does not directly decrease the cost of running the applications since you are still dealing with the servers. Further transition to serverless improves both scalability and flexibility while decreasing the cost. Therefore, it is essential to learn about and implement serverless architectures for future-proof applications. In the following section, the implementation of serverless architecture, namely **Function as a Service (FaaS)**, will be presented.

Function as a Service (FaaS)

FaaS is the most popular and widely adopted implementation of serverless architecture. All major cloud providers have FaaS products, such as AWS Lambda, Google Cloud Functions, and Azure Functions. As its name implies, the unit of deployment and management in FaaS is the function. Functions in this context are no different from any other function in any other programming language. They are expected to take some arguments and return values to implement business needs. FaaS platforms handle the management of servers and make it possible to run event-driven, scalable functions. The essential properties of a FaaS offering are these:

- **Stateless**: Functions are designed to be stateless and ephemeral operations where no file is saved to disk and no caches are managed. At every invocation of a function, it starts quickly with a new environment, and it is removed when it is done.

- **Event-triggered**: Functions are designed to be triggered directly and based on events such as `cron` time expressions, HTTP requests, message queues, and database operations. For instance, it is possible to call the `startConversation` function via an HTTP request when a new chat is started. Likewise, it is possible to launch the `syncUsers` function when a new user is added to a database.

- **Scalable**: Functions are designed to run as much as needed in parallel so that every incoming request is answered and every event is covered.

- **Managed**: Functions are governed by their platform so that the servers and underlying infrastructure is not a concern for FaaS users.

These properties of functions are covered by cloud providers' offerings, such as **AWS Lambda**, **Google Cloud Functions**, and **Azure Functions**; and on-premises offerings, such as **Kubeless**, **Apache OpenWhisk**, and **OpenFass**. With its high popularity, the term FaaS is mostly used interchangeably with the term serverless. In the following exercise, we will create a function to handle HTTP requests and illustrate how a serverless function should be developed.

Exercise 1: Creating an HTTP Function

In this exercise, we will create an HTTP function to be a part of a serverless platform and then invoke it via an HTTP request. In order to execute the steps of the exercise, you will use Docker, text editors, and a terminal.

> **Note**
>
> The code files for the exercises in this chapter can be found here: https://github. com/TrainingByPackt/Serverless-Architectures-with-Kubernetes/tree/master/ Lesson01/Exercise1.

To successfully complete the exercise, we need to ensure the following steps are executed:

1. Create a file named **function.go** with the following content in your favorite text editor:

```go
package main

import (
    "fmt"
    "net/http"
)
func WelcomeServerless(w http.ResponseWriter, r *http.Request) {
    fmt.Fprintf(w, "Hello Serverless World!")
}
```

In this file, we have created an actual function handler to respond when this function is invoked.

2. Create a file named **main.go** with the following content:

```go
package main

import (
    "fmt"
    "net/http"
)

func main() {
    fmt.Println("Starting the serverless environment..")
```

```
http.HandleFunc("/", WelcomeServerless)
fmt.Println("Function handlers are registered.")

http.ListenAndServe(":8080", nil)
}
```

In this file, we have created the environment to serve this function. In general, this part is expected to be handled by the serverless platform.

3. Start a Go development environment with the following command in your terminal:

```
docker run -it --rm -p 8080:8080 -v "$(pwd)":/go/src --workdir=/go/src
golang:1.12.5
```

With that command, a shell prompt will start inside a Docker container for Go version **1.12.5**. In addition, port **8080** of the host system is mapped to the container, and the current working directory is mapped to **/go/src**. You will be able to run commands inside the started Docker container:

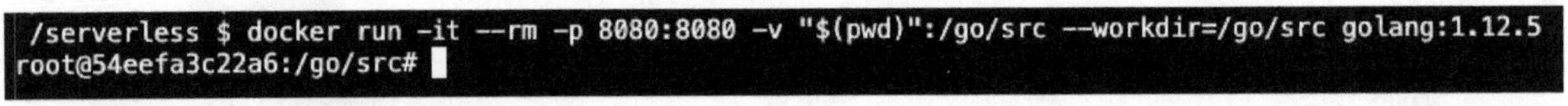

```
/serverless $ docker run -it --rm -p 8080:8080 -v "$(pwd)":/go/src --workdir=/go/src golang:1.12.5
root@54eefa3c22a6:/go/src#
```

Figure 1.10: The Go development environment inside the container

4. Start the function handlers with the following command in the shell prompt opened in *step* 3: **go run *.go**.

With the start of the applications, you will see the following lines:

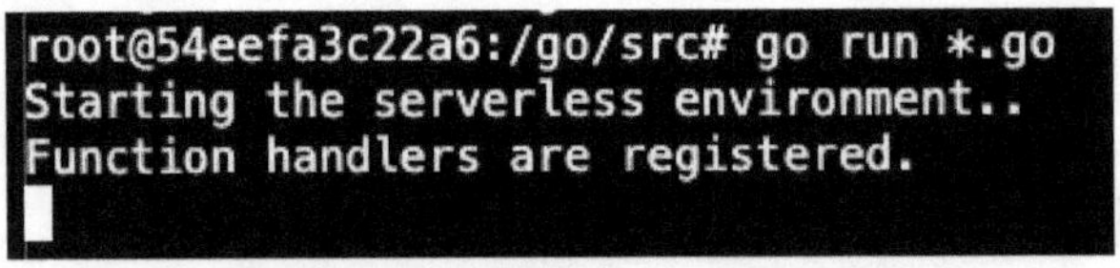

```
root@54eefa3c22a6:/go/src# go run *.go
Starting the serverless environment..
Function handlers are registered.
```

Figure 1.11: The start of the function server

These lines indicate that the **main** function inside the **main.go** file is running as expected.

5. Open **http://localhost:8080** in your browser:

Hello Serverless World!

Figure 1.12: The WelcomeServerless output

The message displayed on the web page reveals that the **WelcomeServerless** function is successfully invoked via the HTTP request and the response is retrieved.

6. Press *Ctrl* + C to exit the function handler and then write **exit** to stop the container:

```
root@54eefa3c22a6:/go/src# go run *.go
Starting the serverless environment..
Function handlers are registered.
^Csignal: interrupt
root@54eefa3c22a6:/go/src# exit
exit
 /serverless $ 
```

Figure 1.13: Exiting the function handler and container

With this exercise, we demonstrated how we can create a simple function. In addition, the serverless environment was presented to show how functions are served and invoked. In the following section, an introduction to Kubernetes and the serverless environment is given to connect the two cloud computing phenomena.

Kubernetes and Serverless

Serverless and Kubernetes arrived on the cloud computing scene at about the same time, in 2014. AWS supports serverless through **AWS Lambda**, whereas **Kubernetes** became open source with the support of Google and its long and successful history in container management. Organizations started to create AWS Lambda functions for their short-lived temporary tasks, and many start-ups have been focused on products running on the serverless infrastructure. On the other hand, Kubernetes gained dramatic adoption in the industry and became the de facto container management system. It enables running both stateless applications, such as web frontends and data analysis tools, and stateful applications, such as databases, inside containers. The containerization of applications and microservices architectures have proven to be effective for both large enterprises and start-ups.

Therefore, running microservices and containerized applications is a crucial factor for successful, scalable, and reliable cloud-native applications. Also, the following two essential elements strengthen the connection between Kubernetes and serverless architectures:

- **Vendor lock-in**: Kubernetes isolates the cloud provider and creates a managed environment for running serverless workloads. In other words, it is not straightforward to run your AWS Lambda functions in Google Cloud Functions if you want to move to a new provider next year. However, if you use a Kubernetes-backed serverless platform, you will be able to quickly move between cloud providers or even on-premises systems.

- **Reuse of services**: As the mainstream container management system, Kubernetes runs most of its workload in your cloud environment. It offers an opportunity to deploy serverless functions side by side with existing services. It makes it easier to operate, install, connect, and manage both serverless and containerized applications.

Cloud computing and deployment strategies are always evolving to create more developer-friendly environments with lower costs. Kubernetes and containerization adoption has already won the market and the love of developers such that any cloud computation without Kubernetes won't be seen for a very long time. By providing the same benefits, serverless architectures are gaining popularity; however, this does not pose a threat to Kubernetes. On the contrary, serverless applications will make containerization more accessible, and consequently, Kubernetes will profit. Therefore, it is essential to learn how to run serverless architectures on Kubernetes to create future-proof, cloud-native, scalable applications. In the following exercise, we will combine functions and containers and package our functions as containers.

Possible answers:

- Serverless – data preparation
- Serverless – ephemeral API operations
- Kubernetes – databases
- Kubernetes – server-related operations

Exercise 2: Packaging an HTTP Function as a Container

In this exercise, we will package the HTTP function from *Exercise 1* as a container to be a part of a Kubernetes workload. Also, we will run the container and trigger the function via its container.

> **Note**
>
> The code files for the exercises in this chapter can be found here: https://github.com/TrainingByPackt/Serverless-Architectures-with-Kubernetes/tree/master/Lesson01/Exercise2.

To successfully complete the exercise, we need to ensure the following steps are executed:

1. Create a file named **Dockerfile** in the same folder as the files from *Exercise 1*:

```
FROM golang:1.12.5-alpine3.9 AS builder
ADD . .
RUN go build *.go

FROM alpine:3.9
COPY --from=builder /go/function ./function
RUN chmod +x ./function
ENTRYPOINT ["./function"]
```

In this multi-stage **Dockerfile**, the function is built inside the **golang:1.12.5-alpine3.9** container. Then, the binary is copied into the **alpine:3.9** container as the final application package.

2. Build the Docker image with the following command in the terminal: `docker build . -t hello-serverless`.

   Each line of **Dockerfile** is executed sequentially, and finally, with the last step, the Docker image is built and tagged: `Successfully tagged hello-serverless:latest`:

```
/serverless $ docker build . -t hello-serverless
Sending build context to Docker daemon  12.29kB
Step 1/7 : FROM golang:1.12.5-alpine3.9 AS builder
 ---> c7330979841b
Step 2/7 : ADD . .
 ---> Using cache
 ---> 6db2bdb89661
Step 3/7 : RUN go build *.go
 ---> Using cache
 ---> 5141352f7996
Step 4/7 : FROM alpine:3.9
 ---> cdf98d1859c1
Step 5/7 : COPY --from=builder /go/function ./function
 ---> Using cache
 ---> c6a601b16edc
Step 6/7 : RUN chmod +x ./function
 ---> Using cache
 ---> e745ec8ba6ac
Step 7/7 : ENTRYPOINT ["./function"]
 ---> Using cache
 ---> a3a4c43208ed
Successfully built a3a4c43208ed
Successfully tagged hello-serverless:latest
/serverless $ ▊
```

Figure 1.14: The build of the Docker container

3. Start a Docker container from the **hello-serverless** image with the following command in your Terminal: `docker run -it --rm -p 8080:8080 hello-serverless`.

   With that command, an instance of the Docker image is instantiated with port **8080** mapping the host system to the container. Furthermore, the **--rm** flag will remove the container when it is exited. The log lines indicate that the container of the function is running as expected:

```
/serverless $ docker run -it --rm -p 8080:8080 hello-serverless
Starting the serverless environment..
Function handlers are registered.
▊
```

Figure 1.15: The start of the function container

4. Open **http://localhost:8080** in your browser:

Figure 1.16: The WelcomeServerless output

It reveals that the **WelcomeServerless** function running in the container was successfully invoked via the HTTP request, and the response is retrieved.

5. Press *Ctrl + C* to exit the container:

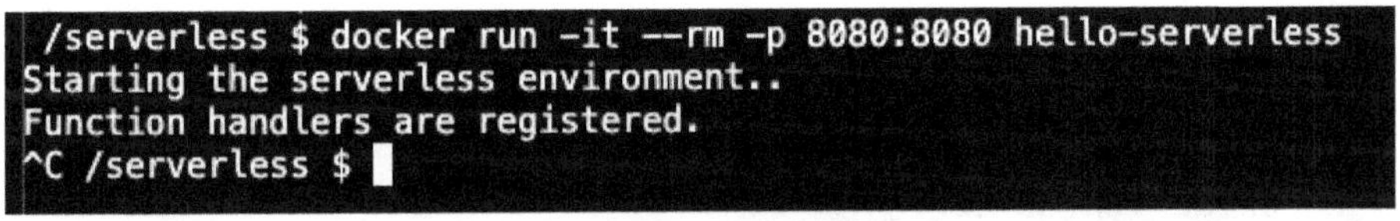

```
/serverless $ docker run -it --rm -p 8080:8080 hello-serverless
Starting the serverless environment..
Function handlers are registered.
^C /serverless $ █
```

Figure 1.17: Exiting the container

In this exercise, we saw how we can package a simple function as a container. In addition, the container was started and the function was triggered with the help of Docker's networking capabilities. In the following exercise, we will implement a parameterized function to show how to pass values to functions and return different responses.

Exercise 3: Parameterized HTTP Functions

In this exercise, we will convert the **WelcomeServerless** function from *Exercise 2* into a parameterized HTTP function. Also, we will run the container and trigger the function via its container.

> **Note**
>
> The code files for the exercises in this chapter can be found here: https://github.com/TrainingByPackt/Serverless-Architectures-with-Kubernetes/tree/master/Lesson01/Exercise3.

To successfully complete the exercise, we need to ensure that the following steps are executed:

1. Change the contents of **function.go** from *Exercise 2* to the following:

```go
package main

import (
        "fmt"
        "net/http"
)

func WelcomeServerless(w http.ResponseWriter, r *http.Request) {

        names, ok := r.URL.Query()["name"]

    if ok && len(names[0]) > 0 {
       fmt.Fprintf(w, names[0] + ", Hello Serverless World!")
    } else {
            fmt.Fprintf(w, "Hello Serverless World!")
    }
}
```

   In the new version of the **WelcomeServerless** function, we now take URL parameters and return responses accordingly.

2. Build the Docker image with the following command in your terminal: **docker build . -t hello-serverless**.

   Each line of **Dockerfile** is executed sequentially, and with the last step, the Docker image is built and tagged: **Successfully tagged hello-serverless:latest**:

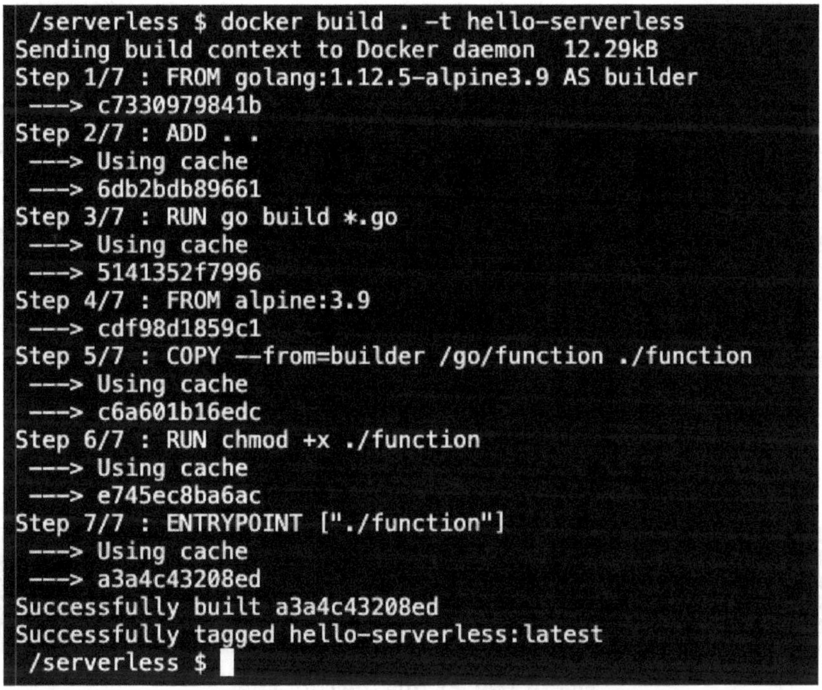

```
/serverless $ docker build . -t hello-serverless
Sending build context to Docker daemon  12.29kB
Step 1/7 : FROM golang:1.12.5-alpine3.9 AS builder
---> c7330979841b
Step 2/7 : ADD . .
---> Using cache
---> 6db2bdb89661
Step 3/7 : RUN go build *.go
---> Using cache
---> 5141352f7996
Step 4/7 : FROM alpine:3.9
---> cdf98d1859c1
Step 5/7 : COPY --from=builder /go/function ./function
---> Using cache
---> c6a601b16edc
Step 6/7 : RUN chmod +x ./function
---> Using cache
---> e745ec8ba6ac
Step 7/7 : ENTRYPOINT ["./function"]
---> Using cache
---> a3a4c43208ed
Successfully built a3a4c43208ed
Successfully tagged hello-serverless:latest
/serverless $
```

Figure 1.18: The build of the Docker container

3. Start a Docker container from the **hello-serverless** image with the following command in the terminal: **docker run -it -rm -p 8080:8080 hello-serverless**.

   With that command, the function handlers will start on port **8080** of the host system:

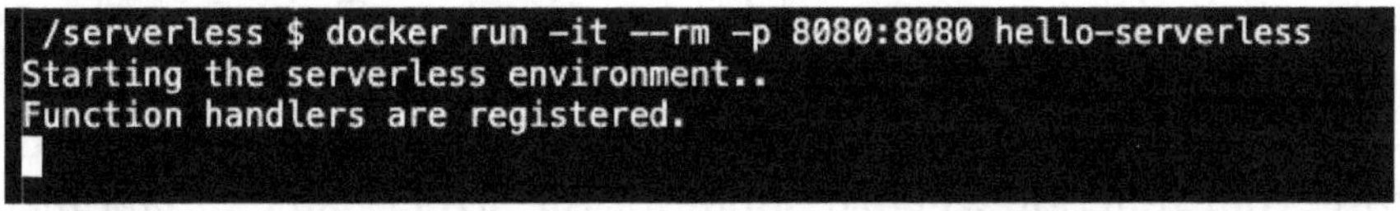

```
/serverless $ docker run -it --rm -p 8080:8080 hello-serverless
Starting the serverless environment..
Function handlers are registered.
```

Figure 1.19: The start of the function container

4. Open **http://localhost:8080** in your browser:

Hello Serverless World!

Figure 1.20: The WelcomeServerless output

It reveals the same response as in the previous exercise. If we provide URL parameters, we should get personalized **Hello Serverless World** messages.

5. Change the address to **http://localhost:8080?name=Ece** in your browser and reload the page. We are now expecting to see a personalized **Hello Serverless World** message with the name provided in URL parameters:

Figure 1.21: Personalized WelcomeServerless output

6. Press *Ctrl* + C to exit the container:

```
/serverless $ docker run -it --rm -p 8080:8080 hello-serverless
Starting the serverless environment..
Function handlers are registered.
^C /serverless $ █
```

Figure 1.22: Exiting the container

In this exercise, how generic functions are used with different parameters was shown. Personal messages based on input values were returned by a single function that we deployed. In the following activity, a more complex function will be created and managed as a container to show how they are implemented in real life.

Activity 1: Twitter Bot Backend for Bike Points in London

The aim of this activity is to create a real-life function for a Twitter bot backend. The Twitter bot will be used to search for available bike points in London and the number of available bikes in the corresponding locations. The bot will answer in a natural language form; therefore, your function will take input for the street name or landmark and output a complete human-readable sentence.

Transportation data for London is publicly available and accessible via the **Transport for London (TFL) Unified API** (https://api.tfl.gov.uk). You are required to use the TFL API and run your functions inside containers.

Once completed, you will have a container running for the function:

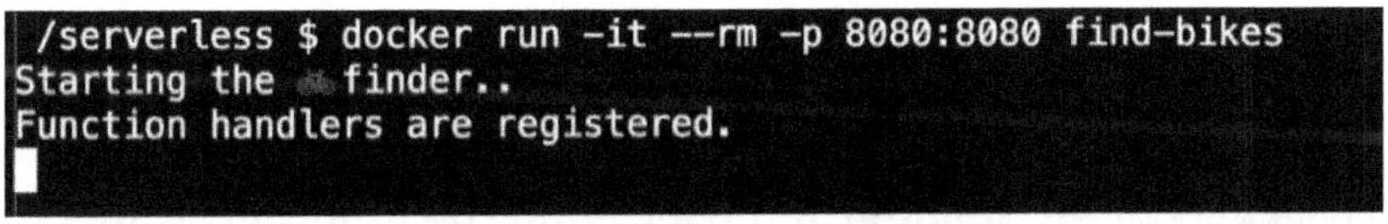

```
/serverless $ docker run -it --rm -p 8080:8080 find-bikes
Starting the  finder..
Function handlers are registered.
```

Figure 1.23: The running function inside the container

When you query via an HTTP REST API, it should return sentences similar to the following when bike points are found with available bikes:

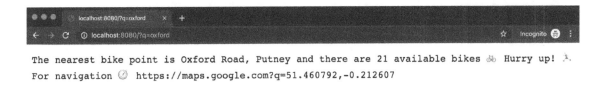

The nearest bike point is Oxford Road, Putney and there are 21 available bikes 🚲 Hurry up! 🏃
For navigation 🧭 https://maps.google.com?q=51.460792,-0.212607

Figure 1.24: Function response when bikes are available

When there are no bike points found or no bikes are available at those locations, the function will return a response similar to the following:

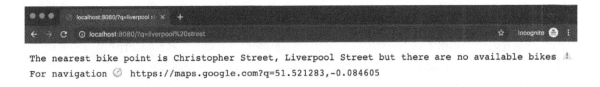

The nearest bike point is Christopher Street, Liverpool Street but there are no available bikes ⚠
For navigation 🧭 https://maps.google.com?q=51.521283,-0.084605

Figure 1.25: Function response when a bike point is located but no bike is found

The function may also provide the following response:

Sorry, no bike points are found for this location!

Figure 1.26: Function response when no bike point or bike is found

Execute the following steps to complete this activity:

1. Create a **main.go** file to register function handlers, as in *Exercise 1*.

2. Create a **function.go** file for the **FindBikes** function.

3. Create a **Dockerfile** for building and packaging the function, as in *Exercise 2*.

4. Build the container image with Docker commands.

5. Run the container image as a Docker container and make the ports available from the host system.

6. Test the function's HTTP endpoint with different queries.

7. Exit the container.

> **Note**
>
> The files **main.go**, **function.go** and **Dockerfile** can be found here: https://github. com/TrainingByPackt/Serverless-Architectures-with-Kubernetes/tree/master/ Lesson01/Activity1.
>
> The solution for the activity can be found on page 372.

In this activity, we built the backend of a Twitter bot. We started by defining **main** and **FindBikes** functions. Then we built and packaged this serverless backend as a Docker container. Finally, we tested it with various inputs to find the closest bike station. With this real-life example, the background operations of a serverless platform and how to write serverless functions were illustrated.

Summary

In this chapter, we first described the journey from traditional to serverless software development. We discussed how software development has changed over the years to create a more developer-friendly environment. Following that, we presented the origin of serverless technology and its official manifesto. Since serverless is a popular term in the industry, defining some rules helps to design better serverless applications that integrate easily into various platforms. We then listed use cases for serverless technology to illustrate how serverless architectures can be used to create any modern application.

Following an introduction to serverless, FaaS was explored as an implementation of serverless architectures. We showed how applications are designed in traditional, microservices, and serverless designs. In addition, the benefits of the transition to serverless architectures were discussed in detail.

Finally, Kubernetes and serverless technologies were discussed to show how they support each other. As the mainstream container management system, Kubernetes was presented, which involved looking at the advantages of running serverless platforms with it. Containerization and microservices are highly adopted in the industry, and therefore running serverless workloads as containers was covered, with exercises. Finally, a real-life example of functions as a backend for a Twitter bot was explored. In this activity, functions were packaged as containers to show the relationship between microservices-based, containerized, and FaaS-backed designs.

In the next chapter, we will be introducing serverless architecture in the cloud and working with cloud services.

Introduction to Serverless in the Cloud

Learning Objectives

By the end of this chapter, you will be able to:

- Evaluate the criteria for choosing the best serverless FaaS provider
- Identify the supported languages, trigger types, and cost structure of major cloud service providers
- Deploy serverless functions to cloud providers and integrate functions with other cloud services

In this chapter, we will explain the serverless FaaS products of cloud providers, create our first serverless functions in the cloud, and integrate with other cloud services.

Introduction

In the previous chapter, the architectural evolution of traditional architectures to serverless designs was discussed. In addition, the origin and benefits of serverless were presented to explain its high adoption and success in the industry. In this chapter, the focus will be on the serverless platforms of cloud providers. Let's start with the evolution of cloud technology offerings over the years.

At the start of cloud computing, the primary offering of cloud providers was its provisioned and ready-to-use hardware, namely the **infrastructure**. Cloud providers manage hardware and networking operations, and therefore, the product they were offering was **Infrastructure-as-a-Service** (**IaaS**), as illustrated in the following diagram. All cloud providers are still offering IaaS products as their core functionality, such as **Amazon Elastic Compute Cloud (Amazon EC2)** in AWS and **Google Compute Engine** in GCP.

In the following years, cloud providers started to offer platforms where developers could only run their applications. With this abstraction, manual server provisioning, security updates, and server failures became the concerns of the cloud provider. These offerings are known as **Platform-as-a-Service** (**PaaS**) since they only focus on running applications and their data on their platforms. **Heroku** is the most popular PaaS provider, although each cloud provider has its own PaaS products, such as **AWS Elastic Beanstalk** or **Google App Engine**. Similar to IaaS, PaaS is still in use in software development.

In the top-level abstraction, the functions of the applications operate as the unit of control in serverless architectures. This known as **Function-as-a-Service** (**FaaS**) and is offered by all the significant cloud providers in recent years. The abstraction levels from IaaS to PaaS, and finally to FaaS, can be seen in the following diagram:

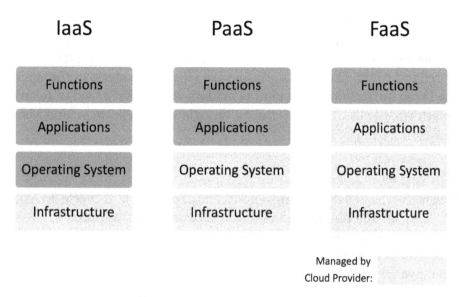

Figure 2.1: IaaS to PaaS and FaaS transition

Serverless and the Cloud Evaluation Criteria

In order to analyze the FaaS products on the market, it is beneficial to define some criteria so that we can compare products in a structured way. The following topics are essential for every FaaS platform and need detailed investigation before you choose a cloud provider:

- **Programming languages**: Functions are deployed and managed inside the cloud provider environments. Therefore, cloud providers define the programming

  languages that are supported. It is one of the most significant decision factors since implementing the functions in another language is not feasible in most circumstances.

- **Function triggers:** Functions are designed to be triggered by cloud provider services and external methods. The conventional techniques are scheduled calls, on-demand calls, and integration with other cloud services, such as databases, queues, and API gateways.

- **Cost:** The most compelling characteristic of the serverless architecture is its cost-effectiveness and the mainstream way of calculating the price, that is, pay per request. It is essential to calculate the actual and projected costs for the feasibility of long-running projects.

Cloud providers are expected to be cost-effective, provide as many programming languages as possible, and support various function triggers. There are also additional criteria, such as monitoring, operations, and in-house knowledge level, but these are not directly related to the serverless products of cloud providers. In the upcoming sections, the three most dominant cloud providers will be discussed in terms of their serverless platforms: Amazon Web Services, Google Cloud Platform, and Microsoft Azure.

AWS Lambda

AWS Lambda is the first FaaS offering, and it also created the serverless hype in the industry. It was made public in 2014 and has been widely adopted in the cloud computing world by all levels of organizations. It made it possible for start-ups to create new products in a short amount of time. It also enabled large enterprises such as **Netflix** to move event-based triggers to serverless functions. With the opportunity of removing the server operation burden, AWS Lambda and serverless became the next trend in the industry. In this section, we will discuss AWS Lambda for programming language support, trigger types, and cost structure. In addition, our very first serverless function will be deployed.

> **Note**
>
> The official website of AWS Lambda can be found here if you wish to find out more: https://aws.amazon.com/lambda.

AWS Lambda supports the **Java**, **Python**, **Node.js**, **C#**, **Ruby**, and **Go** programming languages when it comes to serverless functions. Furthermore, AWS Lambda provides an API called AWS Lambda Runtime Interface to enable the integration of any language as a custom runtime. Therefore, it could be stated that AWS Lambda natively supports a rich set of popular languages while allowing an extension to other programming languages.

AWS Lambda is designed to have event-triggered functions. This is where the functions process the events that have been retrieved from event sources. Within the AWS ecosystem, various services can be an event source, including the following:

- **Amazon S3** file storage for instances when new files are added
- **Amazon Alexa** to implement new skills for voice assistance

- **Amazon CloudWatch Events** for the events that occur in the state changes of cloud resources

- **Amazon CodeCommit** for when developers push new commits to the code repository

In addition to these services, the essential AWS service for the serverless event source is the **Amazon API Gateway**. It has the REST API ability to invoke Lambda functions over HTTPS, and it permits the management of multiple Lambda functions for different methods, such as `GET`, `POST`, `PATCH`, and `DELETE`. In other words, API Gateway creates a layer between the serverless functions and the outside world. This layer also handles the security of the Lambda functions by protecting them against **Distributed Denial of Service** (**DDoS**) attacks and defining throttles. The trigger types and the environment are highly configurable for AWS Lambda functions if you want to integrate with other AWS services or make them public via the API Gateway.

For the pricing of AWS Lambda, there are two critical points to take note of: the first one is the **request charges** and the second one is the **compute charges**. Request charges are based on the number of function invocations, while compute charges are calculated as GB per second. The compute charge is the multiplication of memory size and execution time:

- **Memory Size (GB):** This is the configured allocated memory for the functions.

- **Execution time (ms):** This is the realized execution time that the functions will be running for.

In addition, there is a free tier where the first 1 million request charges and 400,000 GB per second of compute charges are waived monthly. A simple calculation, including the free tier, can show how cheap running a serverless function could be.

Let's assume that your function is called 30 million times in a month. You have allocated 128 MB of memory, and on average, the function runs for 200 ms:

Request charges:

Price: $0.20 per 1 M requests

Free tier: 1 M

Monthly request: 30 M

Monthly request charge: 29 M x $0.20 / M = $5.80

Compute charges:

Price: $0.0000166667 per GB per second

Free tier: 400,000 GB per second

Monthly compute: 30 M x 0.2 second x 128 MB / 1024 = 750,000 GB per second

Monthly compute charge: 350,000 x $0.0000166667 = $5.83

Monthly total cost: $5.80 + $5.83 = $11.63

This calculation shows that it is possible to run a serverless AWS Lambda environment where you receive 1 *million daily function calls at a monthly cost of $11.63*. This indicates both how cheap it is to run serverless workloads and the essential characteristics to consider in serverless economics. In the following exercise, our very first serverless function will be deployed to AWS Lambda and will be invoked to show the operational view of the platform.

> **Note**
>
> In order to complete this exercise, you will need to have an active Amazon Web Services account. You can create an account at https://aws.amazon.com/.

Exercise 4: Creating a Function in AWS Lambda and Invoking It via the AWS Gateway API

In this exercise, we will be creating our first AWS Lambda function and connecting it to AWS Gateway API so that we can invoke over its HTTP endpoint.

To successfully complete this exercise, we need to ensure that the following steps are executed:

1. Open the AWS Management Console, write **Lambda** in the **Find Services** search box, and click **Lambda - Run Code without Thinking about Servers**. The console will look as follows:

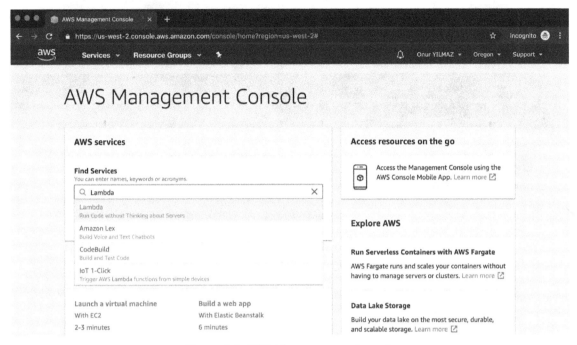

Figure 2.2: AWS Management Console

2. Click on **Create function** in the Lambda functions list, as shown in the following screenshot:

Figure 2.3: AWS Lambda – functions list

3. Select **Author from scratch** in the **Create function** view. Write `hello-from-lambda` as the function name and `Python 3.7` as the runtime. Click **Create function** at the bottom of the screen, as shown in the following screenshot:

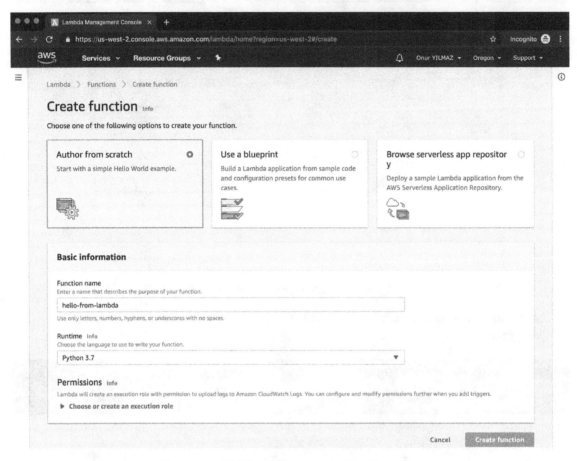

Figure 2.4: AWS Lambda – Create function view

4. You will be directed to the **hello-from-lambda** function view, which is where you

5. can edit the **Function code**, as shown in the following screenshot:

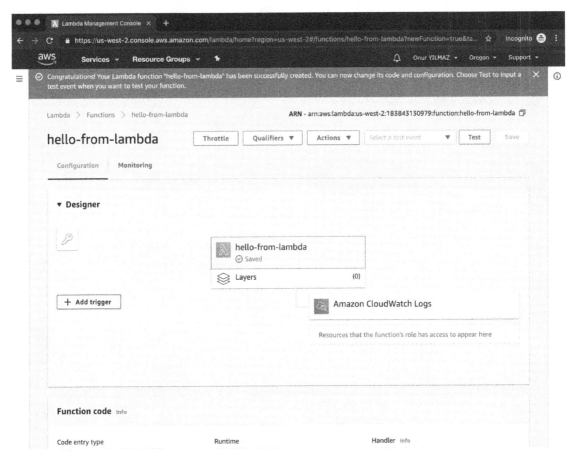

Figure 2.5: AWS Lambda – hello-from-lambda

6. Change the `lambda_handler` function as follows:

```
import json

def lambda_handler(event, context):
    return {
        'statusCode': '200',
        'body': json.dumps({"message": "hello", "platform": "lambda"}),
        'headers': {
            'Content-Type': 'application/json',
        }
    }
```

7. Click **Save** at the top of the screen, as shown in the following screenshot:

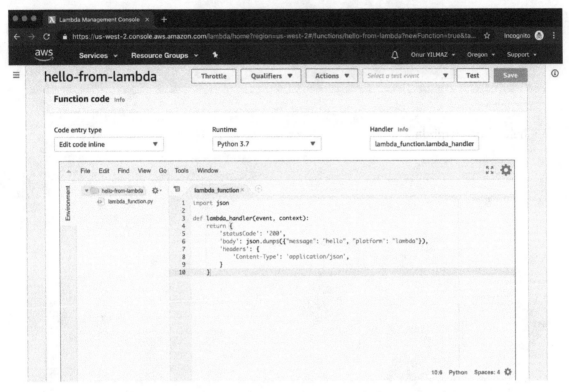

Figure 2.6: AWS Lambda – hello-from-lambda function code

8. Open the **Designer** view and click **Add trigger**, as shown in the following screenshot:

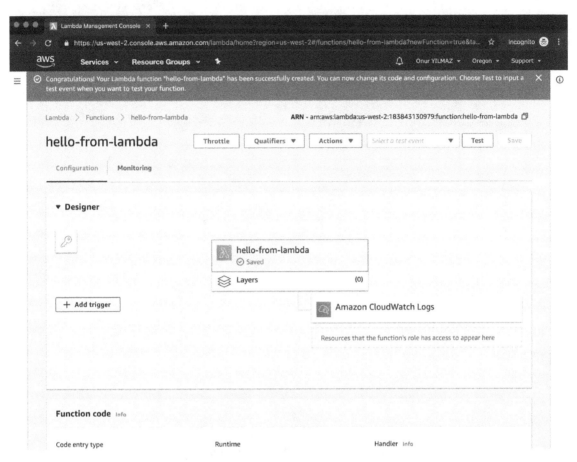

Figure 2.7: AWS Lambda – hello-from-lambda designer view

9. Select **API Gateway** from the triggers list, as shown in the following screenshot:

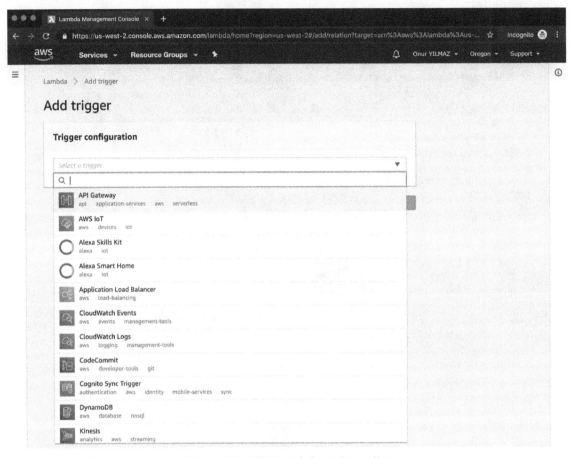

Figure 2.8: AWS Lambda – trigger list

10. Select **Create a new API** for the API and **Open** for the **Security** configurations on the trigger configuration screen, as shown in the following screenshot:

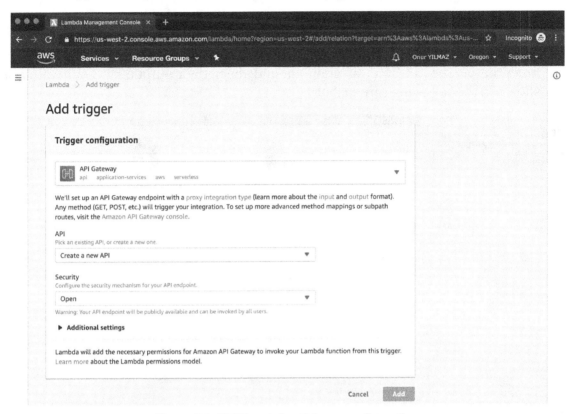

Figure 2.9: AWS Lambda – Trigger configuration

On this screen, a new API has been defined in the API Gateway with open security for the `hello-from-lambda` function. This configuration ensures that an endpoint will be created and that it will be accessible without any authentication.

11. Click **Add** at the bottom of the screen.

    You will be redirected to the `hello-from-lambda` function, with a notification saying **The function is now receiving events from the trigger**. In the **Designer** view, the function from Lambda is connected to the API Gateway for triggering and Amazon CloudWatch Logs for logging. In other words, it is now possible to trigger functions via the API Gateway endpoint and check their outputs in CloudWatch, as shown in the following screenshot:

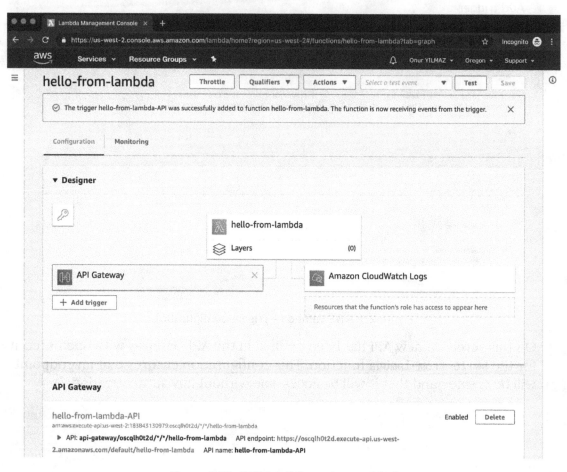

Figure 2.10: AWS Lambda – trigger added

12. Get the API Gateway endpoint from the API Gateway section, as shown in the following screenshot:

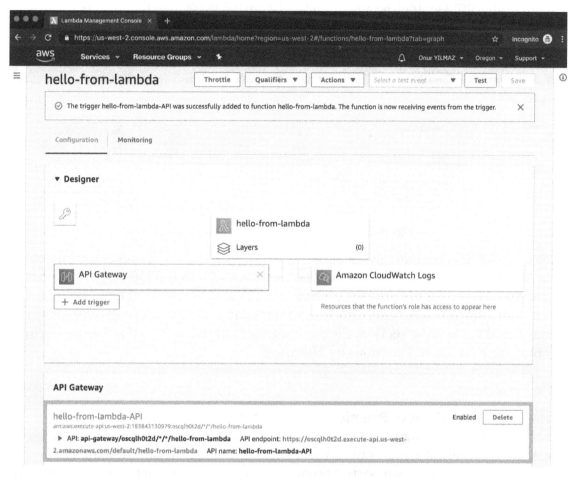

Figure 2.11: AWS Lambda – trigger URL

13. Open the URL in a new tab to trigger the function and get the response, as shown in the following screenshot:

Figure 2.12: AWS Lambda – function response

This JSON response indicates that the AWS Lambda function is connected via the API Gateway and working as expected.

14. Return to the **Functions** list from Step 2, select `hello-from-lambda`, and choose **Delete** from **Actions**. Then, click **Delete** in the pop-up window to remove the function from Lambda, as shown in the following screenshot:

Figure 2.13: AWS Lambda – function deletion

In this exercise, the general flow of creating an AWS Lambda function and connecting to the AWS Gateway API for HTTP access was shown. In less than 10 steps, it is possible to have running production-ready services in an AWS Lambda cloud environment. This exercise has shown you how serverless platforms can make software development fast and easy. In the following section, the analysis of cloud provider serverless platforms will continue with Azure Functions by Microsoft.

Azure Functions

Microsoft announced **Azure Functions** in 2016 as the serverless platform in the **Microsoft Azure** cloud. Azure Functions extends its cloud platform with event triggers from Azure or external services to run serverless workloads. It differentiates by focusing on the Microsoft supported programming languages and tools that are highly prevalent in the industry. In this section, Azure Functions will be discussed in terms of the supported programming languages, trigger types, and cost. Finally, we will deploy a function that takes parameters from endpoints to Azure Functions to illustrate its operational side.

> **Note**
>
> The official website of Azure Functions can be found here if you wish to find out more: https://azure.microsoft.com/en-us/services/functions/.

The latest version of Azure Functions supports **C#**, **JavaScript** in the **Node.js** runtime, **F#**, **Java**, **PowerShell**, **Python**, and **Typescript**, which is transpired into **JavaScript**. In addition, a language extensibility interface is provided for the communication between the functions runtime and the worker processes over **gRPC** as a messaging layer. It is valuable to check the generally available, experimental, and extendible programming languages supported by Azure Functions before we start utilizing it.

> **Note**
>
> gRPC is a **remote procedure call** (**RPC**) system that was initially developed at Google. It is an open source system that enables cross-platform communication without language or platform limitations.

Azure Functions are designed to be triggered by various types, such as timers, HTTP, file operations, queue messages, and events. In addition, input and output bindings can be specified for functions. These bindings define the input arguments for the functions and output values to send other services. For instance, it is possible to create a scheduled function to read files from Blob Storage and create Cosmos DB documents as outputs. In this example, the function could be defined with a **timer trigger**, **Blob Storage** input binding, and **Cosmos DB** output binding. Triggers and bindings make Azure Functions easily integrate to Azure services and the external world.

There are two differences between the cost calculation method and the current prices of Azure Functions compared to AWS Lambda. The first difference is that the current computation price of Azure Functions is slightly cheaper, at $0.000016/GB per second. The second difference is that Azure Functions calculates using observed memory consumption while the memory limit is preconfigured in AWS Lambda.

In the following exercise, the very first serverless function will be deployed to Azure Functions and will be invoked to show the operational view of the platform.

> **Note**
>
> In order to complete this exercise, you need to have an active Azure account. You can create an account at https://signup.azure.com/.

Exercise 5: Creating a Parameterized Function in Azure Functions

In this exercise, we aim to create a parameterized function in Azure and invoke it over its HTTP endpoint with different parameters.

To successfully complete this exercise, we need to ensure the following steps are executed:

1. Click on **Function App** in the left menu of the **Azure** home page, as shown in the following screenshot:

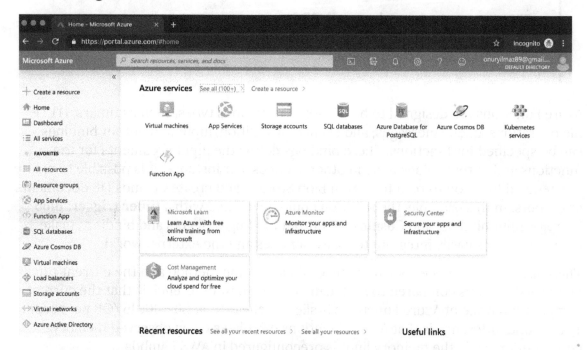

Figure 2.14: Azure home page

2. Click on **Create Function App** from the **Function App** list, as shown in the following screenshot:

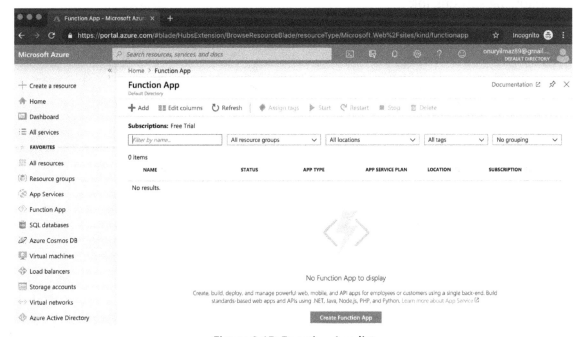

Figure 2.15: Function App list

3. Give the app a unique name, such as **hello-from-azure**, and select **Node.js** as the **Runtime Stack**. Click on **Create** at the bottom of the page, as shown in the following screenshot:

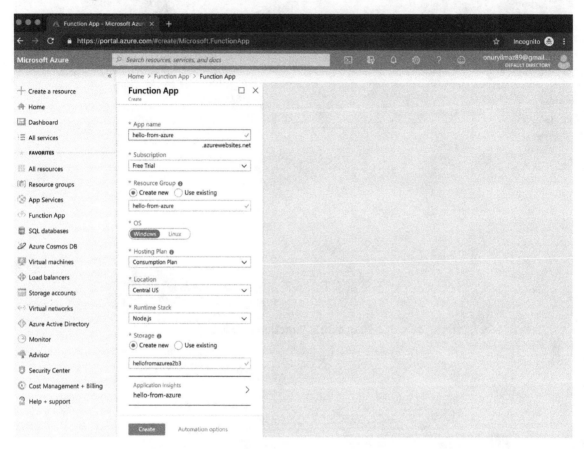

Figure 2.16: Creating a Function App

4. You will be redirected to the **Function App** list view. Check for a notification at the top of the menu. You will see **Deployment to resource group 'hello-from-azure' is in progress**, as shown in the following screenshot:

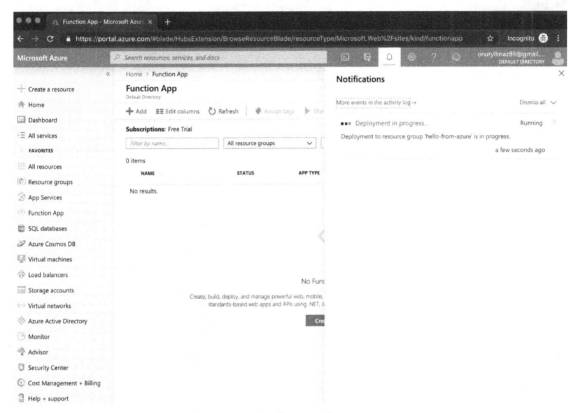

Figure 2.17: Deployment in progress

Wait a couple of minutes until the deployment is complete:

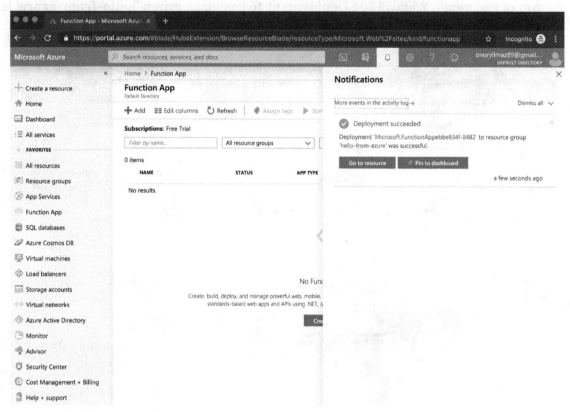

Figure 2.18: Successful deployment

5. Click on **+ New Function** in the `hello-from-azure` function app view, as shown in the following screenshot:

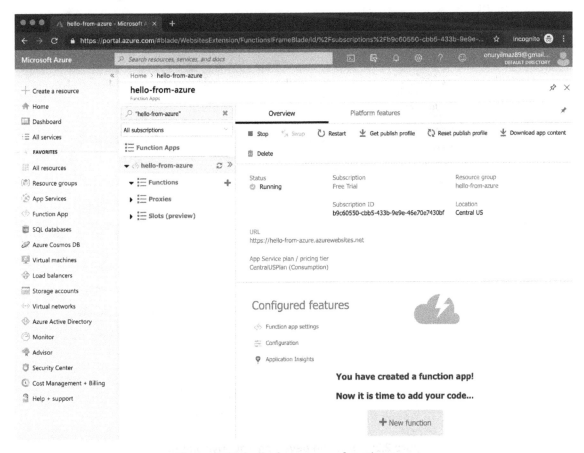

Figure 2.19: hello-from-azure function app

6. Select **In-portal** for function creation inside the Azure web portal as a development environment and click **Continue**, as shown in the following screenshot:

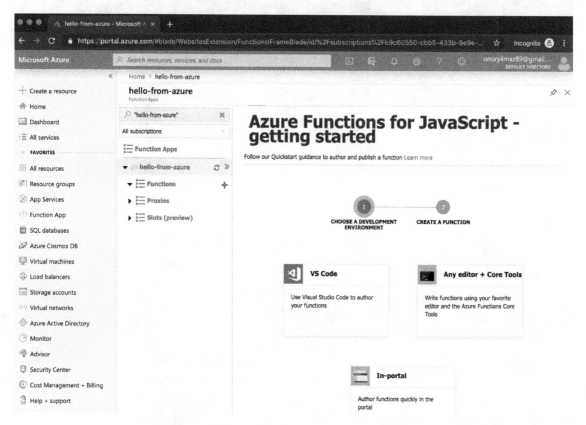

Figure 2.20: Function development environment

7. Select **Webhook + API** and click **Create**, as shown in the following screenshot:

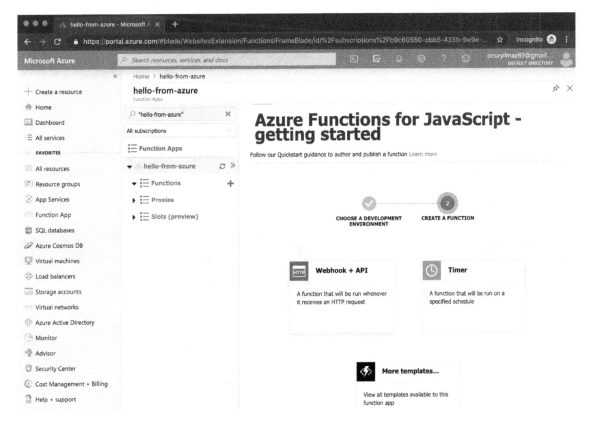

Figure 2.21: Function trigger types

In this view, it is possible to create functions from templates such as webhooks, timers, or collaborative templates from the marketplace.

8. Write the following function into `index.js` and click **Save**:

```
module.exports = async function (context, req) {
    context.log('JavaScript HTTP trigger function processed a request.');

    if (req.query.name || (req.body && req.body.name)) {
        context.res = {
            status: 200,
            body: "Hello " + (req.query.name || req.body.name) +", it is
your function in Azure!"
        };
    }
```

```
    else {
        context.res = {
            status: 400,
            body: "Please pass a name on the query string or in the
request body."
        };
    }
};
```

This code exports a function that accepts parameters from the request. The function creates a personalized message and sends it as output to the users. The code should be inserted into the code editor, as shown in the following screenshot:

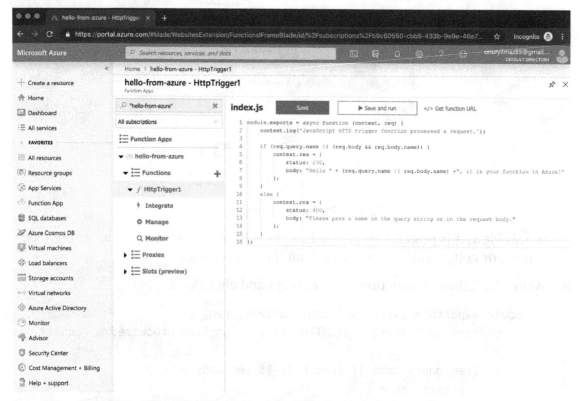

Figure 2.22: index.js of the hello-from-azure function

9. Click on **Get function URL** and copy the URL inside the popup, as shown in the

10. following screenshot:

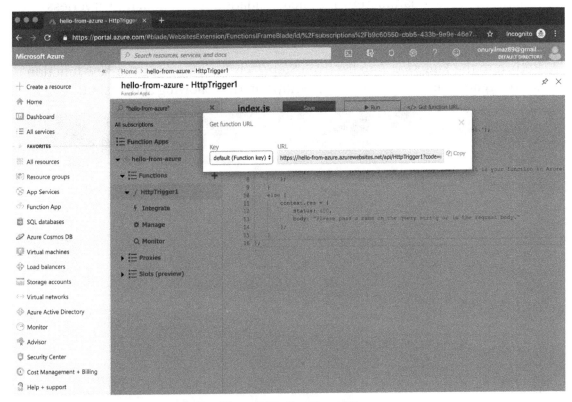

Figure 2.23: Function URL

11. Open the URL you copied in *Step* 7 into a new tab in the browser, as shown in the following screenshot:

Please pass a name on the query string or in the request body.

Figure 2.24: Function response without parameter

Add **&name=** and your name to the end of the URL and reload the tab, for example, `https://hello-from-azure.azurewebsites.net/api/HttpTrigger?code=nNrck...&name=Onur`, as shown in the following screenshot:

Hello Onur, it is your function in Azure!

Figure 2.25: Function response with parameter

These responses show that it is possible to validate and pass parameters to functions. Passing parameters and their validation is essential for serverless functions and when considering the possibility of various integration points as triggers and bindings.

12. Return to the **Function App** list from *Step* 2, click **...** alongside the new function we've created, and select **Delete**, as shown in the following screenshot:

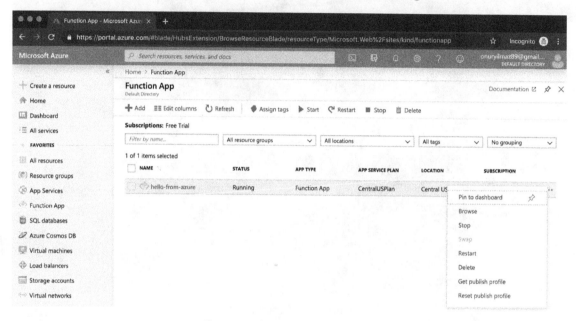

Figure 2.26: Deleting a function

Type the name of the function into the pop-up view and click **Delete** to delete all the resources. In the confirmation view, a warning indicates that deletion of the function application is irreversible, as you can see in the following screenshot:

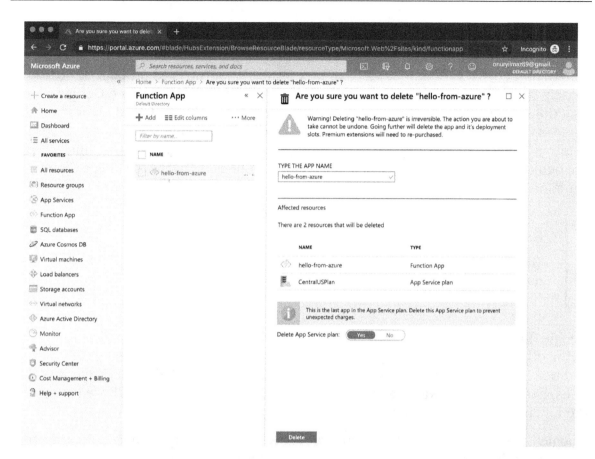

Figure 2.27: Deleting the function and its resources

In the following section, Google Cloud Functions will be discussed in a similar way, and a more complicated function will be deployed to the cloud provider.

Google Cloud Functions

Google Cloud Functions was made public in 2017 just after AWS Lambda and Azure Functions. Serverless functions were already available for the PaaS product of Google, namely **Firebase**, before the release of Google Cloud Functions. However, Google Cloud Functions was made available to all the services inside the Google Cloud Platform as its core serverless cloud product. In this section, Google Cloud Functions will be discussed in terms of the supported programming languages, trigger types, and cost. Finally, we will deploy a function that is periodically invoked by cloud services to Google Cloud Functions to illustrate its operational side.

> **Note**
>
> The official website of Google Cloud Functions can be found here if you wish to find out more: https://cloud.google.com/functions/.

Google Cloud Functions (**GCF**) can be developed in **Node.js**, **Python**, and **Go**. Compared to the other major cloud providers, GCF supports a small subset of languages. In addition, there are no publicly available language extension or APIs supported by GCF. Thus, it is essential to evaluate whether the languages supported by GCF are feasible for the functions you will develop.

Google Cloud Functions are designed to be associated with triggers and events. Events happen within your cloud services, such as database changes, new files in the storage system, or when provisioning new virtual machines. Triggers are the declaration of the services and related events as inputs to functions. It is possible to create triggers as **HTTP** endpoints, **Cloud Pub/Sub** queue messages, or storage services such as **Cloud Storage** and **Cloud Firestore**. In addition, functions can be connected to the big data and machine learning services that are provided in the Google Cloud Platform.

The cost calculation of Google Cloud Platform is slightly complex compared to other cloud providers. This is because it takes the invocations, computation time, and outbound network data into consideration, while other cloud providers focus only on invocations and compute time:

- **Invocations:** Function invocations are charged $0.40 for every one million requests.

- **Compute time:** The computation times of the functions are measured from the time of invocation to their completion in 100 ms increments. For instance, if your function takes 240 ms to complete, you will be charged for 300 ms of computation time. There are two units that are used in this calculation – **GB per second** and **GHz per second**. 1 GB of memory is provisioned for a function running for 1 second, and the price of 1 GB per second is $0.0000025. Also, 1 GHz of CPU is provisioned for a function running for 1 second, and the price of 1 GHz per second is $0.0000100.

- **Outbound network data:** Data that's transferred from the function to the outside is measured in GB and charged at $0.12 for every GB of data.

GCF's free tier provides 2 million invocations, 400,000 GB per second, 200,000 GHz per second of computation time, and 5 GB of outbound network traffic per month. Compared to AWS or Azure, GCP will cost slightly more since it has higher prices and more sophisticated calculation methods.

Let's assume that your function is called 30 million times in a month. You have allocated 128 MB of memory, 200 MHz CPU, and on average, the function runs for 200 ms, similar to the example for AWS Lambda:

Request charges:

Price: $0.40 per 1 M request

Free tier: 2 M

Monthly request: 30 M

Monthly request charge = 28 M x $0.40 / M = $11.2

Compute charges – Memory:

Price: $0.0000025 per GB-second

Free tier: 400,000 GB-Seconds

Monthly compute: 30 M x 0.2 second x 128 MB / 1024 = 750,000 GB-second

Monthly memory charge: 350,000 x $0.0000025 = $0.875

Compute charges – CPU:

Price: $0.0000100 per GHz-second

Free tier: 200,000 GB-Seconds

Monthly compute: 30 M x 0.2 second x 200 MHz / 1000 GHz = 1,200,000 GHz-second

Monthly CPU charge: 1,000,000 x $0.0000100 = $10

Monthly total cost= $11.2 + $0.875 + $10 = $22.075

Since the unit prices are slightly higher than AWS and Azure, the total monthly cost of running the same function is more than $22 in GCP, while it was around $11 for AWS and Azure. Also, any outbound network from the functions to the outside world is critical when it comes to potential extra costs. Therefore, pricing methods and unit prices should be analyzed in depth before you choose a serverless cloud platform.

In the following exercise, our very first serverless function will be deployed to GCF and will be invoked by a scheduled trigger to show the operational view of the platform.

> **Note**
>
> In order to complete this exercise, you need to have an active Google account. You can create an account at https://console.cloud.google.com/start.

Exercise 6: Creating a Scheduled Function in GCF

In this exercise, we aim to create a scheduled function in Google Cloud Platform and check its invocation by using cloud scheduler services.

To successfully complete this exercise, we need to ensure the following steps are executed:

1. Click on **Cloud Functions** in the left menu, which can be found in the **Compute** group on the Google Cloud Platform home page, as shown in the following screenshot:

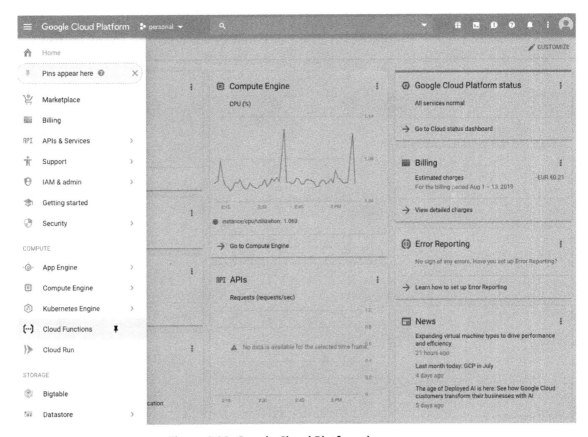

Figure 2.28: Google Cloud Platform home page

2. Click on **Create function** on the **Cloud Functions** page, as shown in the following screenshot:

Figure 2.29: Cloud Functions page

3. In the function creation form, change the function name to **HelloWorld** and select 128 MB for the memory allocation. Ensure that **HTTP** is selected as the trigger method and that **Go 1.11** is selected as the runtime, as shown in the following screenshot:

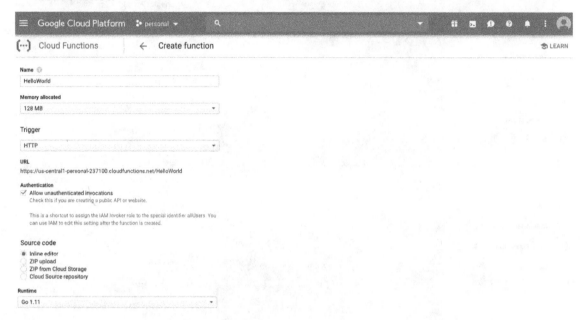

Figure 2.30: Function creation form

4. Change **function.go** using the inline editor inside the browser so that it has the following content:

```go
package p

import (
        "fmt"
        "net/http"
)

func HelloWorld(w http.ResponseWriter, r *http.Request) {
        fmt.Fprint(w, "Hello World from Google Cloud Functions!")
        return
}
```

This code segment creates a **HelloWorld** function with a static message printed to the output. The code should be inserted into **function.go** in the code editor, as shown in the following screenshot:

Figure 2.31: Function inline editor

5. Copy the URL in the form below the **Trigger** selection box to invoke the function, as shown in the following screenshot:

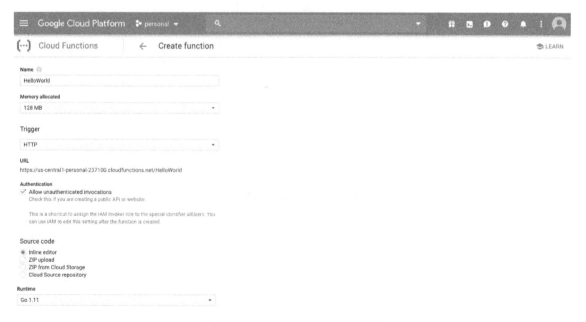

Figure 2.32: Function trigger URL

6. Click on the **Create** button at the end of the form. With this configuration, the code from step 4 will be packaged and deployed to Google Cloud Platform. In addition, a trigger URL will be assigned to the function to be reachable from outside, as shown in the following screenshot:

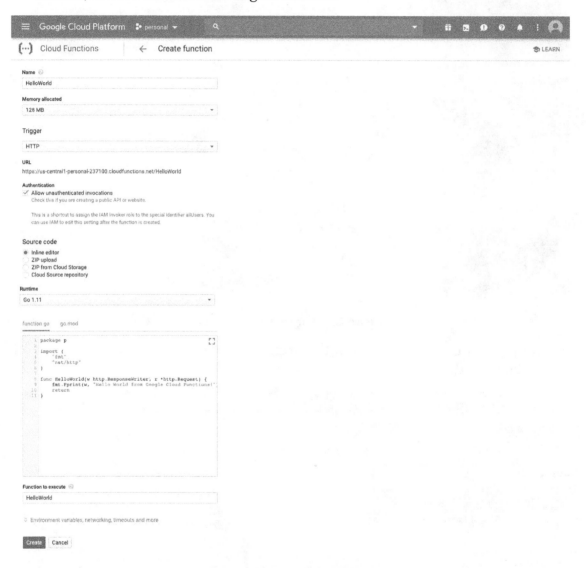

Figure 2.33: Function creation

Wait a couple of minutes until the **HelloWorld** function in the function list has a green check icon next to it, as shown in the following screenshot:

Figure 2.34: Function deployment

7. Open the URL you copied in step 5 into a new tab in your browser, as shown in the following screenshot:

Figure 2.35: Function response

The response shows that the function has been successfully deployed and is running as expected.

8. Click on **Cloud Scheduler** in the left menu, under **TOOLS**, as shown in the following screenshot:

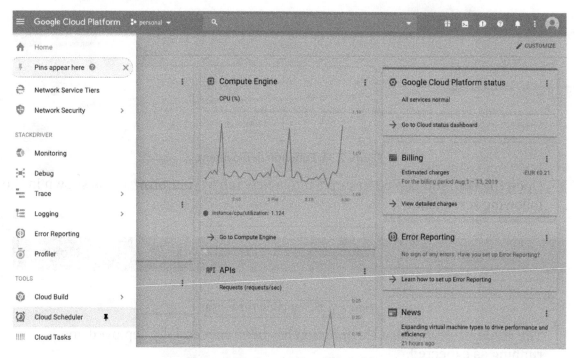

Figure 2.36: Google Cloud Tools Menu

9. Click on **Create job** on the **Cloud Scheduler** page, as shown in the following screenshot:

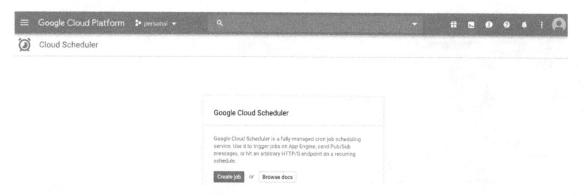

Figure 2.37: Cloud Scheduler page

10. Select a region if you are using **Cloud Scheduler** for the first time in your Google Cloud project and click **Next**, as shown in the following screenshot:

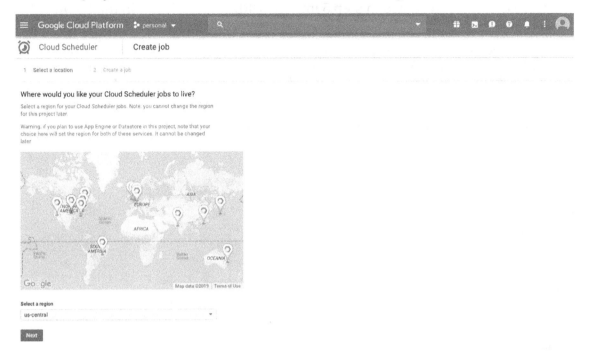

Figure 2.38: Cloud Scheduler – region selection

Wait for a couple of minutes if you see the following notification:

We are initializing Cloud Scheduler in your selected region. This usually takes about a minute.

11. Set the job name as **HelloWorldEveryMinute** and the frequency as * * * * *, which means the job will be triggered every minute. Select HTTP as the target and paste the URL you copied in step 5 into the URL box, as shown in the following screenshot:

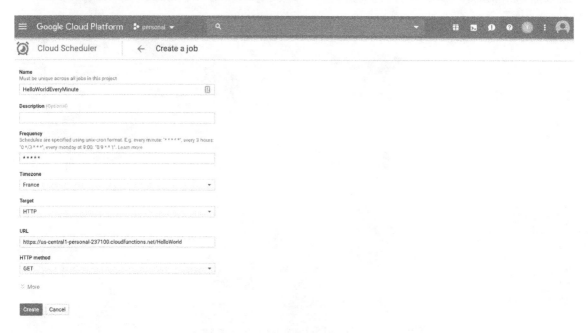

Figure 2.39: Scheduler job creation

12. You will be redirected to the **Cloud Scheduler** list, as shown in the following screenshot:

Figure 2.40: Cloud Scheduler page

Wait for a couple of minutes and click the **Refresh** button. The list will show the **Last run** timestamp and its result for `HelloWorldEveryMinute`, as shown in the following screenshot:

Figure 2.41: Cloud Scheduler page with run information

This indicates that the cloud scheduler triggered our function at `Aug 13, 2019, 3:44:00 PM` and that the result was successful.

13. Return to the function list from step 7 and click **...** for the `HelloWorld` function. Then, click **Logs**, as shown in the following screenshot:

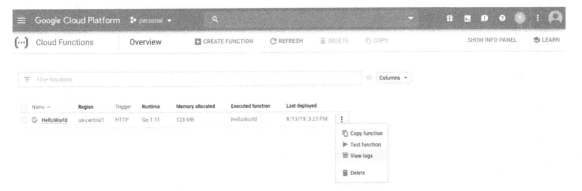

Figure 2.42: Settings menu for the function

You will be redirected to the logs of the function, where you will see that, every minute, **Function execution started** and the corresponding success logs are listed, as shown in the following screenshot:

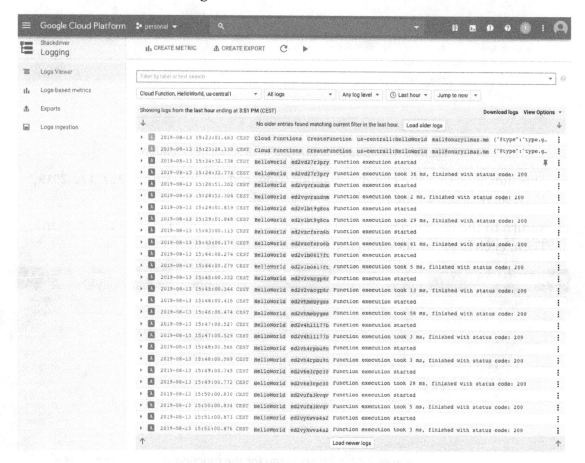

Figure 2.43: Function logs

As you can see, the cloud scheduler is invoking the function as planned and that the function is running successfully.

14. Return to the Cloud Scheduler page from Step 13, choose **HelloWorldEveryMinute**, click **Delete** on the menu, and then confirm this in the popup, as shown in the following screenshot:

Figure 2.44: Cloud Scheduler – job deletion

15. Return to the **Cloud Functions** page from step 7, choose **HelloWorld**, click **Delete** on the menu, and then confirm this in the popup, as shown in the following screenshot:

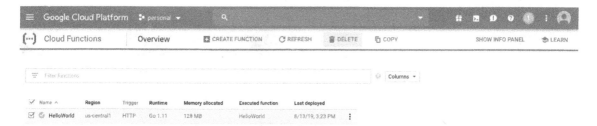

Figure 2.45: Cloud Functions – function deletion

In this exercise, we created a **Hello World** function and deployed it to GCF. In addition, a cloud scheduler job was created to trigger the function with specific intervals such as every minute. Now, the function is connected to another cloud service so that the function can trigger the service. It is essential to integrate functions with other cloud services and evaluate their integration capabilities prior to choosing a cloud FaaS provider.

In the following activity, you will develop a real-life daily stand-up reminder function. You will connect a function and function trigger service you wish to invoke on your specific stand-up meeting time. In addition, this reminder will send a specific message to a cloud-based collaboration tool, namely *Slack*.

Activity 2: Daily Stand-Up Meeting Reminder Function for Slack

The aim of this activity is to create a real-life function for stand-up meeting reminders in Slack. This reminder function will be invoked at specific times for your team to remind everyone in your team about the next stand-up meeting. The reminder will work with Slack since it is a popular collaboration tool that's been adopted by numerous organizations worldwide.

> **Note**
>
> In order to complete this activity, you need to access a Slack workplace. You can use your existing Slack workspace or create a new one for free at https://slack.com/create.

Once completed, you will have deployed a daily stand-up reminder function to GCF, as shown in the following screenshot:

Figure 2.46: Daily reminder function

In addition, you will need an integration environment for invoking the function at specified meeting times. Stand-up meetings generally take place at a specific time on workdays. Thus, a scheduler job will be connected to trigger your function according to your meeting time, as shown in the following screenshot:

Figure 2.47: Daily reminder scheduler

Finally, when the scheduler invokes the function, you will have reminder messages in your Slack channel, as shown in the following screenshot:

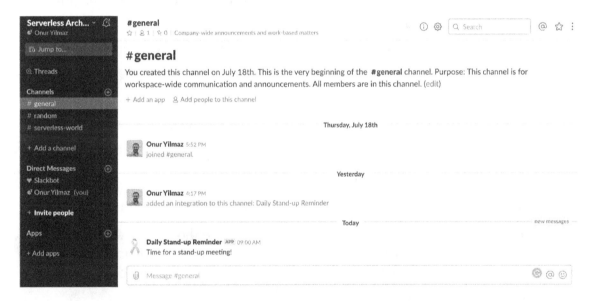

Figure 2.48: Slack message for meeting reminder

Note

In order to complete this activity, you should configure Slack by following the Slack Setup steps.

Slack Setup

Execute the following steps to configure Slack:

1. In the **Slack** workspace, click on your username and select **Customize Slack**.

2. Click on **Configure apps** in the open window.

3. Click on **Browse the App Directory** to add a new application from the directory.

4. Find **Incoming WebHooks** from the search box in **App Directory**.

5. Click on **Add Configuration** for the **Incoming WebHooks** application.

6. Fill in the configuration for the incoming webhook with your specific channel name and icon.

7. Open your Slack workspace and channel. You will see an integration message.

> **Note**
>
> Detailed screenshots of the Slack setup steps can be found on page 376.

Execute the following steps to complete this activity:

1. Create a new function in GCF to call the Slack webhook when it is invoked.

    The code should send a JSON request to the Slack webhook URL with a similar object: **{"text": "Time for a stand-up meeting"}**. You can implement the code in any language that's supported by GCF. The code snippet is as follows:

    ```
    package p

    import (
        "bytes"
        "net/http"
    )

    func Reminder(http.ResponseWriter, *http.Request) {
        url := "https://hooks.slack.com/services/TLJB82G8L/BMAUKCJ9W/
    Q02YZFDiaTRdyUBTImE7MXn1"

        var jsonStr = []byte('{"text": "Time for a stand-up meeting!"}')
        req, err := http.NewRequest("POST", url, bytes.NewBuffer(jsonStr))

        client := &http.Client{}
    ```

```
        _, err = client.Do(req)
        if err != nil {
            panic(err)
        }
    }
```

2. Create a scheduler job in **GCP** with the trigger URL of the function and specify the schedule based on your stand-up meeting times.

   Check the Slack channel when the time that's been defined with the schedule has arrived for the reminder message.

3. Delete the schedule job and function from the cloud provider.

> **Note**
>
> The solution to this activity can be found on page 376.

Summary

In this chapter, we described the evolution of cloud technology offerings, including how the cloud products have changed over the years and how responsibilities are distributed among organizations, starting with IaaS and PaaS and, finally, FaaS. Following that, criteria were presented for evaluating serverless cloud offerings.

Programming language support, function triggers, and the cost structure of serverless products were listed so that we could compare the various cloud providers, that is, AWS Lambda, Azure Functions, and GCF. In addition, we deployed a serverless function to all three cloud providers. This showed you how cloud functions can be integrated with other cloud services, such as the AWS API Gateway for REST API operations. Furthermore, a parameterized function was deployed to Azure Functions to show how we can process inputs from users or other systems. Finally, we deployed a scheduled function to GCF to show integration with other cloud services. At the end of this chapter, we implemented a real-life Slack reminder using serverless functions and cloud schedulers.

In the next chapter, we will cover serverless frameworks and learn how to work with them.

3

Introduction to Serverless Frameworks

Learning Objectives

By the end of this chapter, you will be able to:

- Compare and effectively utilize different serverless functions
- Set up a cloud-agnostic and container-native serverless framework
- Create, deploy, and invoke a function using the Fn framework
- Deploy serverless functions to cloud providers using serverless frameworks
- Create a real-life serverless application and run it on multiple cloud platforms in the future

In this chapter, we will explain serverless frameworks, create our first serverless functions using these frameworks, and deploy them to various cloud providers.

Introduction

Let's imagine that you are developing a complex application with many functions in one cloud provider. It may not be feasible to move to another cloud provider, even if the new one is cheaper, faster, or more secure. This situation of vendor dependency is known as **vendor lock-in** in the industry, and it is a very critical decision factor in the long run. Fortunately, serverless frameworks are a simple and efficient solution to vendor lock-in.

In the previous chapter, all three major cloud providers and their serverless products were discussed. These products were compared based on their programming language support, trigger capabilities, and cost structure. However, there is still one unseen critical difference between all three products: *operations*. Creating functions, deploying them to cloud providers, and their management are all different for each cloud provider. In other words, you cannot use the same function in AWS Lambda, Google Cloud Functions, and Azure Functions. Various changes are required so that we can fulfil the requirements of cloud providers and their runtime.

Serverless frameworks are **open source**, **cloud-agnostic** platforms for running serverless applications. The first difference between the cloud provider and serverless products is that their serverless frameworks are open source and public. They are free to install on the cloud or on on-premise systems and operate on their own. The second characteristic is that serverless frameworks are **cloud agnostic**. This means that it is possible to run the same serverless functions on different cloud providers or your own systems. In other words, the cloud provider where the functions will be executed is just a configuration parameter in serverless frameworks. All cloud providers are equalized behind a shared API so that cloud-agnostic functions can be developed and deployed by serverless frameworks.

Cloud serverless platforms such as AWS Lambda increased the hype of serverless architectures and empowered their adoption in the industry. In the previous chapter, the evolution of cloud technology offerings over the years and significant cloud serverless platforms were discussed in depth. In this chapter, we will discuss open source serverless frameworks and talk about their featured characteristics and functionalities. There are many popular and upcoming serverless frameworks on the market. However, we will focus on two prominent frameworks with differences in terms of priorities and architecture. In this chapter, a container-native serverless framework, namely **Fn**, will be presented. Following that, a more comprehensive framework with multiple cloud provider support, namely, the **Serverless Framework**, will be discussed in depth. Although both frameworks create a cloud-agnostic and open source environment for running serverless applications, their differences in terms of implementation and developer experience will be illustrated.

Fn Framework

Fn was announced in 2017 by **Oracle** at the *JavaOne* 2017 conference as an event-driven and open source **Function-as-a-Service** (**FaaS**) platform. The key characteristics of the framework are as follows:

- **Open source:** All the source code of the **Fn** project is publicly available at https://github.com/fnproject/fn, and the project is hosted at https://fnproject.io. It has an active community on GitHub, with more than 3,300 commits and 1,100 releases, as shown in the following screenshot:

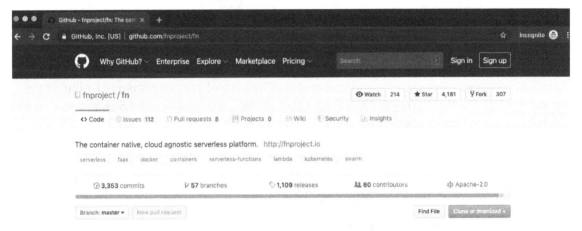

Figure 3.1: Fn at GitHub

- **Container-native:** Containers and microservices have changed the manner of software development and operations. **Fn** is container-native, meaning that each function is packaged and deployed as a Docker container. Also, it is possible to create your own Docker container and run them as functions.

- **Language support:** The framework officially supports **Go**, **Java**, **Node.js**, **Ruby**, and **Python**. In addition, **C#** is supported by the community.

- **Cloud-agnostic:** **Fn** can run on every cloud provider or on-premise system, as long as Docker is installed and running. This is the most critical characteristic of **Fn**, since it avoids the vendor lock-in problem completely. If the functions do not depend on any cloud-specific service, it is possible to move between cloud providers and on-premise systems quickly.

As a cloud-agnostic and container-native platform, **Fn** is a developer-focused framework. It enhances developer experience and agility since you can develop, test, and debug locally and deploy to cloud with the same tooling. In the following exercise, we will install and configure **Fn** so that we can start using the framework.

> **Note**
>
> Docker **17.10.0-ce** or later should be installed and running on your computer before you start the next exercise, since this is a prerequisite for **Fn**.

Exercise 7: Getting Started with the Fn Framework

In this exercise, you will install and configure a cloud-agnostic and container-native serverless framework on your local computer. The aim of this exercise is to illustrate how straightforward it is to configure and install the Fn Framework so that you can get started with serverless frameworks.

To complete this exercise successfully, we need to ensure that the following steps are executed:

1. In your Terminal, type the following command:

    ```
    curl -LSs https://raw.githubusercontent.com/fnproject/cli/master/install |
    sh
    ```

    This command downloads and installs the Fn framework. Once this is complete, the version number is printed out, as shown in the following screenshot:

Figure 3.2: Installation of Fn

2. Start the **Fn** server by using the following command in your Terminal:

```
fn start -d
```

This command downloads the Docker image of the **Fn** server and starts it inside a container, as shown in the following screenshot:

```
/serverless $ fn start -d
2019/08/20 13:11:46 ¡¡¡ 'fn start' should NOT be used for PRODUCTION !!! see https://github.com/fnproject/fn-helm/
Unable to find image 'fnproject/fnserver:latest' locally
latest: Pulling from fnproject/fnserver
ff3a5c916c92: Pull complete
1a649ea86bca: Pull complete
ce35f4d5f86a: Pull complete
b6206661264b: Pull complete
b8b71dba24d3: Pull complete
3873004a68ee: Pull complete
f4205b132661: Pull complete
91a85eeeb257: Pull complete
93c96d032b32: Pull complete
bb761748d6e1: Pull complete
81f6c51c4ac2: Pull complete
2ba715696dba: Pull complete
f46c2b56aaf3: Pull complete
2ba9f20888b7: Pull complete
f6ff7826500c: Pull complete
Digest: sha256:4ed57ea2731a16eb3e9070d9a36ad0a65c21b9460f278b90c1f7c1b187a7f0b1
Status: Downloaded newer image for fnproject/fnserver:latest
d7e26fc891cec0ee9f1a6f21b8f744bbc4b2d92d46588de0e63fb8046f854ec7
/serverless $
```

Figure 3.3: Starting the Fn server

3. Check the client and server version by using the following command in your Terminal:

```
fn version
```

The output should be as follows:

```
/serverless $ fn version
Client version is latest version: 0.5.84
Server version:  0.3.729
/serverless $
```

Figure 3.4: Fn server and client version

This output shows that both the client and server side are running and interacting with each other.

4. Update the current Fn context and set a local development registry:

```
fn use context default && fn update context registry serverless
```

The output is shown in the following screenshot:

```
/serverless $ fn use context default && fn update context registry serverless
Now using context: default
Current context updated registry with serverless
/serverless $
```

Figure 3.5: Registry setup for the current context

As the output indicates, the **default** context is set, and the registry is updated to **serverless**.

5. Start the **Fn** dashboard by using the following command in your Terminal:

```
docker run -d --link fnserver:api -p 4000:4000 -e "FN_API_URL=http://
api:8080" fnproject/ui
```

This command downloads the **fnproject/ui** image and starts it in **detached** mode. In addition, it links **fnserver:api** to itself and publishes the **4000** port, as shown in the following screenshot:

```
/serverless $ docker run -d --link fnserver:api -p 4000:4000 -e "FN_API_URL=http://api:8080" fnproject/ui
Unable to find image 'fnproject/ui:latest' locally
latest: Pulling from fnproject/ui
b56ae66c2937: Pull complete
e93c4ef66dd7: Pull complete
a9e499bf0a12: Pull complete
ba1608f40908: Pull complete
6464d2649fbf: Pull complete
ebc7db4cf098: Pull complete
f34c1cd5ef21: Pull complete
dc688e6ebaad: Pull complete
Digest: sha256:82c5b2fd02d702d2294bb107c1c022dba699241f64e4e14b77519d4c25bbb5f9
Status: Downloaded newer image for fnproject/ui:latest
ceb0cdd70e88f843aa6ee1eea5253758d296598213702e98999f985c59be719b
/serverless $
```

Figure 3.6: Starting the Fn UI

6. Check the running Docker containers with the following command:

```
docker ps
```

As expected, two containers are running for **Fn** with the image names **fnproject/ui** and **fnproject/fnserver:latest**, respectively, as shown in the following screenshot:

```
/serverless $ docker ps
CONTAINER ID   IMAGE                        COMMAND        CREATED          STATUS          PORTS                                    NAMES
ceb0cdd70e88   fnproject/ui                 "npm start"    2 minutes ago    Up 2 minutes    0.0.0.0:4000->4000/tcp                   thirsty_chaplygin
d7e26fc891ce   fnproject/fnserver:latest    "./fnserver"   15 minutes ago   Up 15 minutes   2375/tcp, 0.0.0.0:8080->8080/tcp         fnserver
/serverless $
```

Figure 3.7: Docker containers

7. Open **http://localhost:4000** in your browser to check the Fn UI.

    The Fn Dashboard lists the applications and function statistics as a web application, as shown in the following screenshot:

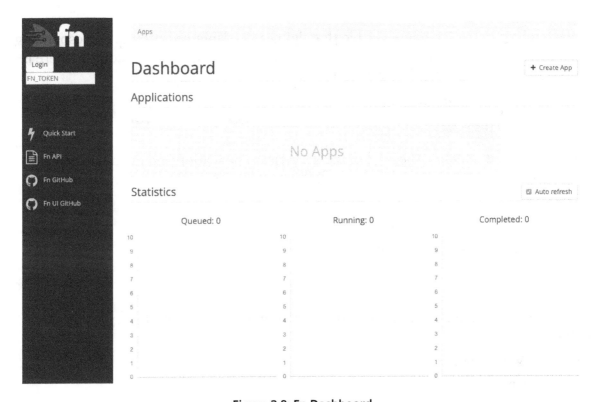

Figure 3.8: Fn Dashboard

With this exercise, we have installed the **Fn** framework, along with its client, server, and dashboard. Since **Fn** is a cloud-agnostic framework, it is possible to install any cloud or on-premise system with the illustrated steps. We will continue discussing the **Fn** framework in terms of how the functions are configured and deployed.

The **Fn** framework is designed to work with applications, where each application is a group of functions with their own route mappings. For instance, let's assume you have grouped your functions into a folder, as follows:

- app.yaml

- func.yaml

- func.go

- go.mod

- products/

    - func.yaml

```
    - func.js
  - suppliers/
    - func.yaml
    - func.rb
```

In each folder, there is a **func.yaml** file that defines the function with the corresponding implementation in **Ruby**, **Node.js**, or any other supported language. In addition, there is an **app.yaml** file in the root folder to define the application.

Let's start by checking the content of **app.yaml**:

```
name: serverless-app
```

app.yaml is used to define the root of the serverless application and includes the name of the application. There are also three additional files for the function in the root folder:

- **func.go**: Go implementation code
- **go.mod**: Go dependency definitions
- **func.yaml**: Function definition and trigger information

For a function with an HTTP trigger and Go runtime, the following **func.yaml** file is defined:

```
name: serverless-app
version: 0.0.1
runtime: go
entrypoint: ./func
triggers:
- name: serverless-app
  type: http
  source: /serverless-app
```

When you deploy all of these functions to Fn, they will be accessible via the following URLs:

```
http://serverless-kubernetes.io/            -> root function
http://serverless-kubernetes.io/products    -> function in products/
directory
http://serverless-kubernetes.io/suppliers   -> function in suppliers/
directory
```

In the following exercise, the content of the **app.yaml** and **func.yaml** files, as well as their function implementation, will be illustrated with a real-life example.

Exercise 8: Running Functions in the Fn Framework

In this exercise, we aim to create, deploy, and invoke a function using the **Fn** framework.

To complete this exercise successfully, we need to ensure that the following steps are executed:

1. In your Terminal, run the following commands to create an application:

    ```
    mkdir serverless-app
    cd serverless-app
    echo "name: serverless-app" > app.yaml
    cat app.yaml
    ```

    The output should be as follows:

    ```
    /serverless $ mkdir serverless-app
    /serverless $ cd serverless-app
    /serverless $ echo "name: serverless-app" > app.yaml
    /serverless $ cat app.yaml
    name: serverless-app
    /serverless $ █
    ```

    Figure 3.9: Creating the application

    These commands create a folder called **serverless-app** and then change the directory so that it's in this folder. Finally, a file called **app.yaml** is created with the content **name: serverless-app**, which is used to define the root of the application.

2. Run the following command in your Terminal to create a root function that's available at the **"/"** of the application URL:

    ```
    fn init --runtime ruby --trigger http
    ```

    This command will create a Ruby function with an HTTP trigger at the root of the application, as shown in the following screenshot:

    ```
    /serverless $ fn init --runtime ruby --trigger http
    Function boilerplate generated.
    func.yaml created.
    /serverless $ █
    ```

    Figure 3.10: Ruby function creation

3. Create a subfunction by using the following commands in your Terminal:

```
fn init --runtime go --trigger http hello-world
```

This command initializes a Go function with an HTTP trigger in the **hello-world** folder of the application, as shown in the following screenshot:

```
/serverless $ fn init --runtime go --trigger http hello-world
Creating function at: ./hello-world
Function boilerplate generated.
func.yaml created.
/serverless $
```

Figure 3.11: Go function creation

4. Check the directory of the application by using the following command in your Terminal:

```
ls -l ./*
```

This command lists the files in the root and child folders, as shown in the following screenshot:

```
/serverless $ ls -l ./*
-rw-r--r-- 1 root root   21 Aug 20 14:39 ./app.yaml
-rw-r--r-- 1 root root  252 Aug 20 14:40 ./func.rb
-rw-r--r-- 1 root root  172 Aug 20 14:40 ./func.yaml
-rw-r--r-- 1 root root   62 Aug 20 14:40 ./Gemfile

./hello-world:
total 12
-rw-r--r-- 1 root root 469 Aug 20 14:40 func.go
-rw-r--r-- 1 root root 155 Aug 20 14:40 func.yaml
-rw-r--r-- 1 root root  13 Aug 20 14:40 go.mod
/serverless $
```

Figure 3.12: Folder structure

As expected, there is a Ruby function in the root folder with three files: **func.rb** for the implementation, **func.yaml** for the function definition, and **Gemfile** to define Ruby function dependencies.

Similarly, there is a Go function in the **hello-world** folder with three files: **func.go** for the implementation, **func.yaml** for the function definition, and **go.mod** for Go dependencies.

5. Deploy the entire application by using the following command in your Terminal:

```
fn deploy --create-app --all --local
```

This command deploys all the functions by creating the app and using a local development environment, as shown in the following screenshot:

```
/serverless $ fn deploy --create-app --all --local
Successfully created app:  serverless-app
Deploying serverless-app to app: serverless-app
Bumped to version 0.0.2
Building image serverless/serverless-app:0.0.2 .....................................
Updating function serverless-app using image serverless/serverless-app:0.0.2...
Successfully created function: serverless-app with serverless/serverless-app:0.0.2
Successfully created trigger: serverless-app
Trigger Endpoint: http://localhost:8080/t/serverless-app/serverless-app
Deploying hello-world to app: serverless-app
Bumped to version 0.0.2
Building image serverless/hello-world:0.0.2 .....................................
Updating function hello-world using image serverless/hello-world:0.0.2...
Successfully created function: hello-world with serverless/hello-world:0.0.2
Successfully created trigger: hello-world
Trigger Endpoint: http://localhost:8080/t/serverless-app/hello-world
/serverless $ 
```

Figure 3.13: Application deployment to Fn

Firstly, the function for **serverless-app** is built, and then the function and trigger are created. Similarly, the **hello-world** function is built and deployed with the corresponding function and trigger.

6. List the triggers of the application with the following command and copy the **Endpoints** for **serverless-app-trigger** and **hello-world-trigger**:

```
fn list triggers serverless-app
```

This command lists the triggers of **serverless-app**, along with function, type, source, and endpoint information, as shown in the following screenshot:

```
/serverless $ fn list triggers serverless-app
FUNCTION        NAME           ID                           TYPE   SOURCE         ENDPOINT
hello-world     hello-world    01DJQQYAM7NG8G00GZJ0000005    http   /hello-world   http://localhost:8080/t/serverless-app/hello-world
serverless-app  serverless-app 01DJQQX36XNG8G00GZJ0000003    http   /serverless-app http://localhost:8080/t/serverless-app/serverless-app
/serverless $ 
```

Figure 3.14: Trigger list

7. Trigger the endpoints by using the following commands in your Terminal:

> **Note**
>
> For the **curl** commands, do not forget to use the endpoints that we copied in *Step 5*.

```
curl -d Ece http://localhost:8080/t/serverless-app/serverless-app
```

The output should be as follows:

```
/serverless $ curl -d Ece http://localhost:8080/t/serverless-app/serverless-app
{"message":"Hello Ece!"}
/serverless $ 
```

Figure 3.15: Invocation of the serverless-app trigger

This command will invoke the **serverless-app** trigger located at the **root** of the application. Since it was triggered with the **name** payload, it responded with a personal message: **Hello Ece!**:

```
curl http://localhost:8080/t/serverless-app/hello-world
```

This command will invoke the **hello-world** trigger without any payload and, as expected, it responded with **Hello World**, as shown in the following screenshot:

```
/serverless $ curl http://localhost:8080/t/serverless-app/hello-world
{"message":"Hello World"}
```

Figure 3.16: Invocation of the hello-world trigger

8. Check the application and function statistics from the **Fn** Dashboard by opening `http://localhost:4000` in your browser.

On the home screen, your applications and their overall statistics can be seen, along with auto-refreshed charts, as shown in the following screenshot:

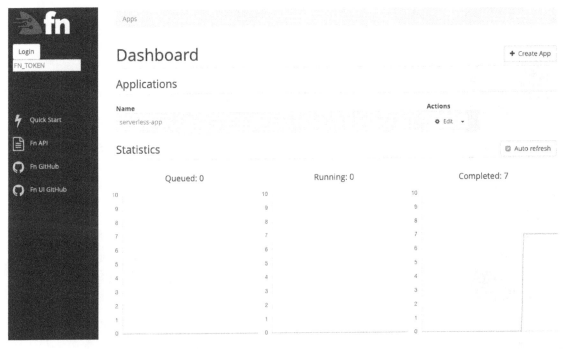

Figure 3.17: Fn Dashboard – Home

Click on **serverless-app** from the applications list to view more information about the functions of the application, as shown in the following screenshot:

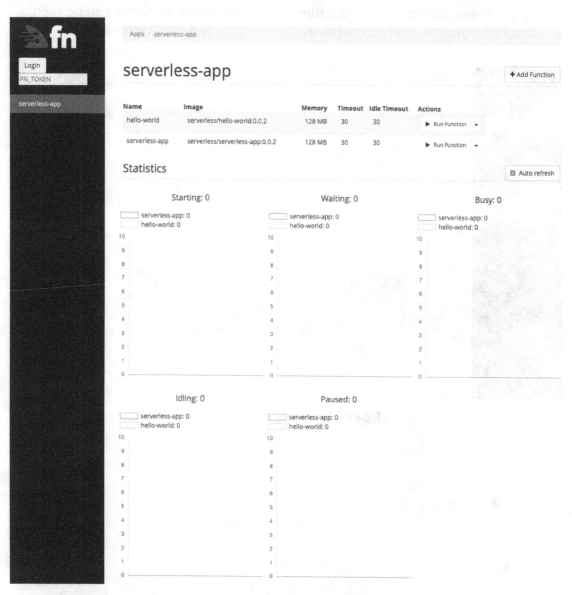

Figure 3.18: Fn Dashboard – Application

9. Stop the **Fn** server by using the following command in your Terminal:

```
fn stop
```

This command will stop the **Fn** server, including all the function instances, as shown in the following screenshot:

```
/serverless $ fn stop
Successfully stopped 'fnserver'
/serverless $ ▮
```

Figure 3.19: Fn server stop

In this exercise, we created a two-function application in the **Fn** framework and deployed it. We have shown you how to build functions as Docker containers using the **fn** client and by creating functions. In addition, the triggers of the functions were invoked via HTTP, and the statistics were checked from the **Fn** dashboard. As a container-native and cloud-agnostic framework, the functions of the framework are Docker containers, and they can run on any cloud provider or local system. In the next section, another serverless framework, namely, the **Serverless Framework**, which focuses more on cloud-provider integration, will be presented.

The Serverless Framework

The Serverless Framework was announced in 2015 with the name **JavaScript Amazon Web Services (JAWS)**. It was initially developed in Node.js to make it easier for people to develop AWS Lambda functions. In the same year, it changed the name to **Serverless Framework** and expanded its scope to other cloud providers and serverless frameworks, including **Google Cloud Functions**, **Azure Functions**, **Apache OpenWhisk**, **Fn**, and many more.

Serverless Framework is open source, and its source code is available at GitHub: https://github.com/serverless/serverless. It is a very popular repository with more than 31,000 stars, as shown in the following screenshot:

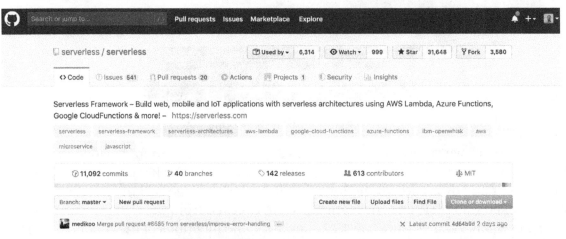

Figure 3.20: Serverless Framework GitHub repository

The official website of the framework is available at https://serverless.com and provides extensive documentation, use cases, and examples. The main features of the Serverless Framework can be grouped into four main topics:

- **Cloud-agnostic**: The Serverless Framework aims to create a cloud-agnostic serverless application development environment so that vendor lock-in is not a concern.

- **Reusable Components**: Serverless functions that are developed in the Serverless Framework are open source and available. These components help us to create complex applications quickly.

- **Infrastructure-as-code**: All the configuration and source code that's developed in the Serverless Framework is explicitly defined and can be deployed with a single command.

- **Developer Experience**: The Serverless Framework aims to enhance developer experience via its CLI, configuration parameters, and active community.

These four characteristics of the Serverless Framework make it the most well-known framework for creating serverless applications in the cloud. In addition, the framework focuses on the management of the complete life cycle of serverless applications:

- **Develop**: It is possible to develop apps locally and reuse open source plugins via the framework CLI.

- **Deploy**: The Serverless Framework can deploy to multiple cloud platforms and roll out and roll back versions from development to production.

- **Test**: The framework supports testing the functions out of the box by using the command-line client functions.

- **Secure**: The framework handles secrets for running the functions and cloud-specific authentication keys for deployments.

- **Monitor**: The metrics and logs of the serverless applications are available with the serverless runtime and client tools.

In the following exercise, a serverless application will be created, configured, and deployed to AWS using the Serverless Framework. The framework will be used inside a Docker container to show how easy it is to get started with serverless applications.

> **Note**
>
> The Serverless Framework can be downloaded and installed to a local computer with **npm**. A Docker container, including the Serverless Framework installation, will be used in the following exercise so that we have a fast and reproducible setup.

In the following exercise, the `hello-world` function will be deployed to AWS Lambda using the Serverless Framework. In order to complete this exercise, you need to have an active Amazon Web Services account. You can create an account at https://aws.amazon.com/.

Exercise 9: Running Functions with the Serverless Framework

In this exercise, we aim to configure the Serverless Framework and deploy our very first function using it. With the Serverless Framework, it is possible to create cloud-agnostic serverless applications. In this exercise, we will deploy the functions to AWS Lambda. However, it is possible to deploy the same functions to different cloud providers.

To successfully complete this exercise, we need to ensure that the following steps are executed:

1. In your Terminal, run the following command to start the Serverless Framework development environment:

   ```
   docker run -it --entrypoint=bash onuryilmaz/serverless
   ```

   This command will start a Docker container in interactive mode. In the following steps, actions will be taken inside this Docker container, as shown in the following screenshot:

   ```
   /serverless $ docker run -it --entrypoint=bash onuryilmaz/serverless
   root@139132ab576a:/#
   ```

   Figure 3.21: Starting a Docker container for serverless

2. Run the following command to check the framework version:

   ```
   serverless version
   ```

   This command lists the Framework, Plugin, and SDK versions, and getting a complete output indicates that everything is set up correctly, as shown in the following screenshot:

   ```
   root@139132ab576a:/# serverless version
   Framework Core: 1.50.0
   Plugin: 1.3.8
   SDK: 2.1.0

   root@139132ab576a:/#
   ```

   Figure 3.22: Framework version

3. Run the following command to use the framework interactively:

   ```
   serverless
   ```

Press **Y** to create a new project and choose **AWS Node.js** from the dropdown, as shown in the following screenshot:

```
root@139132ab576a:/# serverless

Serverless: No project detected. Do you want to create a new one? Yes
Serverless: What do you want to make? (Use arrow keys)
> AWS Node.js
  AWS Python
  Other
```

Figure 3.23: Creating a new project in the framework

4. Set the name of the project to **hello-world** and press **Enter**. The output is as follows:

```
root@139132ab576a:/# serverless

Serverless: No project detected. Do you want to create a new one? Yes
Serverless: What do you want to make? AWS Node.js
Serverless: What do you want to call this project? hello-world

Project successfully created in 'hello-world' folder.

No AWS credentials were found on your computer, you need these to host your application.

Serverless: Do you want to set them up now? (Y/n)
```

Figure 3.24: Successful creation of the project

5. Press **Y** for the AWS credential setup question, and then press **Y** again for the **Do you have an AWS account?** question. The output will be as follows:

```
root@44cdf31c8502:/# serverless

Serverless: No project detected. Do you want to create a new one? Yes
Serverless: What do you want to make? AWS Node.js
Serverless: What do you want to call this project? hello-world

Project successfully created in 'hello-world' folder.

No AWS credentials were found on your computer, you need these to host your application.

Serverless: Do you want to set them up now? Yes
Serverless: Do you have an AWS account? Yes
------------------------------------------------
  Unable to open browser automatically
Please open your browser & open the URL below to login:
https://console.aws.amazon.com/iam/home?region=us-east-1#/users$new?step=final&accessKey&userNames=serverless&permissionType
=policies&policies=arn:aws:iam::aws:policy%2FAdministratorAccess
------------------------------------------------
Serverless: Press Enter to continue after creating an AWS user with access keys
```

Figure 3.25: AWS account setup

You now have a URL for creating a serverless user. Copy and save the URL; we'll need it later.

6. Open the URL from *Step 4* in your browser and start adding users to the AWS console. The URL will open the **Add user** screen with predefined selections. Click **Next: Permissions** at the end of the screen, as shown in the following screenshot:

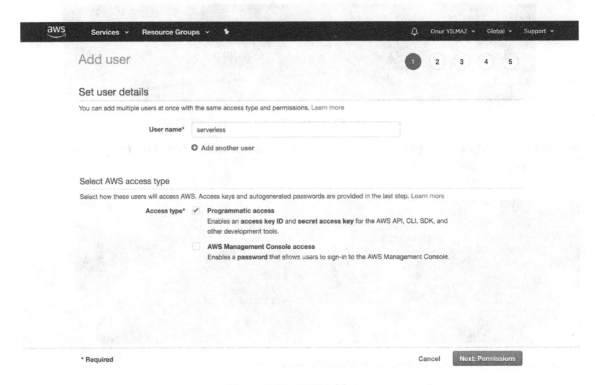

Figure 3.26: AWS Add user

7. The **AdministratorAccess** policy should be selected automatically. Click **Next: Tags** at the bottom of the screen, as shown in the following screenshot:

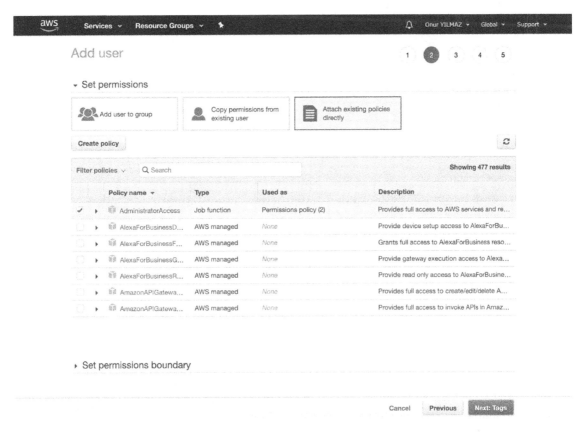

Figure 3.27: AWS Add user – Permissions

8. If you want to tag your users, you can add optional tags in this view. Click **Next: Review**, as shown in the following screenshot:

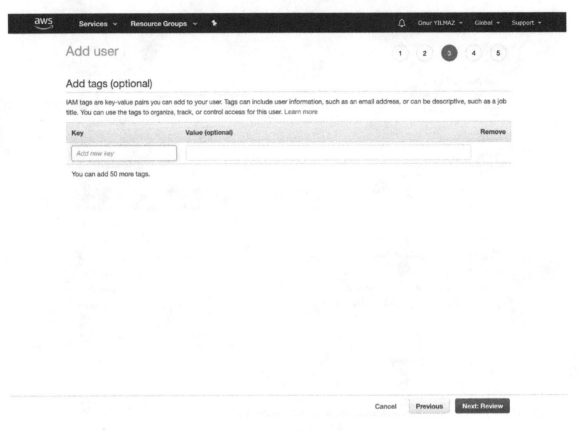

Figure 3.28: AWS Add user – Tags

9. This view shows the summary of the new user. Click **Create User**, as shown in the following screenshot:

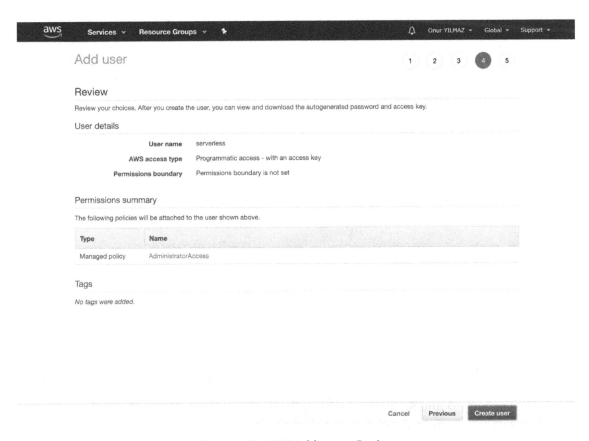

Figure 3.29: AWS Add user – Review

You will be redirected to a success page with an **Access Key ID** and **secret**, as shown in the following screenshot:

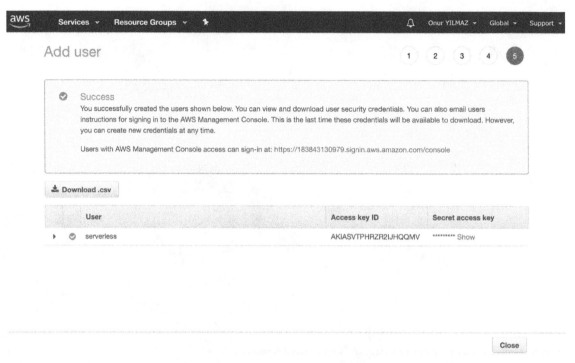

Figure 3.30: AWS Add user – Success

10. Copy the key ID and secret access key so that you can use it in the following steps of this exercise and the activity for this chapter. You need to click **Show** to reveal the secret access key.

11. Return to your Terminal and press **Enter** to enter the key ID and secret information, as shown in the following screenshot:

```
Please open your browser & open the URL below to login:
https://console.aws.amazon.com/iam/home?region=us-east-1#/users$new?step=final&accessKey&userNames=serverless&permissionType
=policies&policies=arn:aws:iam::aws:policy%2FAdministratorAccess
-------------------------------
Serverless: Press Enter to continue after creating an AWS user with access keys
Serverless: AWS Access Key Id: AKIASVTPHRZR2IJHQQMV
Serverless: AWS Secret Access Key: E********************************n

AWS credentials saved on your machine at ~/.aws/credentials. Go there to change them at any time.
```

Figure 3.31: AWS Credentials in the framework

12. Press **Y** for the Serverless account enable question and select **register** from the dropdown, as shown in the following screenshot:

```
You can monitor, troubleshoot, and test your new service with a free Serverless account.

Serverless: Would you like to enable this? Yes

You are not logged in or you do not have a Serverless account.

Serverless: Do you want to login or register? (Use arrow keys)
> register
  login
```

Figure 3.32: Serverless account enabled

13. Write your email and a password to create a Serverless Framework account, as shown in the following screenshot:

```
You can monitor, troubleshoot, and test your new service with a free Serverless account.

Serverless: Would you like to enable this? Yes

You are not logged in or you do not have a Serverless account.

Serverless: Do you want to login or register? register
Serverless: email: mail@onuryilmaz.me
Serverless: password: [hidden]
There's already registered account for given email address. Please try different email address
Serverless: email: *** @onuryilmaz.me
Serverless: password: [hidden]

Successfully registered your new account

Your project is setup for monitoring, troubleshooting and testing

Deploy your project and monitor, troubleshoot and test it:
- Run "serverless deploy" to deploy your service.
- Run "serverless dashboard" to view the dashboard.

root@44cdf31c8502:/#
```

Figure 3.33: Serverless account register

14. Run the following commands to change the directory and deploy the function:

```
cd hello-world
serverless deploy -v
```

These commands will make the Serverless Framework deploy the function into AWS, as shown in the following screenshot:

```
root@44cdf31c8502:/# cd hello-world/
root@44cdf31c8502:/hello-world# serverless deploy -v
Serverless: Packaging service...
Serverless: Excluding development dependencies...
Serverless: Creating Stack...
Serverless: Checking Stack create progress...
CloudFormation - CREATE_IN_PROGRESS - AWS::CloudFormation::Stack - hello-world-dev
CloudFormation - CREATE_IN_PROGRESS - AWS::S3::Bucket - ServerlessDeploymentBucket
CloudFormation - CREATE_IN_PROGRESS - AWS::S3::Bucket - ServerlessDeploymentBucket
CloudFormation - CREATE_COMPLETE - AWS::S3::Bucket - ServerlessDeploymentBucket
CloudFormation - CREATE_COMPLETE - AWS::CloudFormation::Stack - hello-world-dev
Serverless: Stack create finished...
Serverless: Uploading CloudFormation file to S3...
Serverless: Uploading artifacts...
Serverless: Uploading service hello-world.zip file to S3 (67.43 KB)...
Serverless: Validating template...
Serverless: Updating Stack...
Serverless: Checking Stack update progress...
CloudFormation - UPDATE_IN_PROGRESS - AWS::CloudFormation::Stack - hello-world-dev
CloudFormation - CREATE_IN_PROGRESS - AWS::Logs::LogGroup - HelloLogGroup
CloudFormation - CREATE_IN_PROGRESS - AWS::IAM::Role - IamRoleLambdaExecution
CloudFormation - CREATE_IN_PROGRESS - AWS::Logs::LogGroup - HelloLogGroup
CloudFormation - CREATE_IN_PROGRESS - AWS::IAM::Role - IamRoleLambdaExecution
CloudFormation - CREATE_COMPLETE - AWS::Logs::LogGroup - HelloLogGroup
CloudFormation - CREATE_IN_PROGRESS - AWS::IAM::Role - EnterpriseLogAccessIamRole
CloudFormation - CREATE_IN_PROGRESS - AWS::IAM::Role - EnterpriseLogAccessIamRole
CloudFormation - CREATE_IN_PROGRESS - AWS::Logs::SubscriptionFilter - CloudWatchLogsSubscriptionFilterHelloLogGroup
CloudFormation - CREATE_IN_PROGRESS - AWS::Logs::SubscriptionFilter - CloudWatchLogsSubscriptionFilterHelloLogGroup
CloudFormation - CREATE_COMPLETE - AWS::Logs::SubscriptionFilter - CloudWatchLogsSubscriptionFilterHelloLogGroup
CloudFormation - CREATE_COMPLETE - AWS::IAM::Role - IamRoleLambdaExecution
CloudFormation - CREATE_COMPLETE - AWS::IAM::Role - EnterpriseLogAccessIamRole
CloudFormation - CREATE_IN_PROGRESS - AWS::Lambda::Function - HelloLambdaFunction
CloudFormation - CREATE_IN_PROGRESS - AWS::Lambda::Function - HelloLambdaFunction
CloudFormation - CREATE_COMPLETE - AWS::Lambda::Function - HelloLambdaFunction
CloudFormation - CREATE_IN_PROGRESS - AWS::Lambda::Version - HelloLambdaVersiono4eakM4SwChE4T14HkHFyrGIAir5xsDT8U3h7gKYxE
CloudFormation - CREATE_IN_PROGRESS - AWS::Lambda::Version - HelloLambdaVersiono4eakM4SwChE4T14HkHFyrGIAir5xsDT8U3h7gKYxE
CloudFormation - CREATE_COMPLETE - AWS::Lambda::Version - HelloLambdaVersiono4eakM4SwChE4T14HkHFyrGIAir5xsDT8U3h7gKYxE
CloudFormation - UPDATE_COMPLETE_CLEANUP_IN_PROGRESS - AWS::CloudFormation::Stack - hello-world-dev
CloudFormation - UPDATE_COMPLETE - AWS::CloudFormation::Stack - hello-world-dev
Serverless: Stack update finished...
Service Information
service: hello-world
stage: dev
region: us-east-1
stack: hello-world-dev
resources: 7
api keys:
  None
endpoints:
  None
functions:
  hello: hello-world-dev-hello
layers:
  None

Stack Outputs
EnterpriseLogAccessIamRole: arn:aws:iam::183843130979:role/hello-world-dev-EnterpriseLogAccessIamRole-18BOJJQJVWVWU
HelloLambdaFunctionQualifiedArn: arn:aws:lambda:us-east-1:183843130979:function:hello-world-dev-hello:1
ServerlessDeploymentBucketName: hello-world-dev-serverlessdeploymentbucket-d00xroqat6me

Serverless: Publishing service to the Serverless Dashboard...
Serverless: Successfully published your service to the Serverless Dashboard: https://dashboard.serverless.com/tenants/onurx/
applications/hello-world-app/services/hello-world/stage/dev/region/us-east-1
root@44cdf31c8502:/hello-world# 
```

Figure 3.34: Serverless Framework deployment output

Note

The output logs start by packaging the service and creating AWS resources for the source code, artifacts, and functions. After all the resources have been created, the **Service Information** section will provide a summary of the functions and URLs.

At the end of the screen, you will find the **Serverless Dashboard URL** for the deployed function, as shown in the following screenshot:

Figure 3.35: Stack Outputs

Copy the dashboard URL so that you can check the function metrics in the upcoming steps.

15. Invoke the function by using the following command in your Terminal:

```
serverless invoke --function hello
```

This command invokes the deployed function and prints out the response, as shown in the following screenshot:

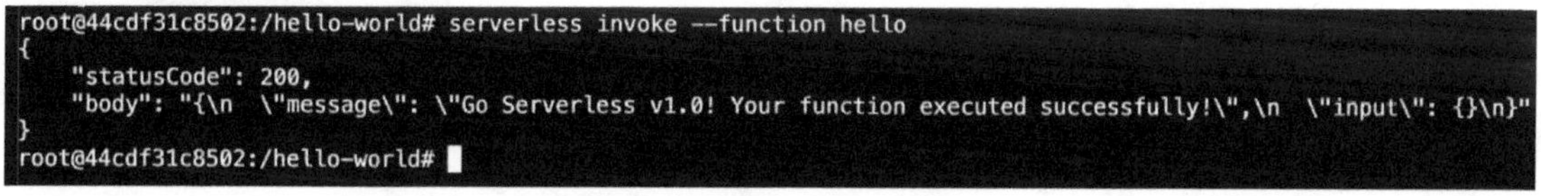

Figure 3.36: Function output

As the output shows, **statusCode** is **200**, and the body of the response indicates that the function has responded successfully.

16. Open the Serverless Dashboard URL you copied at the end of Step 8 into your browser, as shown in the following screenshot:

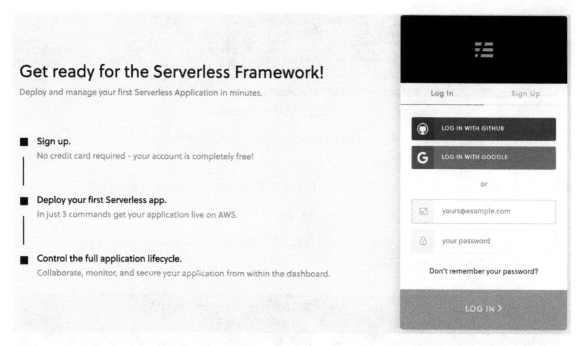

Figure 3.37: Serverless Dashboard login

17. Log in with the email and password you created in *Step* 5.

You will be redirected to the application list. Expand **hello-world-app** and click on the **successful deployment** line, as shown in the following screenshot:

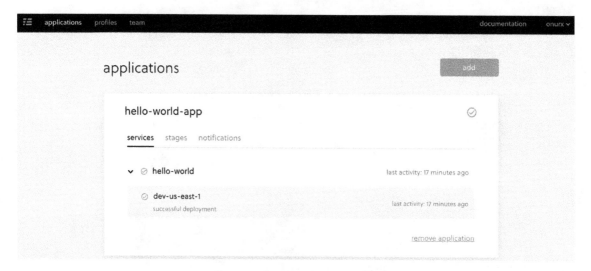

Figure 3.38: Serverless Dashboard application list

In the function view, all the runtime information, including API endpoints, variables, alerts, and metrics, are available. Scroll down to see the number of invocations. The output should be as follows:

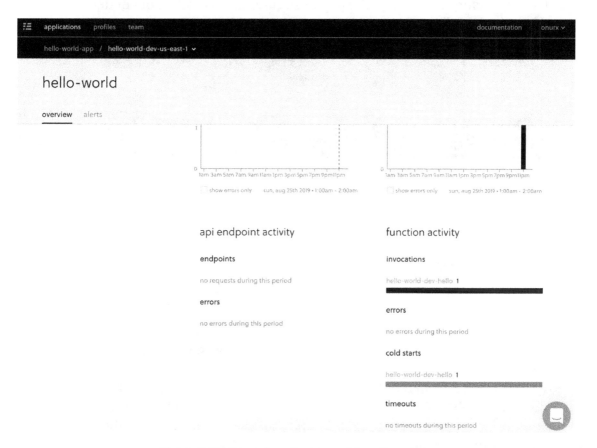

Figure 3.39: Serverless Dashboard function view

Since we have only invoked the function once, you will only see **1** in the charts.

18. Return to your Terminal and delete the function with the following command:

```
serverless remove
```

This command will remove the deployed function and all its dependencies, as shown in the following screenshot:

```
root@44cdf31c8502:/hello-world# serverless remove
Serverless: Getting all objects in S3 bucket...
Serverless: Removing objects in S3 bucket...
Serverless: Removing Stack...
Serverless: Checking Stack removal progress...
.............
Serverless: Stack removal finished...
Serverless: Publishing service to the Serverless Dashboard...
Serverless: Successfully published your service to the Serverless Dashboard: https://dashboard.serverless.com/tenants/onurx/
applications/hello-world-app/services/hello-world/stage/dev/region/us-east-1
root@44cdf31c8502:/hello-world#
```

Figure 3.40: Removing the function

Exit the Serverless Framework development environment container by writing **exit** in the Terminal, as shown in the following screenshot:

```
root@44cdf31c8502:/hello-world# exit
exit
/serverless $
```

Figure 3.41: Exiting the container

In this exercise, we have created, configured, and deployed a serverless function using the Serverless Framework. Furthermore, the function is invoked via a CLI, and its metrics are checked from the Serverless Dashboard. The Serverless Framework creates a comprehensive abstraction for cloud providers so that it is only passed as credentials to the platform. In other words, where to deploy is just a matter of configuration with the help of serverless frameworks.

In the following activity, a real-life serverless daily weather application will be developed. You will create a serverless framework application with an invocation schedule and deploy it to a cloud provider. In addition, the weather status messages will be sent to a cloud-based collaboration tool known as *Slack*.

> **Note**
>
> In order to complete the following activity, you need to be able to access a Slack workplace. You can use your existing Slack workspace or create a new one for free at https://slack.com/create.

Activity 3: Daily Weather Status Function for Slack

The aim of this activity is to create a real-life serverless application that sends weather status messages in specific *Slack* channels. The function will be developed with the **Serverless Framework** so that it can run on multiple cloud platforms in the future. The function will be designed to run at particular times for your team so that they're informed about the weather status, such as early in the morning before their morning commute. These messages will be published on *Slack* channels, which is the main communication tool within the team.

In order to get the weather status to share within the team, you can use **wttr.in** (https://github.com/chubin/wttr.in), which is a free-to-use weather data provider. Once completed, you will have deployed a function to a cloud provider, namely, **AWS Lambda**:

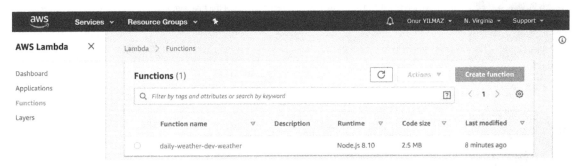

Figure 3.42: Daily weather function

Finally, when the scheduler invokes the function, or when you invoke it manually, you will get messages regarding the current weather status in your Slack channel:

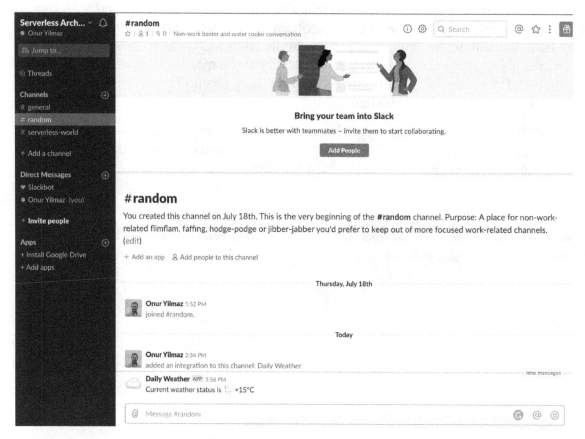

Figure 3.43: Slack message with the current weather status

> **Note**
>
> In order to complete this activity, you should configure Slack by following the Slack setup steps.

Slack Setup

Execute the following steps to configure Slack:

1. In your Slack workspace, click your username and select **Customize Slack**.

2. Click **Configure apps** in the opened window.

3. Click on **Browse the App Directory** to add a new application from the directory.

4. Find **Incoming WebHooks** from the search box in App Directory.

5. Click on **Set Up** for the **Incoming WebHooks** application.

6. Fill in the configuration for incoming webhooks with your specific channel name and icon.

7. Open your Slack workspace and the channel you configured in Step 6 to be able to check the integration message.

> **Note**
>
> Detailed screenshots of the Slack setup steps can be found on page 387.

Execute the following steps to complete this activity.

1. In your Terminal, create a Serverless Framework application structure in a folder called **daily-weather**.

2. Create a **package.json** file to define the Node.js environment in the **daily-weather** folder.

3. Create a **handler.js** file to implement the actual functionality in the **daily-weather** folder.

4. Install the Node.js dependencies for the serverless application.

5. Export the AWS credentials as environment variables.

6. Deploy the serverless application to AWS using the Serverless Framework.

7. Check AWS Lambda for the deployed functions in the AWS Console.

8. Invoke the function with the Serverless Framework client tools.

9. Check the Slack channel for the posted weather status.

10. Return to your Terminal and delete the function with the Serverless Framework.

11. Exit the Serverless Framework development environment container.

> **Note**
>
> The solution to this activity can be found on page 387.

Summary

In this chapter, we provided an overview of serverless frameworks by discussing the differences between the serverless products of cloud providers. Following that, one container-native and one cloud-native serverless framework were discussed in depth. Firstly, the **Fn** framework was discussed, which is an open source, container-native, and cloud-agnostic platform. Secondly, the Serverless Framework was presented, which is a more cloud-focused and comprehensive framework. Furthermore, both frameworks were installed and configured locally. Serverless applications were created, deployed, and run in both serverless frameworks. The functions were invoked with the capabilities of serverless frameworks, and the necessary metrics checked for further analysis.

At the end of this chapter, a real-life, daily weather Slack bot was implemented as a cloud-agnostic, explicitly defined application using serverless frameworks. Serverless frameworks are essential for the serverless development world with their cloud-agnostic and developer-friendly characteristics.

Kubernetes Deep Dive

Learning Objectives

By the end of this chapter, you will be able to:

- Set up a local Kubernetes cluster on your computer
- Access a Kubernetes cluster using the dashboard and the Terminal
- Identify the fundamental Kubernetes resources, the building blocks of Kubernetes applications
- Install complex applications on a Kubernetes cluster

In this chapter, we will explain the basics of the Kubernetes architecture, the methods of accessing the Kubernetes API, and fundamental Kubernetes resources. In addition to that, we will deploy a real-life application into Kubernetes.

Introduction to Kubernetes

In the previous chapter, we studied serverless frameworks, created serverless applications using these frameworks, and deployed these applications to the major cloud providers.

As we have seen in the previous chapters, Kubernetes and serverless architectures started to gain traction at the same time in the industry. Kubernetes got a high level of adoption and became the de facto container management system with its design principles based on scalability, high availability, and portability. For serverless applications, Kubernetes provides two essential benefits: **removal of vendor lock-in** and **reuse of services**.

Kubernetes creates an infrastructure layer of abstraction to remove vendor lock-in. Vendor lock-in is a situation where transition from one service provider to another is very difficult or even infeasible. In the previous chapter, we studied how serverless frameworks make it easy to develop cloud-agnostic serverless applications. Let's assume you are running your serverless framework on an **AWS EC2** instance and want to move to **Google Cloud**. Although your serverless framework creates a layer between the cloud provider and serverless applications, you are still deeply attached to the cloud provider for the infrastructure. Kubernetes breaks this connection by creating an abstraction between the infrastructure and the cloud provider. In other words, serverless frameworks running on Kubernetes are unaware of the underlying infrastructure. If your serverless framework runs on Kubernetes in AWS, it is expected to run on **Google Cloud Platform** (**GCP**) or Azure.

As the defacto container management system, Kubernetes manages most microservices applications in the cloud and in on-premise systems. Let's assume you have already converted your big monolith application to cloud-native microservices and you're running them on Kubernetes. And now you've started developing serverless applications or turning some of your microservices to serverless *nanoservices*. At this stage, your serverless applications will need to access the data and other services. If you can run your serverless applications in your Kubernetes clusters, you will have the chance to reuse the services and be close to your data. Besides, it will be easier to manage and operate both microservices and serverless applications.

As a solution to vendor lock-in, and for potential reuse of data and services, it is crucial to learn how to run serverless architectures on Kubernetes. In this chapter, a Kubernetes recap is presented to introduce the origin and design of Kubernetes. Following that, we will install a local Kubernetes cluster, and you will be able to access the cluster by using a dashboard or a client tool such as `kubectl`. In addition to that, we will discuss the building blocks of Kubernetes applications, and finally, we'll deploy a real-life application to the cluster.

Kubernetes Design and Components

Kubernetes, which is also known as **k8s**, is a platform for managing containers. It is a complex system focused on the complete life cycle of containers, including configuration, installation, health checking, troubleshooting, and scaling. With Kubernetes, it is possible to run microservices in a scalable, flexible, and reliable way. Let's assume you are a DevOps engineer at a fin-tech company, focusing on online banking for your customers.

You can configure and install the complete backend and frontend of an online bank application to Kubernetes in a secure and cloud-native way. With the Kubernetes controllers, you can manually or automatically scale your services up and down to match customer demand. Also, you can check the logs, perform health checks on each service, and even SSH into the containers of your applications.

In this section, we will focus on how Kubernetes is designed and how its components work in harmony.

Kubernetes clusters consist of one or more servers, and each server is assigned with a set of logical roles. There are two essential roles assigned to the servers of a cluster: **master** and **node**. If the server is in the **master** role, **control plane** components of the Kubernetes run on these nodes. Control plane components are the primary set of services used to run the Kubernetes API, including REST operations, authentication, authorization, scheduling, and cloud operations. With the recent version of Kubernetes, four services are running as the control plane:

- **etcd**: **etcd** is an open source key/value store, and it is the database of all Kubernetes resources.

- **kube-apiserver**: API server is the component that runs the Kubernetes REST API. It is the most critical component for interacting with other parts of the plane and client tools.

- **kube-scheduler**: A scheduler assigns workloads to nodes based on the workload requirements and node status.

- **kube-controller-manager**: `kube-controller-manager` is the control plane component used to manage core controllers of Kubernetes resources. *Controllers* are the primary life cycle managers of the Kubernetes resources. For each Kubernetes resource, there is one or more controller that works in the **observe**, **decide**, and **act** loop diagrammed in *Figure 4.1*. Controllers check the current status of the resources in the observe stage and then analyze and decide on the required actions to reach the desired state. In the act stage, they execute the actions and continue to observe the resources.

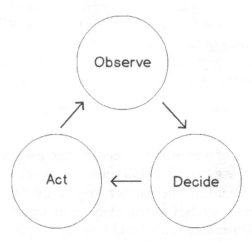

Figure 4.1: Controller loop in Kubernetes

Servers with the **node** role are responsible for running the workload in Kubernetes. Therefore, there are two essential Kubernetes components required in every node:

- **kubelet**: `kubelet` is the management gateway of the control plane in the nodes. `kubelet` communicates with the API server and implements actions needed on the nodes. For instance, when a new workload is assigned to a node, `kubelet` creates the container by interacting with the container runtime, such as Docker.

- **kube-proxy**: Containers run on the server nodes, but they interact with each other as they are running in a unified networking setup. `kube-proxy` makes it possible for containers to communicate, although they are running on different nodes.

The control plane and the roles, such as master and node, are logical groupings of components. However, it is recommended to have a highly available control plane with multiple master role servers. Besides, servers with node roles are connected to the control plane to create a scalable and cloud-native environment. The relationship and interaction of the control plane and the master and node servers are presented in the following figure:

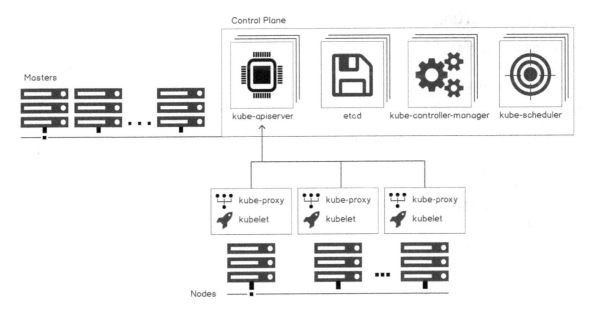

Figure 4.2: The control plane and the master and node servers in a Kubernetes cluster

In the following exercise, a Kubernetes cluster will be created locally, and Kubernetes components will be checked. Kubernetes clusters are sets of servers with master or worker nodes. On these nodes, both control plane components and user applications are running in a scalable and highly available way. With the help of local Kubernetes cluster tools, it is possible to create single-node clusters for development and testing. `minikube` is the officially supported and maintained local Kubernetes solution, and it will be used in the following exercise.

> **Note**
>
> You will use `minikube` in the following exercise as the official local Kubernetes solution, and it runs the Kubernetes components on hypervisors. Hence you must install a hypervisor such as **Virtualbox**, **Parallels**, **VMWareFusion**, **Hyperkit**, or **VMWare**. Refer to this link for more information:
>
> https://kubernetes.io/docs/tasks/tools/install-minikube/#install-a-hypervisor

Exercise 10: Starting a Local Kubernetes Cluster

In this exercise, we will install `minikube` and use it to start a one-node Kubernetes cluster. When the cluster is up and running, it will be possible to check the master and node components.

To complete the exercise, we need to ensure the following steps are executed:

1. Install `minikube` to the local system by running these commands in your Terminal:

    ```
    # Linux
    curl -Lo minikube https://storage.googleapis.com/minikube/releases/latest/
    minikube-linux-amd64
    # MacOS
    curl -Lo minikube https://storage.googleapis.com/minikube/releases/latest/
    minikube-darwin-amd64
    chmod +x minikube
    sudo mv minikube /usr/local/bin
    ```

    These commands download the binary file of `minikube`, make it executable, and move it into the `bin` folder for Terminal access.

2. Start the `minikube` cluster by running the following command:

    ```
    minikube start
    ```

    This command downloads the images and creates a single-node virtual machine. Following that, it configures the machine and waits until the Kubernetes control plane is up and running, as shown in the following figure:

```
/serverless $ minikube start
   minikube v1.3.1 on Darwin 10.14.5
   Downloading VM boot image ...
minikube-v1.3.0.iso.sha256: 65 B / 65 B [--------------------] 100.00% ? p/s 0s
minikube-v1.3.0.iso: 131.07 MiB / 131.07 MiB [--------] 100.00% 21.31 MiB p/s 6s
   Creating virtualbox VM (CPUs=2, Memory=2000MB, Disk=20000MB) ...
   Preparing Kubernetes v1.15.2 on Docker 18.09.8 ...
   Downloading kubeadm v1.15.2
   Downloading kubelet v1.15.2
   Pulling images ...
   Launching Kubernetes ...
   Waiting for: apiserver proxy etcd scheduler controller dns
   Done! kubectl is now configured to use "minikube"
/serverless $ 
```

Figure 4.3: Starting a new cluster in minikube

3. Check the status of Kubernetes cluster:

`minikube status`

As the output in the following figure indicates, the host system, **kubelet**, and **apiserver** are running:

```
/serverless $ minikube status
host: Running
kubelet: Running
apiserver: Running
kubectl: Correctly Configured: pointing to minikube-vm at 192.168.99.100
/serverless $ ▊
```

Figure 4.4: Kubernetes cluster status

4. Connect to the virtual machine of **minikube** by running the following command:

`minikube ssh`

You should see the output shown in the following figure:

Figure 4.5: minikube virtual machine

5. Check for the four control-plane components with the following command:

```
pgrep -l etcd && pgrep -l kube-apiserver && pgrep -l kube-scheduler &&
pgrep -l controller
```

This command lists the processes and captures the mentioned command names. There are total of four lines corresponding to each control plane component and its process IDs, as depicted in the following figure:

```
$ pgrep -l etcd && pgrep -l kube-apiserver && pgrep -l kube-scheduler && pgrep -l controller
3824 etcd
3787 kube-apiserver
3726 kube-scheduler
3811 kube-controller
$ ▊
```

Figure 4.6: Control plane components

6. Check for the node components with the following command:

```
pgrep -l kubelet && pgrep -l kube-proxy
```

This command lists two components running in the node role, with their process IDs, as shown in the following figure:

```
$ pgrep -l kubelet && pgrep -l kube-proxy
3364 kubelet
4437 kube-proxy
$
```

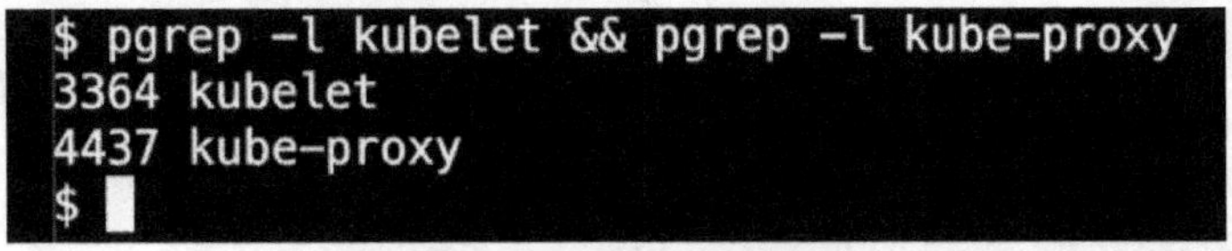

Figure 4.7: Node components

7. Exit the terminal started in *Step 4* with the following command:

```
exit
```

You should see the output shown in the following figure:

```
$ exit
logout
 /serverless $
```

Figure 4.8: Exiting the minikube virtual machine

In this exercise, we installed a single-node Kubernetes cluster using `minikube`. In the next section, we will discuss using the official client tool of Kubernetes to connect to and operate the cluster from the previous exercise.

Kubernetes Client Tool: kubectl

The Kubernetes control plane runs a REST API server for accessing Kubernetes resources and undertaking operational activities. Kubernetes comes with an open source official command-line tool named **kubectl** in order to consume the REST API. It is installed on the local system and configured to connect remote clusters securely and reliably. **kubectl** is the primary tool for the complete life cycle of applications running in Kubernetes. For instance, say you deploy a **WordPress** blog in your cluster. First, you start creating your database passwords as secrets using **kubectl**. Following that, you deploy your blog application and check its status. In addition to that, you may trace the logs of your applications or even SSH into the containers for further analysis. Therefore, it is a powerful CLI tool that can handle both basic **create, read, update, and delete (CRUD)** actions and troubleshooting.

In addition to application management, **kubectl** is also a powerful tool for cluster operations. It is possible to check the Kubernetes API status or the status of the servers in the cluster using **kubectl**. Let's assume you need to restart a server in your cluster and you need to move the workload to other nodes. Using **kubectl** commands, you can mark the node as *unschedulable* and let the Kubernetes scheduler move the workload to other nodes. When you complete the maintenance, you can mark the node back as **Ready** and let a Kubernetes scheduler assign workloads.

kubectl is a vital command-line tool for daily Kubernetes operations. Therefore, learning the basics and getting hands-on experience with **kubectl** is crucial. In the following exercise, you will install and configure **kubectl** to connect to a local Kubernetes cluster.

Exercise 11: Accessing Kubernetes Clusters Using the Client Tool: kubectl

In this exercise, we aim to access the Kubernetes API using **kubectl** and explore its capabilities.

To complete the exercise, we need to ensure the following steps are executed:

1. Download the **kubectl** executable by running these commands in the Terminal:

    ```
    # Linux
    curl -LO https://storage.googleapis.com/kubernetes-release/release/
    v1.15.0/bin/linux/amd64/kubectl
    # MacOS
    curl -LO https://storage.googleapis.com/kubernetes-release/release/
    v1.15.0/bin/darwin/amd64/kubectl
    chmod +x kubectl
    sudo mv kubectl /usr/local/bin
    ```

    These commands download the binary of **kubectl**, make it executable, and move it into the **bin** folder for Terminal access.

2. Configure **kubectl** to connect to the **minikube** cluster:

    ```
    kubectl config use-context minikube
    ```

    This command configures **kubectl** to use the **minikube** context, which is the set of credentials used to connect to the **kubectl** cluster, as shown in the following figure:

```
/serverless $ kubectl config use-context minikube
Switched to context "minikube".
/serverless $
```

Figure 4.9: kubectl context setting

3. Check the available nodes with the following command:

   `kubectl get nodes`

   This command lists all the nodes connected to the cluster. As a single-node cluster, there is only one node, named **minikube**, as shown in the following figure:

```
/serverless $  kubectl get nodes
NAME        STATUS    ROLES     AGE    VERSION
minikube    Ready     master    24h    v1.15.2
/serverless $
```

Figure 4.10: kubectl get nodes

4. Get more information about the **minikube** node with the following command:

`kubectl describe node minikube`

This command lists all the information about the node, starting with its metadata, such as **Roles**, **Labels**, and **Annotations**. The role of this node is specified as **master** in the **Roles** section, as shown in the following figure:

```
/serverless $ kubectl describe node minikube
Name:               minikube
Roles:              master
Labels:             beta.kubernetes.io/arch=amd64
                    beta.kubernetes.io/os=linux
                    kubernetes.io/arch=amd64
                    kubernetes.io/hostname=minikube
                    kubernetes.io/os=linux
                    node-role.kubernetes.io/master=
Annotations:        kubeadm.alpha.kubernetes.io/cri-socket: /var/run/dockershim.sock
                    node.alpha.kubernetes.io/ttl: 0
                    volumes.kubernetes.io/controller-managed-attach-detach: true
CreationTimestamp:  Sat, 14 Sep 2019 14:41:51 +0200
Taints:             <none>
Unschedulable:      false
```

Figure 4.11: Node metadata

Following the metadata, **Conditions** lists the health status of the node. It is possible to check available memory, disk, and process IDs in tabular form, as shown in the following figure.

```
Conditions:
  Type             Status  LastHeartbeatTime                 LastTransitionTime                Reason                       Message
  ----             ------  -----------------                 ------------------                ------                       -------
  MemoryPressure   False   Sun, 15 Sep 2019 15:00:05 +0200   Sat, 14 Sep 2019 14:41:46 +0200   KubeletHasSufficientMemory   kubelet has sufficient memory available
  DiskPressure     False   Sun, 15 Sep 2019 15:00:05 +0200   Sat, 14 Sep 2019 14:41:46 +0200   KubeletHasNoDiskPressure     kubelet has no disk pressure
  PIDPressure      False   Sun, 15 Sep 2019 15:00:05 +0200   Sat, 14 Sep 2019 14:41:46 +0200   KubeletHasSufficientPID      kubelet has sufficient PID available
  Ready            True    Sun, 15 Sep 2019 15:00:05 +0200   Sat, 14 Sep 2019 14:41:46 +0200   KubeletReady                 kubelet is posting ready status
Addresses:
  InternalIP:  10.0.2.15
  Hostname:    minikube
```

Figure 4.12: Node conditions

Then, available and allocatable capacity and system information are listed, as shown in the following figure:

```
Capacity:
 cpu:                       2
 ephemeral-storage:         17784772Ki
 hugepages-2Mi:             0
 memory:                    1989472Ki
 pods:                      110
Allocatable:
 cpu:                       2
 ephemeral-storage:         16390445849
 hugepages-2Mi:             0
 memory:                    1887072Ki
 pods:                      110
System Info:
 Machine ID:                d78ca5cc2d404e57a604153f20f5095c
 System UUID:               EC8117B5-2001-4A3B-BB28-BA975502B20C
 Boot ID:                   fe4852a7-751a-4c97-8065-029b44f06bfe
 Kernel Version:            4.15.0
 OS Image:                  Buildroot 2018.05.3
 Operating System:          linux
 Architecture:              amd64
 Container Runtime Version: docker://18.9.8
 Kubelet Version:           v1.15.2
 Kube-Proxy Version:        v1.15.2
```

Figure 4.13: Node capacity information

Finally, the running workload on the node and allocated resources are listed, as shown in the following figure:

```
Non-terminated Pods:        (9 in total)
  Namespace                 Name                                CPU Requests  CPU Limits  Memory Requests  Memory Limits  AGE
  ---------                 ----                                ------------  ----------  ---------------  -------------  ---
  kube-system               coredns-5c98db65d4-s5565            100m (5%)     0 (0%)      70Mi (3%)        170Mi (9%)     24h
  kube-system               coredns-5c98db65d4-sddcB            100m (5%)     0 (0%)      70Mi (3%)        170Mi (9%)     24h
  kube-system               etcd-minikube                       0 (0%)        0 (0%)      0 (0%)           0 (0%)         24h
  kube-system               kube-addon-manager-minikube         5m (0%)       0 (0%)      50Mi (2%)        0 (0%)         24h
  kube-system               kube-apiserver-minikube             250m (12%)    0 (0%)      0 (0%)           0 (0%)         24h
  kube-system               kube-controller-manager-minikube    200m (10%)    0 (0%)      0 (0%)           0 (0%)         100m
  kube-system               kube-proxy-x4zb9                     0 (0%)        0 (0%)      0 (0%)           0 (0%)         24h
  kube-system               kube-scheduler-minikube             100m (5%)     0 (0%)      0 (0%)           0 (0%)         24h
  kube-system               storage-provisioner                 0 (0%)        0 (0%)      0 (0%)           0 (0%)         24h
Allocated resources:
  (Total limits may be over 100 percent, i.e., overcommitted.)
  Resource                  Requests         Limits
  --------                  --------         ------
  cpu                       755m (37%)       0 (0%)
  memory                    190Mi (10%)      340Mi (18%)
  ephemeral-storage         0 (0%)           0 (0%)
Events:                     <none>
```

Figure 4.14: Node workload information

5. Get the supported API resources with the following command:

```
kubectl api-resources -o name
```

You should see the output shown in the following figure:

```
/serverless $ kubectl api-resources -o name
bindings
componentstatuses
configmaps
endpoints
events
limitranges
namespaces
nodes
persistentvolumeclaims
persistentvolumes
pods
podtemplates
replicationcontrollers
resourcequotas
secrets
serviceaccounts
services
mutatingwebhookconfigurations.admissionregistration.k8s.io
validatingwebhookconfigurations.admissionregistration.k8s.io
customresourcedefinitions.apiextensions.k8s.io
apiservices.apiregistration.k8s.io
controllerrevisions.apps
daemonsets.apps
deployments.apps
replicasets.apps
statefulsets.apps
tokenreviews.authentication.k8s.io
localsubjectaccessreviews.authorization.k8s.io
selfsubjectaccessreviews.authorization.k8s.io
selfsubjectrulesreviews.authorization.k8s.io
subjectaccessreviews.authorization.k8s.io
horizontalpodautoscalers.autoscaling
cronjobs.batch
jobs.batch
certificatesigningrequests.certificates.k8s.io
leases.coordination.k8s.io
events.events.k8s.io
daemonsets.extensions
deployments.extensions
ingresses.extensions
networkpolicies.extensions
podsecuritypolicies.extensions
replicasets.extensions
ingresses.networking.k8s.io
networkpolicies.networking.k8s.io
runtimeclasses.node.k8s.io
poddisruptionbudgets.policy
podsecuritypolicies.policy
clusterrolebindings.rbac.authorization.k8s.io
clusterroles.rbac.authorization.k8s.io
rolebindings.rbac.authorization.k8s.io
roles.rbac.authorization.k8s.io
priorityclasses.scheduling.k8s.io
csidrivers.storage.k8s.io
csinodes.storage.k8s.io
storageclasses.storage.k8s.io
volumeattachments.storage.k8s.io
/serverless $
```

Figure 4.15: Output of kubectl api-resources

This command lists all the resources supported by the Kubernetes cluster. The length of the list indicates the power and comprehensiveness of Kubernetes in the senseof application management. In this exercise, the official Kubernetes client tool was installed, configured, and explored. In the following section, the core building block resources from the resource list will be presented.

Kubernetes Resources

Kubernetes comes with a rich set of **resources** to define and manage cloud-native applications as containers. In the Kubernetes API, every container, secret, configuration, or custom definition is defined as a **resource**. The control plane manages these resources while the node components try to achieve the *desired state* of the applications. The *desired state* could be running 10 instances of the application or mounting disk volumes to database applications. The control plane and node components work in harmony to make all resources in the cluster reach their *desired state*.

In this section, we will study the fundamental Kubernetes resources used to run serverless applications.

Pod

The **pod** is the building block resource for computation in Kubernetes. A pod consists of containers scheduled to run into the same node as a single application. Containers in the same pod share the same resources, such as network and memory resources. In addition, the containers in the pod share life cycle events such as scaling up or down. A pod can be defined with an **ubuntu** image and the **echo** command as follows:

```
apiVersion: v1
kind: Pod
metadata:
  name: echo
spec:
  containers:
  - name: main
    image: ubuntu
    command: ['sh', '-c', 'echo Serverless World! && sleep 3600']
```

When the **echo** pod is created in Kubernetes API, the scheduler will assign it to an available node. Then the **kubelet** in the corresponding node will create a container and attach networking to it. Finally, the container will start to run the **echo** and **sleep** commands. Pods are the essential Kubernetes resource for creating applications, and Kubernetes uses them as building blocks for more complex resources. In the following resources, the pod will be encapsulated to create more complex cloud-native applications.

Deployment

Deployments are the most commonly used Kubernetes resource to manage highly available applications. Deployments enhance pods by making it possible to scale up, scale down, or roll out new versions. The deployment definition looks similar to a pod with two important additions: **labels** and **replicas**.

Consider the following code:

```
apiVersion: apps/v1
kind: Deployment
metadata:
 name: webserver
 labels:
    app: nginx
spec:
 replicas: 5
 selector:
   matchLabels:
     app: server
 template:
   metadata:
     labels:
       app: server
   spec:
     containers:
     - name: nginx
```

```
      image: nginx:1.7.9

      ports:

      - containerPort: 80
```

The deployment named **webserver** defines five **replicas** of the application running with the label **app:server**. In the **template** section, the application is defined with the exact same label and one **nginx** container. The deployment controller in the control plane ensures that five instances of this application are running inside the cluster. Let's assume you have three nodes, A, B, and C, with one, two, and two instances of webserver application running, respectively. If node C goes offline, the deployment controller will ensure that the two lost instances will be recreated in nodes A and B. Kubernetes ensures that scalable and highly available applications are running reliably as deployments. In the following section, Kubernetes resources for stateful applications such as databases will be presented.

StatefulSet

Kubernetes supports running both stateless ephemeral applications and stateful applications. In other words, it is possible to run database applications or disk-oriented applications in a scalable way inside your clusters. The **StatefulSet** definition is similar to deployment with volume-related additions.

Consider the following code snippet:

```
apiVersion: apps/v1

kind: StatefulSet

metadata:

  name: mysql

spec:

  selector:

    matchLabels:

      app: mysql

  serviceName: mysql

  replicas: 1

  template:

    metadata:

      labels:

        app: mysql

    spec:
```

```
    containers:
    - name: mysql
      image: mysql:5.7
      env:
      - name: MYSQL_ROOT_PASSWORD
        value: "root"
      ports:
      - name: mysql
        containerPort: 3306
      volumeMounts:
      - name: data
        mountPath: /var/lib/mysql
        subPath: mysql
  volumeClaimTemplates:
  - metadata:
      name: data
    spec:
      accessModes: ["ReadWriteOnce"]
      resources:
        requests:
          storage: 1Gi
```

The **mysql StatefulSet** state creates a MySQL database with 1 GB volume data. The volume is created by Kubernetes and attached to the container at **/var/lib/mysql**. With the **StatefulSet** controllers, it is possible to create applications that need disk access in a scalable and reliable way. In the following section, we'll discuss how to connect applications in a Kubernetes cluster.

Service

In Kubernetes, multiple applications run in the same cluster and connect to each other. Since each application has multiple pods running on different nodes, it is not straightforward to connect applications. In Kubernetes, **Service** is the resource used to define a set of pods, and you access them by using the name of the **Service**. Service resources are defined using the labels of the pods.

Consider the following code snippet:

```
apiVersion: v1
kind: Service
metadata:
  name: my-database
spec:
  selector:
    app: mysql
  ports:
    - protocol: TCP
      port: 3306
      targetPort: 3306
```

With the **my-database** service, the pods with the label **app: mysql** are grouped. When the **3306** port of **my-database** address is called, Kubernetes networking will connect to the **3306** port of a pod with the label **app:mysql**. Service resources create an abstraction layer between applications and enable decoupling. Let's assume you have a three-instance backend and a three-instance frontend in your application. Frontend pods can easily connect to backend instances using the **Service** resource without knowing where the backend instances are running. It creates abstraction and decoupling between the applications running in the cluster. In the following section, resources focusing on tasks and scheduled tasks will be presented.

Job and CronJob

Kubernetes resources such as **deployments** and **StatefulSets** focus on running applications and keeping them up and running. However, Kubernetes also provides **Job** and **CronJob** resources to run applications to completion. For instance, if your application needs to do one-time tasks, you can create a **Job** resource as follows:

```
apiVersion: batch/v1
kind: Job
metadata:
  name: echo
spec:
  template:
    spec:
      restartPolicy: OnFailure
```

```
      containers:
      - name: echo
        image: busybox
        args:
        - /bin/sh
        - -c
        - echo Hello from the echo Job!
```

When the **echo** Job is created, Kubernetes will create a pod, schedule it, and run it. When the container terminates after the **echo** command, Kubernetes will not try to restart it or keep it running.

In addition to one-time tasks, it is possible to run scheduled jobs using the **CronJob** resource, as shown in the following code snippet:

```
apiVersion: batch/v1beta1
kind: CronJob
metadata:
  name: hourly-echo
spec:
  schedule: "0 * * * *"
  jobTemplate:
    spec:
      template:
        spec:
          containers:
          restartPolicy: OnFailure
          - name: hello
            image: busybox
            args:
            - /bin/sh
            - -c
            - date; echo It is time to say echo!
```

With the **hourly-echo** CronJob, an additional **schedule** parameter is provided. With the schedule of **"0 * * * *"**, Kubernetes will create a new Job instance of this CronJob and run it every hour. Jobs and CronJobs are Kubernetes-native ways of handling manual and automated tasks required for your applications. In the following exercise, Kubernetes resources will be explored using **kubectl** and a local Kubernetes cluster.

Exercise 12: Installing a Stateful MySQL Database and Connecting inside Kubernetes

In this exercise, we will install a MySQL database as **StatefulSet**, check its status, and connect to the database using a job for creating tables.

To complete the exercise, we need to ensure the following steps are executed:

1. Create a file named **mysql.yaml** on your local computer with the following content:

```
apiVersion: apps/v1
kind: StatefulSet
metadata:
  name: mysql
spec:
  selector:
    matchLabels:
      app: mysql
  serviceName: mysql
  replicas: 1
  template:
    metadata:
      labels:
        app: mysql
    spec:
      containers:
      - name: mysql
        image: mysql:5.7
        env:
        - name: MYSQL_ROOT_PASSWORD
          value: "root"
        - name: MYSQL_DATABASE
          value: "db"
        - name: MYSQL_USER
          value: "user"
        - name: MYSQL_PASSWORD
          value: "password"
```

```
      ports:
      - name: mysql
        containerPort: 3306
      volumeMounts:
      - name: data
        mountPath: /var/lib/mysql
        subPath: mysql
  volumeClaimTemplates:
  - metadata:
      name: data
    spec:
      accessModes: ["ReadWriteOnce"]
      resources:
        requests:
          storage: 1Gi
```

> **Note**
>
> **mysql.yaml** is available on GitHub at https://github.com/TrainingByPackt/Serverless-Architectures-with-Kubernetes/blob/master/Lesson04/Exercise12/mysql.yaml.

2. Deploy the **StatefulSet** MySQL database with the following command in your Terminal:

   kubectl apply -f mysql.yaml

   This command submits the **mysql.yaml** file, which includes a **StatefulSet** called **mysql** and a 1 GB volume claim. The output will look like this:

   ```
   /serverless $ kubectl apply -f mysql.yaml
   statefulset.apps/mysql created
   /serverless $
   ```

   Figure 4.16: StatefulSet creation

3. Check the pods with the following command:

   kubectl get pods

   This command lists the running pods, and we expect to see the one instance of **mysql**, as shown in the following figure:

```
/serverless $ kubectl get pods
NAME        READY   STATUS    RESTARTS   AGE
mysql-0     1/1     Running   0          2m
/serverless $ █
```

Figure 4.17: Pod listing

> **Note**
>
> If the pod status is **Pending**, wait a couple of minutes until it becomes **Running** before continuing to the next step.

4. Check the persistent volumes with the following command:

   ```
   kubectl get persistentvolumes
   ```

   This command lists the persistent volumes, and we expect to see the one-volume instance created for the **StatefulSet**, as shown in the following figure:

```
/serverless $ kubectl get persistentvolumes
NAME                                       CAPACITY   ACCESS MODES   RECLAIM POLICY   STATUS   CLAIM
pvc-b1477955-d94c-11e9-8be9-aa8fc9a68c1f   1Gi        RWO            Delete           Bound    default/data-mysql-0
/serverless $ █
```

Figure 4.18: Persistent volume listing

5. Create the **service.yaml** file with the following content:

   ```yaml
   apiVersion: v1
   kind: Service
   metadata:
     name: my-database
   spec:
     selector:
       app: mysql
     ports:
       - protocol: TCP
         port: 3306
         targetPort: 3306
   ```

> **Note**
>
> **service.yaml** is available on GitHub at https://github.com/TrainingByPackt/
> Serverless-Architectures-with-Kubernetes/blob/master/Lesson04/Exercise12/
> service.yaml.

6. Deploy the **my-database** service with the following command in your Terminal:

```
kubectl apply -f service.yaml
```

This command submits the **Service** named **my-database** to group pods with the label **app:mysql**:

```
/serverless $ kubectl apply -f service.yaml
service/my-database created
/serverless $
```

Figure 4.19: Service creation

7. Create the **create-table.yaml** file with the following content:

```
apiVersion: batch/v1
kind: Job
metadata:
  name: create-table
spec:
  template:
    spec:
      restartPolicy: OnFailure
      containers:
      - name: create
        image: mysql:5.7
        args:
        - /bin/sh
        - -c
        - mysql -h my-database -u user -ppassword db -e 'CREATE TABLE IF
NOT EXISTS messages (id INT)';
```

> **Note**
>
> **create-table.yaml** is available on GitHub at https://github.com/TrainingByPackt/
> Serverless-Architectures-with-Kubernetes/blob/master/Lesson04/Exercise12/
> create-table.yaml.

8. Deploy the job with the following command:

```
kubectl apply -f create-table.yaml
```

This command submits the Job named **create-table** and within a couple of minutes, the pod will be created to run the **CREATE TABLE** command, as shown in the following figure:

```
/serverless $ kubectl apply -f create-table.yaml
job.batch/create-table created
/serverless $
```

Figure 4.20: Job creation

9. Check for the pods with the following command:

    kubectl get pods

    This command lists the running pods, and we expect to see the one instance of **create-table**, as shown in the following figure:

```
/serverless $ kubectl get pods
NAME                  READY   STATUS      RESTARTS   AGE
create-table-v7fsd    0/1     Completed   0          37s
mysql-0               1/1     Running     0          4m
/serverless $
```

Figure 4.21: Pod listing

> **Note**
>
> If the pod status is **Pending** or **Running**, wait a couple of minutes until it becomes **Completed** before continuing to the next step.

10. Run the following command to check the tables in the MySQL database:

    ```
    kubectl run mysql-client --image=mysql:5.7 -i -t --rm --restart=Never \
    -- mysql -h my-database -u user -ppassword  db -e "show tables;"
    ```

    This command runs a temporary instance of the **mysql:5.7** image and runs the **mysql** command, as shown in the following figure:

```
/serverless $ kubectl run mysql-client --image=mysql:5.7 -i -t --rm --restart=Never \
> -- mysql -h my-database -u user -ppassword  db -e"show tables;"

mysql: [Warning] Using a password on the command line interface can be insecure.
+-----------------+
| Tables_in_db |
+-----------------+
| messages        |
+-----------------+
pod "mysql-client" deleted
/serverless $
/serverless $
```

Figure 4.22: Table listing

In the MySQL database, a table with the name **messages** is available, as shown in the preceding output. It shows that **MySQL StatefulSet** is up and running the database successfully. In addition, the **create-table** Job has created a pod, connected to the database using the service, and created the table.

11. Clean the resources by running the following command:

```
kubectl delete -f create-table.yaml,service.yaml,mysql.yaml
```

You should see the output shown in the following figure:

```
/serverless $ kubectl delete -f create-table.yaml,service.yaml,mysql.yaml
job.batch "create-table" deleted
service "my-database" deleted
statefulset.apps "mysql" deleted
/serverless $
```

Figure 4.23: Cleanup

In the following activity, the database will be filled with the information retrieved by automated tasks in Kubernetes.

> **Note**
>
> You will need a Docker Hub account to push the images into the registry in the following activity. Docker Hub is a free service, and you can sign up to it at https://hub.docker.com/signup.

Activity 4: Collect Gold Prices in a MySQL Database in Kubernetes

The aim of this activity to create a real-life serverless application that runs in a Kubernetes cluster using Kubernetes-native resources. The serverless function will get gold prices from the live market and will push the data to the database. The function will run with predefined intervals to keep a history and make statistical analyses. Gold prices can be retrieved from the *CurrencyLayer* API, which provides a free API for exchange rates. Once completed, you will have a CronJob running every minute:

> **Note**
>
> In order to complete the following activity, you need to have a CurrencyLayer API access key. It is a free currency and exchange rate service, and you can sign up to it on the official website.

```
/serverless $ kubectl get pods
NAME                                    READY   STATUS      RESTARTS   AGE
gold-price-to-mysql-1568864100-gcmh6    0/1     Completed   0          2m
gold-price-to-mysql-1568864160-zd8ms    0/1     Completed   0          1m
gold-price-to-mysql-1568864220-2sxtd    0/1     Completed   0          42s
mysql-0                                 1/1     Running     0          12m
 /serverless $
```

Figure 4.24: Kubernetes Job for gold price

Finally, with each run of the Kubernetes Job, you will have a real-time gold price in the database:

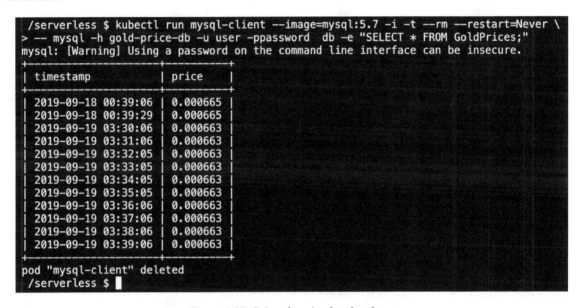

```
/serverless $ kubectl run mysql-client --image=mysql:5.7 -i -t --rm --restart=Never \
> -- mysql -h gold-price-db -u user -ppassword  db -e "SELECT * FROM GoldPrices;"
mysql: [Warning] Using a password on the command line interface can be insecure.
+---------------------+----------+
| timestamp           | price    |
+---------------------+----------+
| 2019-09-18 00:39:06 | 0.000665 |
| 2019-09-18 00:39:29 | 0.000665 |
| 2019-09-19 03:30:06 | 0.000663 |
| 2019-09-19 03:31:06 | 0.000663 |
| 2019-09-19 03:32:05 | 0.000663 |
| 2019-09-19 03:33:05 | 0.000663 |
| 2019-09-19 03:34:05 | 0.000663 |
| 2019-09-19 03:35:05 | 0.000663 |
| 2019-09-19 03:36:06 | 0.000663 |
| 2019-09-19 03:37:06 | 0.000663 |
| 2019-09-19 03:38:06 | 0.000663 |
| 2019-09-19 03:39:06 | 0.000663 |
+---------------------+----------+
pod "mysql-client" deleted
 /serverless $
```

Figure 4.25: Price data in the database

Execute the following steps to complete this activity:

1. Create an application to retrieve the gold price from *CurrencyLayer* and insert it into the MySQL database. It is possible to implement this function in Go with the following structure in a **main.go** file:

```
//only displaying the function here//


func main() {
    db, err := sql.Open("mysql", ...
    r, err := http.Get(fmt.Sprintf("http://apilayer.net/api/...
    stmt, err := db.Prepare("INSERT INTO GoldPrices(price) VALUES(?)")_,
      err = stmt.Exec(target.Quotes.USDXAU)
    log.Printf("Successfully inserted the price: %v", target.Quotes.
USDXAU)
}
```

In the **main** function, first you need to connect to the database, and then retrieve the price from *CurrencyLayer*. Then you need to create a SQL statement and execute on the database connection. The complete code for main.go can be found here: https://github.com/TrainingByPackt/Serverless-Architectures-with-Kubernetes/blob/master/Lesson04/Activity4/main.go.

2. Build the application as a Docker container.

3. Push the Docker container to the Docker registry.

4. Deploy the MySQL database into the Kubernetes cluster.

5. Deploy a Kubernetes service to expose the MySQL database.

6. Deploy a **CronJob** to run every minute.

7. Wait for a couple of minutes and check the instances of **CronJob**.

8. Connect to the database and check for the entries.

9. Clean the database and automated tasks from Kubernetes.

> **Note**
>
> The solution of the activity can be found on page 403.

Summary

In this chapter, we first described the origins and characteristics of Kubernetes. Following that, we studied the Kubernetes design and components with the details of master and node components. Then, we installed a local single-node Kubernetes cluster and checked the Kubernetes components. Following the cluster setup, we studied the official Kubernetes client tool, **kubectl**, which is used to connect to a cluster. We also saw how **kubectl** is used to manage clusters and the life cycle of applications. Finally, we discussed the fundamental Kubernetes resources for serverless applications, including pods, deployments, and **StatefulSets**. In addition to that, we also studied how to connect applications in a cluster using services. Kubernetes resources for one-time and automated tasks were presented using **Jobs** and **CronJobs**. At the end of this chapter, we developed a real-time data collection function using Kubernetes-native resources.

In the next chapter, we will be studying the features of Kubernetes clusters and using a popular cloud platform to deploy them.

5

Production-Ready Kubernetes Clusters

Learning Objectives

By the end of this chapter, you will be able to:

- Identify the requirements of Kubernetes cluster setup
- Create a production-ready Kubernetes cluster in Google Cloud Platform (GCP)
- Manage cluster autoscaling to add new servers to a Kubernetes cluster
- Migrate applications in production clusters

In this chapter, we will learn about the key considerations for the setup of Kubernetes. Following that, we will also study the different Kubernetes platform options. Then, we move on to creating a production-ready Kubernetes cluster in cloud platforms and performing administrative tasks.

Introduction

In the previous chapter, we created Kubernetes clusters for the development environment and installed applications into it. In this chapter, the focus will be on production-ready Kubernetes clusters and how to administer them for better availability, reliability, and cost optimization.

Kubernetes is the de facto system for managing microservices running as containers in the cloud. It is widely adopted in the industry by both start-ups and large enterprises for running various kinds of applications, including **data analysis tools**, **serverless apps**, and **databases**. Scalability, high availability, reliability, and security are the key features of Kubernetes that enable its adoption. Let's assume that you have decided to use Kubernetes, and hence you need a reliable and observable cluster setup for development and production. There are critical considerations that depend on your requirements, budget, and team before choosing a Kubernetes provider and how to operate the applications. There are four key considerations to analyze:

- **Service Quality:** Kubernetes runs microservices in a *highly available* and reliable way. However, it is critical to install and operate Kubernetes reliably and robustly. Let's assume you have installed the Kubernetes control plane into a single node in the cluster, and it was disconnected due to a network problem. Since you have lost the Kubernetes API server connectivity, you will not be able to check the status of your applications and operate them. Therefore, it is essential to evaluate the service quality of the Kubernetes cluster you need for your production environment.

- **Monitoring:** Kubernetes runs containers that are distributed to the nodes and enables checking their logs and statuses. Let's assume that you rolled out a new version of your application yesterday. Today, you want to check how the latest version is working for any errors, crashes, and response time. Therefore, you need a monitoring system integrated into your Kubernetes cluster to capture logs and metrics. The collected data is essential for troubleshooting and diagnosis in a production-ready cluster.

- **Security:** Kubernetes components and client tools work in a secure way to manage the applications running in the cluster. However, you need to have specific roles and authorization levels defined for your organization to operate Kubernetes clusters securely. Hence, it is essential to choose a Kubernetes provider platform that you can securely connect to and share with your customers and colleagues.

- **Operations:** Kubernetes is the host of all applications, including services with data compliance, auditing, and enterprise-level requirements. Let's assume you are running the backend and frontend of your online banking application system on Kubernetes. For a chartered bank in your county, the audit logs of your applications should be accessible. Since you have deployed your entire system on Kubernetes, the platform should enable fetching audit logs, archiving them, and storing them. Therefore, the operational capability of the Kubernetes platform is essential for the production-ready cluster setup.

In order to decide how to install and operate your Kubernetes clusters, these considerations will be discussed for the Kubernetes platform options in this chapter.

Kubernetes Setup

Kubernetes is a flexible system that can be installed on various platforms from **Raspberry Pi** to high-end servers in **data centers**. Each platform comes with its advantages and disadvantages in terms of service quality, monitoring, security, and operations. Kubernetes manages applications as containers and creates an abstraction layer on the infrastructure. Let's imagine that you set up Kubernetes on the three old servers in your basement and then install the **Proof of Concept** (**PoC**) of your new project. When the project becomes successful, you want to scale your application and move to a cloud provider such as **Amazon Web Services** (**AWS**). Since your application is designed to run on Kubernetes and does not depend on the infrastructure, porting to another Kubernetes installation is straightforward.

In the previous chapter, we studied the development environment setup using `minikube`, the official method of Kubernetes. In this section, production-level Kubernetes platforms will be presented. The Kubernetes platforms for production can be grouped into threes, with the following abstraction layers:

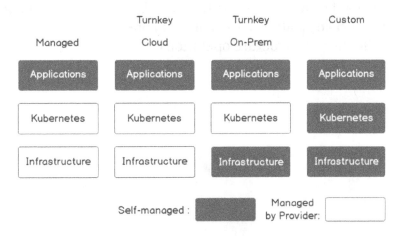

Figure 5.1: Kubernetes platforms

Let's now look at each of these types, one by one.

Managed Platforms

Managed platforms provide **Kubernetes as a Service**, and all underlying services run under the control of cloud providers. It is easy to set up and scale these clusters since the cloud providers handle all infrastructural operations. Leading cloud providers such as GCP, AWS, and Microsoft Azure have managed Kubernetes solution applications, intending to integrate other cloud services such as container registries, identity services, and storage services. The most popular managed Kubernetes solutions are as follows:

- **Google Kubernetes Engine (GKE)**: GKE is the most mature managed service on the market, and Google provides it as a part of GCP.

- **Azure Kubernetes Service (AKS)**: AKS is the Kubernetes solution provided by Microsoft as a part of the Azure platform.

- **Amazon Elastic Container Service for Kubernetes (EKS)**: EKS is the managed Kubernetes of AWS.

Turnkey Platforms

Turnkey solutions focus on installing and operating the Kubernetes control plane in the cloud or in on-premise systems. Users of turnkey platforms provide information about the infrastructure, and the turnkey platforms handle the Kubernetes setup. Turnkey platforms offer better flexibility in setup configurations and infrastructure options. These platforms are mostly designed by organizations with rich experience in Kubernetes and cloud systems such as **Heptio** or **CoreOS**.

If turnkey platforms are installed on cloud providers such as AWS, the infrastructure is managed by the cloud provider, and the turnkey platform manages Kubernetes. However, when the turnkey platform is installed on on-premise systems, in-house teams should handle the infrastructure operations.

Custom Platforms

Custom installation of Kubernetes is possible if your use case does not fit into any managed or turnkey solutions. For instance, you can use **Gardener** (https://gardener. cloud) or **OpenShift** (https://www.openshift.com) to install Kubernetes clusters to cloud providers, on-premise data centers, on-premise virtual machines (VMs), or bare-metal servers. While the custom platforms offer more flexible Kubernetes installations, they also come with special operations and maintenance efforts.

In the following sections, we will create a managed Kubernetes cluster in GKE and administer it. GKE offers the most mature platform and the superior customer experience on the market.

Google Kubernetes Engine

GKE provides a managed Kubernetes platform backed by the experience that Google has of running containerized services for more than a decade. GKE clusters are production-ready and scalable, and they support upstream Kubernetes versions. In addition, GKE focuses on improving the development experience by eliminating the installation, management, and operation needs of Kubernetes clusters.

While GKE improves developer experience, it tries to minimize the cost of running Kubernetes clusters. It only charges for the nodes in the cluster and provides a Kubernetes control plane free of charge. In other words, GKE delivers a reliable, scalable, and robust Kubernetes control plane without any cost. For the servers that run the workload of your applications, the usual GCP Compute Engine pricing is applied. For instance, let's assume that you will start with two **n1-standard-1 (vCPUs: 1, RAM: 3.75 GB)** nodes:

The calculation would be as follows:

1,460 total hours per month

Instance type: n1-standard-1

GCE Instance Cost: USD 48.54

Kubernetes Engine Cost: USD 0.00

Estimated Component Cost: USD 48.54 per 1 month

If your application requires scalability with the higher usage and if you need 10 servers instead of 2, the cost will also scale linearly:

7,300 total hours per month

Instance type: n1-standard-1

GCE Instance Cost: USD 242.72

Kubernetes Engine Cost: USD 0.00

Estimated Component Cost: USD 242.72 per 1 month

This calculation shows that GKE does not charge for the Kubernetes control plane and provides a reliable, scalable, and robust Kubernetes API for every cluster. In addition, the cost linearly increases for scaling clusters, which makes it easier to plan and operate Kubernetes clusters.

In the following exercise, you will create a managed Kubernetes cluster in GKE and connect to it.

> **Note**
>
> In order to complete this exercise, you need to have an active GCP account. You can create an account on its official website: https://console.cloud.google.com/start.

Exercise 13: Creating a Kubernetes Cluster on GCP

In this exercise, we will create a Kubernetes cluster in GKE and connect to it securely to check node statuses. The Google Cloud Platform dashboard and CLI tools maintain a high level of developer experience. Therefore, if you need a production-ready Kubernetes cluster, you will have a fully functioning control plane and server nodes in less than 10 minutes.

To complete the exercise, we need to ensure the following steps are executed:

1. Click **Kubernetes Engine** in the left menu under **Compute** on the Google Cloud Platform home page, as shown in the following figure:

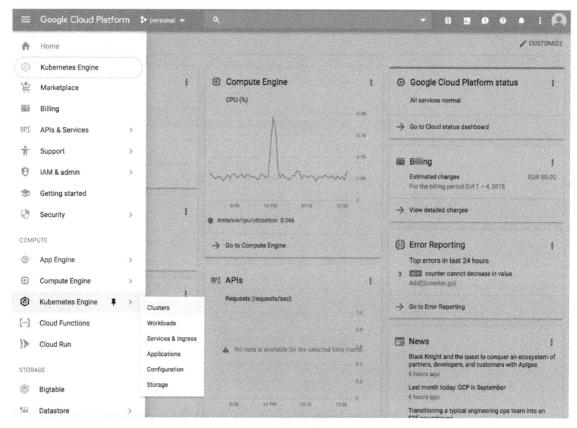

Figure 5.2: Google Cloud Platform home page

2. Click **Create Cluster** on the **Clusters** page, as shown in the following figure:

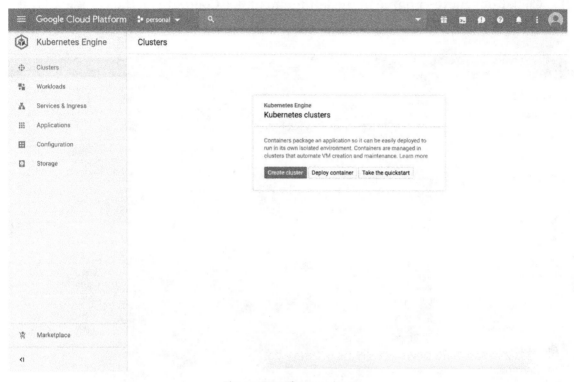

Figure 5.3: Cluster view

3. Select **Your first cluster** in the left from **Cluster templates** and write `serverless` as the name. Click **Create** at the end of the page, as shown in the following figure:

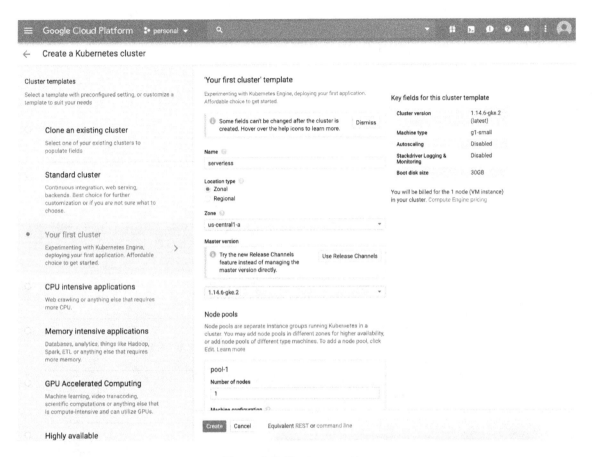

Figure 5.4: Cluster creation

4. Wait a couple of minutes until the cluster icon becomes green and then click the **Connect** button, as you can see in the following figure:

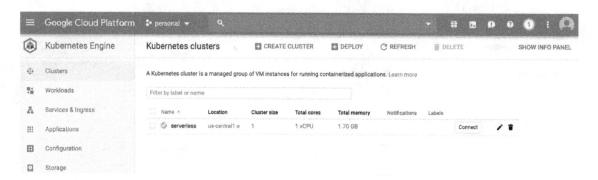

Figure 5.5: Cluster list

5. Click **Run in Cloud Shell** in the **Connect to the cluster** window, as shown in the following figure:

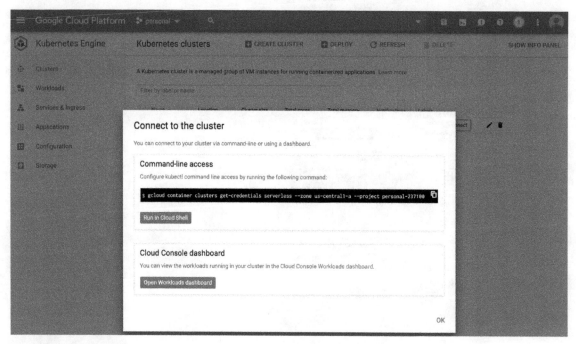

Figure 5.6: Connect to the cluster view

6. Wait until the cloud shell is open and available and press *Enter* when the command is shown, as you can see in the following figure:

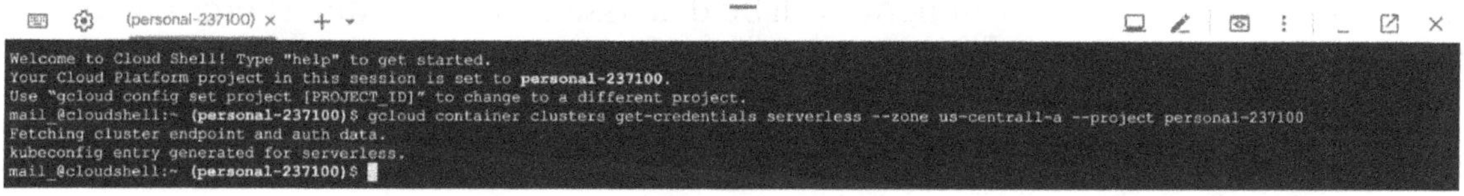

Figure 5.7: Cloud shell

The output shows that the authentication data for the cluster is fetched, and the **kubeconfig** entry is ready to use.

7. Check the nodes with the following command in the cloud shell:

```
kubectl get nodes
```

Since the cluster is created with a single node pool of one node, there is only one node connected to the cluster, as you can see in the following figure:

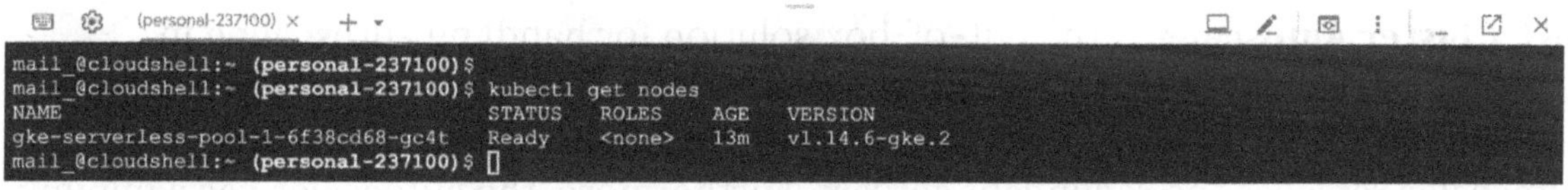

Figure 5.8: Node list

8. Check for the pods running in the cluster with the following command in the cloud shell:

```
kubectl get pods --all-namespaces
```

Since GKE manages the control plane, there are no pods for **api-server**, **etcd**, or **scheduler** in the **kube-system** namespace. There are only networking and metrics pods running in the cluster, as shown in the following screenshot:

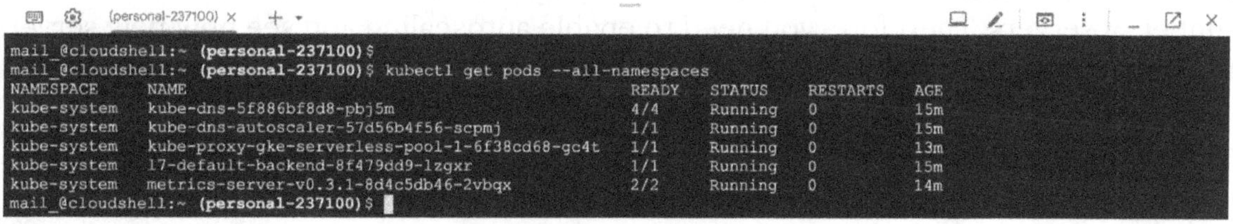

Figure 5.9: Pod list

With this exercise, you have created a production-ready Kubernetes cluster on GKE. Within a couple of minutes, GKE created a managed Kubernetes control plane and connected the servers to the cluster. In the following sections, administrating the clusters for production environments will be discussed, and the Kubernetes cluster from this exercise will be expanded.

Autoscaling Kubernetes Clusters

Kubernetes clusters are designed to run scalable applications reliably. In other words, if the Kubernetes cluster runs **10 instances** of your application today, it should also support running **100 instances** in the future. There are two mainstream methods to reach this level of flexibility: *redundancy* and *autoscaling*. Let's assume that the 10 instances of your application are running on 3 servers in your cluster. With the redundancy, you need at least 27 extra idle servers to be capable of running 100 instances in the future. It also means paying for the empty servers as well as operational and maintenance costs. With autoscaling, you need automated procedures to create or remove servers. Autoscaling ensures that there are no excessive idle servers and minimizes the costs while meeting the scalability requirements.

GKE Cluster Autoscaler is the out-of-box solution for handling autoscaling in Kubernetes clusters. When it is enabled, it automatically adds new servers if there is no capacity left for the workload. Similarly, when the servers are underutilized, the autoscaler removes the redundant servers. Furthermore, the autoscaler has a minimum and maximum number of servers defined to avoid limitless increases or decreases. In the following exercise, the GKE cluster autoscaler will be enabled for the Kubernetes cluster. Then the automatic scaling of the servers will be demonstrated by changing the workload in the cluster.

Exercise 14: Autoscaling a GKE Cluster in Production

In this exercise, we will enable and utilize the GKE cluster autoscaler in a production cluster. Let's assume that you need a large number of replicas of your application running in the cluster. However, it is not currently possible since you have a low number of servers. Therefore, you need to enable autoscaling and see how new servers are created automatically.

To successfully complete the exercise, we need to ensure the following steps are executed:

1. Install **nginx** in the cluster by running the following command in the cloud shell:

   ```
   kubectl create deployment workload --image=nginx
   ```

   This command creates a deployment named **workload** from the **nginx** image, as depicted in the following figure:

Figure 5.10: Deployment creation

2. Scale the **workload** deployment to 25 replicas by running the following command in the cloud shell:

   ```
   kubectl scale deployment workload --replicas=25
   ```

   This command increases the number of replicas of the workload deployment, as shown in the following figure:

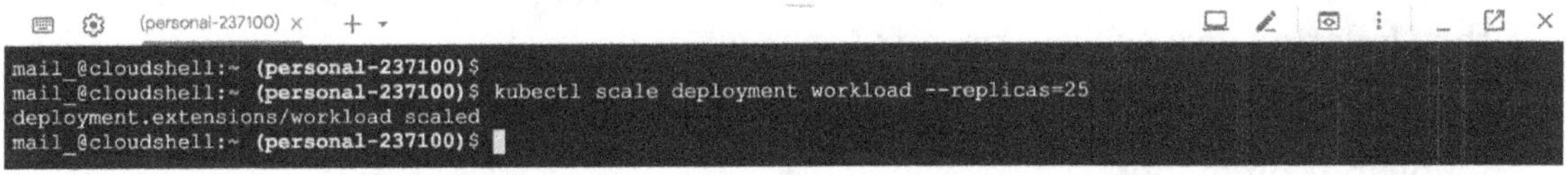

Figure 5.11: Deployment scaling up

3. Check the number of running pods with the following command:

   ```
   kubectl get deployment workload
   ```

   Since there is only 1 node in the cluster, 25 replicas of **nginx** could not run in the cluster. Instead, only 5 instances are running currently, as shown in the following figure:

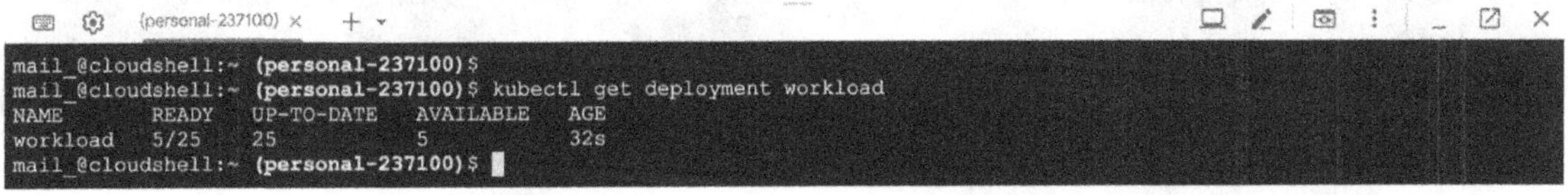

Figure 5.12: Deployment status

4. Enable autoscaling for the node pool of the cluster using the following command:

```
gcloud container clusters update serverless --enable-autoscaling  \
  --min-nodes 1 --max-nodes 10 --zone us-central1-a  \
  --node-pool pool-1
```

> **Note**
>
> Change the **zone** parameter if your cluster is running in another zone.

This command enables autoscaling for the Kubernetes cluster with a minimum of 1 and a maximum of 10 nodes, as shown in the following figure:

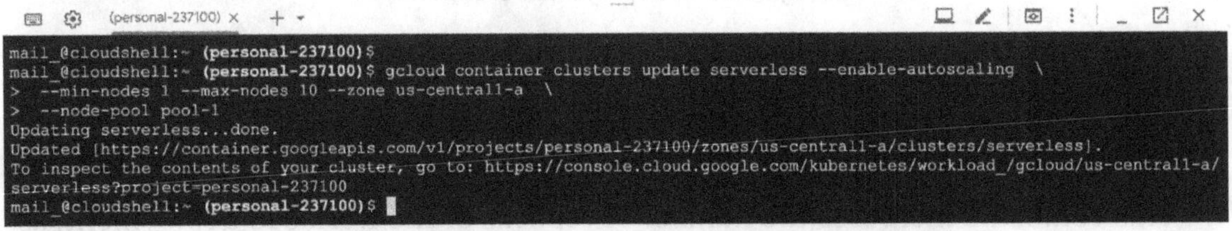

Figure 5.13: Enabling autoscaler

This command can take a couple of minutes to create the required resources with the **Updating serverless...** prompt.

5. Wait a couple of minutes and check for the number of nodes by using the following command:

```
kubectl get nodes
```

With autoscaling enabled, GKE ensures that there are enough nodes to run the workload in the cluster. The node pool is scaled up to four nodes, as shown in the following figure:

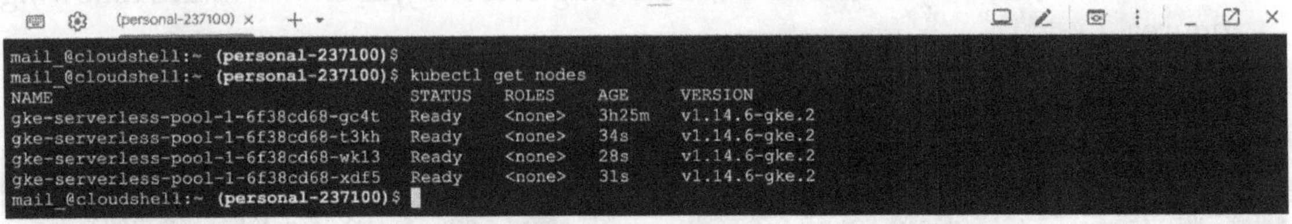

Figure 5.14: Node list

6. Check the number of running pods with the following command:

   ```
   kubectl get deployment workload
   ```

   Since there are 4 nodes in the cluster, 25 replicas of **nginx** could run in the cluster, as shown in the following figure:

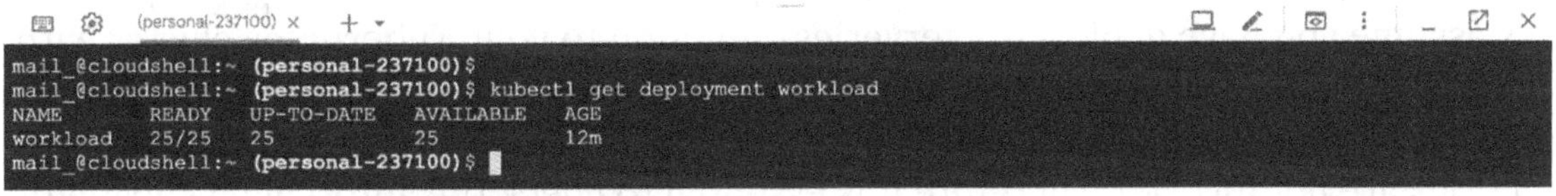

Figure 5.15: Deployment status

7. Delete the deployment with the following command:

   ```
   kubectl delete deployment workload
   ```

   The output should be as follows:

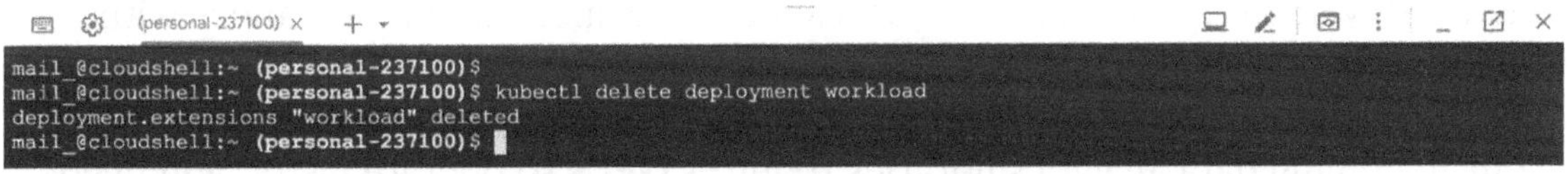

Figure 5.16: Deployment deletion

8. Disable autoscaling for the node pool of the cluster by using the following command:

   ```
   gcloud container clusters update serverless --no-enable-autoscaling \
   --node-pool pool-1 --zone us-central1-a
   ```

   > **Note**
   >
   > Change the **zone** parameter if your cluster is running in another zone.

   You should see the output shown in the following figure:

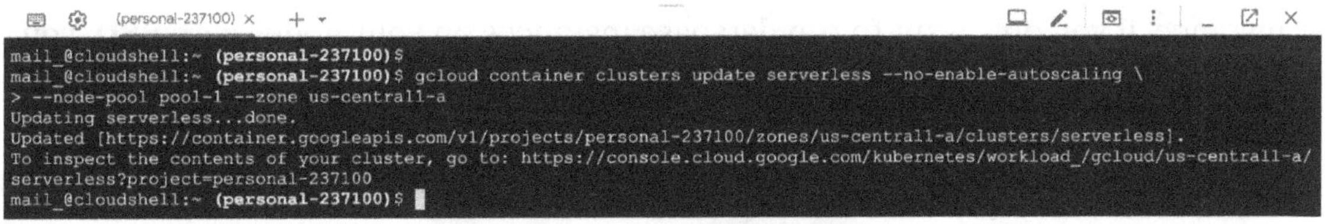

Figure 5.17: Disabling autoscaling

In this exercise, we saw the GKE cluster autoscaler in action. When the autoscaler is enabled, it increases the number of servers when the cluster is out of capacity for the current workload. Although it seems straightforward, it is a compelling feature of Kubernetes platforms. It removes the burden of manual operations to check your cluster utilization and take action. It is even more critical for serverless applications where user demand is highly variable.

Let's assume you have deployed a serverless function to your Kubernetes cluster with autoscaling enabled. The cluster autoscaler will automatically increase the number of nodes when your functions are called frequently and then delete the nodes when your functions are not invoked. Therefore it is essential to check the autoscaling capability of the Kubernetes platform for serverless applications. In the following section, migrating applications in production environments will be discussed, as it is another important cluster administration task.

Application Migration in Kubernetes Clusters

Kubernetes distributes applications to servers and keeps them running reliably and robustly. Servers in the cluster could be VMs or bare-metal server instances with different technical specifications. Let's assume you have connected only standard VMs to your Kubernetes cluster and they are running various types of applications. If one of your upcoming data analytics libraries requires **GPUs** to operate faster, you need to connect servers with **GPUs**. Similarly, if your database application requires **SSD** disks for faster I/O operations, you need to connect servers with **SSD** access. These kinds of application requirements result in having different node pools in your cluster. Also, you need to configure the Kubernetes workload to run on the particular nodes. In addition to marking some nodes reserved for special types of workloads, **taints** are used. Similarly, pods are marked with **tolerations** if they are running specific types of workloads. Kubernetes supports workload distribution to special nodes with **taints** and **tolerations** working in harmony:

- **Taints** are applied to nodes to indicate that the node should not have any pods that do not tolerate the taints.

- **Tolerations** are applied to pods to allow pods to be scheduled on nodes with taints.

For instance, if you only want to run database instances on your nodes with **SSD**, you need first to taint your nodes:

```
kubectl taint nodes disk-node-1 ssd=true:NoSchedule
```

With this command, **disk-node-1** will only accept pods that have the following tolerations in their definition:

```
tolerations:
- key: "ssd"
  operator: "Equal"
  value: "true"
  effect: "NoSchedule"
```

Taints and tolerations work in harmony to assign pods to specific nodes as a part of the Kubernetes scheduler. In addition, Kubernetes supports securely removing the servers from the cluster by using the **kubectl drain** command. It is particularly helpful if you want to take some nodes for maintenance or retirement. In the following exercise, an application running in the Kubernetes cluster will be migrated to a particular set of new nodes.

Exercise 15: Migrating Applications Running in a GKE Cluster

This exercise aims to teach us to perform migration activities in a production cluster. Let's assume that you are running a backend application in your Kubernetes cluster. With the recent changes, you have enhanced your application with better memory management and want to run on servers with higher memory optimization. Therefore, you will create a new node pool and migrate your application instances into it.

To successfully complete the exercise, we need to ensure the following steps are executed:

1. Install the backend application to the cluster by running the following command in the cloud shell:

   ```
   kubectl create deployment backend --image=nginx
   ```

   This command creates a deployment named **backend** from an **nginx** image, as you can see in the following figure:

Figure 5.18: Deployment creation

2. Scale the **backend** deployment to **10** replicas by running the following command in the cloud shell:

```
kubectl scale deployment backend --replicas=10
```

This command increases the number of replicas of the backend deployment, as shown in the following figure:

Figure 5.19: Deployment scaling up

3. Check the number of running **pods** and their nodes with the following command:

```
kubectl get pods -o wide
```

All 10 replicas of the deployment are running successfully on the 4 nodes, as you can see in the following figure:

```
mail_@cloudshell:~ (personal-237100)$
mail_@cloudshell:~ (personal-237100)$ kubectl get pods -o wide
NAME                       READY   STATUS    RESTARTS   AGE    IP            NODE                                        NOMINATED NODE   READINESS GATES
backend-59b85ff57d-22kkr   1/1     Running   0          71s    10.60.2.11    gke-serverless-pool-1-6f38cd68-t3kh         <none>           <none>
backend-59b85ff57d-2r9qv   1/1     Running   0          72s    10.60.0.12    gke-serverless-pool-1-6f38cd68-gc4t         <none>           <none>
backend-59b85ff57d-ch9tz   1/1     Running   0          71s    10.60.1.11    gke-serverless-pool-1-6f38cd68-xdf5         <none>           <none>
backend-59b85ff57d-hmx2k   1/1     Running   0          72s    10.60.1.12    gke-serverless-pool-1-6f38cd68-xdf5         <none>           <none>
backend-59b85ff57d-ltf2x   1/1     Running   0          71s    10.60.0.13    gke-serverless-pool-1-6f38cd68-gc4t         <none>           <none>
backend-59b85ff57d-lznnk   1/1     Running   0          72s    10.60.3.8     gke-serverless-pool-1-6f38cd68-wk13         <none>           <none>
backend-59b85ff57d-nnhdg   1/1     Running   0          71s    10.60.2.12    gke-serverless-pool-1-6f38cd68-t3kh         <none>           <none>
backend-59b85ff57d-p6hpr   1/1     Running   0          2m8s   10.60.2.10    gke-serverless-pool-1-6f38cd68-t3kh         <none>           <none>
backend-59b85ff57d-r2tcn   1/1     Running   0          71s    10.60.3.7     gke-serverless-pool-1-6f38cd68-wk13         <none>           <none>
backend-59b85ff57d-r8kf4   1/1     Running   0          71s    10.60.1.10    gke-serverless-pool-1-6f38cd68-xdf5         <none>           <none>
mail_@cloudshell:~ (personal-237100)$
```

Figure 5.20: Deployment status

4. Create a node pool in GCP with a higher memory:

```
gcloud container node-pools create high-memory-pool --cluster=serverless \
--zone us-central1-a --machine-type=n1-highmem-2 --num-nodes=2
```

> **Note**
>
> Change the **zone** parameter if your cluster is running in another zone.

This command creates a new node pool named **high-memory-pool** in the serverless cluster with the machine type **n1-highmem-2** and two servers, as you can see in the following figure:

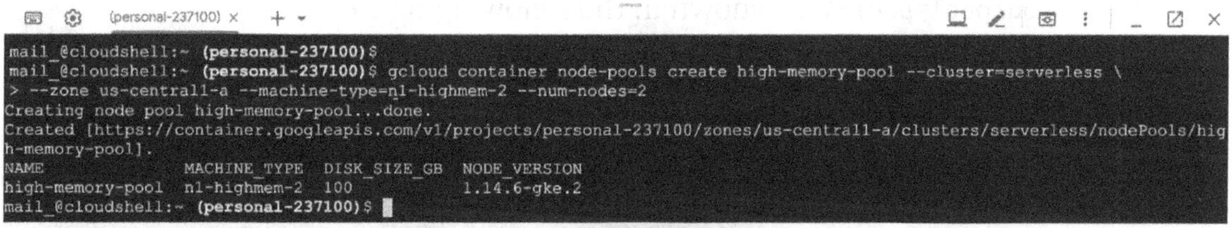

Figure 5.21: Node pool creation

This command can take a couple of minutes to create the required resources with the **Creating node pool high-memory-pool** prompt.

5. Wait for a couple of minutes and check the nodes in the cluster:

    ```
    kubectl get nodes
    ```

    This command lists the nodes in the cluster, and we expect to see two extra **high-memory** nodes, as shown in the following figure:

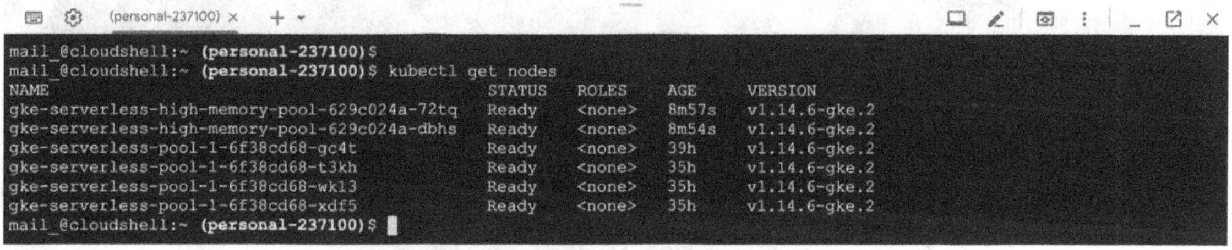

Figure 5.22: Cluster nodes

6. Drain the old nodes so that Kubernetes will migrate applications to new nodes:

```
kubectl drain -l cloud.google.com/gke-nodepool=pool-1
```

This command removes the workloads from all nodes with the label **cloud.google.com/gke-nodepool=pool-1**, as shown in the following figure:

Figure 5.23: Node removal

7. Check the running pods and their nodes with the following command:

```
kubectl get pods -o wide
```

All 10 replicas of the deployment are running successfully on the new **high-memory** node, as shown in the following figure:

Figure 5.24: Deployment status

8. Delete the old node pool with the following command:

```
gcloud container node-pools delete pool-1 --cluster serverless --zone
us-central1-a
```

> **Note**
>
> Change the **zone** parameter if your cluster is running in another zone.

This command deletes the old node pool, which is not being used, as you can see in the following figure:

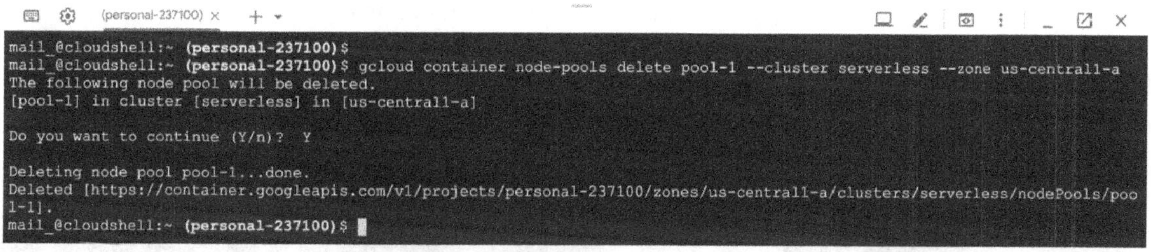

Figure 5.25: Node pool deletion

In this exercise, we have migrated the running application to new nodes with better technical specs. Using the Kubernetes primitives and GKE node pools, it is possible to migrate applications to a particular set of nodes without downtime. In the following activity, you will use autoscaling and Kubernetes taints to run serverless functions while minimizing the cost.

Activity 5: Minimizing the Costs of Serverless Functions in a GKE Cluster

The aim of this activity to take administrative tasks on production clusters to run serverless functions while minimizing the costs. Let's assume that your backend application is already running in your Kubernetes cluster. Now you want to install some serverless functions to connect to the backend. However, backend instances are running memory-optimized servers, which are costly for also running serverless functions. Therefore, you need to add *preemptible* servers, which are cheaper. Preemptible VMs are already available in GCP; however, they have low service quality and a maximum lifespan of 24 hours. Therefore, you should configure the node pool to be autoscaled and only to run serverless functions. Otherwise, your backend instances could also be scheduled on preemptible VMs and degrade the overall performance.

At the end of the activity, you will have functions connecting to the backend instances, as shown in the following figure:

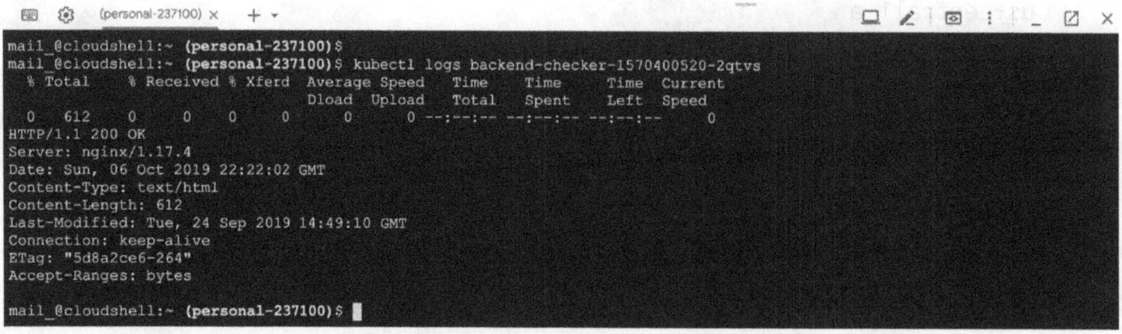

Figure 5.26: Backend checker functions

Backend instances will run on high-memory nodes and function instances will run on preemptible servers, as shown in the following figure:

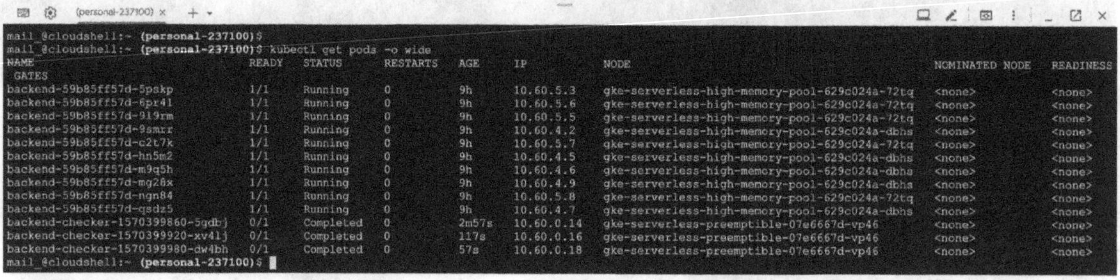

Figure 5.27: Kubernetes pods and the corresponding nodes

> **Note**
>
> In order to complete the activity, you should use the cluster from *Exercise 15* with backend deployments running.

Execute the following steps to complete the activity:

1. Create a new node pool with preemptible servers.

2. Taint the preemptible servers to run only serverless functions.

3. Create a Kubernetes service to reach backend pods.

4. Create a CronJob to connect to the backend service every minute. The CronJob definition should have tolerations to run on preemptible servers.

5. Check the node assignments of the CronJob functions.

6. Check the logs of the CronJob function instances.

7. Clean the backend deployment and the serverless functions.

8. Remove the Kubernetes cluster if you do not need it anymore.

> **Note**
>
> The solution to the activity can be found on page 412.

Summary

In this chapter, we first described the four key considerations to analyze the requirements for the Kubernetes cluster setup. Then we studied the three groups of Kubernetes platforms: managed, turnkey, and custom. Each Kubernetes platform has been explained, along with their responsibility levels on infrastructure, Kubernetes, and applications. Following that, we created a production-ready Kubernetes cluster on GKE. Since Kubernetes is designed to run scalable applications, we studied how to deal with increasing or decreasing workload by autoscaling. Furthermore, we also looked at application migration without downtime in production clusters to illustrate how to move your applications to the servers with higher memory. Finally, we performed autoscaling and migration activities with a serverless function running in a production cluster to minimize the costs. Kubernetes and serverless applications work together to create reliable, robust, and scalable future-proof environments. Therefore, it is essential to know how to install and operate Kubernetes clusters for production.

In the next chapter, we will be studying the upcoming serverless features in Kubernetes. We will also study virtual kubelets in detail and deploy stateless containers on GKE.

Upcoming Serverless Features in Kubernetes

Learning Objectives

By the end of this chapter, you will be able to:

- Utilize the concepts and components of Knative to deploy applications

- Set up Knative on a GKE cluster

- Deploy applications on Knative and configure autoscaling

- Deploy applications on Google Cloud Run

- Set up Virtual Kubelet on Azure

- Deploy applications with Virtual Kubelet

This chapter covers Knative, Google Cloud Run, and Virtual Kubelet, which offers the advantages of serverless on top of a Kubernetes cluster.

Introduction to Serverless with Kubernetes

In the previous chapter, we extensively studied the various setup options and platforms used in Kubernetes. We also covered the autoscaling feature of Kubernetes and implemented it in an application deployed on a cluster.

Kubernetes and serverless are two of the trending topics in the IT industry, but these two topics are often discussed independently of each other. Kubernetes is a platform for managing containerized applications, and serverless is an execution model that abstracts away the infrastructure so software developers can focus on their application logic. However, a combination of these two concepts will achieve the same goal of making the software developer's life much easier.

A few platforms have emerged recently that bring serverless features to containers by abstracting away the complexities of managing containers and any underlying infrastructure. These platforms run serverless workloads on Kubernetes clusters and provide many benefits, including autoscaling, scale to zero, per-usage billing, event-driven capabilities, integrated monitoring, and integrated logging features.

In this chapter, we will be discussing three technologies that offer the benefits of serverless on top of a Kubernetes cluster:

- Knative
- Google Cloud Run
- Virtual Kubelet

Introduction to Knative

Knative is an open source project started by Google with contributions from over 50 other companies, including Pivotal, Red Hat, IBM, and SAP. Knative extends Kubernetes by introducing a set of components to build and run serverless applications on top of it. This framework is great for application developers who are already using Kubernetes. Knative provides tools for them to focus on their code without worrying about the underlying architecture of Kubernetes. It introduces features such as automated container builds, autoscaling, scale to zero, and an eventing framework, which allows developers to get the benefits of serverless on top of Kubernetes.

The Knative framework is described as a "*Kubernetes-based platform to deploy and manage modern serverless workloads*" on the Knative website. The framework helps to bridge the gap between containerized applications and serverless applications by introducing serverless features such as autoscaling and scale to zero to the Kubernetes platform.

Knative consists of three main components:

- Build
- Serving
- Eventing

> **Note**
>
> The Build component has been deprecated in favor of Tekton Pipelines in the latest version of Knative. The final release of the Knative Build component is available in version 0.7.

Build is the process of building the container images from the source code and running them on a Kubernetes cluster. The Knative Serving component allows the deployment of serverless applications and functions. This enables serving traffic to containers and autoscaling based on the number of requests. The serving component is also responsible for taking snapshots of the code and configurations whenever a change is made to them. The Knative Eventing component helps us to build event-driven applications. This component allows the applications to produce events for and consume events from event streams.

The following diagram illustrates a Knative framework with its dependencies and the stakeholders of each component:

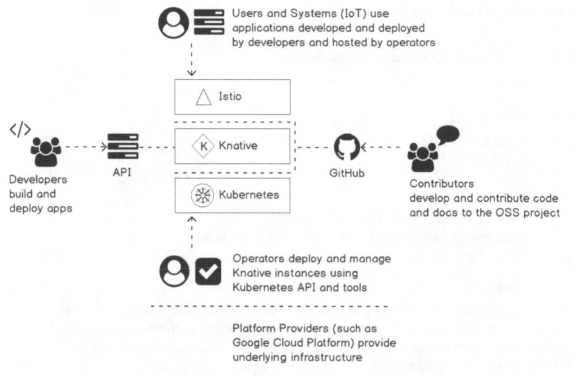

Users and Systems (IoT) use applications developed and deployed by developers and hosted by operators

Istio

Developers build and deploy apps

API

K Knative

GitHub

Contributors develop and contribute code and docs to the OSS project

Kubernetes

Operators deploy and manage Knative instances using Kubernetes API and tools

Platform Providers (such as Google Cloud Platform) provide underlying infrastructure

Figure 6.1: Knative dependencies and stakeholders

The bottom layer represents the Kubernetes framework, which is used as the container orchestration layer by the Knative framework. Kubernetes can be deployed on any infrastructure, such as Google Cloud Platform or an on-premises system. Next, we have the **Istio** service mesh layer, which manages network routing within the cluster. This layer provides many benefits, including traffic management, observability, and security. At the top layer, Knative runs on top of a Kubernetes cluster with **Istio**. In the Knative layer, at one end we can see contributors who contribute code to the Knative framework through the GitHub project, and at the other end we can see the application developers who build and deploy applications on top of the Knative framework.

> **Note**
>
> For more information on Istio, please refer to https://istio.io/.

Now that we have this understanding of Knative, let's look at how to install Knative on a Kubernetes cluster in the following section.

Getting Started with Knative on GKE

In this section, we will take you through the process of installing Knative on a Kubernetes cluster. We will be using Google Kubernetes Engine (GKE) to set up a Kubernetes cluster. GKE is the managed Kubernetes cluster service in the Google cloud. It allows us to run Kubernetes clusters without the burden of installing, managing and operating our own clusters.

We need to have the following prerequisites installed and configured to continue with this section:

- A Google Cloud account

- The gcloud CLI

- The kubectl CLI (v1.10 or newer)

First, we need to set a few environment variables that we will be using with the **gcloud** CLI. You should update **<your-gcp-project-name>** with the name of your GCP project. We will be using **us-central1-a** as the GCP zone. Execute the following commands in your terminal window to set the required environment variables:

```
$ export GCP_PROJECT=<your-gcp-project-name>

$ export GCP_ZONE=us-central1-a

$ export GKE_CLUSTER=knative-cluster
```

The output should be as follows:

```
/serverless $ export GCP_PROJECT=serverless-kubernetes-project
/serverless $ export GCP_ZONE=us-central1-a
/serverless $ export GKE_CLUSTER=knative-cluster
/serverless $
```

Figure 6.2: Setting environment variables

Set our GCP project as the default project to be used by the **gcloud** CLI commands:

```
$ gcloud config set core/project $GCP_PROJECT
```

The output should be as follows:

```
/serverless $ gcloud config set core/project $GCP_PROJECT
Updated property [core/project].
```

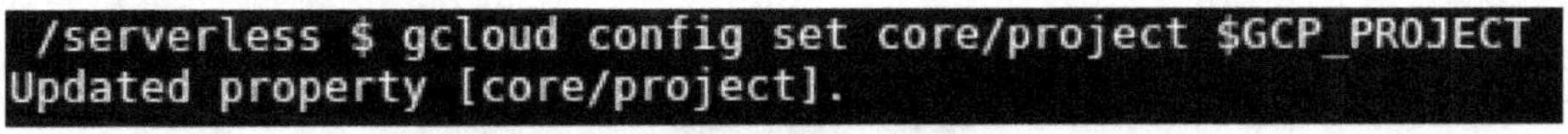

Figure 6.3: Setting the default GCP project

Now we can create the GKE cluster using the **gcloud** command. Knative requires a Kubernetes cluster with version 1.11 or newer. We will be using the **Istio** plugin provided by GKE for this cluster. The following is the recommended configuration for a Kubernetes cluster to run Knative components:

- Kubernetes version 1.11 or newer

- Kubernetes nodes with four vCPUs (n1-standard-4)

- Node autoscaling enabled for up to 10 nodes

- API scopes for `cloud-platform`

Execute the following command to create a GKE cluster compatible with these requirements:

```
$ gcloud beta container clusters create $GKE_CLUSTER \
--zone=$GCP_ZONE \
--machine-type=n1-standard-4 \
--cluster-version=latest \
--addons=HorizontalPodAutoscaling,HttpLoadBalancing,Istio \
--enable-stackdriver-kubernetes \
--enable-ip-alias \
--enable-autoscaling --min-nodes=1 --max-nodes=10 \
--enable-autorepair \
--scopes cloud-platform
```

The output should be as follows:

```
/serverless $ gcloud beta container clusters create $GKE_CLUSTER \
>       --zone=$GCP_ZONE \
>       --machine-type=n1-standard-4 \
>       --cluster-version=latest \
>       --addons=HorizontalPodAutoscaling,HttpLoadBalancing,Istio \
>       --enable-stackdriver-kubernetes \
>       --enable-ip-alias \
>       --enable-autoscaling --min-nodes=1 --max-nodes=10 \
>       --enable-autorepair \
>       --scopes cloud-platform
```

Figure 6.4: Creating a GKE cluster

It may take a few minutes to set up the Kubernetes cluster. Once the cluster is ready, we will use the command **gcloud container clusters get-credentials** to fetch the credentials of the new cluster and configure the **kubectl** CLI as you can see in the following code snippet:

```
$ gcloud container clusters get-credentials $GKE_CLUSTER --zone $GCP_ZONE
--project $GCP_PROJECT
```

The output should be as follows:

```
/serverless $ gcloud container clusters get-credentials $GKE_CLUSTER --zone
$GCP_ZONE --project $GCP_PROJECT
Fetching cluster endpoint and auth data.
kubeconfig entry generated for knative-cluster.
/serverless $
```

Figure 6.5: Fetching credentials for the GKE cluster

Now you have successfully created the GKE cluster with **Istio** and configured **kubectl** to access the newly created cluster. We can now proceed with the next step of installing Knative. We will be installing Knative version 0.8, which is the latest available version at the time of writing this book.

We will use the **kubectl** CLI to apply the Knative components to the Kubernetes cluster. First, run the **kubectl apply** command with the **-l knative.dev/crd-install=true** flag to prevent race conditions during the installation process:

```
$ kubectl apply --selector knative.dev/crd-install=true \

    -f https://github.com/knative/serving/releases/download/v0.8.0/serving.
yaml \

    -f https://github.com/knative/eventing/releases/download/v0.8.0/release.
yaml \

    -f https://github.com/knative/serving/releases/download/v0.8.0/monitoring.
yaml
```

Next, run the command again without the **-l knative.dev/crd-install=true** flag to complete the installation:

```
$ kubectl apply -f https://github.com/knative/serving/releases/download/
v0.8.0/serving.yaml \

    -f https://github.com/knative/eventing/releases/download/v0.8.0/release.
yaml \

    -f https://github.com/knative/serving/releases/download/v0.8.0/monitoring.
yaml
```

Once the command is completed, execute the following commands to check the status of the installation. Make sure that all pods have a status of **Running**:

```
$ kubectl get pods --namespace knative-serving
```

```
$ kubectl get pods --namespace knative-eventing
```

```
$ kubectl get pods --namespace knative-monitoring
```

The output should be as follows:

```
/serverless $ kubectl get pods --namespace knative-serving
NAME                                READY   STATUS    RESTARTS   AGE
activator-c9b79cc45-hcdbl           2/2     Running   2          4m37s
autoscaler-65d66f8ff-6t6pv          2/2     Running   1          4m34s
autoscaler-hpa-86f678798d-5kbv9     1/1     Running   2          4m35s
controller-8f6bcc4fd-r5kkq          1/1     Running   0          4m23s
networking-istio-67f87c4989-686nn   1/1     Running   0          4m22s
webhook-57bfcccfcb-rpc6j            1/1     Running   0          4m21s
/serverless $
/serverless $ kubectl get pods --namespace knative-eventing
NAME                                        READY   STATUS    RESTARTS   AGE
eventing-controller-77b4f76d56-nzx5q        1/1     Running   0          3m59s
eventing-webhook-f5d57b487-5dmm9            1/1     Running   0          3m57s
imc-controller-65bb5ddf-vh7dh               1/1     Running   0          3m47s
imc-dispatcher-dd84879d7-shxmh              1/1     Running   0          3m46s
in-memory-channel-controller-6f74d5c8c8-n7lm8  1/1  Running   0          3m42s
in-memory-channel-dispatcher-8db675949-ks858   1/1  Running   0          3m38s
sources-controller-79c4bf8b86-pchw5         1/1     Running   0          3m58s
/serverless $
/serverless $ kubectl get pods --namespace knative-monitoring
NAME                                  READY   STATUS    RESTARTS   AGE
elasticsearch-logging-0               1/1     Running   0          3m36s
elasticsearch-logging-1               1/1     Running   0          3m13s
fluentd-ds-b7kq4                      1/1     Running   0          3m29s
fluentd-ds-f4cbm                      1/1     Running   0          3m29s
fluentd-ds-pvzq8                      1/1     Running   0          3m29s
grafana-6b74545565-5f5c2              1/1     Running   0          2m54s
kibana-logging-7cb6b64bff-rpnz2       1/1     Running   0          3m34s
kube-state-metrics-56f68467c9-fctkw   4/4     Running   0          3m5s
node-exporter-2gv4p                   2/2     Running   0          3m6s
node-exporter-mh668                   2/2     Running   0          3m6s
node-exporter-wxknb                   2/2     Running   0          3m6s
prometheus-system-0                   1/1     Running   0          2m39s
prometheus-system-1                   1/1     Running   0          2m39s
/serverless $
```

Figure 6.6: Verifying Knative installation

At this stage, you have set up a Kubernetes cluster on GKE and installed Knative. Now we are ready to deploy our first application on Knative.

Exercise 16: Deploying a Sample Application on Knative

In the previous section, we successfully deployed Knative on top of Kubernetes and **Istio**. In this exercise, we will deploy our first application on the Knative framework. For this deployment, we are going to use a sample web application written with Node. js. A Docker image of this application is available in Google Container Registry at **gcr. io/knative-samples/helloworld-nodejs**. These steps can be adapted to deploy our own Docker image on Docker Hub or any other container registry.

This sample "hello world" application will read an environment variable named **TARGET** and print **Hello <VALUE_OF_TARGET>!** as the output. It will print **NOT SPECIFIED** as the output if no value is defined for the **TARGET** environment variable.

Let's start by creating the service definition file for our application. This file defines application-related information including the application name and the application Docker image:

> **Note**
>
> Knative service objects and Kubernetes Service objects are two different types.

1. Create a file named **hello-world.yaml** with the following content. This Knative service object defines values such as the namespace to deploy this service in, the Docker image to use for the container, and any environment variables:

```yaml
apiVersion: serving.knative.dev/v1alpha1
kind: Service
metadata:
  name: helloworld-nodejs
  namespace: default
spec:
  runLatest:
    configuration:
      revisionTemplate:
        spec:
          container:
            image: gcr.io/knative-samples/helloworld-nodejs
            env:
              - name: TARGET
                value: "Knative NodeJS App"
```

2. Once the **hello-world.yaml** file is ready, we can deploy our application with the **kubectl apply** command:

```
$ kubectl apply -f hello-world.yaml
```

The output should be as follows:

```
/serverless $ kubectl apply -f hello-world.yaml
service.serving.knative.dev/helloworld-nodejs created
/serverless $
```

Figure 6.7: Deploying the helloworld-nodejs application

3. The previous command will create multiple objects, including the Knative service, configuration, revision, route, and Kubernetes Deployment. We can verify the application by listing the newly created objects as in the following commands:

```
$ kubectl get ksvc
$ kubectl get configuration
$ kubectl get revision
$ kubectl get route
$ kubectl get deployments
```

The output should be as follows:

```
/serverless $ kubectl get ksvc
NAME                URL                                          LATESTCREATED
        LATESTREADY                READY   REASON
helloworld-nodejs   http://helloworld-nodejs.default.example.com   helloworld-nodejs-
kpnfg   helloworld-nodejs-kpnfg   True
/serverless $
/serverless $ kubectl get configuration
NAME                LATESTCREATED            LATESTREADY                READY   REASO
N
helloworld-nodejs   helloworld-nodejs-kpnfg   helloworld-nodejs-kpnfg   True
/serverless $
/serverless $ kubectl get revision
NAME                    CONFIG NAME       K8S SERVICE NAME          GENERATION
READY   REASON
helloworld-nodejs-kpnfg   helloworld-nodejs   helloworld-nodejs-kpnfg   1
True
/serverless $
/serverless $ kubectl get route
NAME                URL                                          READY   REASON
helloworld-nodejs   http://helloworld-nodejs.default.example.com   True
/serverless $
/serverless $ kubectl get deployment
NAME                            READY   UP-TO-DATE   AVAILABLE   AGE
helloworld-nodejs-kpnfg-deployment   1/1     1            1           4m3s
/serverless $
```

Figure 6.8: Verifying helloworld-nodejs application deployment

4. Once our application is deployed successfully, we can invoke this application using an HTTP request. For this, we need to identify the external IP address of the Kubernetes cluster. Execute the following command to export the value of **EXTERNAL-IP** into an environment variable named **EXTERNAL_IP**:

```
$ export EXTERNAL_IP=$(kubectl get svc istio-ingressgateway --namespace
istio-system --output 'jsonpath={.status.loadBalancer.ingress[0].ip}')
```

The output should be as follows:

```
/serverless $ export EXTERNAL_IP=$(kubectl get svc istio-ingressgateway
--namespace istio-system --output 'jsonpath={.status.loadBalancer.ingress
[0].ip}')
/serverless $
```

Figure 6.9: Exporting the external IP of the istio-ingressgateway service

Next, we need to find the host URL of the **helloworld-nodejs** application. Execute the following command and take note of the value of the **URL** column. This URL takes the form **http://<application-name>.<namespace>.example.com**:

```
$ kubectl get route helloworld-nodejs
```

The output should be as follows:

```
/serverless $ kubectl get route helloworld-nodejs
NAME                URL                                         READY   REASON
helloworld-nodejs   http://helloworld-nodejs.default.example.com   True
/serverless $
```

Figure 6.10: Listing the helloworld-nodejs route

5. Now we can invoke our application using the **EXTERNAL_IP** and **URL** values that we noted in the earlier steps. Let's make a **curl** request with the following command:

```
$ curl -H "Host: helloworld-nodejs.default.example.com" http://${EXTERNAL_
IP}
```

The output should be as follows:

```
/serverless $ curl -H "Host: helloworld-nodejs.default.example.com"
http://${EXTERNAL_IP}
Hello Knative NodeJS App! /serverless $
/serverless $
```

Figure 6.11: Invoking the helloworld-nodejs application

You should receive the expected output as **Hello Knative NodeJS App!**. This indicates that we have successfully deployed and invoked our first application on the Knative platform.

Knative Serving Component

In the previous section, we deployed our first Knative application using a YAML file of the service type. When deploying the service, it created multiple other objects, including configuration, revision, and route objects. In this section, let's discuss each of these objects:

There are four resource types in the Knative Serving component:

- **Configuration**: Defines the desired state of the application
- **Revision**: Read-only snapshots that track the changes in configurations
- **Route**: Provides traffic routing to revisions
- **Service**: Top-level container for routes and configurations

The following diagram illustrates the relationship between each of these components:

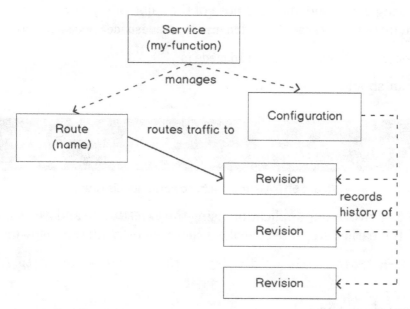

Figure 6.12: Relationship between Knative services, routes, configurations, and revisions

The **configuration** is used to define the desired state of the application. This will define the container image used for the application and any other configuration parameters that are required. A new **Revision** will be created each time a **Configuration** is updated. **Revision** refers to a snapshot of the code and the **Configuration**. This is used to record the history of **Configuration** changes. A **Route** is used to define the traffic routing policy of the application and provides an HTTP endpoint for the application. By default, the **Route** will send traffic to the latest **Revision** created by the **Configuration**. The **Route** can also be configured for more advanced scenarios, including sending traffic to a specific **Revision** or splitting traffic to different revisions based on defined percentages. **Service** objects are used to manage the whole life cycle of the application. While deploying a new application, it is required to create **Configuration** and **Route** objects manually, but the **Service** can be used to simplify this by creating and managing **Configuration** and **Route** objects automatically.

In the following section, we will be using canary deployment to deploy applications with Knative. Let's first understand what exactly canary deployment is.

Canary Deployment

Canary deployment is a deployment strategy used when rolling out a new version of code to a production environment. This is a fail-safe process of deploying a new version of code into a production environment and switching a small percentage of traffic to the new version. This way, the development and deployment teams can verify the new version of the code with minimal impact on production traffic. Once the verifications are done, all traffic will be switched to the new version. In addition to canary deployments, there are several other deployment types, such as big bang deployments, rolling deployments, and blue-green deployments.

In the `helloworld-nodejs` application that we deployed in *Exercise 16, Deploying a Sample App on Knative*, we used the Service object with the `spec.runLatest` field, which directs all traffic to the latest available revision. In the following exercise, we will be using separate configuration and route objects instead of the service object.

> **Note**
>
> For more information on canary deployment technique, refer to https://dev.to/mostlyjason/intro-to-deployment-strategies-blue-green-canary-and-more-3a3.

Exercise 17: Canary Deployment with Knative

In this exercise, we will be implementing a canary deployment strategy to deploy applications with Knative. First, we will deploy an initial version (version 1) of an application and route 100% traffic to that version. Next, we will create version 2 of the application and route 50% of traffic to version 1 and the remaining 50% to version 2. Finally, we will update the routes to send 100% of traffic to version 2.

The following steps will help you complete the exercise:

1. First, start by creating the initial version (**v1**) of the application. Create a file named **canary-deployment.yaml** with the following content. This application uses the same Docker image (**gcr.io/knative-samples/helloworld-nodejs**) that we used previously and sets the **TARGET** environment variable as **This is the first version - v1**:

```
apiVersion: serving.knative.dev/v1alpha1
kind: Configuration
metadata:
  name: canary-deployment
  namespace: default
spec:
  template:
    spec:
      containers:
        - image: gcr.io/knative-samples/helloworld-nodejs
          env:
            - name: TARGET
              value: "This is the first version - v1"
```

2. Deploy the first version of the application with the **kubectl apply** command using the YAML file created in the previous step:

```
$ kubectl apply -f canary-deployment.yaml
```

The output should be as follows:

```
/serverless $ kubectl apply -f canary-deployment.yaml
configuration.serving.knative.dev/canary-deployment created
/serverless $
```

Figure 6.13: Creating canary-deployment

3. Let's get the revision name created by this configuration as we need this value in the next step. Execute the **kubectl get configurations** command and retrieve the value of the **latestCreatedRevisionName** field:

```
$ kubectl get configurations canary-deployment -o=jsonpath='{.status.
latestCreatedRevisionName}'
```

The output should be as follows:

```
/serverless $ kubectl get configurations canary-deployment -o=jsonpath=
'{.status.latestCreatedRevisionName}'
canary-deployment-xgvl8 /serverless $
/serverless $
```

Figure 6.14: Getting the latest revision of the canary-deployment configuration

For me, the value returned from the preceding command is **canary-deployment-xgvl8**. Note that your value will be different.

4. The next step is to create the route object. Let's create a file named **canary-deployment-route.yaml** with the following content (please remember to replace **canary-deployment-xgvl8** with the revision name that you noted in the previous step). Under the **spec.traffic** section, you can see that 100% of traffic is routed to the revision that we created previously:

```
apiVersion: serving.knative.dev/v1alpha1
kind: Route
metadata:
  name: canary-deployment
  namespace: default
spec:
  traffic:
    - revisionName: canary-deployment-xgvl8
      percent: 100
```

5. Create the route object with the **kubectl apply** command:

```
$ kubectl apply -f canary-deployment-route.yaml
```

The output should be as follows:

```
/serverless $ kubectl apply -f canary-deployment-route.yaml
route.serving.knative.dev/canary-deployment created
/serverless $
```

Figure 6.15: Creating the canary-deployment route

6. Make a request to the application and observe the expected output of **Hello This is the first version - v1!**:

```
$ curl -H "Host: canary-deployment.default.example.com" "http://${EXTERNAL_IP}"
```

The output should be as follows:

```
/serverless $ curl -H "Host: canary-deployment.default.example.com"
"http://${EXTERNAL_IP}"
Hello This is the first version - v1! /serverless $
/serverless $
```

Figure 6.16: Invoking canary-deployment

7. Once the application is successfully invoked, we can deploy version 2 of the application. Update **canary-deployment.yaml** with the following content. In version 2 of the application, we only need to update the value of the **TARGET** environment variable from **This is the first version - v1** to **This is the second version - v2**:

```
apiVersion: serving.knative.dev/v1alpha1
kind: Configuration
metadata:
  name: canary-deployment
  namespace: default
spec:
  template:
    spec:
      containers:
        - image: gcr.io/knative-samples/helloworld-nodejs
          env:
            - name: TARGET
              value: "This is the second version - v2"
```

8. Apply the updated configuration with **kubectl apply**:

```
$ kubectl apply -f canary-deployment.yaml
```

The output should be as follows:

```
/serverless $ kubectl apply -f canary-deployment.yaml
configuration.serving.knative.dev/canary-deployment configured
/serverless $
```

Figure 6.17: Updating canary-deployment to version 2

9. Now we can check the revisions created, while updating the configuration, using the **kubectl get revisions** command:

```
$ kubectl get revisions
```

The output should be as follows:

```
/serverless $ kubectl get revisions
NAME                        CONFIG NAME          K8S SERVICE NAME             GENERATION
   READY    REASON
canary-deployment-8pp4s     canary-deployment    canary-deployment-8pp4s      2
   True
canary-deployment-xgvl8     canary-deployment    canary-deployment-xgvl8      1
   True
/serverless $
```

Figure 6.18: Getting the revisions of canary-deployment

10. Let's get the latest revision created by the **canary-deployment** configuration:

```
$ kubectl get configurations canary-deployment -o=jsonpath='{.status.
latestCreatedRevisionName}'
```

The output should be as follows:

```
/serverless $ kubectl get configurations canary-deployment -o=jsonpath=
'{.status.latestCreatedRevisionName}'
canary-deployment-8pp4s /serverless $
/serverless $
```

Figure 6.19: Getting the latest revision of the canary-deployment configuration

11. Now it's time to send some traffic to our new version of the application. Update the **spec.traffic** section of **canary-deployment-route.yaml** to send 50% of the traffic to the old revision and 50% to the new revision:

```
apiVersion: serving.knative.dev/v1alpha1
kind: Route
metadata:
  name: canary-deployment
  namespace: default
spec:
  traffic:
    - revisionName: canary-deployment-xgvl8
      percent: 50
    - revisionName: canary-deployment-8pp4s
      percent: 50
```

12. Apply changes to the route using the following command:

```
$ kubectl apply -f canary-deployment-route.yaml
```

The output should be as follows:

```
/serverless $ kubectl apply -f canary-deployment-route.yaml
route.serving.knative.dev/canary-deployment configured
/serverless $
```

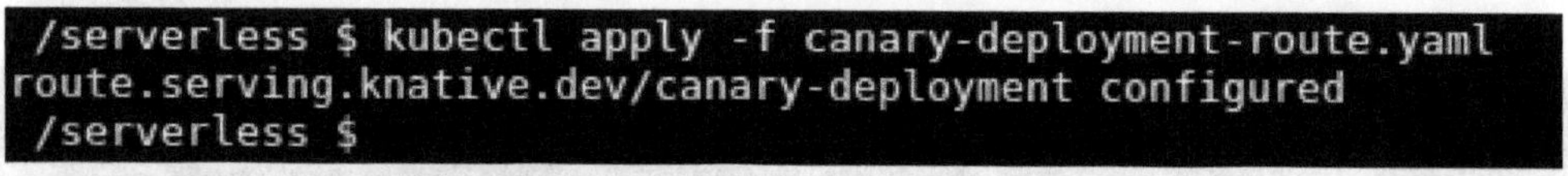

Figure 6.20: Updating the canary-deployment route

13. Now we can invoke the application multiple times to observe how traffic splits between two revisions:

```
$ curl -H "Host: canary-deployment.default.example.com"
"http://${EXTERNAL_IP}"
```

14. Once we verify version 2 of the application successfully, we can update **canary-deployment-route.yaml** to route 100% of the traffic to the latest revision:

```
apiVersion: serving.knative.dev/v1alpha1
kind: Route
metadata:
  name: canary-deployment
  namespace: default
spec:
  traffic:
    - revisionName: canary-deployment-xgvl8
      percent: 0
    - revisionName: canary-deployment-8pp4s
      percent: 100
```

15. Apply the changes to the route using the following command:

```
$ kubectl apply -f canary-deployment-route.yaml
```

The output should be as follows:

```
/serverless $ kubectl apply -f canary-deployment-route.yaml
route.serving.knative.dev/canary-deployment configured
/serverless $
```

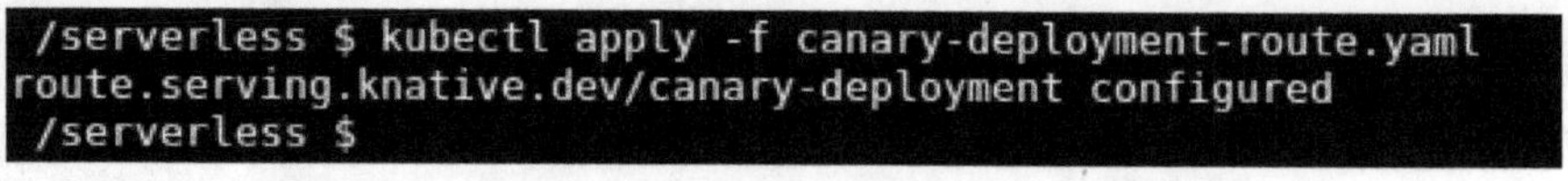

Figure 6.21: Updating the canary-deployment route

16. Now invoke the application multiple times to verify that all traffic goes to version 2 of the application:

```
$ curl -H "Host: blue-green-deployment.default.example.com"
"http://${EXTERNAL_IP}"
```

In this exercise, we have successfully used configuration and route objects to perform a canary deployment with Knative.

Knative Monitoring

Knative comes with Grafana pre-installed, which is an open source metric analytics and visualization tool. The Grafana pod is available in the **knative-monitoring** namespace and can be listed with the following command:

```
$ kubectl get pods -l app=grafana -n knative-monitoring
```

The output should be as follows:

```
/serverless $ kubectl get pods -l app=grafana -n knative-monitoring
NAME                         READY   STATUS    RESTARTS   AGE
grafana-6b74545565-5f5c2     1/1     Running   0          87m
/serverless $
```

Figure 6.22: Listing the Grafana pod

We can expose the Grafana UI with the **kubectl port-forward** command, which will forward local port **3000** to the port **3000** of the Grafana pod. Open a new terminal and execute the following command:

```
$ kubectl port-forward $(kubectl get pod -n knative-monitoring -l app=grafana
-o jsonpath='{.items[0].metadata.name}') -n knative-monitoring 3000:3000
```

The output should be as follows:

```
/serverless $ kubectl port-forward $(kubectl get pod -n knative-monitoring -l app=
grafana -o jsonpath='{.items[0].metadata.name}') -n knative-monitoring 3000:3000
Forwarding from 127.0.0.1:3000 -> 3000
Forwarding from [::1]:3000 -> 3000
```

Figure 6.23: Port forwarding to the Grafana pod

Now we can navigate the Grafana UI from our web browser on `http://127.0.0.1:3000`. The output should be as follows:

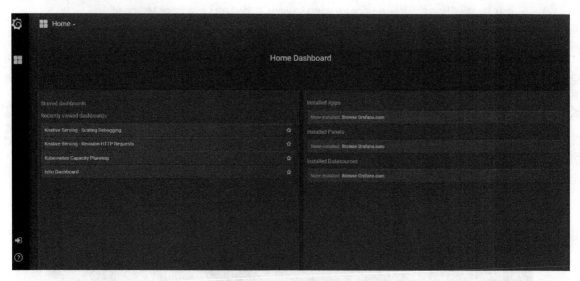

Figure 6.24: The Grafana UI

Knative's Grafana dashboard comes with multiple dashboards, including the following:

Dashboard Name	Dashboard Metrics
Nodes	CPU, memory, disk, and network usage stats of Kubernetes nodes
Pods	CPU, memory, and network usage stats of Kubernetes pods
Knative Serving - Revision CPU and Memory Usage	CPU usage and memory usage by the revision
Knative Serving - Revision HTTP Requests	Request volume, request volume by revision, request volume by response code, and request volume by the response time
Knative Serving - Scaling Debugging	Revision pod count, resource usages, autoscaler metrics, and activator metrics
Knative Serving - Control Plane Efficiency	Namespace CPU usage, namespace memory usage, control plane versus data plane CPU usage, and control plane versus data plane memory usage

Figure 6.25: Dashboards

Knative Autoscaler

Knative has a built-in autoscaling feature that automatically scales the application pods based on the number of HTTP requests it receives. This will increase the pod count when there is increased demand and decrease the pod count when the demand decreases. The pod count will scale to zero when pods are idle and there are no incoming requests.

Knative uses two components, the autoscaler, and the activator, to achieve the previously mentioned functionality. These components are deployed as pods in the **knative-serving** namespace, as you can see in the following snippet:

```
NAME                          READY   STATUS    RESTARTS   AGE
activator-7c8b59d78-9kgk5     2/2     Running   0          15h
autoscaler-666c9bfcc6-vwrj6   2/2     Running   0          15h
controller-799cd5c6dc-p47qn   1/1     Running   0          15h
webhook-5b66fdf6b9-cbllh      1/1     Running   0          15h
```

The activator component is responsible for collecting information about the number of concurrent requests to a revision and reporting these values to the autoscaler. The autoscaler component will increase or decrease the number of pods based on the metrics reported by the activator. By default, the autoscaler will try to maintain 100 concurrent requests per pod by scaling pods up or down. All Knative autoscaler-related configurations are stored in a configuration map named **config-autoscaler** in the **knative-serving** namespace. Knative can also be configured to use the **Horizontal Pod Autoscaler** (**HPA**), which is provided by Kubernetes. HPA will autoscale pods based on CPU usage.

Exercise 18: Autoscaling with Knative

In this exercise, we will perform Knative pod autoscaling by deploying a sample application:

1. Create an **autoscale-app.yaml** service definition file with the following content. This file defines a service named **autoscale-app**, which will use the **gcr.io/knative-samples/autoscale-go:0.1** sample Docker image. **autoscaling.knative.dev/target** is used to configure the target number of concurrent requests per pod:

    ```
    apiVersion: serving.knative.dev/v1alpha1
    kind: Service
    metadata:
      name: autoscale-app
    spec:
      runLatest:
    ```

```
configuration:
  revisionTemplate:
    metadata:
      annotations:
        autoscaling.knative.dev/target: "10"
    spec:
      container:
        image: "gcr.io/knative-samples/autoscale-go:0.1"
```

2. Apply the service definition with the **kubectl apply** command:

   ```
   $ kubectl apply -f autoscale-app.yaml
   ```

   The output should be as follows:

   ```
   /serverless $ kubectl apply -f autoscale-app.yaml
   service.serving.knative.dev/autoscale-app created
   /serverless $
   ```

   Figure 6.26: Creating autoscale-app

3. Once the application is ready, we can generate a load to the **autoscale-app** application to observe the autoscaling. For this, we will use a load generator named **hey**. Download the **hey** binary using the following **curl** command.

   ```
   $ curl -Lo hey https://storage.googleapis.com/hey-release/hey_linux_amd64
   ```

   The output should be as follows:

   ```
   /serverless $ curl -Lo hey https://storage.googleapis.com/hey-release/hey_linux_amd64
     % Total    % Received % Xferd  Average Speed   Time    Time     Time  Current
                                    Dload  Upload   Total   Spent    Left  Speed
   100 9864k  100 9864k    0     0   833k      0  0:00:11  0:00:11 --:--:--  894k
   /serverless $
   ```

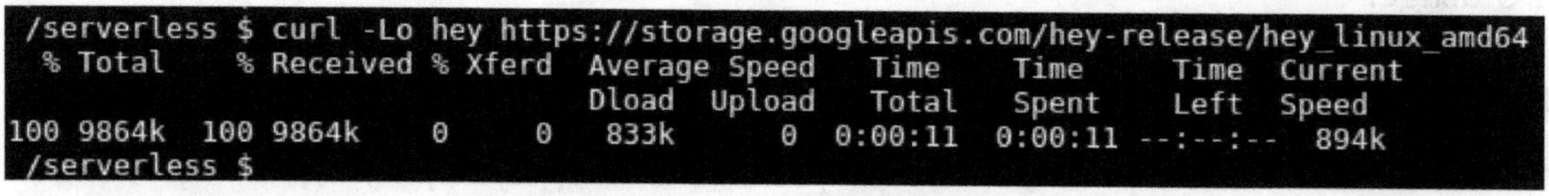

   Figure 6.27: Installing hey

4. Add execution permission to the **hey** binary and move it into the **/usr/local/bin/** path:

```
$ chmod +x hey
$ sudo mv hey /usr/local/bin/
```

The output should be as follows:

```
/serverless $ chmod +x hey
/serverless $ sudo mv hey /usr/local/bin/
/serverless $
```

Figure 6.28: Moving hey to /usr/local/bin

5. Now we are ready to generate a load with the **hey** tool. The **hey** tool supports multiple options when generating a load. For this scenario, we will use a load with a concurrency of 50 (with the **-c flag**) for a duration of 60 seconds (with the **-z flag**):

```
$ hey -z 60s -c 50 \
    -host "autoscale-app.default.example.com" \
    "http://${EXTERNAL_IP?}?sleep=1000"
```

6. In a separate terminal, watch for the number of pods created during the load:

```
$ kubectl get pods --watch
```

You will see output similar to the following:

```
NAME                                                  READY   STATUS
RESTARTS    AGE
autoscale-app-7jt29-deployment-9c9c4b474-4ttl2        3/3     Running   0
58s
autoscale-app-7jt29-deployment-9c9c4b474-6pmjs        3/3     Running   0
60s
autoscale-app-7jt29-deployment-9c9c4b474-7j52p        3/3     Running   0
63s
autoscale-app-7jt29-deployment-9c9c4b474-dvcs6        3/3     Running   0
56s
autoscale-app-7jt29-deployment-9c9c4b474-hmkzf        3/3     Running   0
62s
```

7. Open the **Knative Serving – Scaling Debugging** dashboard from Grafana to observe how autoscaling increased the pod count during the load and decreased the pod count back to zero once the load stopped, as you can see in the following screenshots:

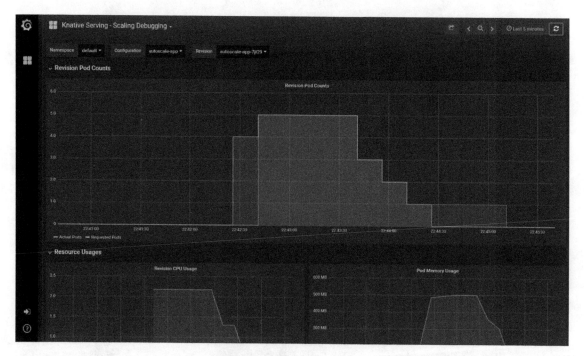

Figure 6.29: Revision pod count metrics

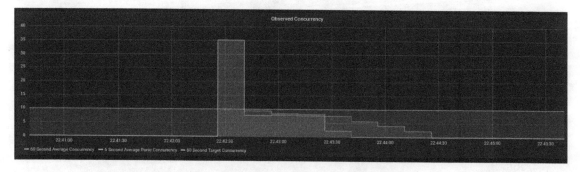

Figure 6.30: Observed concurrency metrics

We have successfully configured Knative's autoscaler and observed autoscaling with the Grafana dashboard.

Google Cloud Run

In the previous sections, we discussed Knative. We learned how to install Istio and Knative on top of a Kubernetes cluster and how to run Docker images with Knative. But the advantages of the Knative platform come with the operational overhead of managing the underlying Kubernetes cluster with Istio. GKE, which is the managed Kubernetes service from Google Cloud, will help us manage the Kubernetes master components, but still, we have to manage all the Kubernetes nodes ourselves.

In order to abstract away all the infrastructure management tasks from the developer, Google introduced a new service named Cloud Run. This is a fully managed platform, built on the Knative project, to run stateless HTTP-driven containers. Cloud Run offers the same set of features as Knative, including autoscaling, scale to zero, versioning, and events. Cloud Run was introduced in the Google Cloud Next '19 conference as the newest member of Google Cloud's serverless compute stack. At the time of writing this book, the Cloud Run service is still in beta and only available in a limited number of regions.

Let's now perform an exercise to deploy containers on Google Cloud Run.

Exercise 19: Deploying Containers on Google Cloud Run

In this exercise, we will be deploying a pre-built Docker image on the Google Cloud Run platform.

The following steps will help you complete the exercise:

1. Navigate to your GCP console from your browser and select **Cloud Run** from the menu (in the **Compute** category) as shown in the following figure:

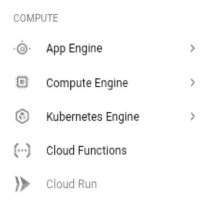

Figure 6.31: GCP menu for Cloud Run

2. Click on the **CREATE SERVICE** button to create a new service.

3. Fill the create service form with the following values:

   Container Image URL: <u>gcr.io/knative-samples/helloworld-nodejs</u>

   Deployment platform: **Cloud Run** (fully managed)

   Location: Select any region you prefer from the options

   Service name: **hello-world**

   Authentication: **Allow unauthenticated invocations**

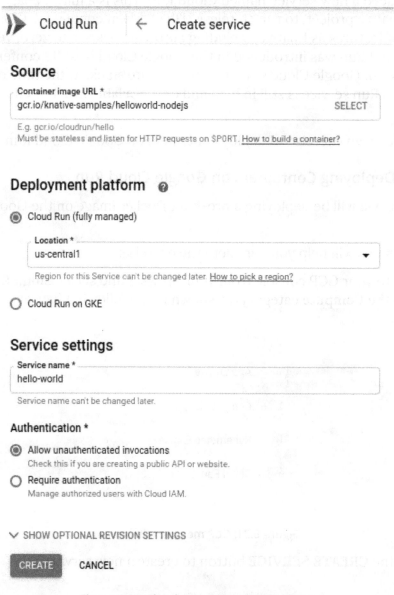

Figure 6.32: Cloud Run create service form

4. Click on the **CREATE** button.

5. Now we will be redirected to the deployed service page, which includes details about the newly deployed **hello-world** service. We can see that a revision has been created called **hello-world-00001**, as shown in the following figure:

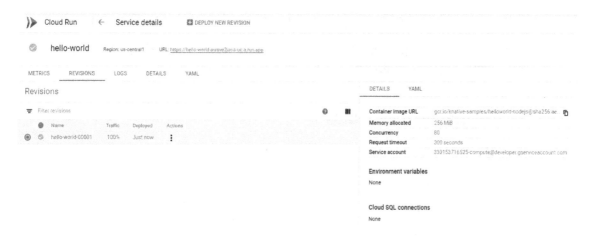

Figure 6.33: Service details page

6. Click on the URL link displayed to run the container. Note that the URL will be different for every new instance:

Figure 6.34: Invoking the hello-world app

7. Next, we are going to deploy a new revision of the application by updating the **TARGET** environment variable. Navigate back to the **GCP** console and click on the **DEPLOY NEW REVISION** button.

8. From the **Deploy revision to hello-world (us-central1)** form, click on the **SHOW OPTIONAL REVISION SETTINGS** link, which will point us to the additional setting section:

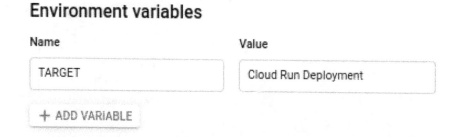

∨ SHOW OPTIONAL REVISION SETTINGS

Figure 6.35: Optional revision settings

9. Under the environment variables section, create a new environment variable named **TARGET** with the value `Cloud Run Deployment`:

Environment variables

Name

TARGET

Value

Cloud Run Deployment

+ ADD VARIABLE

Figure 6.36: Setting the TARGET environment variable

10. Click on the **DEPLOY** button.

11. Now we can see the new revision of the **hello-world** application called `hello-world-00002` with 100% of traffic being routed to the latest revision:

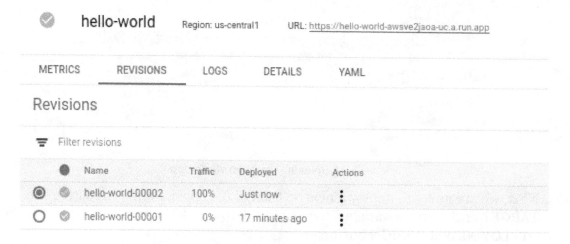

Figure 6.37: The hello-world app's new revision

12. Click on the URL again to run the updated revision:

Figure 6.38: Invoking the hello-world app

We have successfully deployed a pre-built Docker image on the Google Cloud Run platform.

Introduction to Virtual Kubelet

Virtual Kubelet is an open source implementation of Kubernetes' kubelet that acts as a kubelet. This is a sandbox project from the **Cloud Native Computing Foundation** (**CNCF**), and the first major version (v 1.0) of Virtual Kubelet was released on July 8, 2019.

Before diving further into Virtual Kubelet, let's recap what a kubelet is in the Kubernetes architecture. A kubelet is an agent that runs on each node in a Kubernetes cluster and is responsible for managing pods within the nodes. A kubelet takes instructions from the Kubernetes API to identify the pods to be scheduled on the node and interacts with the underlying container runtime (for example, Docker) of the nodes to ensure that the desired number of pods are running and that they are healthy.

In addition to managing pods, the kubelet performs several other tasks:

- Updating the Kubernetes API with the current status of the pods

- Monitoring and reporting node health metrics such as CPU, memory, and disk utilization to the Kubernetes master

- Pulling Docker images from the Docker registry for the assigned pods

- Creating and mounting volumes for pods

- Providing an interface for the API server to execute commands such as **kubectl logs**, **kubectl exec**, and **kubectl attach** for the pods

The following figure displays a Kubernetes cluster with standard and virtual kubelets:

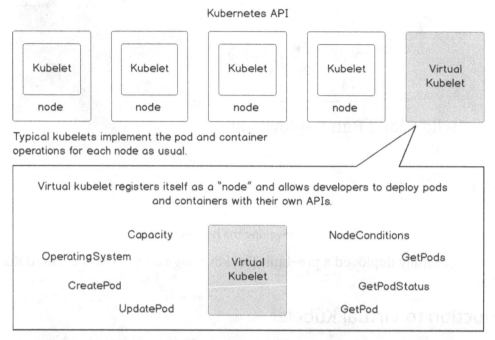

Figure 6.39: Kubernetes cluster with standard kubelets and Virtual Kubelets

Virtual Kubelet will appear as a traditional kubelet from the viewpoint of the Kubernetes API. This will run in the existing Kubernetes cluster and register itself as a node within the Kubernetes API. Virtual Kubelet will run and manage the pods in the same way a kubelet does. But in contrast to the kubelet, which runs pods within the nodes, Virtual Kubelet will utilize external services to run the pods. This connects the Kubernetes cluster to other services such as serverless container platforms. Virtual Kubelet supports a growing number of providers, including the following:

- Alibaba Cloud **Elastic Container Instance** (**ECI**)
- AWS Fargate
- Azure Batch
- **Azure Container Instances** (**ACI**)
- Kubernetes **Container Runtime Interface** (**CRI**)
- Huawei **Cloud Container Instance** (**CCI**)
- HashiCorp Nomad
- OpenStack Zun

Running pods on these platforms come with the benefits of the serverless world. We do not have to worry about the infrastructure as it is managed by the cloud provider. Pods will scale up and down automatically based on the number of requests received. Also, we have to pay only for the utilized resources.

Exercise 20: Deploying Virtual Kubelet on AKS

In this exercise, we are going to configure Virtual Kubelet on **Azure Kubernetes Service** (**AKS**) with the ACI provider. For this exercise, we will be using the following services available in Azure.

- AKS: AKS is a managed Kubernetes service on Azure.

- ACI: ACI provides a managed service for running containers on Azure.

- Azure Cloud Shell: An interactive, browser-based shell that supports both Bash and PowerShell.

You need to have the following prerequisites for this exercise:

- A Microsoft Azure account

- The Azure CLI

- The kubectl CLI

- Helm

We will be using Azure Cloud Shell, which has all the previously mentioned CLIs pre-installed:

1. Navigate to https://shell.azure.com/ to open Cloud Shell in a browser window. Select **Bash** from the **Welcome to Azure Cloud Shell** window:

Welcome to Azure Cloud Shell

Select Bash or PowerShell. You can change shells any time via the environment selector in the Cloud Shell toolbar. The most recently used environment will be the default for your next session.

Bash   PowerShell

Figure 6.40: The Welcome to Azure Cloud Shell window

2. Click on the **Create storage** button to create a storage account for Cloud Shell. Note that this is a one-time task purely for when we are using Cloud Shell for the first time:

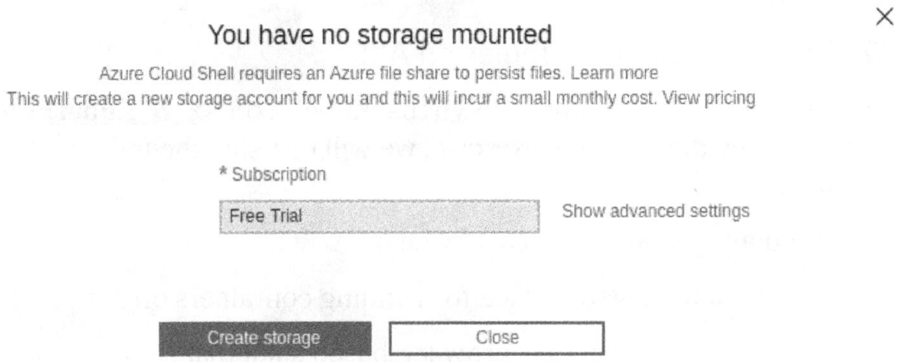

You have no storage mounted   ✕

Azure Cloud Shell requires an Azure file share to persist files. Learn more
This will create a new storage account for you and this will incur a small monthly cost. View pricing

* Subscription

| Free Trial | Show advanced settings

Create storage   Close

Figure 6.41: Mounting storage for Cloud Shell

The Cloud Shell window will look as follows:

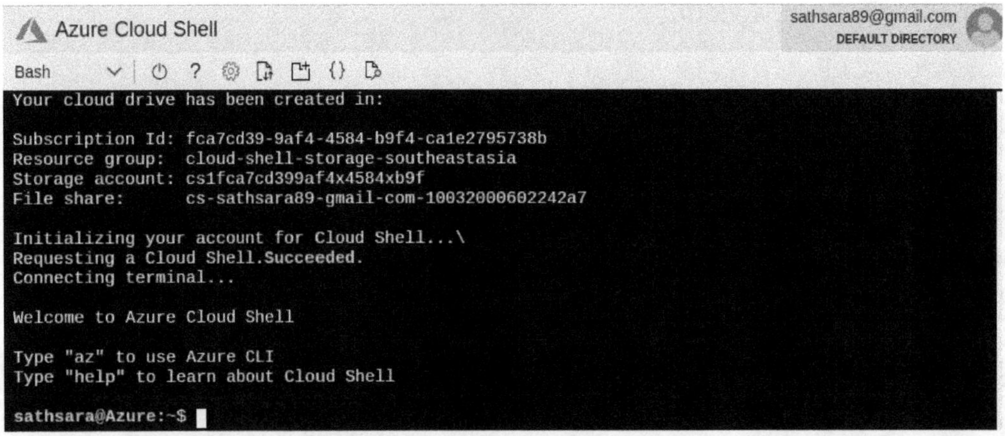

Figure 6.42: Cloud Shell window

3. Once Cloud Shell is ready, we can start creating the AKS cluster.

First, we need to create an Azure resource group that allows us to group related Azure resources logically. Execute the following command to create a resource group named **serverless-kubernetes-group** in the West US (**westus**) region:

```
$ az group create --name serverless-kubernetes-group --location westus
```

The output should be as follows:

```
sathsara@Azure:~$ az group create --name serverless-kubernetes-group --location westus
{
  "id": "/subscriptions/ecb726f1-4082-464b-87a5-ef5bbc8baba9/resourceGroups/serverless-kubernetes-group",
  "location": "westus",
  "managedBy": null,
  "name": "serverless-kubernetes-group",
  "properties": {
    "provisioningState": "Succeeded"
  },
  "tags": null,
  "type": "Microsoft.Resources/resourceGroups"
}
sathsara@Azure:~$
```

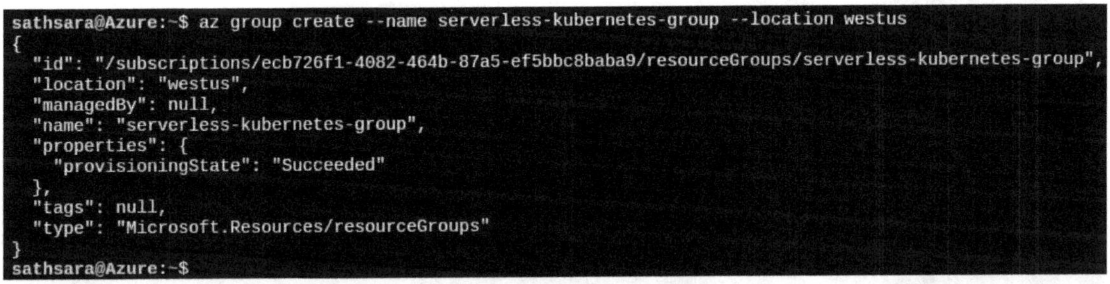

Figure 6.43: Creating an Azure resource group

4. Register your subscription to use the **Microsoft.Network** namespace:

```
$ az provider register --namespace Microsoft.Networks
```

The output should be as follows:

```
sathsara@Azure:~$ az provider register --namespace Microsoft.Network
Registering is still on-going. You can monitor using 'az provider show -n Microsoft.Network'
sathsara@Azure:~$
```

Figure 6.44: Registering the subscription

5. Next, we will create an Azure Kubernetes cluster. The following command will create an AKS cluster named **virtual-kubelet-cluster** with one node. This command will take a few minutes to execute:

```
$ az aks create --resource-group serverless-kubernetes-group --name
virtual-kubelet-cluster --node-count 1 --node-vm-size Standard_D2
--network-plugin azure --generate-ssh-keys
```

Once AKS cluster creation is successful, the preceding command will return some JSON output with the details of the cluster:

```
sathsara@Azure:~$ az aks create --resource-group serverless-kubernetes-group --name virt
--network-plugin azure --generate-ssh-keys
- Running ..
{
  "aadProfile": null,
  "addonProfiles": null,
  "agentPoolProfiles": [
    {
      "availabilityZones": null,
      "count": 1,
      "enableAutoScaling": null,
      "enableNodePublicIp": null,
      "maxCount": null,
      "maxPods": 30,
      "minCount": null,
      "name": "nodepool1",
      "nodeTaints": null,
      "orchestratorVersion": "1.13.12",
      "osDiskSizeGb": 100,
      "osType": "Linux",
      "provisioningState": "Succeeded",
      "scaleSetEvictionPolicy": null,
      "scaleSetPriority": null,
      "type": "VirtualMachineScaleSets",
      "vmSize": "Standard_D2",
      "vnetSubnetId": null
    }
  ],
```

Figure 6.45: Creating the AKS cluster

6. Next, we need to configure the kubectl CLI to communicate with the newly created AKS cluster. Execute the `az aks get-credentials` command to download the credentials and configure the kubectl CLI to work with the `virtual-kubelet-cluster` cluster with the following command:

> **Note**
>
> We are not required to install the kubectl CLI because Cloud Shell comes with kubectl pre-installed.

```
$ az aks get-credentials --resource-group serverless-kubernetes-group
--name virtual-kubelet-cluster
```

The output should be as follows:

```
sathsara@Azure:~$ az aks get-credentials --resource-group serverless-kuberne
tes-group --name virtual-kubelet-cluster
Merged "virtual-kubelet-cluster" as current context in /home/sathsara/.kube/
config
sathsara@Azure:~$
```

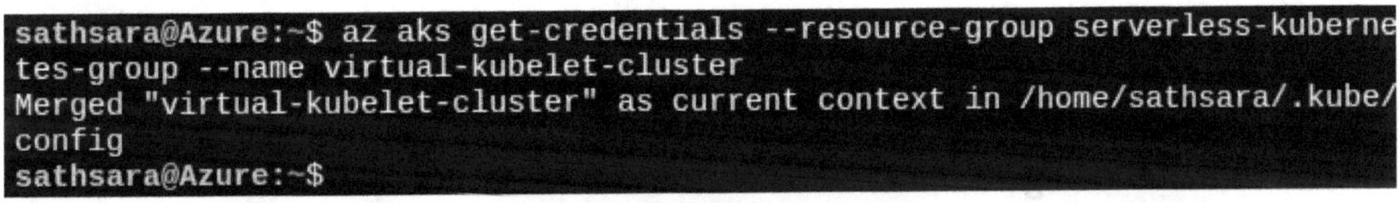

Figure 6.46: Configuring kubectl

7. Now we can verify the connection to the cluster from Cloud Shell by executing the `kubectl get nodes` command, which will list the nodes available in the AKS cluster:

```
$ kubectl get nodes
```

The output should be as follows:

```
sathsara@Azure:~$ kubectl get nodes
NAME                                STATUS   ROLES   AGE     VERSION
aks-nodepool1-37650960-vmss000000   Ready    agent   8m18s   v1.13.12
sathsara@Azure:~$
```

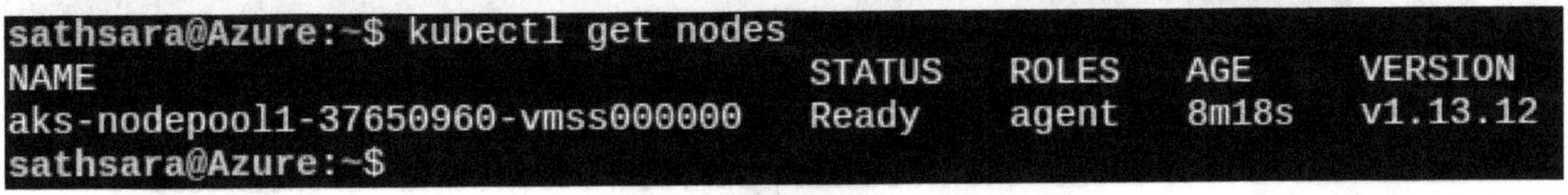

Figure 6.47: Listing Kubernetes nodes

8. If this is the first time you are using the ACI service, you need to register the **Microsoft.ContainerInstance** provider with your subscription. We can check the registration state of the **Microsoft.ContainerInstance** provider with the following command:

```
$ az provider list --query "[?contains(namespace,'Microsoft.
ContainerInstance')]" -o table
```

The output should be as follows:

```
sathsara@Azure:~$ az provider list --query "[?contains(namespace,'Microsoft.
ContainerInstance')]" -o table
Namespace                      RegistrationState     RegistrationPolicy
---------------------------    -------------------   --------------------
Microsoft.ContainerInstance    NotRegistered         RegistrationRequired
sathsara@Azure:~$
```

Figure 6.48: Checking the registration status of the Microsoft.ContainerInstance provider

9. If the **RegistrationStatus** column contains a value of **NotRegistered**, execute the **az provider register** command to register the **Microsoft.ContainerInstance** provider. If the **RegistrationStatus** column contains a value of **Registered**, you can continue to the next step:

```
$ az provider register --namespace Microsoft.ContainerInstance
```

The output should be as follows:

```
sathsara@Azure:~$ az provider register --namespace Microsoft.ContainerInstance
Registering is still on-going. You can monitor using 'az provider show -n Micro
soft.ContainerInstance'
sathsara@Azure:~$
```

Figure 6.49: Registering for Microsoft.ContainerInstance provider

10. The next step is to create the necessary **ServiceAccount** and **ServiceAccount** objects for the tiller. Create a file named **tiller-rbac.yaml** with the following code:

```
apiVersion: v1
kind: ServiceAccount
metadata:
  name: tiller
```

```
      namespace: kube-system
---
apiVersion: rbac.authorization.k8s.io/v1
kind: ClusterRoleBinding
metadata:
  name: tiller
roleRef:
  apiGroup: rbac.authorization.k8s.io
  kind: ClusterRole
  name: cluster-admin
subjects:
  - kind: ServiceAccount
    name: tiller
    namespace: kube-system
```

11. Then execute the **kubectl apply** command to create the necessary **ServiceAccount** and **ClusterRoleBinding** objects:

```
$ kubectl apply -f tiller-rbac.yaml
```

The output should be as follows:

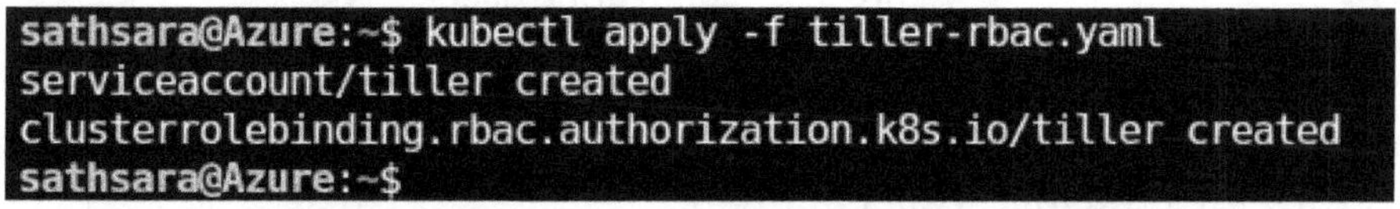

```
sathsara@Azure:~$ kubectl apply -f tiller-rbac.yaml
serviceaccount/tiller created
clusterrolebinding.rbac.authorization.k8s.io/tiller created
sathsara@Azure:~$
```

Figure 6.50: Creating the ServiceAccount and ClusterRoleBinding objects

12. Now we can configure Helm to use the tiller service account that we created in the previous step:

```
$ helm init --service-account tiller
```

The output should be as follows:

```
sathsara@Azure:~$ helm init --service-account tiller
Creating /home/sathsara/.helm
Creating /home/sathsara/.helm/repository
Creating /home/sathsara/.helm/repository/cache
Creating /home/sathsara/.helm/repository/local
Creating /home/sathsara/.helm/plugins
Creating /home/sathsara/.helm/starters
Creating /home/sathsara/.helm/cache/archive
Creating /home/sathsara/.helm/repository/repositories.yaml
Adding stable repo with URL: https://kubernetes-charts.storage.googleapis
.com
Adding local repo with URL: http://127.0.0.1:8879/charts
$HELM_HOME has been configured at /home/sathsara/.helm.

Tiller (the Helm server-side component) has been installed into your Kube
rnetes Cluster.

Please note: by default, Tiller is deployed with an insecure 'allow unaut
henticated users' policy.
To prevent this, run `helm init` with the --tiller-tls-verify flag.
For more information on securing your installation see: https://docs.helm
.sh/using_helm/#securing-your-helm-installation
sathsara@Azure:~$
```

Figure 6.51: Configuring tiller

13. Once all configurations are done, we can install Virtual Kubelet using the **az aks install-connector** command. We will be deploying both Linux and Windows connectors with the following command:

```
$ az aks install-connector \
    --resource-group serverless-kubernetes-group \
    --name virtual-kubelet-cluster \
    --connector-name virtual-kubelet \
    --os-type Both
```

The output should be as follows:

```
sathsara@Azure:~$ az aks install-connector \
>      --resource-group serverless-kubernetes-group \
>      --name virtual-kubelet-cluster \
>      --connector-name virtual-kubelet \
>      --os-type Both
This command is in preview. It may be changed/removed in a future release
.
Merged "virtual-kubelet-cluster" as current context in /tmp/tmpzxdtq2vn
Deploying the ACI connector for 'Linux' using Helm
NAME:   virtual-kubelet-linux-westus
LAST DEPLOYED: Tue Nov 12 07:24:18 2019
NAMESPACE: default
STATUS: DEPLOYED

RESOURCES:
==> v1/Pod(related)
NAME                                                            READY  S
TATUS          RESTARTS   AGE
virtual-kubelet-linux-westus-virtual-kubelet-for-aks-6f8689kfff  0/1     C
ontainerCreating  0           1s

==> v1/Secret
NAME                                                  TYPE    DATA  AGE
virtual-kubelet-linux-westus-virtual-kubelet-for-aks  Opaque  3     1s

==> v1/ServiceAccount
NAME                                                  SECRETS  AGE
virtual-kubelet-linux-westus-virtual-kubelet-for-aks  1        1s

==> v1beta1/ClusterRoleBinding
NAME                                                  AGE
```

Figure 6.52: Installing Virtual Kubelet

14. Once the installation is complete, we can verify it by listing the Kubernetes nodes. There will be two new nodes, one for Windows and one for Linux:

```
$ kubectl get nodes
```

The output should be as follows:

```
sathsara@Azure:~$ kubectl get nodes
NAME                                                     STATUS    ROLES    AGE
VERSION
aks-nodepool1-37650960-vmss000000                        Ready     agent    15m
v1.13.12
virtual-kubelet-virtual-kubelet-linux-westus            Ready     agent    3m50s
v1.13.1-vk-v0.9.0-1-g7b92d1ee-dev
virtual-kubelet-virtual-kubelet-windows-westus          Ready     agent    3m47s
v1.13.1-vk-v0.9.0-1-g7b92d1ee-dev
sathsara@Azure:~$
```

Figure 6.53: Listing Kubernetes nodes

15. Now we have Virtual Kubelet installed in the AKS cluster. We can deploy an application to a new node introduced by Virtual Kubelet. We will be creating a Kubernetes Deployment named **hello-world** with the **microsoft/aci-helloworld** Docker image.

We need to add a **nodeSelector** to assign this pod specifically to the Virtual Kubelet node. Note that Virtual Kubelet nodes are tainted by default to prevent unexpected pods from being run on them. We need to add tolerations to the pods to allow them to be scheduled for these nodes.

Let's create a file named **hello-world.yaml** with the following content:

```
apiVersion: apps/v1
kind: Deployment
metadata:
  name: hello-world
spec:
  replicas: 1
  selector:
    matchLabels:
      app: hello-world
  template:
    metadata:
      labels:
        app: hello-world
    spec:
      containers:
      - name: hello-world
```

```
      image: microsoft/aci-helloworld
      ports:
      - containerPort: 80
    nodeSelector:
      kubernetes.io/role: agent
      type: virtual-kubelet
      beta.kubernetes.io/os: linux
    tolerations:
    - key: virtual-kubelet.io/provider
      operator: Equal
      value: azure
      effect: NoSchedule
```

16. Deploy the **hello-world** application with the **kubectl apply** command:

    ```
    $ kubectl apply -f hello-world.yaml
    ```

    The output should be as follows:

    ```
    sathsara@Azure:~$ kubectl apply -f hello-world.yaml
    deployment.apps/hello-world created
    sathsara@Azure:~$
    ```

    Figure 6.54: Creating the hello-world deployment

17. Execute the **kubectl get pods** command with the **-o wide** flag to output a list of pods and their respective nodes. Note that the **hello-world-57f597bc59-q9w9k** pod has been scheduled on the **virtual-kubelet-virtual-kubelet-linux-westus** node:

    ```
    $ kubectl get pods -o wide
    ```

    The output should be as follows:

    ```
    sathsara@Azure:~$ kubectl get pods -o wide
    NAME                                                             READY
    STATUS     RESTARTS    AGE     IP            NODE
                          NOMINATED NODE    READINESS GATES
    hello-world-57f597bc59-q9w9k                                     1/1
    Running    0           23s     13.83.148.91  virtual-kubelet-virtual-kubele
    t-linux-westus    <none>            <none>
    virtual-kubelet-linux-westus-virtual-kubelet-for-aks-6f8689kfff  1/1
    Running    0           5m14s   10.240.0.33   aks-nodepool1-37650960-vmss000
    000               <none>            <none>
    virtual-kubelet-windows-westus-virtual-kubelet-for-aks-65bqzwbw  1/1
    Running    0           5m8s    10.240.0.25   aks-nodepool1-37650960-vmss000
    000               <none>            <none>
    sathsara@Azure:~$
    ```

    Figure 6.55: Listing all pods with the -o wide flag

Thus, we have successfully configured Virtual Kubelet on AKS with ACI and have deployed a pod in the Virtual Kubelet node.

Let's now complete an activity where we will be deploying a containerized application in a serverless environment.

Activity 6: Deploy a Containerized Application in a Serverless Environment

Imagine that you are working for a start-up company and your manager wants you to create an application that can return the current date and time for a given timezone. This application is expected to receive only a few requests during the initial phase but will receive millions of requests in the long run. The application should be able to scale automatically based on the number of requests received without any modifications. Also, your manager does not want to have the burden of managing the infrastructure and expects this application to run with the lowest possible cost.

Execute the following steps to complete this activity:

1. Create an application (in any language you want) that can provide the current date and time based on the given **timezone** value.

   The following is some sample application code written in PHP:

   ```php
   <?php

   if ( !isset ( $_GET['timezone'] ) ) {
       // Returns error if the timezone parameter is not provided
       $output_message = "Error: Timezone not provided";
   } else if ( empty ( $_GET['timezone'] ) ) {
       // Returns error if the timezone parameter value is empty
       $output_message = "Error: Timezone cannot be empty";
   } else {
       // Save the timezone parameter value to a variable
       $timezone = $_GET['timezone'];
   ```

```
    try {
        // Generates the current time for the provided timezone
        $date = new DateTime("now", new DateTimeZone($timezone) );
        $formatted_date_time = $date->format('Y-m-d H:i:s');
        $output_message = "Current date and time for $timezone is
$formatted_date_time";
    } catch(Exception $e) {
        // Returns error if the timezone is invalid
        $output_message = "Error: Invalid timezone value";
    }

}

// Return the output message
echo $output_message;
```

2. Containerize the application according to the guidelines provided by Google Cloud Run.

   The following is the content of a sample Dockerfile:

```
# Use official PHP 7.3 image as base image
FROM php:7.3-apache

# Copy index.php file to the docker image
COPY index.php /var/www/html/

# Replace port 80 with the value from PORT environment variable in apache2
configuration files
RUN sed -i 's/80/${PORT}/g' /etc/apache2/sites-available/000-default.conf
/etc/apache2/ports.conf

# Use the default production configuration file
RUN mv "$PHP_INI_DIR/php.ini-production" "$PHP_INI_DIR/php.ini"
```

3. Push the Docker image to a Docker registry.

4. Run the application with Cloud Run.

The output should be as follows:

Figure 6.56: Deployment of the application in a serverless environment

Note

The solution to the activity can be found on page 417.

Summary

In this chapter, we discussed the advantages of using serverless on Kubernetes. We discussed three technologies that offer the benefits of serverless on top of a Kubernetes cluster. These are Knative, Google Cloud Run, and Virtual Kubelet.

First, we created a GKE cluster with Istio and deployed Knative on top of it. Then we learned how to deploy an application on Knative. Next, we discussed the serving component of Knative and how to perform a canary deployment with configuration and route objects. Then we discussed monitoring on Knative and observed how Knative autoscaling works based on the number of requests received.

We also discussed Google Cloud Run, which is a fully managed platform, built on the Knative project, to run stateless HTTP-driven containers. Then we learned how to deploy an application with the Cloud Run service.

In the final section, we studied Virtual Kubelet, which is an open source implementation of Kubernetes' kubelet. We learned the differences between normal kubelets and Virtual Kubelet. Finally, we deployed Virtual Kubelet on an AKS cluster and deployed an application to a Virtual Kubelet node.

In the next three chapters, we will be focusing on three different Kubernetes serverless frameworks, namely Kubeless, OpenWhisk, and OpenFaaS.

Kubernetes Serverless with Kubeless

Learning Objectives

By the end of this chapter, you will be able to:

- Create a Kubernetes cluster with Minikube
- Install the Kubeless framework on Kubernetes
- Create, update, call, and delete Kubeless functions
- List, describe, debug, and monitor Kubeless functions
- Create HTTP and PubSub triggers for Kubeless functions

In this chapter, we will first learn about the Kubeless architecture. Then, we'll create our first Kubeless function, deploy it, and invoke it. You'll also learn how to debug a Kubeless function in the case of a failure.

Introduction to Kubeless

Kubeless is an open source and Kubernetes-native serverless framework that runs on top of Kubernetes. This allows software developers to deploy code into a Kubernetes cluster without worrying about the underlying infrastructure. **Kubeless** is a project by Bitnami, who is a provider of packaged applications for any platform. Bitnami provides software installers for over 130 applications, which allow you to quickly and efficiently deploy these software applications to any platform.

Kubeless functions support multiple programming languages, including Python, PHP, Ruby, Node.js, Golang, Java, .NET, Ballerina, and custom runtimes. These functions can be invoked with HTTP(S) calls as well as event triggers with Kafka or NATS messaging systems. Kubeless also supports Kinesis triggers to associate functions with the AWS Kinesis service, which is a managed data-streaming service by AWS. Kubeless functions can even be invoked at specified intervals using scheduled triggers.

Kubeless comes with its own Command-Line Interface (CLI) named **kubeless**, which is similar to the **kubectl** CLI offered by Kubernetes. We can create, deploy, list, and delete Kubeless functions using this **kubeless** CLI. Kubeless also has a graphical user interface, which makes the management of the functions much easier.

In this chapter, we will create our first serverless function on Kubernetes using Kubeless. Then, we will invoke this function with multiple mechanisms including HTTP, and PubSub triggers. Once we are familiar with the basics of Kubeless, we will create a more advanced function that can post messages to Slack.

Kubeless Architecture

The Kubeless framework is an extension of the Kubernetes framework, leveraging native Kubernetes concepts such as **Custom Resource Definitions** (**CRDs**) and custom controllers. Since Kubeless is built on top of Kubernetes, it can take advantage of all the great features available in Kubernetes, such as self-healing, autoscaling, load balancing, and service discovery.

> **Note**
>
> Custom resources are extensions of the Kubernetes API. You can find more about Kubernetes' custom resources in the official Kubernetes documentation at https://kubernetes.io/docs/concepts/extend-kubernetes/api-extension/custom-resources/.

Let's take a look at the Kubernetes architecture in order to understand the core concepts behind it:

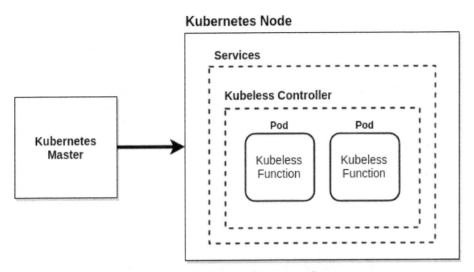

Figure 7.1: Kubeless architecture diagram

The preceding diagram is similar to the standard Kubernetes architecture with Kubernetes masters and nodes. There can be one or more Kubernetes masters that are responsible for overall decision-making in the cluster. Kubernetes nodes are used to host the Kubernetes pods. These pods contain the functions written by the software developers. The source code of the functions will be injected into the pods by the controller using **ConfigMaps**.

These pods will be managed by the **Kubeless controller**. During the Kubeless framework installation process, it will launch an in-cluster controller that will continuously watch for function resources. When a function is being deployed, this controller will create relevant services, deployments, and pods with the provided runtime.

The Kubeless framework has three core concepts:

- Functions
- Triggers
- Runtimes

Functions represent the code blocks executed by the Kubeless framework. During the installation, a CRD named `functions.kubeless.io` will be created to represent the Kubeless functions.

Triggers represent the invocation mechanism of the function. A Kubeless function will be invoked whenever it receives a trigger. A single trigger can be associated with one or many functions. Functions deployed on Kubeless can be triggered using five possible mechanisms:

- HTTP trigger: This executes through HTTP(S)-based invocations such as HTTP GET or POST requests.

- CronJob trigger: This executes through a predefined schedule.

- Kafka trigger: This executes when a message gets published to the Kafka topics.

- NATS trigger: This executes when a message gets published to the NATS topics.

- Kinesis trigger: This executes when records get published to AWS Kinesis data streams.

Runtimes represent different programming languages that can be used to write and execute Kubeless functions. A single programming language will be further divided into multiple runtimes based on the version. As an example, Python 2.7, Python 3.4, Python 3.6, and Python 3.7 are the runtimes supporting the Python programming language. Kubeless supports runtimes in both the stable and incubator stage. A runtime is considered stable once it meets certain technical requirements specified by Kubeless. Incubator runtimes are considered to be in the development stage. Once the specified technical requirements are fulfilled, runtime maintainers can create a "pull" request in the Kubeless GitHub repository to move the runtime from the incubator stage to the stable stage. At the time of writing this book, Ballerina, .NET, Golang, Java, Node.js, PHP, and Python runtimes are available in the stable stage and JVM and Vertx runtimes are available in the incubator stage.

> **Note**
>
> The following document defines the technical requirements for a stable runtime: https://github.com/kubeless/runtimes/blob/master/DEVELOPER_GUIDE. md#runtime-image-requirements.

Creating a Kubernetes Cluster

We need to have a working Kubernetes cluster in order to install the Kubeless framework. You can create your own Kubernetes cluster using tools such as Minikube, Kubeadm, and Kops. You can also create a Kubernetes cluster using the managed Kubernetes cluster services provided by public cloud providers such as **Google Kubernetes Engine** (**GKE**), Microsoft's **Azure Kubernetes Service** (**AKS**), and **Amazon Elastic Kubernetes Service** (**Amazon EKS**). In the following sections, we will create our own Kubernetes cluster using **Minikube**.

Creating a Kubernetes Cluster with Minikube

First, we are going to create our Kubernetes cluster with Minikube. Minikube is a tool that will install and run Kubernetes locally on your PC. This will create a single-node Kubernetes cluster inside a **Virtual Machine** (**VM**). Minikube is used by the software developers who want to try Kubernetes locally, but it is not recommended for running production-grade Kubernetes clusters. We will begin creating our Kubernetes cluster by performing the following steps:

1. Install VirtualBox.

    Since Minikube is running as a VM, we need to install a hypervisor to support the VMs. We will be installing Oracle VirtualBox, which is a free virtualization software developed by Oracle Corporation.

    > **Note**
    >
    > VirtualBox can be installed on Ubuntu 18.04 with the APT package manager by executing the following command in the terminal:
    >
    > ```
    > $ sudo apt install virtualbox -y
    > ```

2. Execute the **virtualbox** command to start <u>**Oracle VM VirtualBox Manager**</u>, as shown in the following screenshot:

```
$ virtualbox
```

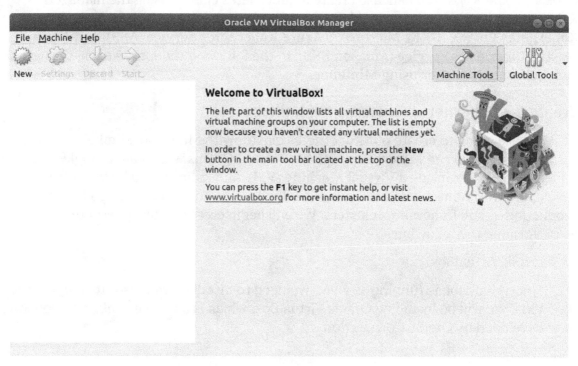

Figure 7.2: Oracle VM VirtualBox Manager

3. Install **minikube**.

Now, we are going to install **Minikube** version 1.2.0, which is the latest version available at the time of writing this book. First, download the **minikube** binaries to your local machine:

```
$ curl -Lo minikube https://storage.googleapis.com/minikube/releases/
v1.2.0/minikube-linux-amd64
```

The output will be as follows:

```
/serverless $ curl -Lo minikube https://storage.googleapis.com/minikube/release
s/v1.2.0/minikube-linux-amd64
  % Total    % Received % Xferd  Average Speed   Time    Time     Time  Current
                                 Dload  Upload   Total   Spent    Left  Speed
100 39.8M  100 39.8M    0     0   911k      0  0:00:44  0:00:44 --:--:--  735k
/serverless $
```

Figure 7.3: Downloading the Minikube binaries

4. Then, add execution permission to the **minikube** binary:

```
$ chmod +x minikube
```

The output is as follows:

```
/serverless $ chmod +x minikube
/serverless $
```

Figure 7.4: Adding execution permissions to Minikube binaries

5. Finally, move the Minikube binary to the **/usr/local/bin/** path location:

```
$ sudo mv minikube /usr/local/bin/
```

The result is shown in the following screenshot:

```
/serverless $ sudo mv minikube /usr/local/bin/
/serverless $
```

Figure 7.5: Moving the Minikube binaries to the path

6. Verify the installation:

```
$ minikube version
```

The result is shown in the following screenshot:

```
/serverless $ minikube version
minikube version: v1.2.0
/serverless $
```

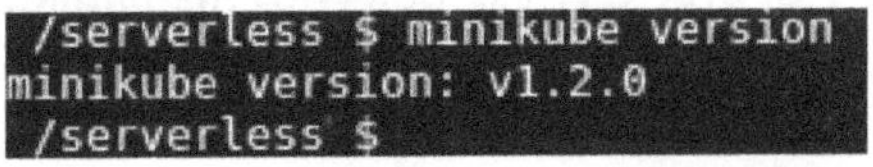

Figure 7.6: Verifying the Minikube version

7. Start the Minikube cluster with the **minikube start** command:

```
$ minikube start
```

This will create a VM for Minikube in VirtualBox, as follows:

```
/serverless $ minikube start
😄  minikube v1.2.0 on linux (amd64)
🔥  Creating virtualbox VM (CPUs=2, Memory=2048MB, Disk=20000MB) ...
🐳  Configuring environment for Kubernetes v1.15.0 on Docker 18.09.6
```

Figure 7.7: Starting Minikube

Now, in the **VirtualBox Manager** window, you can see a VM named `minikube` in the running state:

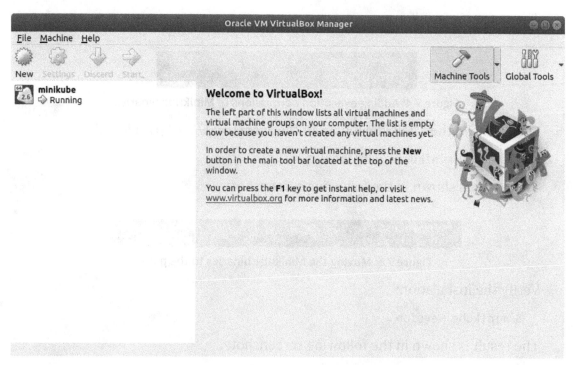

Figure 7.8: Oracle VirtualBox with the Minikube VM

8. Install `kubectl`.

    Now, we are going to install `kubectl` version 1.15.0, which is the latest version available at the time of writing this book. First, download the `kubectl` binaries to your local machine:

    ```
    $ curl -LO https://storage.googleapis.com/kubernetes-release/release/
    v1.15.0/bin/linux/amd64/kubectl
    ```

    This will show the following output:

    ```
    /serverless $ curl -LO https://storage.googleapis.com/kubernetes-release/releas
    e/v1.15.0/bin/linux/amd64/kubectl
      % Total    % Received % Xferd  Average Speed   Time    Time     Time  Current
                                     Dload  Upload   Total   Spent    Left  Speed
    100 40.9M  100 40.9M    0     0   871k      0  0:00:48  0:00:48 --:--:--  921k
    /serverless $
    ```

    Figure 7.9: Downloading the kubectl binaries

9. Then, add execution permissions to the Minikube binary:

```
$ chmod +x kubectl
```

The following screenshot shows the result:

```
/serverless $ chmod +x kubectl
/serverless $
```

Figure 7.10: Adding execution permissions to the kubectl binaries

10. Finally, move the Minikube binary to the **/usr/local/bin/** path location:

```
$ sudo mv kubectl /usr/local/bin/kubectl
```

The output is as follows:

```
/serverless $ sudo mv kubectl /usr/local/bin/kubectl
/serverless $
```

Figure 7.11: Moving the kubectl binaries to the path

11. Verify the installation:

```
$ kubectl version
```

The following will be shown on the screen:

```
/serverless $ kubectl version
Client Version: version.Info{Major:"1", Minor:"15", GitVersion:"v1.15.0", GitCommit
:"e8462b5b5dc2584fdcd18e6bcfe9f1e4d970a529", GitTreeState:"clean", BuildDate:"2019-
06-19T16:40:16Z", GoVersion:"go1.12.5", Compiler:"gc", Platform:"linux/amd64"}
Server Version: version.Info{Major:"1", Minor:"15", GitVersion:"v1.15.0", GitCommit
:"e8462b5b5dc2584fdcd18e6bcfe9f1e4d970a529", GitTreeState:"clean", BuildDate:"2019-
06-19T16:32:14Z", GoVersion:"go1.12.5", Compiler:"gc", Platform:"linux/amd64"}
```

Figure 7.12: Verifying the kubectl version

12. Verify that the **kubectl** CLI is correctly pointed to the Minikube cluster:

```
$ kubectl get pods
```

You should see the following output:

```
/serverless $ kubectl get pods
No resources found.
```

Figure 7.13: Verifying that kubectl is pointed to the Minikube cluster

Installing Kubeless

Once the Minikube Kubernetes environment is ready, we can install Kubeless on top of the Kubernetes cluster. Installing Kubeless consists of installing three components:

- The Kubeless framework
- The Kubeless CLI
- The Kubeless UI

The Kubeless framework will install all the extensions on top of Kubernetes to support Kubeless features. This includes CRDs, custom controllers, and deployments. The Kubeless CLI is used to interact with the Kubeless framework for tasks such as deploying functions, invoking functions, and creating triggers. The Kubeless UI is a GUI for the Kubeless framework, which will help you to view, edit, and run functions.

Installing the Kubeless Framework

We are going to install Kubeless version 1.0.3, which is the latest available release at the time of writing this book.

First, we need to create the **kubeless** namespace using **kubectl create namespace**. This is the default namespace used by Kubeless to store all its objects:

```
$ kubectl create namespace kubeless
```

The result is as follows:

```
/serverless $ kubectl create namespace kubeless
namespace/kubeless created
/serverless $
```

Figure 7.14: Creating the kubeless namespace

In the next step, we will install the Kubeless framework. We will be using one of the YAML manifests provided by Kubeless to install the framework. There are multiple **yaml** files provided by Kubeless and we have to choose the correct **yaml** file based on the Kubernetes environment (for example, **rbac**, **non-rbac**, or **openshift**):

```
$ kubectl create -f https://github.com/kubeless/kubeless/releases/download/
v1.0.3/kubeless-v1.0.3.yaml
```

The screen will display the following:

```
/serverless $ kubectl create -f https://github.com/kubeless/kubeless/releases/down
load/v1.0.3/kubeless-v1.0.3.yaml
configmap/kubeless-config created
deployment.apps/kubeless-controller-manager created
serviceaccount/controller-acct created
clusterrole.rbac.authorization.k8s.io/kubeless-controller-deployer created
clusterrolebinding.rbac.authorization.k8s.io/kubeless-controller-deployer created
customresourcedefinition.apiextensions.k8s.io/functions.kubeless.io created
customresourcedefinition.apiextensions.k8s.io/httptriggers.kubeless.io created
customresourcedefinition.apiextensions.k8s.io/cronjobtriggers.kubeless.io created
/serverless $
```

Figure 7.15: Installing the Kubeless framework

The preceding step will create multiple Kubernetes objects in the **kubeless** namespace. This will create a function object as a **Custom Resource Definition** and Kubeless controller as a deployment. You can verify that these objects are up and running by executing the following commands:

```
$ kubectl get pods -n kubeless
```

```
$ kubectl get deployment -n kubeless
```

```
$ kubectl get customresourcedefinition
```

You will see the following on your screen:

```
/serverless $ kubectl get pods -n kubeless
NAME                                           READY   STATUS    RESTARTS   AGE
kubeless-controller-manager-7456bb44b8-nwm7m   3/3     Running   0          5m5s
/serverless $
/serverless $ kubectl get deployment -n kubeless
NAME                          READY   UP-TO-DATE   AVAILABLE   AGE
kubeless-controller-manager   1/1     1            1           5m15s
/serverless $
/serverless $ kubectl get customresourcedefinition
NAME                          CREATED AT
cronjobtriggers.kubeless.io   2019-07-05T13:31:42Z
functions.kubeless.io         2019-07-05T13:31:42Z
httptriggers.kubeless.io      2019-07-05T13:31:42Z
/serverless $
```

Figure 7.16: Verifying the Kubeless installation

Now, we have completed the installation of the Kubeless framework successfully. In the next section, we will install the Kubeless CLI.

Installing the Kubeless CLI

Kubeless CLI is the command-line interface for running commands against the Kubeless framework. `kubeless function` is the most common one because it allows you to perform tasks such as deploying, calling, updating, or deleting a function. Additionally, you can list and describe the functions. Checking the logs or metrics is also supported through the `kubeless function` command. You can also manage Kubeless triggers, topics, and autoscaling from the Kubeless CLI.

Once you have successfully installed the Kubeless framework, the next step is to install the Kubeless CLI. We are going to use Kubeless CLI version 1.0.3, which is the same version as the Kubeless framework we installed in the previous section.

First, we need to download the Kubeless CLI zip file:

```
$ curl -OL https://github.com/kubeless/kubeless/releases/download/v1.0.3/
kubeless_linux-amd64.zip
```

The result is as follows:

```
/serverless $ curl -OL https://github.com/kubeless/kubeless/releases/download/v1.0
.3/kubeless_linux-amd64.zip
  % Total    % Received % Xferd  Average Speed   Time    Time     Time  Current
                                 Dload  Upload   Total   Spent    Left  Speed
100   614    0   614    0     0    281      0 --:--:--  0:00:02 --:--:--   281
100 9054k  100 9054k    0     0   517k      0  0:00:17  0:00:17 --:--:--  440k
/serverless $
```

Figure 7.17: Downloading the Kubeless binaries

Next, we will extract the zip file:

```
$ unzip kubeless_linux-amd64.zip
```

To understand this better, refer to the following output:

```
/serverless $ unzip kubeless_linux-amd64.zip
Archive:  kubeless_linux-amd64.zip
   creating: bundles/kubeless_linux-amd64/
  inflating: bundles/kubeless_linux-amd64/kubeless
/serverless $
```

Figure 7.18: Extracting the Kubeless binaries

Then, move the Kubeless executable to the **/usr/local/bin/** path location:

```
$ sudo mv bundles/kubeless_linux-amd64/kubeless /usr/local/bin/
```

The following is what you'll see on your screen:

```
/serverless $ sudo mv bundles/kubeless_linux-amd64/kubeless /usr/local/bin/
/serverless $
```

Figure 7.19: Moving the Kubeless binaries to the path

Now, we have successfully installed the Kubeless CLI. We can verify this by running the following command:

```
$ kubeless version
```

Refer to the following screenshot:

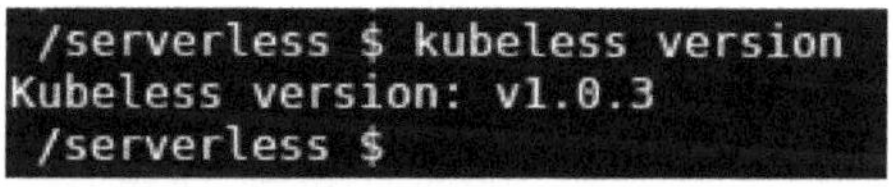

```
/serverless $ kubeless version
Kubeless version: v1.0.3
/serverless $
```

Figure 7.20: Verifying the Kubeless version

The Kubeless UI

The **Kubeless UI** is the GUI for Kubeless. It allows you to create, edit, delete, and execute Kubeless functions with an easy-to-use UI. Execute the following command to install the Kubeless UI in the Kubernetes cluster:

```
$ kubectl create -f https://raw.githubusercontent.com/kubeless/kubeless-ui/master/k8s.yaml
```

This will give you the following output:

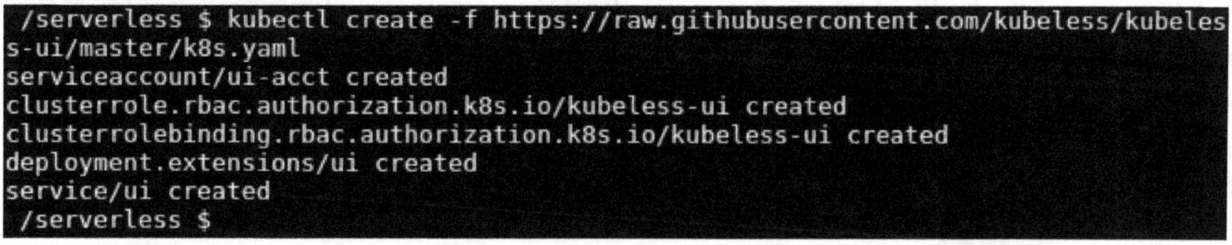

```
/serverless $ kubectl create -f https://raw.githubusercontent.com/kubeless/kubeles
s-ui/master/k8s.yaml
serviceaccount/ui-acct created
clusterrole.rbac.authorization.k8s.io/kubeless-ui created
clusterrolebinding.rbac.authorization.k8s.io/kubeless-ui created
deployment.extensions/ui created
service/ui created
/serverless $
```

Figure 7.21: Installing the Kubeless UI

Once the installation is successful, execute the following command to open the Kubeless UI in a browser window. You can reload the browser window if the Kubeless UI doesn't show up, since creating the service can take a few minutes:

```
$ minikube service ui --namespace kubeless
```

This is shown as follows:

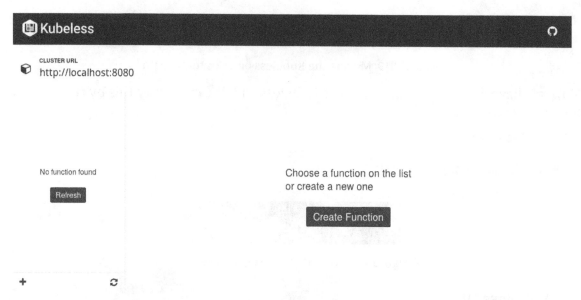

Figure 7.22: The Kubeless GUI

We've just completed the installation of the Kubeless UI, which can be used to create, edit, delete, and execute Kubeless functions that are similar to the Kubeless CLI.

Kubeless Functions

Once Kubeless is successfully installed, you can now forget about the underlying infrastructure, including VMs and containers, and focus only on your function logic. Kubeless functions are code snippets written in one of the supported languages. As we discussed previously, Kubeless supports multiple programming languages and versions. You can execute the **kubeless get-server-config** command to get a list of language runtimes supported by your Kubeless version:

```
$ kubeless get-server-config
```

The result is shown in the following screenshot:

```
/serverless $ kubeless get-server-config
INFO[0000] Current Server Config:
INFO[0000] Supported Runtimes are: ballerina0.981.0, dotnetcore2.0, dotnetcore2.1,
go1.10, java1.8, nodejs6, nodejs8, php7.2, python2.7, python3.4, python3.6, python3
.7, ruby2.3, ruby2.4, ruby2.5, jvm1.8, nodejs_distroless8, nodejsCE8, vertx1.8
/serverless $
```

Figure 7.23: Kubeless server configuration

In the following sections, we are going to create, deploy, list, invoke, update, and delete a Kubeless function.

Creating a Kubeless Function

Every Kubeless function, regardless of the language runtime, has the same format. It receives two arguments as input and returns a string or object as the response. The first argument of the function is an event, which includes all the information about the event source such as the event ID, event time, and event type. The **data** field inside the **event** object contains the body of the function request. The second argument of the function is named **context**, which contains general information about the function, such as its name, timeout, runtime, and memory limits.

The following is a sample Python function that returns the text **Welcome to Kubeless World** as the response:

```
def main(event, context):

    return "Welcome to Kubeless World"
```

You can save the file as **hello.py**.

Deploying the Kubeless Function

Once the function is ready, you can deploy it to the Kubeless framework. You can use the **kubeless function deploy** command to register the function with the Kubeless framework. In order to deploy a function, you need to provide few pieces of information, including the function name, the runtime of the function, the file that contains the function source code, and the method name to be executed when the function is invoked:

```
kubeless function deploy hello --runtime python3.7 \

                    --from-file hello.py \

                    --handler hello.main
```

The output is as follows:

```
/serverless $ kubeless function deploy hello --runtime python3.7 \
>                           --from-file hello.py \
>                           --handler hello.main
INFO[0000] Deploying function...
INFO[0000] Function hello submitted for deployment
INFO[0000] Check the deployment status executing 'kubeless function ls hello'
/serverless $
```

Figure 7.24: Deploying a Kubeless function

Let's break this command up into a few pieces in order to understand what each part of the command does:

- **kubeless function deploy hello**: This tells Kubeless to register a new function named **hello**. We can use this name to invoke this function later.

- **--runtime python3.7**: This tells Kubeless to use the Python 3.7 runtime to run this function.

- **--from-file hello.py**: This tells Kubeless to use the code available in the **hello.py** file to create the **hello** function. If you are not in the current file path when executing the command, you need to specify the full file path.

- **--handler hello.main**: This specifies the name of the code file and the method to execute when this function is invoked. This should be in the format of **<file-name>.<function-name>**. In our case, the filename is **hello** and the function name inside the file is **main**.

You can find the other options that are available when deploying a function by executing the **kubeless function deploy --help** command.

Listing the Kubeless Function

Once you deploy the function, you can verify that the function is deployed successfully by listing the functions with the **kubeless function list** command. You should see the details of all the registered functions as follows:

```
$ kubeless function list
```

The following screenshot reflects the result:

```
/serverless $ kubeless function list
NAME     NAMESPACE      HANDLER          RUNTIME         DEPENDENCIES      STATUS
hello    default        hello.main       python3.7                         1/1 READY
/serverless $
```

Figure 7.25: Listing the Kubeless functions with the Kubeless CLI

> **Note**
>
> The same can be achieved using the **kubeless function ls** command.

If you wish to obtain more detailed information about a specific function, you can use the **kubeless function describe** command:

```
$ kubeless function describe hello
```

It produces the following output:

```
/serverless $ kubeless function describe hello
Name:           hello
Namespace:      default
Handler:        hello.main
Runtime:        python3.7
Label:          {"created-by":"kubeless","function":"hello"}
Envvar:         null
Memory:         0
Dependencies:
/serverless $
```

Figure 7.26: Describing a Kubeless function

Since a Kubeless function is created as a Kubernetes object (that is, a custom resource), you can also use the Kubectl CLI to get the information about the available functions. The following is the output from the **kubectl get functions** command:

```
$ kubectl get functions
```

You will get the following output:

```
/serverless $ kubectl get functions
NAME      AGE
hello     13m
/serverless $
```

Figure 7.27: Listing the Kubeless functions with the kubectl CLI

Invoking the Kubeless Function

Now it's time to invoke our **hello** function. You can use the **kubeless function call** method to invoke the Kubeless function. The **hello** function will return the text **Welcome to Kubeless World** as the response:

```
$ kubeless function call hello
```

The output will be as follows:

```
/serverless $ kubeless function call hello
Welcome to Kubeless World
/serverless $
```

Figure 7.28: Invoking a Kubeless function with the kubeless CLI

Congratulations! You have successfully executed your first Kubeless function.

You can also invoke Kubeless functions with the Kubeless UI. Once you open the Kubeless UI, you can see the list of functions available on the left-hand side. You can click on the **hello** function to open it. Then, click on the **Run** function button to execute the function. You can see the expected response of **Welcome to Kubeless World** underneath the **Response** section:

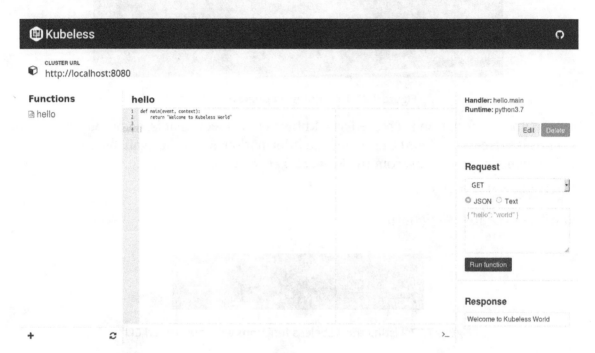

Figure 7.29: Invoking a Kubeless function with the Kubeless UI

> **Note**
>
> Kubeless functions can also be updated or deleted using the Kubeless UI.

Updating the Kubeless Function

After successfully invoking our **hello** function, we are now going to update it to say *hello* to anyone. You can update the **hello.py** file as follows:

```
def main(event, context):
    name = event['data']['name']
    return "Hello " +  name
```

You can then execute the **kubeless function update** command to update the **hello** function that we created earlier:

```
$ kubeless function update hello --from-file hello.py
```

This will give the following output:

```
/serverless $ kubeless function update hello --from-file hello.py
INFO[0000] Redeploying function...
INFO[0000] Function hello submitted for deployment
INFO[0000] Check the deployment status executing 'kubeless function ls hello'
/serverless $
```

Figure 7.30: Updating a Kubeless function with the Kubeless CLI

Now you have to pass the required data when invoking the **hello** function:

```
$ kubeless function call hello --data '{"name":"Kubeless World!"}'
```

This is the output of the preceding code:

```
/serverless $ kubeless function call hello --data '{"name":"Kubeless World!"}'
Hello Kubeless World!
/serverless $
```

Figure 7.31: Invoking updated Kubeless functions

You should be able to see **Hello Kubeless World!** as the output of the preceding command.

Deleting the Kubeless Function

If you want to delete the function, you can execute the **kubeless function delete** command:

```
$ kubeless function delete hello
```

This renders the following:

```
/serverless $ kubeless function delete hello
/serverless $
```

Figure 7.32: Deleting the kubeless function

Once the function is deleted, try listing the function again. It should throw an error, as follows:

```
$ kubeless function list hello
```

We would see the following result:

```
/serverless $ kubeless function list hello
FATA[0000] Error listing function hello: functions.kubeless.io "hello" not found
/serverless $
```

Figure 7.33: Verifying the deletion of the kubeless function

The preceding **kubeless function delete** command will delete not only the **kubeless** function, but, while creating the Kubeless function, the framework creates Kubernetes objects such as pods and deployment. Those objects will also be deleted when we delete the kubeless function. You can verify this with the following command:

```
$ kubectl get pods -l function=hello
```

You can see the result as follows:

```
/serverless $ kubectl get pods -l function=hello
No resources found.
/serverless $
```

Figure 7.34: Verifying the deletion

Now we have learned how to create, deploy, list, invoke, update, and delete Kubeless functions. Let's move on to an exercise about creating your first Kubeless function.

Exercise 21: Creating Your First Kubeless Function

In this exercise, we will create, deploy, invoke, and later delete a Kubeless function. Perform the following steps to complete the exercise:

> **Note**
>
> The code files for this exercise can be found at https://github.com/TrainingByPackt/
> Serverless-Architectures-with-Kubernetes/tree/master/Lesson07/Exercise21.

1. Create a file with a sample **hello** function:

```
$ cat <<EOF >my-function.py
def main(event, context):
    return "Welcome to Serverless Architectures with Kubernetes"
EOF
```

This will render the following output:

```
/serverless $ cat <<EOF >my-function.py
> def main(event, context):
>     return "Welcome to Serverless Architectures with Kubernetes"
> EOF
/serverless $
```

Figure 7.35: Creating the my-function.py file

2. Create the **lesson-7** namespace and deploy the **my-function.py** file created previously:

```
$ kubectl create namespace lesson-7

$ kubeless function deploy my-function --runtime python3.7 \
                            --from-file my-function.py \
                            --handler my-function.main \
                            --namespace lesson-7
```

The output is as follows:

```
/serverless $ kubectl create namespace lesson-7
namespace/lesson-7 created
/serverless $
/serverless $ kubeless function deploy my-function --runtime python3.7 \
>                            --from-file my-function.py \
>                            --handler my-function.main \
>                            --namespace lesson-7
INFO[0000] Deploying function...
INFO[0000] Function my-function submitted for deployment
INFO[0000] Check the deployment status executing 'kubeless function ls my-function'
/serverless $
```

Figure 7.36: Deploying my-function

3. Verify whether **my-function** has been deployed correctly:

```
$ kubeless function list my-function --namespace lesson-7
```

The output rendered is as follows:

```
/serverless $ kubeless function list my-function --namespace lesson-7
NAME          NAMESPACE      HANDLER            RUNTIME      DEPENDENCIES    STATUS
my-function   lesson-7       my-function.main   python3.7                    1/1 READY
/serverless $
```

Figure 7.37: Verifying my-function has successfully deployed

4. Invoke **my-function** with the **kubeless** CLI:

   ```
   $ kubeless function call my-function --namespace lesson-7
   ```

It will look like this:

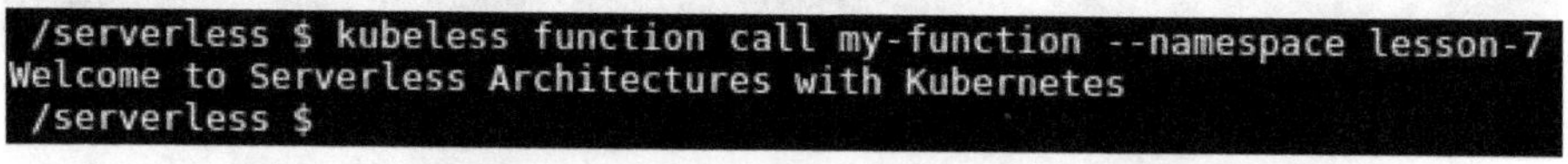

```
/serverless $ kubeless function call my-function --namespace lesson-7
Welcome to Serverless Architectures with Kubernetes
/serverless $
```

Figure 7.38: Invoking my-function with the Kubeless CLI

5. Delete **my-function** and the **lesson-7** namespace:

   ```
   $ kubeless function delete my-function --namespace lesson-7
   $ kubectl delete namespace lesson-7
   ```

The following is what we get:

```
/serverless $ kubeless function delete my-function --namespace lesson-7
/serverless $
```

Figure 7.39: Deleting my-function with the Kubeless CLI

In this exercise, first, we created a simple Python function, which returned the **Welcome to Serverless Architectures with Kubernetes** string as the output and deployed it to Kubeless. Then, we listed the function to make sure it was created successfully. Then, we invoked the **my-function** and successfully returned the expected response of **Welcome to Serverless Architectures with Kubernetes**. Finally, we did the cleanup by deleting the function.

Kubeless HTTP Triggers

In the previous sections, we discussed how to invoke Kubeless functions using the Kubeless CLI. In this section, we are going to demonstrate how to expose these functions to everyone by creating HTTP triggers.

HTTP triggers are used to execute a Kubeless function through HTTP(S)-based invocations such as HTTP **GET** or **POST** requests. When a function is deployed, Kubeless will create a Kubernetes service associated with the function with the **ClusterIP** as the service type; however, these services are not publicly accessible. In order to make the function publicly available, we need to create a Kubeless HTTP trigger. This will expose the Kubeless functions to everyone by using Kubernetes ingress rules.

In order to run the HTTP trigger, your Kubernetes cluster must have a running ingress controller. Once the ingress controller is running in the Kubernetes cluster, you can use the **kubeless trigger http create** command to create an HTTP trigger:

```
$ kubeless trigger http create <trigger-name> --function-name <function-
name>
```

--function-name flag is used to specify the name of the function that will be associated with the HTTP trigger.

> **Note**
>
> There is a number of ingress controller add-ons available for Kubernetes, including NGINX, Kong, Traefik, F5, Contour, and more. You can find them at https://kubernetes.io/docs/concepts/services-networking/ingress-controllers/.

Exercise 22: Creating an HTTP Trigger for a Kubeless Function

In this exercise, we will first enable the ingress plugin for Minikube. Then, we will create a function to be executed with HTTP triggers. Finally, we will create an HTTP trigger and invoke this function with the HTTP trigger.

> **Note**
>
> The code files for this exercise can be found at https://github.com/TrainingByPackt/Serverless-Architectures-with-Kubernetes/tree/master/Lesson07/Exercise22.

Perform the following steps to complete the exercise:

1. First, we need to enable the **ingress** add-on in our Minikube cluster:

   ```
   $ minikube addons enable ingress
   ```

   This shows the following output:

   ```
   /serverless $ minikube addons enable ingress
   ✔  ingress was successfully enabled
   /serverless $
   ```

   Figure 7.40: Enabling the Minikube add-on

2. After a couple of minutes, you should be able to see that the **nginx-ingress-controller** container has been created in the **kube-system** namespace, which is the namespace for the object created by the Kubernetes system:

```
$ kubectl get pod -n kube-system -l app.kubernetes.io/name=nginx-ingress-controller
```

It shows the following:

```
/serverless $ kubectl get pod -n kube-system -l app.kubernetes.io/name=nginx-ingre
ss-controller
NAME                                      READY   STATUS    RESTARTS   AGE
nginx-ingress-controller-7b465d9cf8-mr4xr  1/1     Running   0          6m55s
/serverless $
```

Figure 7.41: Listing the nginx-ingress-controller pod

3. Once the **nginx-ingress-controller** container is in a running state, we will create the function to be executed with the HTTP trigger. Create a Python file named **greetings.py** with the following content:

```python
import datetime as dt

def main(event, context):
    currentHour = dt.datetime.now().hour
    greetingMessage = ''

    if currentHour < 12:
        greetingMessage = 'Hello, Good morning!'
    elif currentHour < 18:
        greetingMessage = 'Hello, Good afternoon!'
    else:
        greetingMessage = 'Hello, Good evening!'

    return greetingMessage
```

4. Create the **lesson-7** namespace and deploy the **greetings.py** created earlier:

```
$ kubectl create namespace lesson-7

$ kubeless function deploy greetings --runtime python3.7 \
                            --from-file greetings.py \
                            --handler greetings.main \
                            --namespace lesson-7
```

Refer to the following output:

```
/serverless $ kubeless function deploy greetings --runtime python3.7 \
>                              --from-file greetings.py \
>                              --handler greetings.main \
>                              --namespace lesson-7
INFO[0000] Deploying function...
INFO[0000] Function greetings submitted for deployment
INFO[0000] Check the deployment status executing 'kubeless function ls greetings'
```

Figure 7.42: Executing the function with an HTTP trigger

5. Invoke the function and verify that the function is providing the expected output:

    ```
    $ kubeless function call greetings --namespace lesson-7
    ```

    Once invoked, the screen will display the following:

```
/serverless $ kubeless function call greetings --namespace lesson-7
Hello, Good afternoon!
 /serverless $
```

Figure 7.43: Output for function

6. Now we can create the **http** trigger for the **hello** function:

    ```
    $ kubeless trigger http create greetings \
                      --function-name greetings \
                      --namespace lesson-7
    ```

    The result is as follows:

```
/serverless $ kubeless trigger http create greetings \
>                      --function-name greetings \
>                      --namespace lesson-7
INFO[0000] HTTP trigger greetings created in namespace lesson-7 successfully!
 /serverless $
```

Figure 7.44: Creating the HTTP trigger

7. List the **http** triggers; you should be able to see the **http** trigger for the **hello** function:

    ```
    $ kubeless trigger http list --namespace lesson-7
    ```

    The list will look something like this:

```
/serverless $ kubeless trigger http list --namespace lesson-7
NAME               NAMESPACE          FUNCTION NAME
greetings          lesson-7           greetings
 /serverless $
```

Figure 7.45: Listing the HTTP triggers

8. This will create an **ingress** object in the Kubernetes layer. We can list the **ingress** objects with the **kubectl** CLI:

```
$ kubectl get ingress --namespace lesson-7
```

This will return the following:

```
/serverless $ kubectl get ingress --namespace lesson-7
NAME          HOSTS                                ADDRESS       PORTS    AGE
greetings     greetings.192.168.99.100.nip.io      10.0.2.15     80       82s
/serverless $
/serverless $
```

Figure 7.46: Listing ingress objects

9. You can see the hostname with the **.nip.io** domain, which we can use to access the **greetings** function over HTTP.

In this case, the hostname is **greetings.192.168.99.100.nip.io**. Once you open this hostname in a web browser, you should be able to see the greeting message in the browser window (note that your output may be different depending on your local time):

Figure 7.47: Invoking the function with the HTTP GET request

Kubeless PubSub Triggers

Kubeless functions can be invoked by sending input messages to **topics** in messaging systems. This method is known as a PubSub mechanism. Currently, Kubeless supports two messaging systems, namely, Kafka and NATS.

In order to create PubSub triggers in Kubeless, we need to have a running Kafka cluster or NATS cluster. Once the Kafka or NATS cluster is ready, we can use **kubeless trigger kafka create** to create a Kafka trigger or **kubeless trigger nats create** to create a NATS trigger and associate our PubSub function with the new trigger:

```
$ kubeless trigger <trigger-type> create <trigger-name> \
                        --function-selector <label-query> \
                        --trigger-topic <topic-name>
```

Let's discuss what each piece of the command does:

- **kubeless trigger <trigger-type> create <trigger-name>**: This tells Kubeless to create a PubSub trigger with the provided name and trigger type. Valid trigger types are **kafka** and **nats**.

- **--function-selector <label-query>**: This tells us which function should be associated with this trigger. Kubernetes labels are used to define this relationship (for example, **--function-selector key1=value1,key2=value2**).

- **--trigger-topic <topic-name>**: The Kafka broker will listen to this topic and the function will be triggered when a message is published to it.

The topic is where messages from the producers get published. The Kubeless CLI allows us to create topics using the **kubeless topic** command. This allows us to create, delete, list topics, and publish messages to topics easily.

Exercise 23: Creating a PubSub Trigger for a Kubeless Function

In this exercise, we will first create a Kafka and Zookeeper cluster within our Minikube environment. Once the Kafka and Zookeeper clusters are ready, we will create a function to be executed with PubSub triggers. Next, we will create the PubSub topic. Publishing messages to the created topic will execute the Kubeless function. Perform the following steps to complete the exercise.

Let's invoke a Kubeless function with the **PubSub** mechanism using Kafka:

1. First, we are going to deploy **Kafka** and **Zookeeper** to our Kubernetes cluster:

    ```
    $ kubectl create -f https://github.com/kubeless/kafka-trigger/releases/
    download/v1.0.2/kafka-zookeeper-v1.0.2.yaml
    ```

    The output will look like the following:

    ```
    /serverless $ kubectl create -f https://github.com/kubeless/kafka-trigger/releases
    /download/v1.0.2/kafka-zookeeper-v1.0.2.yaml
    service/kafka created
    service/zoo created
    deployment.apps/kafka-trigger-controller created
    clusterrole.rbac.authorization.k8s.io/kafka-controller-deployer created
    clusterrolebinding.rbac.authorization.k8s.io/kafka-controller-deployer created
    customresourcedefinition.apiextensions.k8s.io/kafkatriggers.kubeless.io created
    statefulset.apps/kafka created
    service/broker created
    statefulset.apps/zoo created
    service/zookeeper created
    /serverless $
    ```

    Figure 7.48: Installing Kafka and Zookeeper

2. Verify that two **statefulset** named **kafka** and **zoo** are running in the **kubeless** namespace for Kafka and Zookeeper:

    ```
    $ kubectl get statefulset -n kubeless
    $ kubectl get services -n kubeless
    $ kubectl get deployment -n kubeless
    ```

    The following output is seen:

    ```
    /serverless $ kubectl get statefulset -n kubeless
    NAME     DESIRED   CURRENT   AGE
    kafka    1         1         14m
    zoo      1         1         14m
    /serverless $
    /serverless $ kubectl get services -n kubeless
    NAME        TYPE        CLUSTER-IP      EXTERNAL-IP   PORT(S)             AGE
    broker      ClusterIP   None            <none>        9092/TCP            14m
    kafka       ClusterIP   10.59.243.110   <none>        9092/TCP            14m
    zoo         ClusterIP   None            <none>        9092/TCP,3888/TCP   14m
    zookeeper   ClusterIP   10.59.252.232   <none>        2181/TCP            14m
    /serverless $
    /serverless $ kubectl get deployment -n kubeless
    NAME                          DESIRED   CURRENT   UP-TO-DATE   AVAILABLE   AGE
    kafka-trigger-controller      1         1         1            1           15m
    kubeless-controller-manager   1         1         1            1           41h
    /serverless $
    ```

    Figure 7.49: Verifying the Kafka and Zookeeper installation

3. Once our Kafka and Zookeeper deployment is ready, we can create and deploy the function to be triggered by **PubSub** triggers. Create a file named **pubsub.py** and add the following content:

```
def main(event, context):
    return "Invoked with Kubeless PubSub Trigger"
```

4. Let's deploy our function now:

```
$ kubeless function deploy pubsub --runtime python3.7 \
                    --from-file pubsub.py \
                    --handler pubsub.main
```

The deployment will yield the following:

```
/serverless $ kubeless function deploy pubsub --runtime python2.7 \
>                    --from-file pubsub.py \
>                    --handler pubsub.main
INFO[0001] Deploying function...
INFO[0002] Function pubsub submitted for deployment
INFO[0002] Check the deployment status executing 'kubeless function ls pubsub'
/serverless $
```

Figure 7.50: Deploying the pubsub function

5. Once the function is deployed, we can verify the function is successful by listing the function:

```
$ kubeless function list pubsub
```

The listed function will be as follows:

```
/serverless $ kubeless function list pubsub
NAME     NAMESPACE     HANDLER        RUNTIME      DEPENDENCIES     STATUS
pubsub   default       pubsub.main    python2.7                     1/1 READY
/serverless $
```

Figure 7.51: Verifying the pubsub function

6. Now, let's create the **kafka** trigger with the **kubeless trigger kafka create** command and associate our **pubsub** function with the new trigger:

```
$ kubeless trigger kafka create my-trigger \
                        --function-selector function=pubsub \
                        --trigger-topic pubsub-topic
```

It will look as follows:

```
/serverless $ kubeless trigger kafka create my-trigger --function-selector functio
n=pubsub --trigger-topic pubsub-topic
INFO[0001] Kafka trigger my-trigger created in namespace default successfully!
/serverless $
```

Figure 7.52: Creating the kafka trigger for the pubsub function

7. Now we need a Kubeless topic to publish the messages. Let's create a topic with the **kubeless topic create** command. We need to make sure that the topic name is similar to the one we provided as the **--trigger-topic** while creating the **kafka** trigger in the previous step:

```
$ kubeless topic create pubsub-topic
```

8. Okay. Now it's time to test our **pubsub** function by publishing events to **pubsub-topic**:

```
$ kubeless topic publish --topic pubsub-topic --data "My first message"
```

9. Check the **logs** function to verify whether the **pubsub** function is successfully invoked:

```
$ kubectl logs -l function=pubsub
```

You should see the published message in the **output** logs:

```
...
My first message
...
```

To understand this better, check out the following output:

```
10.56.0.1 - - [04/Jul/2019:10:17:54 +0000] "GET /healthz HTTP/1.1" 200 2 "" "kube-probe/1.12+" 0/154
My first message
```

Figure 7.53: Logs of the pubsub function

Monitoring a Kubeless Function

When we have successfully deployed our Kubeless function, we then need to monitor our function. This can be achieved with the **kubeless function top** command. This command will provide us with the following information:

- **NAME**: The name of the Kubeless function
- **NAMESPACE**: The namespace of the function

- **METHOD**: The HTTP method type (for example, GET/POST) when invoking the function

- **TOTAL_CALLS**: The total number of invocations

- **TOTAL_FAILURES**: The number of function failures

- **TOTAL_DURATION_SECONDS**: The total number of seconds this function has executed

- **AVG_DURATION_SECONDS**: The average number of seconds this function has executed

- **MESSAGE**: Any other messages

The following is the **kubeless function top** output for the **hello** function:

```
$ kubeless function top hello
```

The output will be as follows:

Figure 7.54: Viewing the metrics for the hello function

Now that we've monitored the function, it's time to move toward debugging it.

Debugging a Kubeless Function

A Kubeless function can fail at different stages of the function life cycle (for example, from deployment time to function execution time) due to a number of reasons. In this section, we are going to debug a function to identify the cause of failure.

In order to demonstrate multiple error scenarios, first, we are going to create a sample function with the following code block in the **debug.py** file:

```
def main(event, context)
    name = event['data']['name']
    return "Hello " +  name
```

Error Scenario 01

Now, let's try to deploy this function using the **kubeless function deploy** command:

```
$ kubeless function deploy debug --runtime python \
                  --from-file debug.py \
                  --handler debug.main
```

This will result in **Invalid runtime error** and Kubeless will display the supported runtimes. Upon further inspection, we can see that there is a typo in the **--runtime** parameter of the **kubeless function deploy** command.

The resulting output would look like this:

```
/serverless $ kubeless function deploy debug --runtime python \
>                      --from-file debug.py \
>                      --handler debug.main
FATA[0000] Invalid runtime: python. Supported runtimes are: ballerina0.981.0, dotne
tcore2.0, dotnetcore2.1, go1.10, java1.8, nodejs6, nodejs8, php7.2, python2.7, pyth
on3.4, python3.6, python3.7, ruby2.3, ruby2.4, ruby2.5, jvm1.8, nodejs_distroless8,
 nodejsCE8, vertx1.8
/serverless $
```

Figure 7.55: Deploying the debug function – error

Let's correct this typo and rerun the **kubeless function deploy** command with the **python3.7** runtime:

```
$ kubeless function deploy debug --runtime python3.7 \
                   --from-file debug.py \
                   --handler debug.main
```

This time, the function will be successfully deployed into the Kubeless environment. It should look like the following:

```
/serverless $ kubeless function deploy debug --runtime python3.7 \
>                      --from-file debug.py \
>                      --handler debug.main
INFO[0000] Deploying function...
INFO[0000] Function debug submitted for deployment
INFO[0000] Check the deployment status executing 'kubeless function ls debug'
/serverless $
```

Figure 7.56: Deploying the debug function – successful

Error Scenario 02

Now, let's check the status of the function using the **kubeless function ls** command:

```
$ kubeless function ls debug
```

To understand this better, refer to the following output:

```
/serverless $ kubeless function ls debug
NAME    NAMESPACE      HANDLER        RUNTIME        DEPENDENCIES      STATUS
debug   default        debug.main     python3.7                        0/1 NOT READY
/serverless $
```

Figure 7.57: Listing the debug function

You can see that the status is **0/1 NOT READY**. Now, let's check the status of the debug pod using the **kubectl get pods** command:

```
$ kubectl get pods -l function=debug
```

Now, refer to the following screenshot for the output:

```
/serverless $ kubectl get pods -l function=debug
NAME                      READY     STATUS              RESTARTS    AGE
debug-dd8d8b58-f8cpz      0/1       CrashLoopBackOff    5           4m37s
```

Figure 7.58: Listing the debug function pods

Here, debug **pod** is in **CrashLoopBackOff** status. This error commonly occurs due to either a syntax error in the function or the dependencies that we specify.

On closer inspection, we could identify that a colon (:) to mark the end of the function header is missing.

Let's correct this and update our function.

Open the **debug.py** file and add a colon at the end of the function header:

```
def main(event, context):
    name = event['data']['name']
    return  "Hello " +  name
```

We will now execute the **kubeless function update** command to update the function with the new code file:

```
$ kubeless function update debug --from-file debug.py
```

The output is as follows:

```
/serverless $ kubeless function update debug --from-file debug.py
INFO[0003] Redeploying function...
INFO[0003] Function debug submitted for deployment
INFO[0003] Check the deployment status executing 'kubeless function ls debug'
```

Figure 7.59: Updating the debug function

When you execute the **kubeless function ls** debug again, you should be able to see that the function is now ready with the **1/1 READY** status:

```
/serverless $ kubeless function ls debug
NAME    NAMESPACE    HANDLER       RUNTIME      DEPENDENCIES    STATUS
debug   default      debug.main    python2.7                    1/1 READY
```

Figure 7.60: Listing the debug function

Error Scenario 03

Let's create an example error scenario with our **hello** function. For this, you can call the **hello** function by replacing the key name of the **data** section with **username**:

```
$ kubeless function call debug --data '{"username":"Kubeless"}'
```

Now, let's see how it looks on the screen:

```
/serverless $ kubeless function call hello --data '{"username":"Kubeless"}'
ERRO[0001]
FATA[0001] an error on the server ("<!DOCTYPE HTML PUBLIC \"-//IETF//DTD HTML 2.0//EN\">
    <html>
        <head>
            <title>Error: 500 Internal Server Error</title>
            <style type=\"text/css\">
              html {background-color: #eee; font-family: sans;}
              body {background-color: #fff; border: 1px solid #ddd;
                    padding: 15px; margin: 15px;}
              pre {background-color: #eee; border: 1px solid #ddd; padding: 5px;}
            </style>
        </head>
        <body>
            <h1>Error: 500 Internal Server Error</h1>
            <p>Sorry, the requested URL <tt>&#039;http://35.238.152.1/&#039;</tt>
                caused an error:</p>
            <pre>Internal Server Error</pre>
        </body>
    </html>") has prevented the request from succeeding
```

Figure 7.61: Invoking the debug function – error

In order to find the possible cause for this failure, we need to check the function logs. You can execute the **kubeless function logs** command to view the logs of the **hello** function:

```
$ kubeless function logs debug
```

The output would look as follows:

```
10.56.0.1 - - [03/Jul/2019:13:36:17 +0000] "GET /healthz HTTP/1.1" 200 2 "" "kube-p
robe/1.12+" 0/120
10.56.0.1 - - [03/Jul/2019:13:36:47 +0000] "GET /healthz HTTP/1.1" 200 2 "" "kube-p
robe/1.12+" 0/116
10.56.0.1 - - [03/Jul/2019:13:37:17 +0000] "GET /healthz HTTP/1.1" 200 2 "" "kube-p
robe/1.12+" 0/108
Traceback (most recent call last):
  File "/usr/local/lib/python2.7/dist-packages/bottle.py", line 862, in _handle
    return route.call(**args)
  File "/usr/local/lib/python2.7/dist-packages/bottle.py", line 1740, in wrapper
    rv = callback(*a, **ka)
  File "/kubeless.py", line 86, in handler
    raise res
KeyError: 'name'
10.56.0.1 - - [03/Jul/2019:13:37:29 +0000] "POST / HTTP/1.1" 500 739 "" "kubeless/v
0.0.0 (linux/amd64) kubernetes/$Format" 0/10944
```

Figure 7.62: Checking the debug function logs

The first few lines of the output show lines similar to the following code block, which are internal health checks. As per the logs, we can see that all the calls to the **/healthz** endpoint have been successful with the **200** HTTP success response code:

```
10.56.0.1 - - [03/Jul/2019:13:36:17 +0000] "GET /healthz HTTP/1.1" 200 2 ""
"kube-probe/1.12+" 0/120
```

Next, you can see a stack trace of the error messages, as follows, with the possible cause being the **KeyError: 'name'** error. The function was expecting a **'name'** key, which was not found during the function execution:

```
Traceback (most recent call last):
  File "/usr/local/lib/python3.7/dist-packages/bottle.py", line 862, in _
handle
    return route.call(**args)
  File "/usr/local/lib/python3.7/dist-packages/bottle.py", line 1740, in
wrapper
    rv = callback(*a, **ka)
  File "/kubeless.py", line 86, in handler
    raise res
KeyError: 'name'
```

The last line of the error message indicates that HTTP error **500** was returned for the function call:

```
10.56.0.1 - - [03/Jul/2019:13:37:29 +0000] "POST / HTTP/1.1" 500 739 ""
"kubeless/v0.0.0 (linux/amd64) kubernetes/$Format" 0/10944
```

> **Note**
>
> **HTTP 500** is the error code returned by the HTTP protocol, which indicates an **Internal Server Error**. This means that the server was unable to fulfill the request due to unexpected conditions.

Apart from **kubeless function logs**, you can also use the **kubectl logs** command, which will return a similar output. You need to pass the **-l** parameter, which indicates a label, in order to only get the logs for a specific function:

```
$ kubectl logs -l function=hello
```

The following will be the output:

```
/serverless $ kubectl logs -l function=hello
10.56.0.1 - - [03/Jul/2019:13:59:47 +0000] "GET /healthz HTTP/1.1" 200 2 "" "kube-p
robe/1.12+" 0/120
Traceback (most recent call last):
  File "/usr/local/lib/python2.7/dist-packages/bottle.py", line 862, in _handle
    return route.call(**args)
  File "/usr/local/lib/python2.7/dist-packages/bottle.py", line 1740, in wrapper
    rv = callback(*a, **ka)
  File "/kubeless.py", line 86, in handler
    raise res
KeyError: 'name'
10.56.0.1 - - [03/Jul/2019:14:00:08 +0000] "POST / HTTP/1.1" 500 739 "" "kubeless/v
0.0.0 (linux/amd64) kubernetes/$Format" 0/10694
```

Figure 7.63: Checking the debug function logs

Use the **kubectl get functions --show-labels** command to see the labels associated with the Kubeless functions.

This will yield the following:

```
/serverless $ kubectl get functions --show-labels
NAME      AGE    LABELS
hello     45m    created-by=kubeless,function=hello
```

Figure 7.64: Listing the function labels

Let's correct our mistake and pass the correct argument to the **debug** function:

```
$ kubeless function call debug --data '{"name":"Kubeless"}'
```

Now our function has run successfully and has generated **Hello Kubeless** as its output:

```
/serverless $ kubeless function call debug --data '{"name":"Kubeless"}'
Hello Kubeless
```

Figure 7.65: Invoking the debug function – successful

Serverless Plugin for Kubeless

The Serverless Framework is a general framework for deploying serverless applications across different serverless providers. The serverless plugin for Kubeless supports deploying Kubeless functions. Apart from the plugin for Kubeless, the Serverless Framework supports serverless applications such as AWS Lambda, Azure Functions, Google Cloud Functions, Apache OpenWhisk, and Kubeless.

In this section, we will install the serverless framework and create a Kubeless function using the CLI provided by the serverless framework.

Before we start installing the serverless framework, we need to have Node.js version 6.5.0 or later installed as a prerequisite. So, first, let's install Node.js:

```
$ curl -sL https://deb.nodesource.com/setup_12.x | sudo -E bash -
```

```
$ sudo apt-get install nodejs -y
```

The output is as follows:

```
/serverless $ sudo apt-get install nodejs -y
Reading package lists... Done
Building dependency tree
Reading state information... Done
The following packages were automatically installed and are no longer required:
  grub-pc-bin libnuma1
Use 'sudo apt autoremove' to remove them.
The following additional packages will be installed:
  libpython-stdlib libpython2.7-minimal libpython2.7-stdlib python python-minimal pytho
Suggested packages:
  python-doc python-tk python2.7-doc binutils binfmt-support
The following NEW packages will be installed:
  libpython-stdlib libpython2.7-minimal libpython2.7-stdlib nodejs python python-minimal
  python2.7-minimal
0 upgraded, 8 newly installed, 0 to remove and 6 not upgraded.
Need to get 20.8 MB of archives.
After this operation, 98.6 MB of additional disk space will be used.
```

Figure 7.66: Node.js version 6.5.0 installation

Once installed, verify the Node.js version by executing the following command:

```
$ nodejs -v
```

Here is the output:

```
/serverless $ nodejs -v
v12.6.0
/serverless $
```

Figure 7.67: Node.js version verification

Once the Node.js installation is successful, we will then install the Serverless Framework by executing the following command:

```
$ sudo npm install -g serverless
```

Next, we will verify the serverless version:

```
$ serverless -v
```

Check the output, as follows:

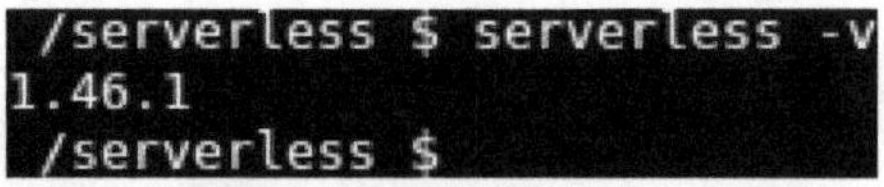

```
/serverless $ serverless -v
1.46.1
/serverless $
```

Figure 7.68: Serverless version verification

We have successfully completed the installation of the Serverless Framework. We can now start creating functions with it.

We can use the **serverless create** command to create a basic service from a template. Let's create a project named **my-kubeless-project**, as follows:

```
$ serverless create --template kubeless-python --path my-kubeless-project
```

Let's break the command into pieces in order to understand it:

- **--template kubeless-python**: Currently, two templates are available for the Kubeless framework. **kubeless-python** creates a Python function and **kubeless-nodejs** creates a Node.js function.

- **--path my-kubeless-project**: This defines that this function should be created under the **my-kubeless-project** directory. Take a look at the output to understand it better:

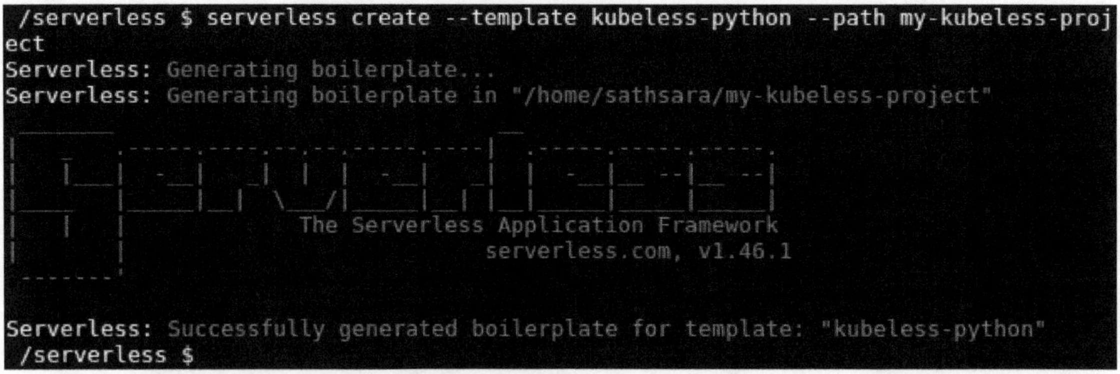

```
/serverless $ serverless create --template kubeless-python --path my-kubeless-proj
ect
Serverless: Generating boilerplate...
Serverless: Generating boilerplate in "/home/sathsara/my-kubeless-project"

 _____                             __
|   _   .-----.----.--.--.-----.----|  .-----.-----.-----.
|   |___|  -__|   _|  |  |  -__|   _|  |  -__|__ --|__ --|
|____   |_____|__|  \___/|_____|__| |__|_____|_____|_____|
|   |   |             The Serverless Application Framework
|       |                   serverless.com, v1.46.1
 -------'

Serverless: Successfully generated boilerplate for template: "kubeless-python"
/serverless $
```

Figure 7.69: Creation of my-kubeless-project

This command will create a directory named **my-kubeless-project** and several files within this directory. First, let's move to the **my-kubeless-project** directory by executing the following command:

```
$ cd my-kubeless-project
```

The following files are in the **my-kubeless-project** directory:

- handler.py
- serverless.yml
- package.json

The **handler.py** file contains a sample Python function, as follows. This is a simple function that returns a JSON object and the status code of 200:

```python
import json


def hello(event, context):
    body = {
        "message": "Go Serverless v1.0! Your function executed
successfully!",
        "input": event['data']
    }


    response = {
        "statusCode": 200,
        "body": json.dumps(body)
    }


    return response
```

It also creates a **serverless.yml** file, which tells the serverless framework to execute the **hello** function inside the **handler.py** file. In the **provider** section, it is mentioned that this is a Kubeless function with a **python2.7** runtime. In the **plugins** section, it defines the custom plugins required, such as the **serverless-kubeless** plugin:

```yaml
# Welcome to Serverless!
#
# For full config options, check the kubeless plugin docs:
#    https://github.com/serverless/serverless-kubeless
#
```

```
# For documentation on kubeless itself:
#    http://kubeless.io

# Update the service name below with your own service name
service: my-kubeless-project

# Please ensure the serverless-kubeless provider plugin is installed
globally.
# $ npm install -g serverless-kubeless
#
# ...before installing project dependencies to register this provider.
# $ npm install

provider:
  name: kubeless
  runtime: python2.7

plugins:
  - serverless-kubeless

functions:
  hello:
    handler: handler.hello
```

Finally, the **package.json** file contains the **npm** packaging information, such as **dependencies**:

```
{
  "name": "my-kubeless-project",
  "version": "1.0.0",
  "description": "Sample Kubeless Python serverless framework service.",
  "dependencies": {
    "serverless-kubeless": "^0.4.0"
  },
```

```
  "scripts": {
    "test": "echo \"Error: no test specified\" && exit 1"
  },
  "keywords": [
    "serverless",
    "kubeless"
  ],
  "author": "The Kubeless Authors",
  "license": "Apache-2.0"
}
```

You can update these files as required to match your business requirements. We are not going to change these files in this example.

Now, we are going to execute the **npm install** command, which installs all **npm** dependencies, such as the **kubeless-serverless** plugin:

```
$ npm install
```

The output for this is as follows:

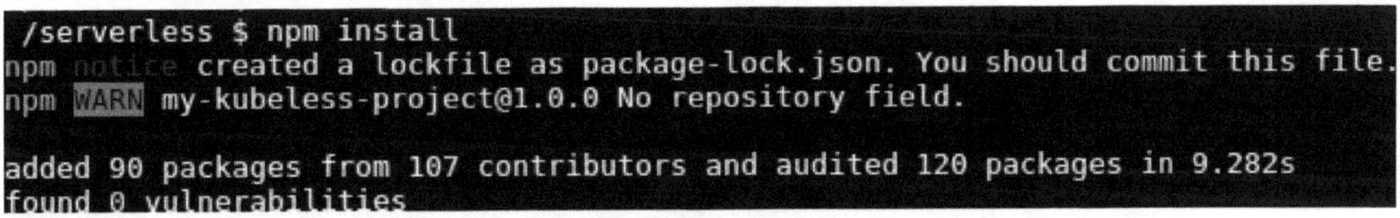

```
/serverless $ npm install
npm notice created a lockfile as package-lock.json. You should commit this file.
npm WARN my-kubeless-project@1.0.0 No repository field.

added 90 packages from 107 contributors and audited 120 packages in 9.282s
found 0 vulnerabilities
```

Figure 7.70: Installing the npm dependencies

Once the dependencies are ready, let's deploy the service:

```
$ serverless deploy -v
```

Deploying the service provides us with the following output:

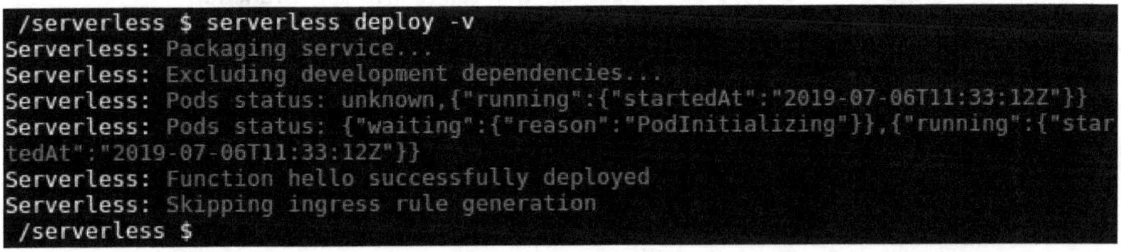

```
/serverless $ serverless deploy -v
Serverless: Packaging service...
Serverless: Excluding development dependencies...
Serverless: Pods status: unknown,{"running":{"startedAt":"2019-07-06T11:33:12Z"}}
Serverless: Pods status: {"waiting":{"reason":"PodInitializing"}},{"running":{"star
tedAt":"2019-07-06T11:33:12Z"}}
Serverless: Function hello successfully deployed
Serverless: Skipping ingress rule generation
/serverless $
```

Figure 7.71: Deploying the service

Then, we can deploy the function using the following command:

```
$ serverless deploy function -f hello
```

The following screenshot shows the output:

```
/serverless $ serverless deploy function -f hello
Serverless: Packaging function: hello...
Serverless: Excluding development dependencies...
Serverless: Redeploying hello...
Serverless: Function hello successfully deployed
/serverless $
```

Figure 7.72: Deploying the function

When the function is successfully deployed, we can invoke the function with the **serverless invoke** command:

```
$ serverless invoke --function hello -l
```

Invoking the function renders the following output:

```
/serverless $ serverless invoke --function hello -l
Serverless: Calling function: hello...
--------------------------------------------------------------
{"body": "{\"input\": \"\", \"message\": \"Go Serverless v1.0! Your function execut
ed successfully!\"}", "statusCode": 200}
/serverless $
```

Figure 7.73: Invoking the function

You can also use the **kubeless function call** command to invoke this function:

```
$ kubeless function call hello
```

Doing this will provide the following output:

```
/serverless $ kubeless function call hello
{"body": "{\"input\": \"\", \"message\": \"Go Serverless v1.0! Your function execut
ed successfully!\"}", "statusCode": 200}
/serverless $
```

Figure 7.74: Using the kubeless function call to invoke the function

Once you are done with the function, use **serverless remove** to delete the function:

```
$ serverless remove
```

Here is the output of the preceding code:

```
/serverless $ serverless remove
Serverless: Removing function: hello...
/serverless $
```

Figure 7.75: Deleting the function

> **Note**
>
> Execute the **serverless logs -f hello** command if you encounter any errors while invoking the function.

Activity 7: Publishing Messages to Slack with Kubeless

Imagine that you need a Slackbot to post messages to your Slack channel. This Slackbot should be able to post messages to a specific Slack channel using the incoming webhook integration method. This bot will print a success message if posting the message to Slack was successful; otherwise, it will print an error message if there were any errors while sending the message to Slack. In this activity, we will be creating a Kubeless function that can post messages to a specific Slack channel.

As a prerequisite to this activity, we need to have a Slack workspace with incoming webhook integration. Execute the following steps to create a Slack workspace and integrate the incoming webhook:

Solution-Slack Setup

1. Create a Slack workspace.

2. Visit https://slack.com/create to create a workspace. Enter your email address and then click on **Create**.

3. You should receive a six-digit confirmation code to the email that you entered on the previous page. Enter the received code on the workspace.

4. Add suitable names for our workspace and Slack channel.

5. You will be asked to fill in email IDs for others who are collaborating on the same project. You can either skip this section or fill in the details and then continue.

6. Now that your Slack channel is ready, click on **See Your Channel in Slack**.

7. Once clicked, we should see our channel.

8. Now we are going to add the **Incoming Webhook** app to our Slack. From the left menu, select **Add apps** under the **Apps** section.

9. Enter **Incoming Webhooks** in the search field and then click on **Install** for **Incoming Webhook** app.

10. Click on **Add Configuration**.

11. Click on **Add Incoming WebHooks Integration**.

12. Save the webhook URL. We will need this when we are writing the Kubeless function.

> **Note**
>
> The detailed steps on creating a Slack workspace with incoming webhook integration, along with the corresponding screenshots, are available on page 422.

Now we are ready to start the activity. Execute the following steps to complete this activity:

Activity Solution

1. Create a function in any language (supported by Kubeless) that can post messages to Slack. In this activity, we will write a Python function that performs the following steps.

2. Use the **requests** library as a dependency.

3. Send a **POST** request to the incoming webhook (created in step 2) with an input message.

4. Print the response of the post request,

5. Deploy the function to the Kubeless framework.

6. Invoke the function.

7. Go to your Slack workspace and verify that the message was successfully posted to the Slack channel. The final output should look like this:

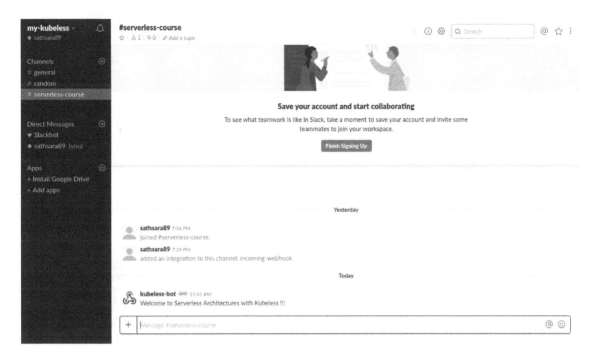

Figure 7.76: Verifying whether the message was successfully posted

> **Note**
>
> The solution to the activity can be found on page 422.

Summary

In this chapter, we learned how to deploy a single-node Kubernetes cluster with Minikube. Then, we installed the Kubeless framework, Kubeless CLI, and Kubeless UI on top of our Minikube cluster. Once the Kubernetes cluster and Kubeless framework were ready, we created our first Kubeless function with Python and deployed it to Kubeless. Then, we discussed multiple ways of invoking Kubeless functions, namely with the Kubeless CLI, the Kubeless UI, HTTP triggers, scheduled triggers, and PubSub triggers. Next, we discussed how to debug common error scenarios that we encounter while deploying Kubeless functions. Then, we discussed how we can use the serverless framework to deploy a Kubeless function. Finally, in the activity, we learned how we can use a Kubeless function to send messages to a Slack channel.

In the next chapter, we shall introduce OpenWhisk, and cover OpenWhisk actions and triggers.

8

Introduction to Apache OpenWhisk

Learning Objectives

By the end of this chapter, you will be able to:

- Run OpenWhisk with IBM Cloud Functions
- Create, list, invoke, update, and delete OpenWhisk actions
- Utilize and invoke OpenWhisk web actions and sequences
- Automate OpenWhisk action invocation with feeds, triggers, and rules

This chapter covers Apache OpenWhisk and how to work with its actions, triggers, and packages.

Introduction to OpenWhisk

Until now in this book, we have learned about the **Kubeless** framework, which is an open source Kubernetes-native serverless framework. We discussed the **Kubeless** architecture, and created and worked with the **Kubeless** functions and triggers. In this chapter, we shall be learning about **OpenWhisk**, which is another open source serverless framework that can be deployed on top of Kubernetes.

OpenWhisk is an open source serverless framework that is part of the Apache Software Foundation. This was originally developed at IBM with the project code name of Whisk, and later branded as **OpenWhisk** once the source code was open sourced. **Apache OpenWhisk** supports many programming languages, including Ballerina, Go, Java, JavaScript, PHP, Python, Ruby, Swift, and .NET Core. It allows us to invoke functions written in these programming languages in response to events. OpenWhisk supports many deployment options, such as on-premises and cloud infrastructure.

There are four core components of OpenWhisk:

- **Actions**: These contain application logic written in one of the supported languages that will be executed in response to events.

- **Sequences**: These link multiple actions together to create more complex processing pipelines.

- **Triggers and rules**: These automate the invocation of actions by binding them to external event sources.

- **Packages**: These combine related actions together for distribution.

The following diagram illustrates how these components interact with each other:

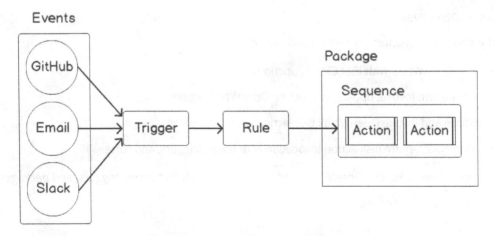

Figure 8.1: OpenWhisk core components

In the next section, we will learn how to run Apache OpenWhisk with IBM Cloud Functions.

Running OpenWhisk with IBM Cloud Functions

OpenWhisk is a framework that can be deployed on-premises or in a cloud infrastructure. However, OpenWhisk is also available as a managed service from IBM, the creator of the OpenWhisk project. **IBM Cloud Functions** is the name for the managed OpenWhisk implementation on the IBM Cloud infrastructure. This book will use this service to deploy our serverless functions because IBM Cloud Functions is the easiest way to start working with OpenWhisk. We will first begin by setting up an IBM Cloud account.

Exercise 24: Setting Up an IBM Cloud Account

In this exercise, we are going to set up an account on IBM Cloud.

> **Note**
>
> A credit card is not required to register with IBM Cloud.

The following steps will help you complete the exercise:

1. First, we need to register on IBM Cloud at https://cloud.ibm.com/registration. Then, fill in the required data and submit the form. It should look similar to the following screenshot:

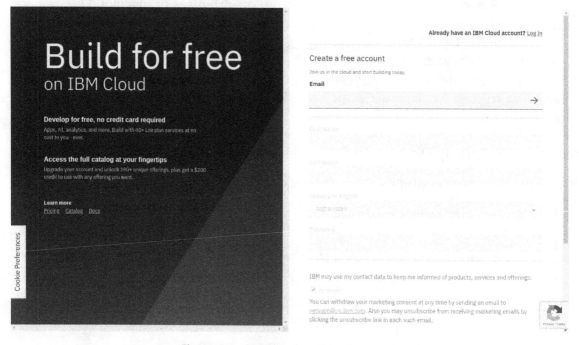

Figure 8.2: IBM Cloud registration page

Once the registration is complete, you should see the following:

Figure 8.3: IBM Cloud registration completion page

2. At this point, we will receive an email with an activation link. Click on the **Confirm account** button to activate your account, as shown in the following figure:

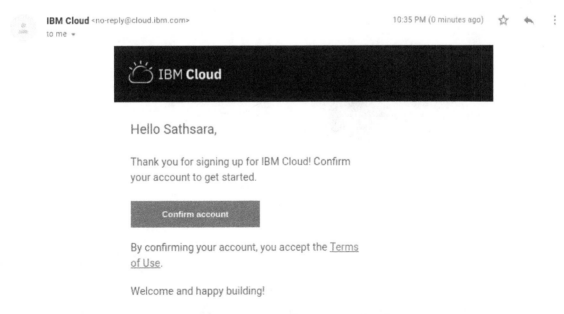

Figure 8.4: IBM Cloud Activation Email

3. When you click on the **Confirm account** button in the email, we will be taken to the IBM Cloud welcome screen. Click on the **Log in** button to log in with the credentials used to register with **IBM Cloud**, as shown in the following figure:

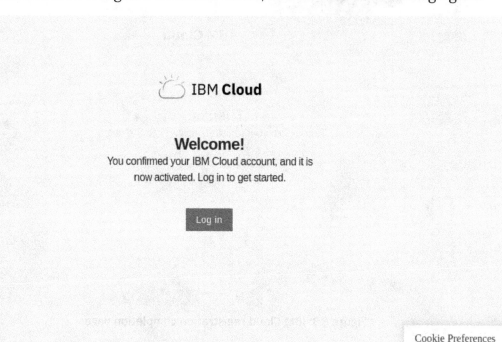

Figure 8.5: IBM Cloud welcome page

4. Acknowledge the privacy data by clicking on the **Proceed** button, as shown in the following figure:

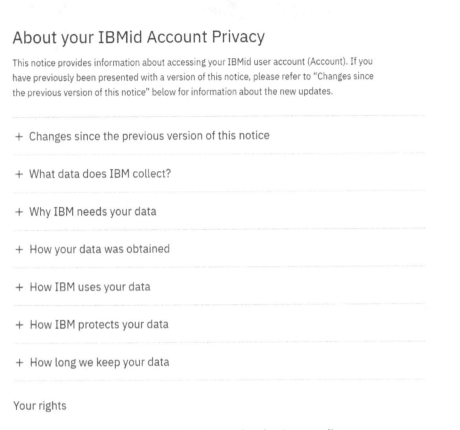

Figure 8.6: IBM Cloud privacy policy

5. You can skip the introduction video and proceed to the home page. Now you can click the **hamburger** icon ( ) in the top-left corner of the screen and select **Functions** from the menu, as shown in the following figure:

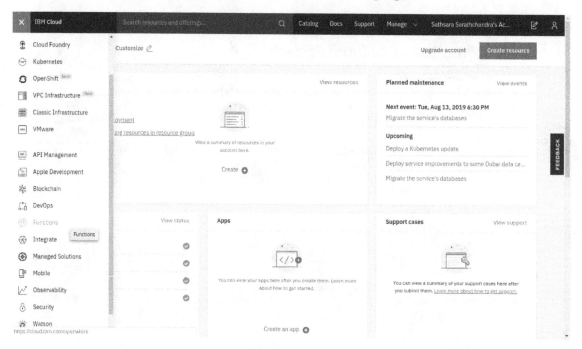

Figure 8.7: IBM Cloud home page

6. This will take you to the **IBM Cloud** functions page (https://cloud.ibm.com/functions/), as shown in the following figure:

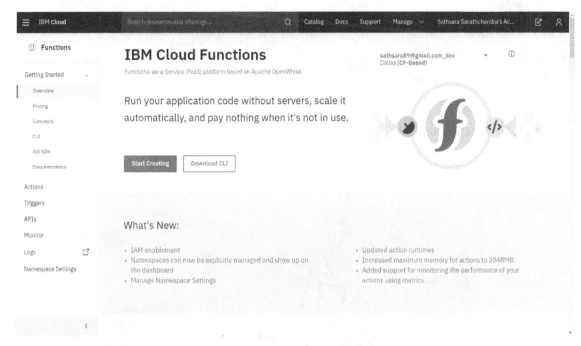

Figure 8.8: IBM Cloud Functions page

OpenWhisk offers a CLI named **wsk** to create and manage OpenWhisk entities. Next, we will install the **OpenWhisk CLI**, which will be used to interact with the OpenWhisk platform.

Exercise 25: Installing the IBM Cloud CLI

In this exercise, we are going to install the IBM Cloud CLI with the Cloud Functions plugin, which supports OpenWhisk:

1. First, we need to download the compressed IBM Cloud CLI file. Use the **curl** command with the **-Lo** flag to download the CLI, as follows:

```
$ curl -Lo ibm-cli.tar.gz  https://clis.cloud.ibm.com/download/bluemix-cli/0.18.0/linux64
```

The output should be as follows:

```
/serverless $ curl -Lo ibm-cli.tar.gz  https://clis.cloud.ibm.com/download/bluemix
-cli/0.18.0/linux64
  % Total    % Received % Xferd  Average Speed   Time    Time     Time  Current
                                 Dload  Upload   Total   Spent    Left  Speed
100   120    0   120    0     0     32       0 --:--:--  0:00:03 --:--:--    32
100 18.7M  100 18.7M    0     0    189k      0  0:01:41  0:01:41 --:--:--   154k
/serverless $
```

Figure 8.9: Downloading the IBM Cloud CLI

2. Next, we will extract the **tar.gz** file using the **tar** command as follows:

    ```
    $ tar zxvf ibm-cli.tar.gz
    ```

The output should be as follows:

```
/serverless $ tar zxvf ibm-cli.tar.gz
Bluemix_CLI/
Bluemix_CLI/bin/
Bluemix_CLI/bin/cfcli/
Bluemix_CLI/bin/cfcli/cf
Bluemix_CLI/bin/ibmcloud
Bluemix_CLI/bin/ibmcloud-analytics
Bluemix_CLI/bin/NOTICE
Bluemix_CLI/bin/LICENSE
Bluemix_CLI/autocomplete/
Bluemix_CLI/autocomplete/bash_autocomplete
Bluemix_CLI/autocomplete/zsh_autocomplete
Bluemix_CLI/install
Bluemix_CLI/uninstall
Bluemix_CLI/install_bluemix_cli
 /serverless $
```

Figure 8.10: Extracting the IBM Cloud CLI

3. Then move the **ibmcloud** executable file to the **/usr/local/bin/** path, as shown in the following command:

    ```
    $ sudo mv Bluemix_CLI/bin/ibmcloud /usr/local/bin/ibmcloud
    ```

The output should be as follows:

```
/serverless $ sudo mv Bluemix_CLI/bin/ibmcloud /usr/local/bin/ibmcloud
/serverless $
```

Figure 8.11: Moving ibmcloud to /usr/local/bin

4. Now we will log in to IBM Cloud using the IBM Cloud CLI. Execute the following command, replacing **<YOUR_EMAIL>** with the email address used when registering to IBM Cloud. Provide the email and password used during the registration phase when prompted and set the region number as **5 (us-south)**, as you can see in the following command:

```
$ ibmcloud login -a cloud.ibm.com -o "<YOUR_EMAIL>" -s "dev"
```

The output should be as follows:

```
/serverless $ ibmcloud login -a cloud.ibm.com -o "sathsara89@gmail.com" -s "dev"
API endpoint: https://cloud.ibm.com

Email> sathsara89@gmail.com

Password>
Authenticating...
OK

Targeted account Sathsara Sarathchandra's Account (478b906284304729bf729e5606ab3538)


Select a region (or press enter to skip):
1. au-syd
2. jp-tok
3. eu-de
4. eu-gb
5. us-south
6. us-east
Enter a number> 5
Targeted region us-south

Targeted Cloud Foundry (https://api.ng.bluemix.net)

Targeted org sathsara89@gmail.com

Targeted space dev


API endpoint:       https://cloud.ibm.com
Region:             us-south
User:               sathsara89@gmail.com
Account:            Sathsara Sarathchandra's Account (478b906284304729bf729e5606ab3538)
Resource group:     No resource group targeted, use 'ibmcloud target -g RESOURCE_GROUP'
CF API endpoint:    https://api.ng.bluemix.net (API version: 2.128.0)
Org:                sathsara89@gmail.com
Space:              dev
 /serverless $
```

Figure 8.12: Logging in to IBM Cloud

5. Now we will install the Cloud Functions plugin using the **ibmcloud** CLI, as shown in the following command. This plugin will be used when we work with OpenWhisk entities:

```
$ ibmcloud plugin install cloud-functions
```

The output should be as follows:

```
/serverless $ ibmcloud plugin install cloud-functions
Looking up 'cloud-functions' from repository 'IBM Cloud'...
Plug-in 'cloud-functions 1.0.32' found in repository 'IBM Cloud'
Attempting to download the binary file...
 13.08 MiB / 13.08 MiB [=======================================================] 100.00% 1m9s
13713558 bytes downloaded
Installing binary...
OK
Plug-in 'cloud-functions 1.0.32' was successfully installed into /home/sathsara/.bluemix/plugins/clou
d-functions. Use 'ibmcloud plugin show cloud-functions' to show its details.
/serverless $
```

Figure 8.13: Installing Cloud Functions

6. Next, we will provide the target organization (the organization name is your email address) and the space (which defaults to **dev**) using the following command:

```
$ ibmcloud target -o <YOUR_EMAIL> -s dev
```

The output should be as follows:

```
/serverless $ ibmcloud target -o sathsara89@gmail.com -s dev
Targeted org sathsara89@gmail.com

Targeted space dev



API endpoint:       https://cloud.ibm.com
Region:             us-south
User:               sathsara89@gmail.com
Account:            Sathsara Sarathchandra's Account (478b906284304729bf729e5606ab3538)
Resource group:     No resource group targeted, use 'ibmcloud target -g RESOURCE_GROUP'
CF API endpoint:    https://api.ng.bluemix.net (API version: 2.128.0)
Org:                sathsara89@gmail.com
Space:              dev
/serverless $
```

Figure 8.14: Setting the target organization and space

7. Now the configurations are done. We can use **ibmcloud wsk** to interact with OpenWhisk entities, as shown in the following command:

```
$ ibmcloud wsk action list
```

The output should be as follows:

```
/serverless $ ibmcloud wsk action list
actions
/serverless $
```

Figure 8.15: Listing OpenWhisk actions

> **Note**
>
> In this book, we will be using the **wsk** command to manage OpenWhisk entities instead of the **ibmcloud wsk** command provided by IBM Cloud Functions. Both of them provide the same functionality. The only difference is that **wsk** is the standard CLI for OpenWhisk and **ibmcloud fn** is from the IBM Cloud Functions plugin.

8. Let's create a Linux alias, **wsk="ibmcloud wsk"**. First, open the **~/.bashrc** file with your favorite text editor. In the following command, we will be using the **vim** text editor to open the file:

```
vim ~/.bashrc
```

Add the following line at the end of the file:

```
alias wsk="ibmcloud wsk"
```

9. Source the **~/.bashrc** file to apply the changes, as shown in the following command:

```
$ source ~/.bashrc
```

The output should be as follows:

```
/serverless $ source ~/.bashrc
```

Figure 8.16: Sourcing the bashrc file

10. Now we should be able to invoke OpenWhisk with the **wsk** command. Execute the following command to verify the installation:

```
$ wsk --help
```

This will print the help page of the **wsk** command, as shown in the following figure:

```
/serverless $ wsk --help
NAME:
cloud-functions, wsk, functions, fn - IBM Cloud CLI plug-in for IBM Cloud Functions

USAGE:
Issue 'ibmcloud cloud-functions' for detailed help

/serverless $
```

Figure 8.17: Output for wsk command

Now, let's proceed to the next section on OpenWhisk actions.

OpenWhisk Actions

In OpenWhisk, actions are code snippets written by developers that will be executed in response to events. These actions can be written in any programming language supported by OpenWhisk:

- Ballerina

- Go

- Java

- JavaScript

- PHP

- Python

- Ruby

- Swift

- .NET Core

Also, we can use a custom Docker image if our preferred language runtime is not supported by OpenWhisk yet. These actions will receive a JSON object as input, then perform the necessary processing within the action, and finally return a JSON object with the processed results. In the following sections, we will focus on how to write, create, list, invoke, update, and delete OpenWhisk actions using the **wsk** CLI.

Writing Actions for OpenWhisk

When writing OpenWhisk actions with your preferred language, there are few standards that you must follow. They are as follows:

- Each action should have a function named **main**, which is the entry point of the action. The source code can have additional functions, but the **main** function will be executed once the action is triggered.

- The function must return a JSON object as the response.

> **Note**
>
> In this chapter, we will be mainly using JavaScript to create the function code.

Let's look at an example in which we create a JavaScript code (**random-number.js**) that conforms to the rules we've just mentioned. This is a simple function that generates a random number between 0 to 1 and returns the generated number as the function's response:

```
function main() {
    var randomNumber = Math.random();
    return { number: randomNumber };
}
```

Here is a PHP function that conforms to the rules:

```
<?php
function main()
{
    $randomNumber = rand();
    return ["number" => $randomNumber];
}
```

Creating Actions on the OpenWhisk Framework

Now it's time to create an action on the OpenWhisk framework by using the action code written in the previous section. We will be using the **wsk action create** command, which has the following format:

```
$ wsk action create <action-name> <action-file-name>
```

<action-name> is the identifier of the action. It should be unique to prevent naming conflicts. **<action-file-name>** is the file that contains the source code of the action. Let's execute the following command to create an OpenWhisk action named **randomNumber** using the action source code in the **random-number.js** file:

```
$ wsk action create randomNumber random-number.js
```

The output we receive from this command looks like this:

```
/serverless $ wsk action create randomNumber random-number.js
ok: created action randomNumber
```

Figure 8.18: Creating a randomNumber action

As we can see in the output, whenever an action is successfully created, the CLI prompt appropriately informs the reader of the status of the action.

The OpenWhisk framework will determine the runtime to execute the action based on the extension of the source code file. In the preceding scenario, the Node.js **10** runtime will be selected for the provided **.js** file. You can use the **--kind** flag with the **wsk action create** command if you want to override the default runtime selected by the OpenWhisk framework:

```
$ wsk action create secondRandomNumber random-number.js --kind nodejs:8
```

The output should be as follows:

```
/serverless $ wsk action create secondRandomNumber random-number.js --kind nodejs:8
ok: created action secondRandomNumber
/serverless $
```

Figure 8.19: Creating a randomNumber action with the nodejs:8 runtime

The preceding output indicates that **secondRandomNumber** was created successfully. At the end of this section, we have deployed two OpenWhisk actions.

Having learned how to create actions on the OpenWhisk framework, next we shall work on listing OpenWhisk actions.

Listing OpenWhisk Actions

In this section, we are going to list the OpenWhisk actions in our environment with the **wsk** CLI using the following command:

```
$ wsk action list
```

The output should be as follows:

```
/serverless $ wsk action list
actions
/sathsara89@gmail.com_dev/secondRandomNumber                          private nodejs:8
/sathsara89@gmail.com_dev/randomNumber                                private nodejs:10
 /serverless $
```

Figure 8.20: Listing all actions

From the preceding output, we can see the two actions we created earlier with the names **randomNumber** and **secondRandomNumber**. The **wsk action list** command lists the actions and the runtime of these actions, such as **nodejs:8** or **nodejs:10**. By default, the action list will be sorted based on the last update time, so the most recently updated action will be at the top of the list. If we want the list to be sorted alphabetically, we can use the **--name-sort** (or **-n**) flag, as shown in the following command:

```
$ wsk action list --name-sort
```

The output should be as follows:

```
/serverless $ wsk action list --name-sort
actions
/sathsara89@gmail.com_dev/randomNumber                                private nodejs:10
/sathsara89@gmail.com_dev/secondRandomNumber                          private nodejs:8
 /serverless $
```

Figure 8.21: Listing all actions sorted by name in ascending order

Invoking OpenWhisk Actions

Now our actions are ready to be invoked. OpenWhisk actions can be invoked in two ways using the **wsk** CLI:

- Request-response
- Fire-and-forget

The **request-response** method is synchronous; the action invocation will wait until the results are available. On the other hand, the **fire-and-forget** method is asynchronous. This will return an ID called the activation ID, which can be used later to get the results.

Here is the standard format of the **wsk** command to invoke the action:

```
$ wsk action invoke <action-name>
```

Request-Response Invocation Method

In the **request-response** method, the `wsk action invoke` command is used with the `--blocking` (or `-b`) flag, which asks the `wsk` CLI to wait for the invocation results:

```
$ wsk action invoke randomNumber --blocking
```

The preceding command will return the following output in the terminal, which contains the result returned from the method with other metadata about the method invocation:

```
ok: invoked /_/randomNumber with id 002738b1acee4abba738b1aceedabb60
{
    "activationId": "002738b1acee4abba738b1aceedabb60",
    "annotations": [
        {
            "key": "path",
            "value": "your_email_address_dev/randomNumber"
        },
        {
            "key": "waitTime",
            "value": 79
        },
        {
            "key": "kind",
            "value": "nodejs:10"
        },
        {
            "key": "timeout",
            "value": false
        },
```

```
    {
        "key": "limits",
        "value": {
            "concurrency": 1,
            "logs": 10,
            "memory": 256,
            "timeout": 60000
        }
    },
    {
        "key": "initTime",
        "value": 39
    }
],
"duration": 46,
"end": 1564829766237,
"logs": [],
"name": "randomNumber",
"namespace": "your_email_address_dev",
"publish": false,
"response": {
    "result": {
        "number": 0.6488215545330562
    },
    "status": "success",
    "success": true
},
"start": 1564829766191,
"subject": "your_email_address",
"version": "0.0.1"
}
```

We can see the output (`"number": 0.6488215545330562`) returned by the main function within the **response** section of the returned JSON object. This is the random number generated by the JavaScript function that we wrote previously. The returned JSON object contains an activation ID (`"activationId": "002738b1acee4abba738b1aceedabb60"`), which we can use to get the results later. This output includes other important values, such as the action invocation status (`"status": "success"`), the start time (`"start": 156482976619`), the end time (`"end": 1564829766237`), and the execution duration (`"duration": 46`) of this action.

> **Note**
>
> We will discuss how to get the activation results using **activationId** in the **Fire-and-Forget Invocation Method** section.

We can use the **--result** (or **-r**) flag if we need to get the result of the action without the other metadata, as shown in the following code:

```
$ wsk action invoke randomNumber --result
```

The output should be as follows:

```
/serverless $ wsk action invoke randomNumber --result
{
    "number": 0.03875445894018004
}
/serverless $
```

Figure 8.22: Invoking the randomNumber action using the request-and-response method

Fire-and-Forget Invocation Method

Action invocations with the **fire-and-forget** method do not wait for the result of the action. Instead, they return an activation ID that we can use to get the results of the action. This invocation method uses a similar command to the request-response method but without the **--blocking** (or **-b**) flag:

```
$ wsk action invoke randomNumber
```

The output should be as follows:

```
/serverless $ wsk action invoke randomNumber
ok: invoked /_/randomNumber with id 2b90ade473e443bc90ade473e4b3bcff
/serverless $
```

Figure 8.23: Invoking the randomNumber action using the fire-and-forget method

In the preceding result, we can see the returned activation ID of **2b90ade473e443bc90ade473e4b3bcff** (please note that your activation ID will be different).

Now we can use the **wsk activation get** command to get the results for a given activation ID:

```
$ wsk activation get "<activation_id>"
```

You need to replace **<activation_id>** with the value returned when you invoked the function using the **wsk action invoke** command:

```
$ wsk activation get 2b90ade473e443bc90ade473e4b3bcff
ok: got activation 2b90ade473e443bc90ade473e4b3bcff
{
    "namespace": "sathsara89@gmail.com_dev",
    "name": "randomNumber",
    "version": "0.0.2",
    "subject": "sathsara89@gmail.com",
    "activationId": "2b90ade473e443bc90ade473e4b3bcff",
    "start": 1564832684116,
    "end": 1564832684171,
    "duration": 55,
    "statusCode": 0,
    "response": {
        "status": "success",
        "statusCode": 0,
        "success": true,
        "result": {
            "number": 0.05105974715780626
        }
    },
    "logs": [],
    "annotations": [
        {
            "key": "path",
            "value": "sathsara89@gmail.com_dev/randomNumber"
```

```
        },
        {
            "key": "waitTime",
            "value": 126
        },
        {
            "key": "kind",
            "value": "nodejs:10"
        },
        {
            "key": "timeout",
            "value": false
        },
        {
            "key": "limits",
            "value": {
                "concurrency": 1,
                "logs": 10,
                "memory": 256,
                "timeout": 60000
            }
        },
        {
            "key": "initTime",
            "value": 41
        }
    ],
    "publish": false
}
```

If you would prefer to retrieve only a summary of the activation, the **--summary** (or **-s**) flag should be provided with the **wsk activation get** command:

```
$ wsk activation get <activation-id> --summary
```

The output from the preceding command will print a summary of the activation details, as shown in the following screenshot:

```
/serverless $ wsk activation get 2b90ade473e443bc90ade473e4b3bcff --summary
activation result for '/sathsara89@gmail.com_dev/randomNumber' (success at 2019-08-
03 17:14:44 +0530 +0530)
{
    "number": 0.05105974715780626
}
```

Figure 8.24: The activation summary

The **wsk activation result** command returns only the results of the action, omitting any metadata:

```
$ wsk activation result <activation-id>
```

The output should be as follows:

```
/serverless $ wsk activation result 2b90ade473e443bc90ade473e4b3bcff
{
    "number": 0.05105974715780626
}
```

Figure 8.25: The activation result

The **wsk activation list** command can be used to list all the activations:

```
$ wsk activation list
```

The output should be as follows:

```
/serverless $ wsk activation list
Datetime          Activation ID                        Kind       Start Duration   Status
 Entity
2019-08-03 17:14:44 2b90ade473e443bc90ade473e4b3bcff nodejs:10 cold  55ms          success
 sathsara89...com_dev/randomNumber:0.0.2
2019-08-03 16:45:38 538319e6054f44a78319e6054fc4a73a nodejs:10 cold  45ms          success
 sathsara89...com_dev/randomNumber:0.0.2
2019-08-03 16:35:19 3c4c192c40034c8a8c192c4003ac8a34 nodejs:10 cold  47ms          success
 sathsara89...com_dev/randomNumber:0.0.2
```

Figure 8.26: Listing activations

The preceding command returns a list of activations sorted by the **datetime** of the activation's invocation. The following table describes the information provided by each column:

Column	Description
Datetime	Date and time of the action invocation.
Activation ID	Activation ID for the action invocation.
Kind	Language runtime.
Start	Start method of the runtime container.
Duration	Number of milliseconds taken to complete the action.
Status	Outcome of the action. Possible values are success, application error, action developer error, and whisk internal error.
Entity	Fully qualified name of the action.

Figure 8.27: Column description

Updating OpenWhisk Actions

In this section, we will learn how to update the source code of an action once it has been created on the OpenWhisk platform. We might want to update the action for several reasons. There could be a bug in the code, or we may simply want to enhance the code. The **wsk action update** command can be used to update an OpenWhisk action using the **wsk** CLI:

```
$ wsk action update <action-name> <action-file-name>
```

We already have an action that prints a random number, which is defined in the **random-number.js** function. This function prints a value between 0 and 1, but what if we want to print a random number between 1 and 100? This can now be done using the following code:

```
function main() {
    var randomNumber = Math.floor((Math.random() * 100) + 1);
    return { number: randomNumber };
}
```

Then, we can execute the **wsk action update** command to update the **randomNumber** action:

```
$ wsk action update randomNumber random-number.js
```

The output should be as follows:

```
/serverless $ wsk action update randomNumber random-number.js
ok: updated action randomNumber
/serverless $
```

Figure 8.28: Updating the randomNumber action

Now we can verify the result of the updated action by executing the following command:

```
$ wsk action invoke randomNumber --result
```

```
/serverless $ wsk action invoke randomNumber --result
{
    "number": 54
}
/serverless $
```

Figure 8.29: Invoking the randomNumber action

As we can see, the **randomNumber** action has returned a number between 1 to 100. We can invoke the **randomNumber** function number multiple times to verify that it returns an output number between 1 and 100.

Deleting OpenWhisk Actions

In this section, we will discuss how to delete an OpenWhisk action. The **wsk action delete** command is used to delete OpenWhisk actions:

```
$ wsk action delete <action-name>
```

Let's execute the **wsk action delete** command to delete the **randomNumber** and **secondRandomNumber** actions we created in the preceding sections:

```
$ wsk action delete randomNumber
```

```
$ wsk action delete secondRandomNumber
```

The output should be as follows:

```
/serverless $ wsk action delete randomNumber
ok: deleted action randomNumber
/serverless $
/serverless $ wsk action delete secondRandomNumber
ok: deleted action secondRandomNumber
/serverless $
```

Figure 8.30: Deleting the randomNumber and secondRandomNumber actions

Now we have learned how to write, create, list, invoke, update, and delete OpenWhisk actions. Let's move on to an exercise in which you will create your first OpenWhisk action.

Exercise 26: Creating Your First OpenWhisk Action

In this exercise, we will first create a JavaScript function that receives exam marks as input and returns the exam results using the following criteria:

- Return **Pass** if marks are equal to or above 60.

- Return **Fail** if marks are below 60.

Next, we will create an action named **examResults** in the OpenWhisk framework with the previously mentioned JavaScript function code. Then, we will invoke the action to verify that it returns the results as expected. Once the action response is verified, we will update the action to return the exam grade with the results based on the following criteria:

- Return **Pass with grade A** if marks are equal to or above 80.

- Return **Pass with grade B** if marks are equal to or above 70.

- Return **Pass with grade C** if marks are equal to or above 60.

- Return **Fail** if marks are below 60.

Again, we will invoke the action to verify the results and finally delete the action.

> **Note**
>
> The code files for this exercise can be found at https://github.com/TrainingByPackt/ Serverless-Architectures-with-Kubernetes/tree/master/Lesson08/Exercise26.

Perform the following steps to complete the exercise:

1. First, let's create a JavaScript function in the **exam-result.js** file that will return the exam results based on the provided exam marks:

```
function main(params) {
    var examResult = '';

    if (params.examMarks < 0 || params.examMarks > 100) {
        examResult = 'ERROR: invalid exam mark';
    } else if (params.examMarks >= 60) {
```

```
      examResult = 'Pass';
    } else {
      examResult = 'Fail';
    }

    return { result: examResult };
  }
```

2. Now, let's create the OpenWhisk action named **examResult** from the **exam-result. js** file created in *step* 1:

```
$ wsk action create examResult exam-result.js
```

The output should be as follows:

```
/serverless $ wsk action create examResult exam-result.js
ok: created action examResult
/serverless $
```

Figure 8.31: Creating the examResult action

3. Once the action creation is successful, we can invoke the **examResult** action by sending a value between 0 to 100 to the **examMarks** parameter:

```
$ wsk action invoke examResult --param examMarks 72 -result
```

The output should be as follows:

```
/serverless $ wsk action invoke examResult --param examMarkes 72 --result
{
    "result": "Pass"
}
/serverless $
```

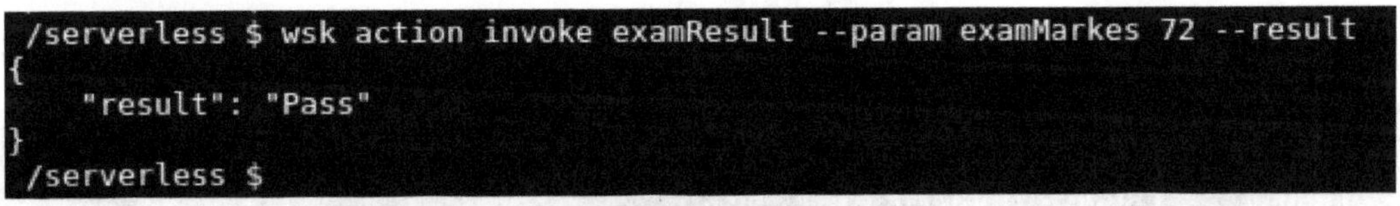

Figure 8.32: Invoking the examResult action

4. At this step, we are going to create a new JavaScript function in **exam-result-02.js** to return the exam results with the **grade** parameter:

```
function main(params) {
    var examResult = '';

    if (params.examMarks < 0 || params.examMarks > 100) {
        examResult = 'ERROR: invalid exam mark';
    } else if (params.examMarks > 80) {
        examResult = 'Pass with grade A';
    } else if (params.examMarks > 70) {
        examResult = 'Pass with grade B';
    } else if (params.examMarks > 60) {
```

```
        examResult = 'Pass with grade C';
    } else {
        examResult = 'Fail';
    }

    return { result: examResult };
}
```

5. Now, let's update the OpenWhisk action with the previously updated **exam-result-02.js** file:

```
$ wsk action update examResult exam-result-02.js
```

The output should be as follows:

```
/serverless $ wsk action update examResult exam-result-02.js
ok: updated action examResult
/serverless $
```

Figure 8.33: Updating the examResult action

6. Once the action is updated, we can invoke the action multiple times with different exam marks as parameters to verify the functionality:

```
$ wsk action invoke examResult --param examMarks 150 --result
$ wsk action invoke examResult --param examMarks 75 --result
$ wsk action invoke examResult --param examMarks 42 -result
```

The output should be as follows:

```
/serverless $ wsk action invoke examResult --param examMarkes 150 --result
{
    "result": "ERROR: invalid exam mark"
}
/serverless $
/serverless $ wsk action invoke examResult --param examMarkes 75 --result
{
    "result": "Pass with grade B"
}
/serverless $
/serverless $ wsk action invoke examResult --param examMarkes 42 --result
{
    "result": "Fail"
}
/serverless $
```

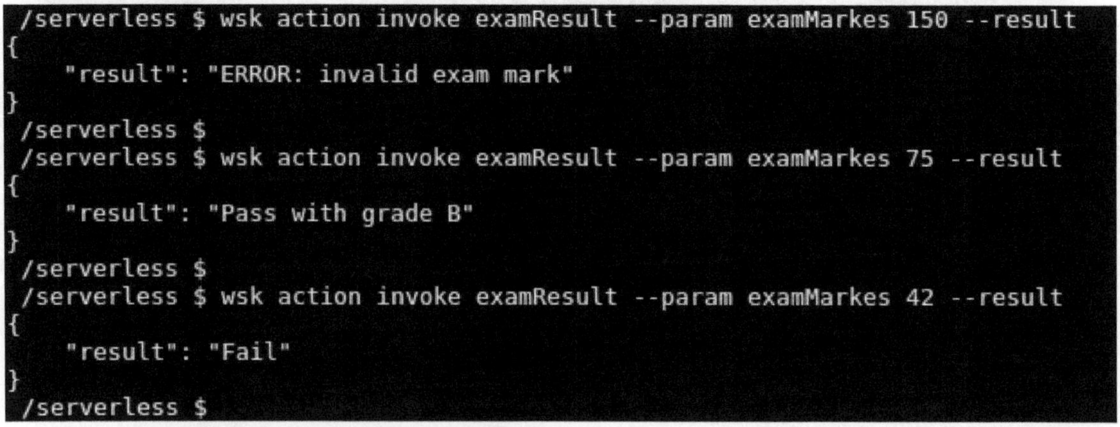

Figure 8.34: Invoking the examResult action with different parameter values

7. Finally, we will delete the **examResult** action:

```
$ wsk action delete examResult
```

The output should be as follows:

```
/serverless $ wsk action delete examResult
ok: deleted action examResult
/serverless $
```

Figure 8.35: Deleting the examResult action

In this exercise, we learned how to create a JavaScript function that follows the standards for OpenWhisk actions. Then we created the action and invoked it with the **wsk** CLI. After that, we changed the logic of the function code and updated the action with the latest function code. Finally, we performed a cleanup by deleting the action.

OpenWhisk Sequences

In OpenWhisk, and in general with programming, functions (known as actions in OpenWhisk) are expected to perform a single focused task. This will help to reduce code duplication by reusing the same function code. But creating complex applications requires connecting multiple actions together to achieve the desired result. OpenWhisk sequences are used to chain multiple OpenWhisk actions (which can be in different programming language runtimes) together and create more complex processing pipelines.

The following diagram illustrates how a sequence can be constructed by chaining multiple actions:

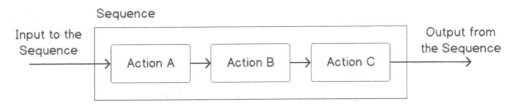

Figure 8.36: OpenWhisk sequence

We can pass parameters (if any) to the sequence, which will be used as the input for the first action. Then, the output of each action will be the input for the next action, and the final action of the sequence will return its result as the output of the sequence. Actions written in different programming languages can also be chained together with sequences.

Sequences can be created using the **wsk action create** command with the **--sequence** flag to provide a comma-separated list of actions to invoke:

```
$ wsk action create <sequence-name> --sequence <action-01>,<action-02>
```

In order to demonstrate the concept of OpenWhisk sequences, we will be creating a sequence named **login** in the following section, which consists of two actions, named **authentication** and **authorization**. The **login** action will be invoked when a user tries to log in to the application. If the user provides correct credentials at login, they can view all the content on the system. But if the user fails to provide the correct login credentials, they can only view the public content of the system.

> **Note**
>
> Authentication is verifying the user's identity, and authorization is granting the required level of access to the system.

First, let's create the **authentication.js** function. This function will receive two parameters, named **username** and **password**. If the username and password match the hardcoded values of **admin** (for the **username** parameter) and **openwhisk** (for the **password** parameter), the function will return **authenticationResult** as **true**. Otherwise, **authenticationResult** will be **false**:

```
function main(params) {
    var authenticationResult = '';

    if (params.username == 'admin' && params.password == 'openwhisk') {
        authenticationResult = 'true';
    } else {
        authenticationResult = 'false';
    }

    return { authenticationSuccess: authenticationResult };
}
```

The next function is **authorization.js**, which takes the **authenticationSuccess** value as input and displays appropriate content to the users. If the user is successfully authenticated (**authenticationSuccess = true**), the **'Authentication Success! You can view all content'** message will be displayed. If authentication failed (**authenticationSuccess != true**), the **'Authentication Failed! You can view only public content'** message will be displayed:

```
function main(params) {
    var contentMessage = '';

    if (params.authenticationSuccess == "true") {
        contentMessage = 'Authentication Success! You can view all content';
    } else {
        contentMessage = 'Authentication Failed! You can view only public
content';
    }

    return { content: contentMessage };
}
```

Now, let's deploy both actions with the **wsk action create** command:

```
$ wsk action create authentication authentication.js
$ wsk action create authorization authorization.js
```

The output should be as follows:

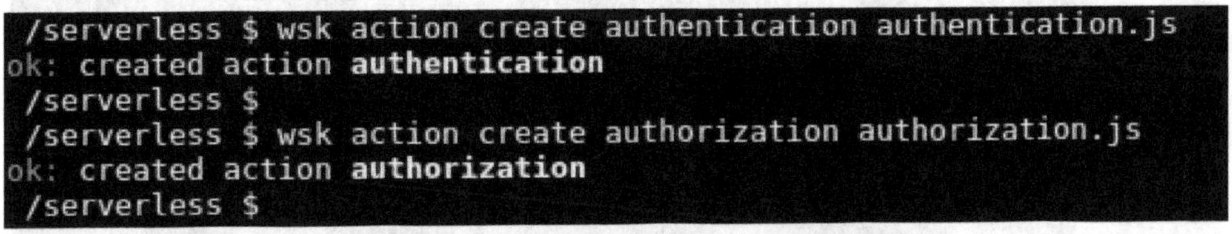

Figure 8.37: Creating authentication and authorization actions

Now both authentication and authorization actions are ready. Let's create a sequence named **login** by combining **authentication** and **authorization** actions:

```
$ wsk action create login --sequence authentication,authorization
```

The output should be as follows:

```
/serverless $ wsk action create login --sequence authentication,authorization
ok: created action login
/serverless $
```

Figure 8.38: Creating a login sequence

Now it's time to test the login sequence. First, we will invoke the login sequence by sending the correct credentials (**username** = **admin** and **password** = **openwhisk**):

```
$ wsk action invoke login --param username admin --param password openwhisk
-result
```

The output should be as follows:

```
/serverless $ wsk action invoke login --param username admin --param
password openwhisk --result
{
    "content": "Authentication Success! You can view all content"
}
/serverless $
```

Figure 8.39: Invoking the login sequence with valid credentials

The expected result for a successful login is shown in the preceding screenshot. Now, let's invoke the login sequence by sending incorrect credentials (**username** = **hacker** and **password** = **hacker**). This time we expect to receive an authentication failure message:

```
$ wsk action invoke login --param username hacker --param password hacker -
result
```

The output should be as follows:

```
/serverless $ wsk action invoke login --param username hacker
--param password hacker --result
{
    "content": "Authentication Failed! You can view only public
content"
}
/serverless $
```

Figure 8.40: Invoking the login sequence with invalid credentials

In this section, we learned about OpenWhisk sequences. We created multiple actions, linked them together using a sequence, and invoked the sequence by sending the required parameters.

Exercise 27: Creating OpenWhisk Sequences

In this exercise, we will create a sequence with two actions written in different languages. The first action, written in Python, receives the marks for two exams and returns the average marks. The second action, written in JavaScript, receives the average marks and returns either pass or fail.

> **Note**
>
> The code files for this exercise can be found at https://github.com/TrainingByPackt/ Serverless-Architectures-with-Kubernetes/tree/master/Lesson08/Exercise27.

The following steps will help you complete the exercise:

1. Write the first function (**calculate-average.py**), which calculates the average marks. This function will receive the marks for two exams as the input:

```python
def main(params):
    examOneMarks = params.get("examOneMarks")
    examTwoMarks = params.get("examTwoMarks")

    fullMarks = examOneMarks + examTwoMarks
    averageMarks =  fullMarks / 2

    return {"averageMarks": averageMarks}
```

2. Create an OpenWhisk action named **calculateAverage** from **calculate-average.py**:

```
$ wsk action create calculateAverage calculate-average.py
```

The output should be as follows:

```
/serverless $ wsk action create calculateAverage calculate-average.py
ok: created action calculateAverage
/serverless $
```

Figure 8.41: Creating the calculateAverage action

3. Check that the **calculateAverage** action is working as expected by invoking it:

```
$ wsk action invoke calculateAverage --param examOneMarks 82 --param
examTwoMarks 68 -result
```

4. The output should be as follows:

```
/serverless $ wsk action invoke calculateAverage --param examOneMarks 82 --param
examTwoMarks 68 --result
{
    "averageMarks": 75
}
/serverless $
```

Figure 8.42: Invoking the calculateAverage action

5. Create the second function (**show-result.js**), which returns the exam result (**Pass** or **Fail**) based on the average marks. The exam results will be based on the logic as marks less than 0 or greater than 100 will return an **Error**; marks greater than or equal to 60 will return **Pass**; else it will return **Fail**.

The code would be as follows:

```
function main(params) {
    var examResult = '';

    if (params.averageMarks < 0 || params.averageMarks > 100) {
        examResult = 'ERROR: invalid average exam mark';
    } else if (params.averageMarks >= 60) {
        examResult = 'Pass';
    } else {
        examResult = 'Fail';
    }

    return { result: examResult };
}
```

6. Create an OpenWhisk action named **showResult** from **show-result.js**:

```
$ wsk action create showResult show-result.js
```

The output should be as follows:

```
/serverless $ wsk action create showResult show-result.js
ok: created action showResult
/serverless $
```

Figure 8.43: Creating the showResult action

7. Check that the **showResult** action is working as expected by invoking it:

   ```
   $ wsk action invoke showResult --param averageMarks 75 -result
   ```

   The output should be as follows:

   ```
   /serverless $ wsk action invoke showResult --param averageMarks 75 --result
   {
       "result": "Pass"
   }
   /serverless $
   ```

   Figure 8.44: Invoking the showResult action

8. Create the **getExamResults** sequence with the **calculateAverage** and **showResult** actions:

   ```
   $ wsk action create getExamResults --sequence calculateAverage,showResult
   ```

   The output should be as follows:

   ```
   /serverless $ wsk action create getExamResults --sequence calculateAverage,
   showResult
   ok: created action getExamResults
   /serverless $
   ```

   Figure 8.45: Creating the getExamResults sequence

9. Invoke the **getExamResults** sequence and verify the result:

   ```
   $ wsk action invoke getExamResults --param examOneMarks 82 --param
   examTwoMarks 68 -result
   ```

   The output should be as follows:

   ```
   /serverless $ wsk action invoke getExamResults --param examOneMarks 82
   --param examTwoMarks 68 --result
   {
       "result": "Pass"
   }
   /serverless $
   ```

   Figure 8.46: Invoking the getExamResults sequence

OpenWhisk Web Actions

So far, we have invoked our OpenWhisk actions through the `wsk` CLI with the `wsk action invoke` command. Even though this invocation method is very simple and suits us well during the development stage, the `wsk` CLI cannot be used by external parties, such as external applications or users, to invoke our actions. As a solution, we can use OpenWhisk web actions, which will allow actions to be invoked through HTTP requests with a publicly available URL.

OpenWhisk standard actions require authentication when invoking the action (this is handled internally by the `wsk` CLI) and must return a JSON payload as the response. In contrast, web actions can be invoked without authentication and can return additional information, such as HTTP headers and non-JSON payloads such as HTML and binary data.

An OpenWhisk standard action can be converted to a web action by sending the `--web true` (or `--web yes`) flag when creating (`wsk action create`) or updating (`wsk action update`) actions with the `wsk` CLI.

Let's create a JavaScript function (`web-action.js`) to be invoked as a web action. This function will return **Hello, Stranger** if we did not pass a value for the name parameter and returns `Hello` with the name when we pass a value for the `name` parameter with the web action URL:

```
function main(params) {
    var helloMessage = ''

    if (params.name) {
        helloMessage = 'Hello, ' + params.name;
    } else {
        helloMessage = 'Hello, Stranger';
    }

    return { result: helloMessage };
}
```

Now we can create a web action by sending the `--web true` flag with the `wsk action create` command:

```
$ wsk action create myWebAction web-action.js --web true
```

The output should be as follows:

```
/serverless $ wsk action create myWebAction web-action.js --web true
ok: created action myWebAction
/serverless $
```

Figure 8.47: Creating myWebAction as a web action

Then, we can invoke the created web action using the web action URL. The general format of a web action URL is as follows:

```
https://{APIHOST}/api/v1/web/{QUALIFIED_ACTION_NAME}.{EXT}
```

Let's discuss each component of this URL:

- **APIHOST**: The **APIHOST** value for IBM Cloud Functions is **openwhisk.ng.bluemix.net**.

- **QUALIFIED_ACTION_NAME**: The fully qualified name of the web action in **<namespace>/<package-name>/<action-name>** format. If the action is not in a named **package**, use **default** as the value of **<package-name>**.

- **EXT**: The extension that represents the expected response type of the web action.

We can use the **--url** flag with the **wsk action get** command to retrieve the URL of a web action:

```
$ wsk action get myWebAction -url
```

The output should be as follows:

```
/serverless $ wsk action get myWebAction --url
ok: got action myWebAction
https://us-south.functions.cloud.ibm.com/api/v1/web/sathsara89%40gmail.com_dev/defa
ult/myWebAction
/serverless $
```

Figure 8.48: Retrieving the public URL of myWebAction

We need to append **.json** as an extension to the preceding URL since our web action is responding with a JSON payload. Now we can either open this URL in a web browser or use the **curl** command to retrieve the output.

Let's invoke in the preceding URL using a web browser:

Figure 8.49: Invoking myWebAction from a web browser without the name parameter

Hello, Stranger is the expected response because we did not pass a value for the **name** parameter in the query.

Now, let's invoke the same URL by appending **?name=OpenWhisk** at the end of the URL:

https://us-south.functions.cloud.ibm.com/api/v1/web/sathsara89%40gmail.com_dev/default/myWebAction.json?name=OpenWhisk

The output should be as follows:

Figure 8.50: Invoking myWebAction from a web browser with the name parameter

We can invoke the same URL as a **curl** request with the following command:

```
$ curl https://us-south.functions.cloud.ibm.com/api/v1/web/
sathsara89%40gmail.com_dev/default/myWebAction.json?name=OpenWhisk
```

The output should be as follows:

```
/serverless $ curl https://us-south.functions.cloud.ibm.com/api/v1/web/sathsara89%
40gmail.com_dev/default/myWebAction.json?name=OpenWhisk
{
  "result": "Hello, OpenWhisk"
} /serverless $
```

Figure 8.51: Invoking myWebAction as a curl command with the name parameter

This command will produce the same output as we saw in the web browser.

As we discussed previously, OpenWhisk web actions can be configured to return additional information including HTTP headers, HTTP status codes, and body content of different types using one or more of the following fields in the JSON response:

- **headers**: This field is used to send HTTP headers in the response. An example would be to send `Content-Type` as `text/html`.

- **statusCode**: This will send a valid HTTP response code. The status code of **200 OK** will be sent unless specified explicitly.

- **body**: This contains the response content, which is either plain text, a JSON object or array, or a base64-encoded string for binary data.

Now we will update the **web-action.js** function to send the response in the format we discussed earlier:

```
function main(params) {
    var helloMessage = ''

    if (params.name) {
        username = params.name;
        httpResponseCode = 200;
    } else {
        username = 'Stranger';
        httpResponseCode = 400;
    }


    var htmlMessage = '<html><body><h3>' + 'Hello, ' + username + '</h3></
body></html>';


    return {
```

```
        headers: {
            'Set-Cookie': 'Username=' + username + '; Max-Age=3600',
            'Content-Type': 'text/html'
        },
        statusCode: httpResponseCode,
        body: htmlMessage
    };
}
```

Then, we will update the **myWebAction** action with the latest function code:

```
$ wsk action update myWebAction web-action.js
```

The output should be as follows:

```
/serverless $ wsk action update myWebAction web-action.js
ok: updated action myWebAction
/serverless $
```

Figure 8.52: Updating myWebAction

Let's invoke the updated action with the following **curl** command. We will provide **name=OpenWhisk** as a query parameter in the URL. Also, the **-v** option is used to print verbose output, which will help us to verify the fields we added to the response:

```
$ curl https://us-south.functions.cloud.ibm.com/api/v1/web/
sathsara89%40gmail.com_dev/default/myWebAction.http?name=OpenWhisk -v
```

Here is the response we received after the preceding **curl** command:

```
*     Trying 104.17.9.194...
* Connected to us-south.functions.cloud.ibm.com (104.17.9.194) port 443 (#0)
* * *
* * *
> GET /api/v1/web/sathsara89%40gmail.com_dev/default/myWebAction.
http?name=OpenWhisk HTTP/1.1
> Host: us-south.functions.cloud.ibm.com
> User-Agent: curl/7.47.0
> Accept: */*
```

```
>
< HTTP/1.1 200 OK
< Date: Sun, 04 Aug 2019 16:32:56 GMT
< Content-Type: text/html; charset=UTF-8
< Transfer-Encoding: chunked
< Connection: keep-alive
< Set-Cookie: __cfduid=d1cb4dec494fb11bd8b60a225c218b3101564936375;
expires=Mon, 03-Aug-20 16:32:55 GMT; path=/; domain=.functions.cloud.ibm.
com; HttpOnly
< X-Request-ID: 7dbce6e92b0a90e313d47e0c2afe203b
< Access-Control-Allow-Origin: *
< Access-Control-Allow-Methods: OPTIONS, GET, DELETE, POST, PUT, HEAD, PATCH
< Access-Control-Allow-Headers: Authorization, Origin, X-Requested-With,
Content-Type, Accept, User-Agent
< x-openwhisk-activation-id: f86aad67a9674aa1aaad67a9674aa12b
< Set-Cookie: Username=OpenWhisk; Max-Age=3600
< IBM_Cloud_Functions: OpenWhisk
< Expect-CT: max-age=604800, report-uri="https://report-uri.cloudflare.com/
cdn-cgi/beacon/expect-ct"
< Server: cloudflare
< CF-RAY: 5011ee17db5d7f2f-CMB
<
* Connection #0 to host us-south.functions.cloud.ibm.com left intact
<html><body><h3>Hello, OpenWhisk</h3></body></html>
```

As expected, we have received **HTTP/1.1 200 OK** as the HTTP response code, **Content-Type: text/html** as a header, a cookie, and **<html><body><h3>Hello, OpenWhisk</h3></body></html>** as the body of the response.

Now, let's invoke the same **curl** request without the **name=OpenWhisk** query parameter. This time, the expected response code is **HTTP/1.1 400 Bad Request** because we did not pass a value for the query parameter. Also, the **curl** command will respond with **<html><body><h3>Hello, Stranger</h3></body></html>** as the HTTP response body code:

```
$ curl https://us-south.functions.cloud.ibm.com/api/v1/web/
sathsara89%40gmail.com_dev/default/myWebAction.http -v
```

Here is the response from the preceding **curl** command:

```
*   Trying 104.17.9.194...
* Connected to us-south.functions.cloud.ibm.com (104.17.9.194) port 443 (#0)
* * *
* * *
* ALPN, server accepted to use http/1.1
> GET /api/v1/web/sathsara89%40gmail.com_dev/default/myWebAction.http HTTP/1.1
> Host: us-south.functions.cloud.ibm.com
> User-Agent: curl/7.47.0
> Accept: */*
>
< HTTP/1.1 400 Bad Request
< Date: Sun, 04 Aug 2019 16:35:09 GMT
< Content-Type: text/html; charset=UTF-8
< Transfer-Encoding: chunked
< Connection: keep-alive
< Set-Cookie: __cfduid=dedba31160ddcdb6791a04ff4359764611564936508;
expires=Mon, 03-Aug-20 16:35:08 GMT; path=/; domain=.functions.cloud.ibm.
com; HttpOnly
< X-Request-ID: 8c2091fae68ab4b678d835a000a21cc2
< Access-Control-Allow-Origin: *
< Access-Control-Allow-Methods: OPTIONS, GET, DELETE, POST, PUT, HEAD, PATCH
< Access-Control-Allow-Headers: Authorization, Origin, X-Requested-With,
Content-Type, Accept, User-Agent
< x-openwhisk-activation-id: 700916ace1d843e78916ace1d813e7c3
< Set-Cookie: Username=Stranger; Max-Age=3600
< IBM_Cloud_Functions: OpenWhisk
```

```
< Expect-CT: max-age=604800, report-uri="https://report-uri.cloudflare.com/
cdn-cgi/beacon/expect-ct"
< Server: cloudflare
< CF-RAY: 5011f1577b7a7f35-CMB
<
* Connection #0 to host us-south.functions.cloud.ibm.com left intact
<html><body><h3>Hello, Stranger</h3></body></html>
```

In this section, we introduced OpenWhisk web actions and discussed the differences between standard actions and web actions. Then, we created a web action using the **wsk** CLI. Next, we learned about the format of the URL exposed by web actions. We invoked the web action with both web browser and **curl** commands. Then, we discussed the additional information that can be returned with web actions. Finally, we updated our web action to include headers, **statusCode**, and the body in the response and invoked the web action using the **curl** command to verify the response.

OpenWhisk Feeds, Triggers, and Rules

In the previous sections, we learned how to invoke actions either with the **wsk** CLI or with HTTP requests using web actions. In this section, we are going to learn how to automate action invocation with OpenWhisk feeds, triggers, and rules. The following diagram illustrates how actions are invoked with events from external event sources using feeds, triggers, and rules:

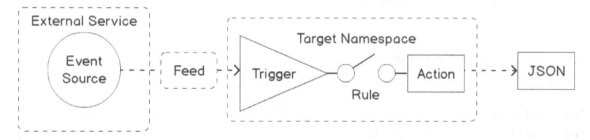

Figure 8.53: OpenWhisk Feeds, triggers, and rules

Triggers are different types of events sent from event sources. These triggers can be fired either manually with the **wsk** CLI or automatically from events occurring in external event sources. Some examples of an event source are a Git repository, an email account, or a Slack channel. As illustrated in the preceding diagram, feeds are used to connect the triggers to external event sources. Examples for feeds are as follows:

- A commit is made to a Git repository.

- Incoming email messages to a particular account.

- Message received by a Slack channel.

As illustrated, the rule is the component that connects triggers with actions. A rule will connect one trigger with one action. Once this link is created, every invocation of the trigger will execute the associated action. The following scenarios are also possible by creating an appropriate set of rules:

- A single trigger to execute multiple actions

- A single action to be executed in response to multiple triggers

Let's start by creating a simple action to be invoked with triggers and rules. Create a file named **triggers-rules.js** and add the following JavaScript function:

```
function main(params) {
    var helloMessage = 'Invoked with triggers and rules';
    return { result: helloMessage };
}
```

Then we will create the action:

```
$ wsk action create triggersAndRules triggers-rules.js
```

Now it's time to create our first trigger. We will use the **wsk trigger create** command to create the trigger using the **wsk** CLI:

```
$ wsk trigger create <trigger-name>
```

Let's create a trigger called **myTrigger**:

```
$ wsk trigger create myTrigger
```

The output should be as follows:

```
/serverless $ wsk trigger create myTrigger
ok: created trigger myTrigger
/serverless $
```

Figure 8.54: Creating myTrigger

We can list the available triggers to make sure that **myTrigger** has been created successfully:

```
$ wsk trigger list
```

The output should be as follows:

```
/serverless $ wsk trigger list
triggers
/sathsara89@gmail.com_dev/myTrigger                    private
/serverless $
```

Figure 8.55: Listing all triggers

Triggers are useless until we connect them with actions through a rule. Now we will be creating an OpenWhisk rule with the **wsk rule create** command, which has the following format:

```
$ wsk rule create <rule-name> <trigger-name> <action-name>
```

Let's create a rule named **myRule** to connect the **myTrigger** and **triggerAndRules** actions together:

```
$ wsk rule create myRule myTrigger triggersAndRules
```

The output should be as follows:

```
/serverless $ wsk rule create myRule myTrigger triggersAndRules
ok: created rule myRule
/serverless $
```

Figure 8.56: Creating myRule to connect myTrigger with the triggersAndRules action

We can get the details about **myRule**, which shows the trigger and action associated with the rule:

```
$ wsk rule get myRule
```

This command will print detailed output about **myRule** as shown in the following screenshot, which includes the **namespace**, **version**, **status**, and associated **triggers** and **actions** of **rule**.

The output should be as follows:

```
/serverless $ wsk rule get myRule
ok: got rule myRule
{
    "namespace": "sathsara89@gmail.com_dev",
    "name": "myRule",
    "version": "0.0.1",
    "status": "inactive",
    "trigger": {
        "name": "myTrigger",
        "path": "sathsara89@gmail.com_dev"
    },
    "action": {
        "name": "triggersAndRules",
        "path": "sathsara89@gmail.com_dev"
    },
    "publish": false
}
/serverless $
```

Figure 8.57: Getting the details of myRule

It's time to see triggers in action once the **action**, **trigger**, and **rule** are ready. Let's fire the trigger using the **wsk trigger fire** command:

```
$ wsk trigger fire myTrigger
```

The output should be as follows:

```
/serverless $ wsk trigger fire myTrigger
ok: triggered /_/myTrigger with id 34118747f8914791918747f891679188
/serverless $
```

Figure 8.58: Firing myTrigger

This will print the ID of the activation for the trigger.

Let's execute the following command to list the last two activations:

```
$ wsk activation list --limit 2
```

The output should be as follows:

```
/serverless $ wsk activation list --limit 2
Datetime              Activation ID                     Kind       Start Duration  Status
  Entity
2019-08-06 13:31:35 85d9d7e50891468299d7e50891d68224 nodejs:10 cold   47ms         success
  sathsara89...com_dev/triggersAndRules:0.0.1
2019-08-06 13:31:35 34118747f8914791918747f891679188 unknown   warm  0s            success
  sathsara89...com_dev/myTrigger:0.0.1
/serverless $
```

Figure 8.59: Listing the last two activations

In the preceding screenshot, we can see that the **myTrigger** trigger activation is recorded, followed by the **triggersAndRules** action activation.

We can print the result of the **triggersAndRules** action activation to make sure that the action was invoked properly by the trigger:

```
$ wsk activation get 85d9d7e50891468299d7e50891d68224 -summary
```

The output should be as follows:

```
/serverless $ wsk activation get 85d9d7e50891468299d7e50891d68224 --summary
activation result for '/sathsara89@gmail.com_dev/triggersAndRules' (success at 2019
-08-06 13:31:35 +0530 +0530)
{
    "result": "Invoked with triggers and rules"
}
/serverless $
```

Figure 8.60: Printing the result of the activation

In this section, we discussed how to automate action invocation with feeds, triggers, and rules. We created an action, a trigger, and then a rule to connect them. Finally, we invoked the action by firing the trigger.

OpenWhisk CronJob Triggers

In the preceding section, we discussed how to fire a trigger with the **wsk trigger fire** command. However, there are situations in which we need to automate the firing of triggers. An example would be performing a periodic task, such as running system backups, log archiving, or database purging. OpenWhisk provides cron-based triggers for invoking serverless functions at fixed intervals. The **/whisk.system/alarms** package provided by OpenWhisk can be used to fire triggers at scheduled intervals.

This package includes the following feeds:

Feed Name	Description
/whisk.system/alarms/once	Fire the trigger on a defined date.
/whisk.system/alarms/interval	Fire the trigger on an interval-based schedule.
/whisk.system/alarms/alarm	Fire the trigger based on a cron.

Figure 8.61: Feeds available in alarms package

In the following exercise, let's learn how to create a cron job-based trigger.

Exercise 28: Creating CronJob Triggers

In this exercise, we are going to create an OpenWhisk action that will be invoked every minute using feeds, triggers, and rules. The function code will print the current date and time as the output so we can verify that the cron job trigger has correctly invoked the action.

> **Note**
>
> The code files for this exercise can be found at https://github.com/TrainingByPackt/ Serverless-Architectures-with-Kubernetes/tree/master/Lesson08/Exercise28.

The following steps will help you to complete the exercise:

1. Let's start by creating the function code. This function will return the current date and time. Create a **date-time.js** file with the following code and create an action called **dateTimeAction**:

```
function main() {
    var currentDateTime = new Date();
    return { currentDateTime: currentDateTime };
}
$ wsk action create dateTimeAction date-time.js
```

The output should be as follows:

```
/serverless $ wsk action create dateTimeAction date-time.js
ok: created action dateTimeAction
/serverless $
```

Figure 8.62: Creating dateTimeAction

2. The next step is to create a trigger with the **/whisk.system/alarms/alarm** feed. The cron value is provided as "* * * * *", which aims to trigger this action every minute:

```
$ wsk trigger create dateTimeCronTrigger \
                    --feed /whisk.system/alarms/alarm \
                    --param cron "* * * * *"
```

Here is the response for the **wsk trigger create** command. Make sure there is **ok: created trigger dateTimeCronTrigger** at the end of the output, which indicates the successful creation of **dateTimeCronTrigger**:

```
ok: invoked /whisk.system/alarms/alarm with id
06f8535f9d364882b8535f9d368882cd
{
    "activationId": "06f8535f9d364882b8535f9d368882cd",
    "annotations": [
        {
            "key": "path",
            "value": "whisk.system/alarms/alarm"
        },
        {
            "key": "waitTime",
            "value": 85
        },
        {
            "key": "kind",
            "value": "nodejs:10"
        },
        {
            "key": "timeout",
            "value": false
        },
        {
            "key": "limits",
            "value": {
                "concurrency": 1,
                "logs": 10,
                "memory": 256,
                "timeout": 60000
            }
        },
        {
            "key": "initTime",
            "value": 338
        }
    ],
    "duration": 594,
    "end": 1565083299218,
    "logs": [],
```

```
            "name": "alarm",
            "namespace": "sathsara89@gmail.com_dev",
            "publish": false,
            "response": {
                "result": {
                    "status": "success"
                },
                "status": "success",
                "success": true
            },
            "start": 1565083298624,
            "subject": "sathsara89@gmail.com",
            "version": "0.0.152"
        }
    ok: created trigger dateTimeCronTrigger
```

3. Create the rule (**dateTimeRule**) to connect the action (**dateTimeAction**) with the trigger (**dateTimeCronTrigger**):

```
$ wsk rule create dateTimeRule dateTimeCronTrigger dateTimeAction
```

The output should be as follows:

```
/serverless $ wsk rule create dateTimeRule dateTimeCronTrigger dateTimeAction
ok: created rule dateTimeRule
/serverless $
```

Figure 8.63: Creating dateTimeRule to connect dateTimeCronTrigger with dateTimeAction

4. This action will now be triggered every minute. Allow the cron job trigger to run for around 5 minutes. We can list the last 6 activations with the following command:

```
$ wsk activation list --limit 6
```

The output should be as follows:

```
/serverless $ wsk activation list --limit 6
Datetime           Activation ID                    Kind          Start Duration   Status
Entity
2019-08-06 15:09:03 04012f4f3e6044ed812f4f3e6054edc4 nodejs:10 warm  2ms          success
sathsara89...com_dev/dateTimeAction:0.0.1
2019-08-06 15:09:03 2807364a7860465487364a7860c65474 unknown   warm  0s           success
sathsara89...com_dev/dateTimeCronTrigger:0.0.1
2019-08-06 15:08:03 c4758e5fa4464d0cb58e5fa446cd0cf7 nodejs:10 cold  67ms         success
sathsara89...com_dev/dateTimeAction:0.0.1
2019-08-06 15:08:03 7bfa3bf838e04880ba3bf838e03880f9 unknown   warm  0s           success
sathsara89...com_dev/dateTimeCronTrigger:0.0.1
2019-08-06 15:07:02 cf78acfd78d044e8b8acfd78d044e89c nodejs:10 cold  142ms        success
sathsara89...com_dev/dateTimeAction:0.0.1
2019-08-06 15:07:02 48104c1e906f44f7904c1e906fb4f78f unknown   warm  0s           success
sathsara89...com_dev/dateTimeCronTrigger:0.0.1
/serverless $
```

Figure 8.64: Listing the last six activations

5. List the summary of the activations of **dateTimeAction** to make sure it has printed the current datetime every minute:

```
$ wsk activation get 04012f4f3e6044ed812f4f3e6054edc4 --summary
```

```
$ wsk activation get c4758e5fa4464d0cb58e5fa446cd0cf7 --summary
```

```
$ wsk activation get cf78acfd78d044e8b8acfd78d044e89c -summary
```

The output should be as follows:

```
/serverless $ wsk activation get 04012f4f3e6044ed812f4f3e6054edc4 --summary
activation result for '/sathsara89@gmail.com_dev/dateTimeAction' (success at
2019-08-06 15:09:03 +0530 +0530)
{
    "currentDateTime": "2019-08-06T09:39:03.203Z"
}
/serverless $
/serverless $ wsk activation get c4758e5fa4464d0cb58e5fa446cd0cf7 --summary
activation result for '/sathsara89@gmail.com_dev/dateTimeAction' (success at
2019-08-06 15:08:03 +0530 +0530)
{
    "currentDateTime": "2019-08-06T09:38:03.974Z"
}
/serverless $
/serverless $ wsk activation get cf78acfd78d044e8b8acfd78d044e89c --summary
activation result for '/sathsara89@gmail.com_dev/dateTimeAction' (success at
2019-08-06 15:07:02 +0530 +0530)
{
    "currentDateTime": "2019-08-06T09:37:02.744Z"
}
/serverless $
```

Figure 8.65: Printing the summary of dateTimeAction activations

Check the value of the `currentDateTime` field, printed for each invocation to verify that this action was invoked every minute as scheduled. In the preceding screenshot, we can see that the action was invoked at **09:37:02**, then again at **09:38:03**, and finally at **09:39:03**.

In this activity, we created a simple function that prints the current date and time. Then, we created a cron job trigger to invoke this action every minute.

OpenWhisk Packages

OpenWhisk packages allow us to organize our actions by bundling the related actions together. As an example, consider that we have multiple actions, such as `createOrder`, `processOrder`, `dispatchOrder`, and `refundOrder`. These actions will perform the relevant application logic when an application user creates an order, processes an order, dispatches an order, and refunds an order respectively. In this case, we can create a package named `order` to group all order-related actions together.

As we learned previously, action names should be unique. Packages help to prevent naming conflicts because we can create multiple actions with the same name by placing them in different packages. As an example, the `retrieveInfo` action from the `order` package may retrieve information about an order, but the `retrieveInfo` action from the customer package can retrieve information about a customer.

So far, we have created many actions without bothering about packages. How was this possible? This is because OpenWhisk places actions into default packages if we do not mention any specific package during action creation.

There are two types of packages in OpenWhisk:

- Built-in packages (packages come with OpenWhisk)
- User-defined packages (other packages created by users)

All the packages available in a namespace can be retrieved with the `wsk package list <namespace>` command.

The output should be as follows:

```
/serverless $ wsk package list /whisk.system
packages
/whisk.system/websocket                    shared
/whisk.system/weather                      shared
/whisk.system/utils                        shared
/whisk.system/slack                        shared
/whisk.system/samples                      shared
/whisk.system/cloudant                     shared
/whisk.system/cos-experimental             shared
/whisk.system/alarms                       shared
/whisk.system/messaging                    shared
/whisk.system/pushnotifications            shared
/whisk.system/watson-textToSpeech          shared
/whisk.system/github                       shared
/whisk.system/combinators                  shared
/whisk.system/watson-speechToText          shared
/whisk.system/watson-translator            shared
/serverless $
```

Figure 8.66: Listing the packages in the /whisk.system namespace

Packages can be created with the **wsk package create** command:

```
$ wsk package create <package-name>
```

In this section, we introduced the concept of packages and discussed the built-in packages and user-defined packages of OpenWhisk. In the next exercise, we will create a package and add an action to the newly created package.

Exercise 29: Creating OpenWhisk Packages

In this exercise, we will create a package named **arithmetic** that contains all arithmetic-related actions, such as add, subtract, multiply, and divide. We will create a function that receives two numbers as input and returns the result by adding the numbers. Then, we will create this action within the **arithmetic** package:

1. Let's start by creating a package named **arithmetic**:

    ```
    $ wsk package create arithmetic
    ```

    The output should be as follows:

    ```
    /serverless $ wsk package create arithmetic
    ok: created package arithmetic
    /serverless $
    ```

    Figure 8.67: Creating the arithmetic package

2. Now we are going to create an action that will be added to our **arithmetic** package. Create a file named **add.js** with the following content:

```
function main(params) {
    var result = params.firstNumber + params.secondNumber;
    return { result: result };
}
```

3. We can create the action and add it to the **arithmetic** package simultaneously with the **wsk action create** command. This will only require us to prefix the action name with the package name. Execute the following command:

```
$ wsk action create arithmetic/add add.js
```

In the output, we can see that the action has been successfully created in the **arithmetic** package.

The output should be as follows:

```
/serverless $ wsk action create arithmetic/add add.js
ok: created action arithmetic/add
/serverless $
```

Figure 8.68: Adding an add action to the arithmetic package

4. Now we can verify that our **add** action has been placed in the arithmetic package using the **wsk action list** command.

```
$ wsk action list --limit 2
```

The output should be as follows:

```
/serverless $ wsk action list --limit 2
actions
/sathsara89@gmail.com_dev/arithmetic/add              private nodejs:10
/sathsara89@gmail.com_dev/dateTimeAction              private nodejs:10
/serverless $
```

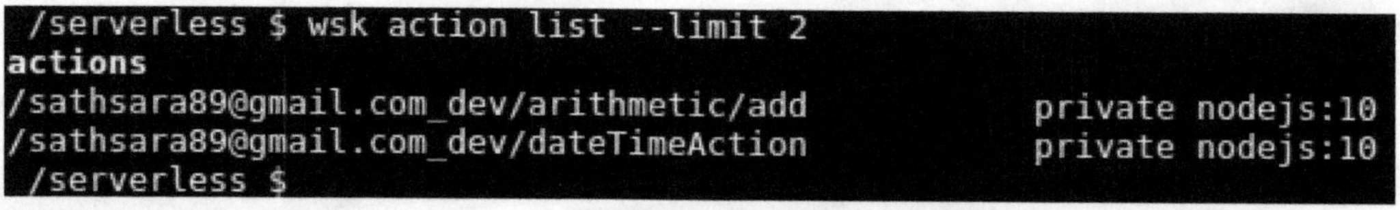

Figure 8.69: Listing the actions

5. The **wsk package get** command will return JSON output that describes the package:

```
$ wsk package get arithmetic
```

The output should be as follows:

```
/serverless $ wsk package get arithmetic
ok: got package arithmetic
{
    "namespace": "sathsara89@gmail.com_dev",
    "name": "arithmetic",
    "version": "0.0.1",
    "publish": false,
    "binding": {},
    "actions": [
        {
            "name": "add",
            "version": "0.0.1",
            "annotations": [
                {
                    "key": "exec",
                    "value": "nodejs:10"
                }
            ]
        }
    ]
}
/serverless $
```

Figure 8.70: Getting a detailed description of the arithmetic package

6. We can use the **--summary** flag if we want to see a summary of the package description, which lists the actions within the package:

    ```
    $ wsk package get arithmetic -summary
    ```

The output should be as follows:

```
/serverless $ wsk package get arithmetic --summary
package /sathsara89@gmail.com_dev/arithmetic
   (parameters: none defined)
 action /sathsara89@gmail.com_dev/arithmetic/add
   (parameters: none defined)
 /serverless $
```

Figure 8.71: Getting the summary description of the arithmetic package

Activity 8: Receive Daily Weather Updates via Email

Imagine that you are working for a disaster management center and need to be updated with weather information. You have decided to create an application that can send you weather updates via email at specified intervals. To achieve this, you have decided to deploy an application that can retrieve the current weather in a specific city and send a daily email at 8.00 AM with the current weather information to a specified email address. In this activity, we will be using external services to retrieve weather information (**OpenWeather**) and send emails (**SendGrid**).

We need to have the following before we start this activity:

- An **OpenWeather** account (to retrieve current weather information)

- A **SendGrid** account (to send emails)

- `npm` installed

- `zip` installed

Execute the following steps to create an **OpenWeather** account and a SendGrid account:

1. Create an **OpenWeather** (https://openweathermap.org/) account to retrieve current weather information and save the API key. Create an **OpenWeather** account at https://home.openweathermap.org/users/sign_up.

    Go to the **API keys** tab (https://home.openweathermap.org/api_keys) and save the API key as this API key is required to fetch the data from the OpenWeather API.

    Test the OpenWeather API using `https://api.openweathermap.org/data/2.5/weather?q=London&appid=<YOUR-API-KEY>` in a web browser. Please note that you need to replace **<YOUR-API-KEY>** with your API key from *step 1*.

2. Create a SendGrid (https://sendgrid.com) account and save the API key. This is used to send emails. Create a SendGrid account at https://signup.sendgrid.com/.

    Go to **Settings > API Keys** and click on the **Create API Key** button.

    Provide a name in the **API Key Name** field, select the **Full Access** radio button, and click on the **Create & View** button to create an API key with full access.

Once the key is generated, copy the API key and save it somewhere safe as you will see this key only once.

> **Note**
>
> Detailed steps on creating an **OpenWeather** account and a SendGrid account are available in the *Appendix* section on page 432.

Now we are ready to start the activity. Execute the following steps to complete this activity:

3. Create a function in any language that you are familiar with (and supported by the OpenWhisk framework) that will take the city name as a parameter and return a JSON object with weather information retrieved from the OpenWeather API.

> **Note**
>
> For this solution, we will be using functions written in JavaScript. However, you can use any language that you are familiar with to write the functions.

Here is an example function written in JavaScript:

```javascript
const request = require('request');
function main(params) {
    const cityName = params.cityName
    const openWeatherApiKey = '<OPEN_WEATHER_API_KEY>';
    const openWeatherUrl = 'https://api.openweathermap.org/data/2.5/
weather?q=' + cityName + '&mode=json&units=metric&appid=' +
openWeatherApiKey ;
    return new Promise(function(resolve, reject) {
        request(openWeatherUrl, function(error, response, body) {
            if (error) {
                reject('Requesting weather data from provider failed '
                        + 'with status code '
                        + response.statusCode + '.\n'
                        + 'Please check the provided cityName argument.');
            } else {
                try {
                    var weatherData = JSON.parse(body);
                    resolve({weatherData:weatherData});
                } catch (ex) {
```

```
                          reject('Error occurred while parsing weather data.');
                }
            }
        });
    });
}
```

4. Create a second function (in any language that you are familiar with and is supported by the OpenWhisk framework) that will take a message as input and send the input message to a specified email address using the SendGrid service.

Here is an example function written in JavaScript:

```javascript
const sendGridMailer = require('@sendgrid/mail');
function main(params) {
    const sendGridApiKey = '<SEND_GRID_API_KEY>';
    const toMail = '<TO_EMAIL>';
    const fromMail = '<FROM_EMAIL>';
    const mailSubject = 'Weather Information for Today';
    const mailContent = params.message;
    return new Promise(function(resolve, reject) {
        sendGridMailer.setApiKey(sendGridApiKey);
        const msg = {
            to: toMail,
            from: fromMail,
            subject: mailSubject,
            text: mailContent,
        };
        sendGridMailer.send(msg, (error, result) => {
            if (error) {
                reject({msg: "Message sending failed."});
            } else {
                resolve({msg: "Message sent!"});
            }
        });
    });
}
exports.main = main;
```

5. Create a third function (in any language that you are familiar with and is supported by the OpenWhisk framework) that will take the JSON object with the weather data and format it as a string message to be sent as the email body.

Here is an example function written in JavaScript:

```javascript
function main(params) {

    return new Promise(function(resolve, reject) {

        if (!params.weatherData) {
            reject("Weather data not provided");
        }

        const weatherData = params.weatherData;
        const cityName = weatherData.name;
        const currentTemperature = weatherData.main.temp;

        weatherMessage = "It's " + currentTemperature
                                + " degrees celsius in " + cityName;

        resolve({message: weatherMessage});

    });
}
```

6. Next, create a sequence connecting all three actions.

7. Finally, create the trigger and rule to invoke the sequence daily at 8.00 AM.

> **Note**
>
> The solution to the activity can be found on page 432.

Summary

In this chapter, we first learned about the history and the core concepts of Apache OpenWhisk. Then, we learned how to set up IBM Cloud Functions with CLI to run our serverless functions. After that, OpenWhisk actions were introduced, which are the code snippets written in one of the languages supported by OpenWhisk. We discussed how to write, create, list, invoke, update, and delete OpenWhisk actions using the wsk CLI. Next, we went over OpenWhisk sequences, which are used to combine multiple actions together to create a more complex processing pipeline. Going forward, we learned how to expose actions publicly using a URL with web actions. We discussed how web actions allow us to return additional information from the action, such as HTTP headers and non-JSON payloads, including HTML and binary data. The next section was on feeds, triggers, and rules that automate action invocation using events from external event sources. Finally, OpenWhisk packages were discussed, which are used to organize related actions by bundling them together.

In the next and final chapter, we shall learn about OpenFaaS and work with an OpenFaaS function.

Going Serverless with OpenFaaS

Learning Objectives

By the end of this chapter, you will be able to:

- Set up the OpenFaaS framework on a Minikube cluster
- Create, build, deploy, list, invoke, and delete functions with the OpenFaaS CLI
- Deploy and invoke OpenFaaS functions from the OpenFaaS portal
- Return an HTML web page from OpenFaaS functions
- Set up the Prometheus and Grafana dashboards to monitor OpenFaaS functions
- Configure function autoscaling to adjust the function count based on demand

In this chapter, we aim to set up the OpenFaaS framework on top of a Minikube cluster and study how we can work with OpenFaaS functions, using both the OpenFaaS CLI and OpenFaaS portal. We will also look into features such as observability and autoscaling with OpenFaaS.

Introduction to OpenFaaS

In the previous chapter, we learned about OpenWhisk, an open source serverless framework, which is part of the Apache Software Foundation. We learned how to create, list, invoke, update, and delete OpenWhisk actions. We also discussed how to automate the action invocation with feeds, triggers, and rules.

In this chapter, we will be studying OpenFaas, another open source framework used to build and deploy serverless functions on top of containers. This was started as a proof-of-concept project by Alex Ellis in October 2016, and the first version of the framework, written in Golang, was committed to GitHub in December 2016.

OpenFaaS was originally designed to work with Docker Swarm, which is the clustering and scheduling tool for Docker containers. Later, the OpenFaaS framework was rearchitected to support the Kubernetes framework, too.

OpenFaaS comes with a built-in UI named **OpenFaaS Portal**, which can be used to create and invoke the functions from the web browser. This portal also offers a CLI named **faas-cli** that allows us to manage functions through the command line. The OpenFaaS framework has built-in support for autoscaling. This will scale up the function when there is increased demand, and it will scale down when demand decreases, or even scale down to zero when the function is idle.

Now, let's take a look at the components of the OpenFaaS framework:

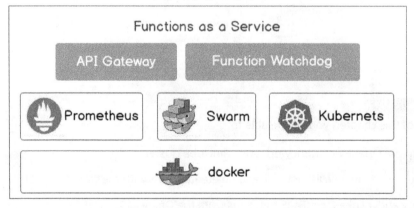

Figure 9.1: OpenFaaS components

OpenFaaS consists of the following components that are running on the underlying Kubernetes or Docker Swarm:

- **API Gateway**:

  The API Gateway is the entry point to the OpenFaaS framework, which exposes the functions externally. It is also responsible for collecting the function metrics such as function invocation count, function execution duration, and number of function replicas. The API Gateway also handles function autoscaling by increasing or decreasing function replicas based on demand.

- **Prometheus**:

  Prometheus, which is an open source monitoring and alerting tool, comes bundled with the OpenFaaS framework. This is used to store the information about the function metrics collected by the API Gateway.

- **Function Watchdog**:

  The Function Watchdog is a tiny Golang web server running alongside each function container. This component is placed between the API Gateway and your function and is responsible for converting message formats between the API Gateway and the function. It converts the HTTP messages sent by the API Gateway to the "standard input" (**stdin**) messages, which the function can understand. This also handles the response path by converting the "standard output" (**stdout**) response sent by the function to an HTTP response.

  The following is an illustration of a function watchdog:

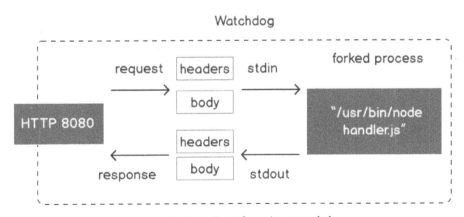

Figure 9.2: OpenFaaS function watchdog

Docker Swarm or Kubernetes can be used as the container orchestration tool with the OpenFaaS framework, which manages the containers running on the underlying Docker framework.

Getting Started with OpenFaas on Your Local Minikube Cluster

In this section, we will set up an OpenFaaS framework and CLI on our local Minikube cluster. Before starting the installation, we need to ensure that the following prerequisites are met:

- Minikube is installed

- Docker (version 17.05 or later) is installed

- Helm is installed

- A Docker Hub account is created

Once these prerequisites are ready, we can continue to install OpenFaaS. The installation of OpenFaas can be broadly classified into three steps, as follows:

1. Installing the OpenFaaS CLI

2. Installing the OpenFaaS framework (on a Minikube cluster)

3. Setting up an environment variable

Let's look at each of these steps in more depth:

Installing the OpenFaaS CLI

faas-cli is the command-line utility for the OpenFaaS framework, which can be used to create and invoke OpenFaaS functions from the Terminal. We can install the latest version of **faas-cli** using the following command:

```
$ curl -sL https://cli.openfaas.com | sudo sh
```

The output should be as follows:

```
/serverless $ curl -sL https://cli.openfaas.com | sudo sh
x86_64
Downloading package https://github.com/openfaas/faas-cli/releases/download/0.9.2/
faas-cli as /tmp/faas-cli
Download complete.

Running as root - Attempting to move faas-cli to /usr/local/bin
New version of faas-cli installed to /usr/local/bin
Creating alias 'faas' for 'faas-cli'.




CLI:
 commit:  893972afffa5ea6672faa6e11743ae46322ec58c
 version: 0.9.2
/serverless $
```

Figure 9.3: Installing faas-cli

Once the installation is complete, we can verify installation with the **faas-cli version** command:

```
$ faas-cli version
```

The output should be as follows:

Figure 9.4: The faas-cli version

As you can see, we have installed the **faas-cli** utility on the cluster and can also check the version number.

Installing the OpenFaaS Framework

Next, we need to install the OpenFaaS framework using the OpenFaaS **helm** repository. First, we need to add the **openfaas helm** repository and update it to pull any new releases. Use the following commands:

```
$ helm repo add openfaas https://openfaas.github.io/faas-netes/
```

```
$ helm repo update
```

The output should be as follows:

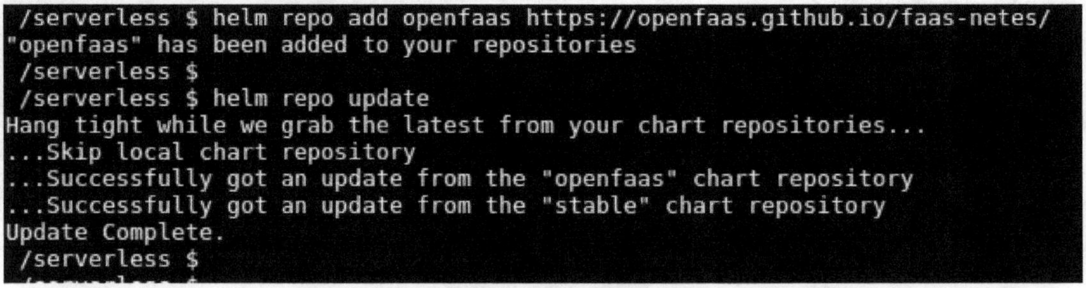

```
/serverless $ helm repo add openfaas https://openfaas.github.io/faas-netes/
"openfaas" has been added to your repositories
/serverless $
/serverless $ helm repo update
Hang tight while we grab the latest from your chart repositories...
...Skip local chart repository
...Successfully got an update from the "openfaas" chart repository
...Successfully got an update from the "stable" chart repository
Update Complete.
/serverless $
```

Figure 9.5: Adding and updating helm charts

Installing OpenFaaS requires two Kubernetes namespaces. The **openfaas** namespace is for the core services of the OpenFaaS framework, and the **openfaas-fn** namespace is for the OpenFaaS functions. Run the following commands to create the namespaces:

```
$ kubectl create namespace openfaas
```

```
$ kubectl create namespace openfaas-fn
```

The output will be as follows:

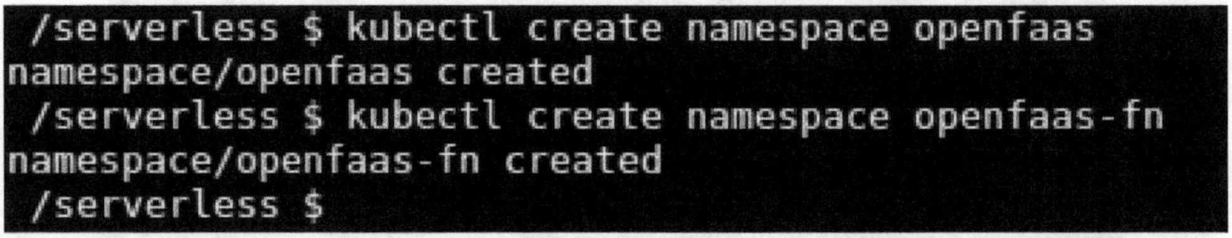

```
/serverless $ kubectl create namespace openfaas
namespace/openfaas created
/serverless $ kubectl create namespace openfaas-fn
namespace/openfaas-fn created
/serverless $
```

Figure 9.6: Creating namespaces

Now we are going to create the Kubernetes secret, which is required to enable basic authentication for the OpenFaaS gateway. First, we will create a random string that will be used as the password. Once the password is generated, we will **echo** the generated password and save it in a secure place as we need it to log in to the API Gateway later on. Run the following commands to generate the password:

```
$ PASSWORD=$(head -c 12 /dev/urandom | shasum| cut -d' ' -f1)
```

```
$ echo $PASSWORD
```

The output will be as follows:

```
/serverless $ PASSWORD=$(head -c 12 /dev/urandom | shasum| cut -d' ' -f1)
/serverless $ echo $PASSWORD
51d75b2602c83bd62d353a8b5a2b02c62a319e3a
/serverless $
```

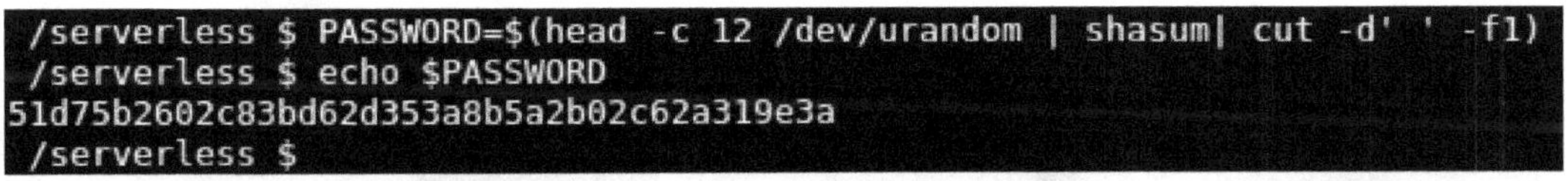

Figure 9.7: Generating the password

After generating the password, we will create a Kubernetes **secret** object to store the password.

> **Note:**
>
> A Kubernetes **secret** object is used to store sensitive data such as a password.

Execute the following command to create a Kubernetes secret named **basic-auth**:

```
$ kubectl -n openfaas create secret generic basic-auth \

    --from-literal=basic-auth-user=admin \

    --from-literal=basic-auth-password="$PASSWORD"
```

The output will be as follows:

```
/serverless $ kubectl -n openfaas create secret generic basic-auth \
>       --from-literal=basic-auth-user=admin \
>       --from-literal=basic-auth-password="$PASSWORD"
secret/basic-auth created
/serverless $
```

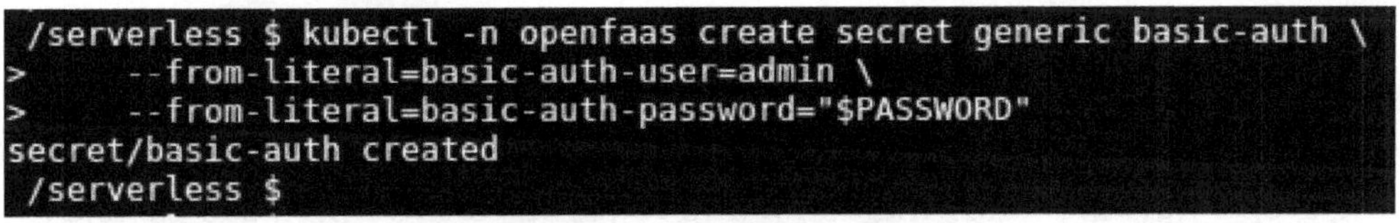

Figure 9.8: Creating the basic-auth secret

We can now deploy the OpenFaaS framework from the **helm** chart. The **helm upgrade openfaas** command starts the deployment of OpenFaaS and will start deploying the OpenFaaS framework on your local Minikube cluster. This will take between 5 and 15 minutes depending on the network speed. Run the following commands to install **OpenFaaS**:

```
$ helm upgrade openfaas \

    --install openfaas/openfaas \

    --namespace openfaas \

    --set functionNamespace=openfaas-fn \

    --set basic_auth=true
```

The preceding command prints a lengthy output, and, at the bottom, it provides a command to verify the installation, as you can see in the following screenshot:

```
NOTES:
To verify that openfaas has started, run:

  kubectl --namespace=openfaas get deployments -l "release=openfaas, app=openfaas"
```

Figure 9.9: OpenFaaS installation

You can verify the deployment state from the following command:

```
$ kubectl --namespace=openfaas get deployments -l "release=openfaas,
app=openfaas"
```

The output will be displayed as follows:

```
/serverless $ kubectl --namespace=openfaas get deployments -l "release=openfaas,
 app=openfaas"
NAME               READY   UP-TO-DATE   AVAILABLE   AGE
alertmanager       1/1     1            1           8m10s
basic-auth-plugin  1/1     1            1           8m10s
faas-idler         1/1     1            1           8m10s
gateway            1/1     1            1           8m10s
nats               1/1     1            1           8m10s
prometheus         1/1     1            1           8m10s
queue-worker       1/1     1            1           8m10s
 /serverless $
```

Figure 9.10: Verifying the OpenFaaS installation

Once the installation has been successfully completed and all services are running, we then have to log in to the OpenFaaS gateway with the credentials we created in the preceding steps. Run the following command to log in to the OpenFaas gateway:

```
$ faas-cli login --username admin --password $PASSWORD
```

The output should be as follows:

```
/serverless $ faas-cli login --username admin --password $PASSWORD
WARNING! Using --password is insecure, consider using: cat ~/faas_pass.txt |
 faas-cli login -u user --password-stdin
Calling the OpenFaaS server to validate the credentials...
WARNING! Communication is not secure, please consider using HTTPS. Letsencry
pt.org offers free SSL/TLS certificates.
credentials saved for admin http://192.168.99.100:31112
 /serverless $
```

Figure 9.11: Logging in to the OpenFaaS gateway

Setting the Environment Variables

There are several environment variables related to OpenFaaS, and we will set two environment variables in this section. These environment variables can be overridden using the command-line flags of **faas-cli**, if necessary.

- **OPENFAAS_URL**: This should point to the API Gateway component.

- **OPENFAAS_PREFIX**: This is the Docker ID of your Docker Hub account.

Open the **~/.bashrc** file with your favorite text editor and add the following two lines at the end of the file. Replace **<your-docker-id>** with your Docker ID in the following commands:

```
export OPENFAAS_URL=$(minikube ip):31112

export OPENFAAS_PREFIX=<your-docker-id>
```

Then, you need to source the **~/.bashrc** file to reload the newly configured environment variables, as shown in the following command:

```
$ source ~/.bashrc
```

The command should appear as follows:

```
/serverless $ source ~/.bashrc
```

Figure 9.12: Source the bashrc file

OpenFaaS Functions

OpenFaaS functions can be written in any language supported by Linux or Windows, and they can then be converted to a serverless function using Docker containers. This is a major advantage of the OpenFaaS framework compared to other serverless frameworks that support only predefined languages and runtimes.

OpenFaaS functions can be deployed with either **faas-cli** or the OpenFaaS portal. In the following sections, we are first going to discuss how we can build, deploy, list, invoke, and delete OpenFaaS functions using the **faas-cli** command-line tool. Then, we will discuss how to deploy and invoke functions with the OpenFaaS portal.

Creating OpenFaaS Functions

As we discussed previously, OpenFaaS functions can be written in any language supported by Linux and Windows. This requires us to create the function code, add any dependencies, and create a **Dockerfile** to build the Docker image. It requires a certain amount of understanding of the OpenFaaS platform in order to be able to perform the previously mentioned tasks. As a solution, OpenFaaS has a template store that includes prebuilt templates for a set of supported languages. This means that you can download these templates from the template store, update the function code, and then the CLI does the rest to build the Docker image.

First of all, we need to pull the OpenFaaS templates with the `faas-cli template pull` command. This will fetch the templates from the official OpenFaaS template repository at https://github.com/openfaas/templates.git.

Now, let's create a new folder and pull the templates to the newly created folder with the following commands:

```
$ mkdir chapter-09
```

```
$ cd chapter-09/
```

```
$ faas-cli template pull
```

The output will be as follows:

```
/serverless $ mkdir chapter-09
/serverless $ cd chapter-09/
/serverless $
/serverless $ faas-cli template pull
Fetch templates from repository: https://github.com/openfaas/templates.git
2019/08/18 09:39:49 Attempting to expand templates from https://github.com/openfaas
/templates.git
2019/08/18 09:39:52 Fetched 17 template(s) : [csharp csharp-armhf dockerfile docker
file-armhf go go-armhf java12 java8 node node-arm64 node-armhf php7 python python-a
rmhf python3 python3-armhf ruby] from https://github.com/openfaas/templates.git
/serverless $
```

Figure 9.13: Creating directories

Let's check the folder structure with the **tree -L 2** command that will print the folder **tree** with two levels of depth, as you can see in the following screenshot:

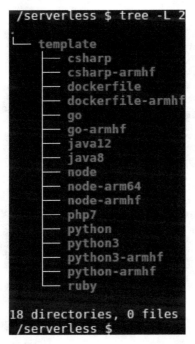

Figure 9.14: The tree view of the folder

Within the template folder, we can see 17 folders each for a specific language template.

Now, we can use the **faas-cli new** command to create the structure and files for a new function using the downloaded templates as follows:

```
$ faas-cli new <function-name> --lang=<function-language>
```

`<function-language>` can be replaced by any programming language supported by OpenFaaS templates. `faas-cli new --list` can be used to get a list of supported programming languages, as displayed in the following figure:

```
/serverless $ faas-cli new --list
Languages available as templates:
- csharp
- csharp-armhf
- dockerfile
- dockerfile-armhf
- go
- go-armhf
- java12
- java8
- node
- node-arm64
- node-armhf
- php7
- python
- python-armhf
- python3
- python3-armhf
- ruby
```

Figure 9.15: Listing supported programming language templates

Let's create our first OpenFaaS function named **hello** with the **go** language template using the following command:

```
$ faas-cli new hello --lang=go
```

The output will be as follows:

```
/serverless $ faas-cli new hello --lang=go
Folder: hello created.




Function created in folder: hello
Stack file written: hello.yml
/serverless $
```

Figure 9.16: Creating the hello function template

As per the output, the preceding command will create multiple files and directories inside the current folder. Let's execute the **tree -L 2** command again to identify the newly created files and directories:

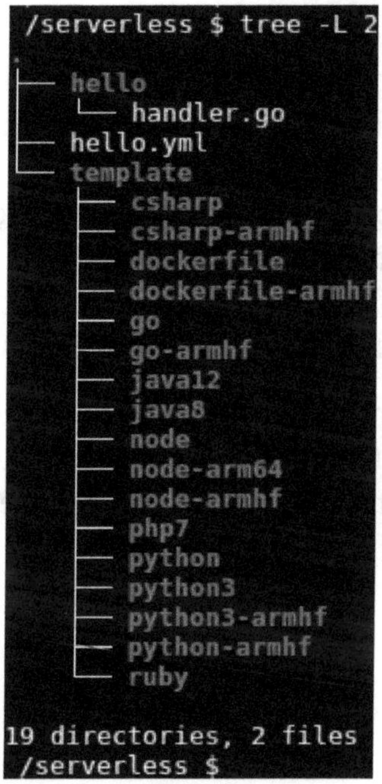

```
/serverless $ tree -L 2
    hello
        handler.go
    hello.yml
    template
        csharp
        csharp-armhf
        dockerfile
        dockerfile-armhf
        go
        go-armhf
        java12
        java8
        node
        node-arm64
        node-armhf
        php7
        python
        python3
        python3-armhf
        python-armhf
        ruby
19 directories, 2 files
/serverless $
```

Figure 9.17: The tree view of the folder

We can see a file named **hello.yml**, a folder named **hello**, and a **handler.go** file inside the **hello** folder.

First, we will look into the **hello.yml** file, which is called the **function definition** file:

```
version: 1.0
provider:
  name: openfaas
  gateway: http://192.168.99.100:31112
functions:
  hello:
    lang: go
    handler: ./hello
    image: sathsarasa/hello:latest
```

This file has three top levels named **version**, **provider**, and **functions**.

Inside the **provider** section, there is a **name: faas** tag, which defines the provider name as **faas**. This is the default and only valid value for the name tag. The next one is the **gateway** tag, which points to the URL where the API Gateway is running. This value can be overridden at deployment time with the **--gateway** flag or the **OPENFAAS_URL** environment variable.

Next is the **functions** section, which is used to define one or more functions to be deployed with the OpenFaaS CLI. In the preceding code, the **hello.yml** file has a single function named **hello** written in the Go language (**lang: go**). The handler of the function is defined with **handler: ./hello** section, which points to the folder where the source code of the **hello** function (**hello/handler.go**) resides. Finally, there is the **image** tag that specifies the name of the output Docker image. The Docker image name is prepended with your Docker image ID configured using the **OPENFAAS_PREFIX** environment variable.

Next, we will discuss the **handler.go** file that was created inside the **hello** folder. This file contains the source code of the function written in the Go language. This function accepts a string parameter and returns the string by prepending it with **Hello, Go. You said:**, as displayed in the following code snippet:

```
package function


import (
    "fmt"
)


// Handle a serverless request
func Handle(req []byte) string {
    return fmt.Sprintf("Hello, Go. You said: %s", string(req))
}
```

This is just a sample function generated by the template. We can update it with our function logics.

Building OpenFaaS Functions

Once the function definition file (**hello.yml**) and function source code (**hello/handler. go**) are ready, the next step is to build the function as a Docker image. The **faas-cli build** CLI command is used to build the Docker image, which has the following format:

```
$ faas-cli build -f <function-definition-file>
```

This initiates the process of building the Docker image and will invoke the **docker build** command internally. A new folder named **build** will be created during this step with all the files required for the build process.

Now, let's build the **hello** function that we created in the previous section:

```
$ faas-cli build -f hello.yml
```

We will receive an output similar to the following:

```
      [0] > Building hello.
  Clearing temporary build folder: ./build/hello/
  Preparing ./hello/ ./build/hello/function
  Building: sathsarasa/hello with go template. Please wait..



  Sending build context to Docker daemon  6.656kB
  Step 1/24 : FROM openfaas/classic-watchdog:0.15.4 as watchdog
   ---> a775beb8ba9f
  ...
  ...
  Successfully built 72c9089a7dd4
  Successfully tagged sathsarasa/hello:latest
  Image: sathsarasa/hello built.
  [0] < Building hello done.
  [0] worker done.
```

Once we receive the build success message, we can list the Docker image using the **docker images** command as follows:

```
$ docker images | grep hello
```

The output is as follows:

Figure 9.18: Verifying the Docker image

Pushing the OpenFaaS Function Image

The next step of the process is to push the Docker image of the function to a Docker registry or to the Docker Hub. We can use either the **faas-cli push** or **docker push** commands to push the image.

> **Note**
>
> Docker Hub is a free service for storing and sharing Docker images.

Let's push the image with the **faas-cli push** command:

```
$ faas-cli push -f hello.yml
```

The output will be as follows:

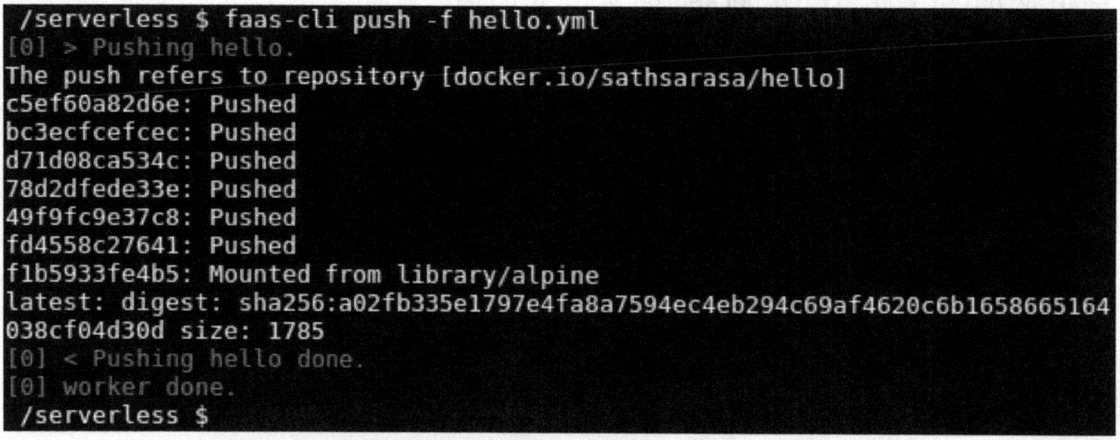

```
/serverless $ faas-cli push -f hello.yml
[0] > Pushing hello.
The push refers to repository [docker.io/sathsarasa/hello]
c5ef60a82d6e: Pushed
bc3ecfcefcec: Pushed
d71d08ca534c: Pushed
78d2dfede33e: Pushed
49f9fc9e37c8: Pushed
fd4558c27641: Pushed
f1b5933fe4b5: Mounted from library/alpine
latest: digest: sha256:a02fb335e1797e4fa8a7594ec4eb294c69af4620c6b1658665164
038cf04d30d size: 1785
[0] < Pushing hello done.
[0] worker done.
/serverless $
```

Figure 9.19: Pushing the Docker image

We can verify that the image is pushed successfully by visiting the Docker Hub page at https://hub.docker.com/.

The output should be as follows:

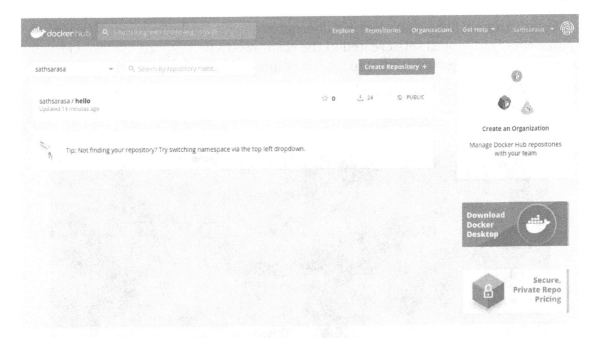

Figure 9.20: Verifying from Docker Hub

Thus, we have successfully pushed the Docker image function to Docker Hub.

Deploying the OpenFaaS Functions

Now, we are ready to deploy the **hello** function into the OpenFaaS framework using the **faas-cli deploy** command. This command also requires the function specification file with the **-f** flag similar to other **faas-cli** commands that we executed previously:

```
$ faas-cli deploy -f hello.yml
```

The output should be as follows:

```
/serverless $ faas-cli deploy -f hello.yml
Deploying: hello.

Deployed. 202 Accepted.
URL: http://192.168.99.100:31112/function/hello

/serverless $
```

Figure 9.21: Deploying the hello function

We will receive a **202 Accepted** output along with the function URL, which we can use to invoke the function.

At this step, there will be a number of Kubernetes objects, including pods, services, deployments, and replica sets created in the **openfaas-fn** namespace. We can view all these Kubernetes objects with the following command:

```
$ kubectl get all -n openfaas-fn
```

The output should be as follows:

```
/serverless $ kubectl get all -n openfaas-fn
NAME                            READY    STATUS     RESTARTS    AGE
pod/hello-6966969bcd-zpbzx      1/1      Running    0           9s


NAME              TYPE         CLUSTER-IP       EXTERNAL-IP    PORT(S)     AGE
service/hello     ClusterIP    10.106.160.250   <none>         8080/TCP    10s


NAME                        READY    UP-TO-DATE    AVAILABLE    AGE
deployment.apps/hello       1/1      1             1            10s

NAME                                    DESIRED    CURRENT    READY    AGE
replicaset.apps/hello-6966969bcd        1          1          1        10s
```

Figure 9.22: Verifying the Kubernetes objects

Hence, we have successfully deployed the **hello** function to the OpenFaaS framework.

Listing the OpenFaaS Functions

The **faas-cli list** command is used to list all the functions deployed on the OpenFaaS framework:

```
$ faas-cli list
```

The output should be as follows:

```
/serverless $ faas-cli list
Function                          Invocations          Replicas
hello                             0                    1
/serverless $
```

Figure 9.23: Listing the OpenFaaS functions

The output of the **faas-cli list** command will include the following columns:

- **Function** – The name of the function

- **Invocations** – The number of times the function has been invoked

- **Replicas** – The number of Kubernetes pod replicas of the function

The value of the **Invocations** column will increase each time we invoke the function. The value of the **Replicas** column will increase automatically if the invocation rate increases.

The **--verbose** flag can be used with **faas-cli list** if you want to get an additional column named **Image**, which lists the Docker image used to deploy the function, as shown in the following command:

```
$ faas-cli list --verbose
```

The output should be as follows:

```
/serverless $ faas-cli list --verbose
Function                          Image
           Invocations       Replicas
hello                             sathsarasa/hello
         0                  1
 /serverless $
```

Figure 9.24: Listing the OpenFaaS functions with the verbose output

If we want to get details about a specific function, we can use the **faas-cli describe** CLI command:

```
$ faas-cli describe hello
```

The output should be as follows:

```
/serverless $ faas-cli describe hello
Name:                hello
Status:              Ready
Replicas:            1
Available replicas:  1
Invocations:         0
Image:               sathsarasa/hello:latest
Function process:
URL:                 http://192.168.99.100:31112/function/hello
Async URL:           http://192.168.99.100:31112/async-function/hello
Labels:              faas_function : hello
Annotations:         prometheus.io.scrape : false
 /serverless $
```

Figure 9.25: Describing an OpenFaaS function

Invoking OpenFaaS Functions

Now, the function is deployed and ready to be invoked. A function can be invoked with the **faas-cli invoke** command, which has the following format:

```
$ faas-cli invoke <function-name>
```

Now, let's invoke the **hello** function we deployed in the previous step.

Run the following command to invoke the **hello** function:

```
$ faas-cli invoke hello
```

Once the function is invoked, it will ask you to enter the input parameters and press *Ctrl + D* to stop reading from the standard input. The output should be as follows:

```
/serverless $ faas-cli invoke hello
Reading from STDIN - hit (Control + D) to stop.
Hello OpenFaaS   Hello, Go. You said: Hello OpenFaaS
/serverless $
```

Figure 9.26: Invoking the hello function

We can also send the input data to the function, as shown in the following command:

```
$ echo "Hello with echo" | faas-cli invoke hello
```

The output should be as follows:

```
/serverless $ echo "Hello with echo" | faas-cli invoke hello
Hello, Go. You said: Hello with echo

/serverless $
```

Figure 9.27: Invoking the hello function with piping the input

The **curl** command can also be used to invoke the functions, as follows:

```
$ curl http://192.168.99.100:31112/function/hello -d "Hello from curl"
```

The output should be as follows:

```
/serverless $ curl http://192.168.99.100:31112/function/hello -d "Hello
from curl"
Hello, Go. You said: Hello from curl
/serverless $
```

Figure 9.28: Invoking the hello function with curl

Hence, we have successfully invoked the **hello** function using both the **faas-cli invoke** command and the **curl** command.

Deleting OpenFaaS Functions

The **faas-cli remove** command is used to delete a function from the OpenFaaS cluster either by specifying the function definition file with the **-f** flag, or by explicitly specifying the function name, as shown in the following command:

```
$ faas-cli remove <function-name>
```

Or, alternatively, with the following command:

```
$ faas-cli remove -f <function-definition-file>
```

We can remove the **hello** function we created earlier with the following command:

```
$ faas-cli remove hello
```

The output should be as follows:

```
/serverless $ faas-cli remove hello
Deleting: hello.
Removing old function.
/serverless $
```

Figure 9.29: Deleting the hello function

In these sections, we learned to create, deploy, list, invoke, and delete OpenFaaS functions using the **faas-cli** command line. Now, let's move on to an exercise where we will be creating our first OpenFaaS function.

Exercise 30: Creating an OpenFaaS Function with Dependencies

In this exercise, we are going to create a Python function that can print the source IP address by invoking an external API. We will be using the **requests** Python module to invoke this API:

1. Create a new function named **ip-info** using the **Python3** template:

```
$ faas-cli new ip-info --lang=python3
```

The output should be as follows:

```
/serverless $ faas-cli new ip-info --lang=python3
Folder: ip-info created.




Function created in folder: ip-info
Stack file written: ip-info.yml
/serverless $
```

Figure 9.30: Creating the ip-info function template

2. Update the **ip-info/requirements.txt** file to add the **requests pip** module, which we need to invoke HTTP requests from our function:

   ```
   requests
   ```

3. Update the **ip-info/handler.py** file to invoke the https://httpbin.org/ip endpoint. This endpoint is a simple service that will return the IP of the originating request. The following code will send an HTTP GET request to the https://httpbin.org/ip endpoint and return the origin IP address:

   ```python
   import requests
   import json

   def handle(req):
       api_response = requests.get('https://httpbin.org/ip')
       json_object = api_response.json()
       origin_ip = json_object["origin"]

       return "Origin IP is " + origin_ip
   ```

4. Build, push, and deploy the **ip-info** function with the **faas-cli up** command. The **faas-cli up** command will execute the **faas-cli build**, **faas-cli push**, and **faas-cli deploy** commands in the background to build the function, push the Docker images to the Docker registry, and deploy the function on the OpenFaaS framework:

   ```
   $ faas-cli up -f ip-info.yml
   ```

The **faas-cli up** command will print the following output, which lists the steps of building, pushing, and deploying the **ip-info** function:

```
[0] > Building ip-info.
Clearing temporary build folder: ./build/ip-info/
Preparing ./ip-info/ ./build/ip-info//function
Building: sathsarasa/ip-info:latest with python3 template. Please wait..
Sending build context to Docker daemon  9.728kB
...
Successfully built 1b86554ad3a2
Successfully tagged sathsarasa/ip-info:latest
Image: sathsarasa/ip-info:latest built.
[0] < Building ip-info done.
[0] worker done.

[0] > Pushing ip-info [sathsarasa/ip-info:latest].
The push refers to repository [docker.io/sathsarasa/ip-info]
...
latest: digest:
sha256:44e0b0e1eeca37f521d4e9daa1c788192cbc0ce6ab898c5e71cb840c6d3b4839
size: 4288
[0] < Pushing ip-info [sathsarasa/ip-info:latest] done.
[0] worker done.

Deploying: ip-info.
WARNING! Communication is not secure, please consider using HTTPS.
Letsencrypt.org offers free SSL/TLS certificates.

Deployed. 202 Accepted.
URL: http://192.168.99.100:31112/function/ip-info
```

5. Invoke the **ip-info** function using the **curl** command as follows:

```
$ curl http://192.168.99.100:31112/function/ip-info
```

The output should be as follows:

```
/serverless $ curl http://192.168.99.100:31112/function/ip-info
Origin IP is 122.255.33.34, 122.255.33.34
/serverless $
```

Figure 9.31: Invoking the ip-info function template

6. Finally, remove the **ip-info** function:

```
$ faas-cli remove ip-info
```

Thus, we have created, deployed, and invoked an OpenFaaS function named **ip-info**, which will print the source IP address of the function invoker.

Deploying and Invoking Functions with OpenFaaS Portal

The OpenFaaS framework comes with a built-in UI that allows us to deploy and invoke functions from the web browser. It can be used to either deploy a custom function or a function from the function store. The OpenFaaS function store is a freely available set of prebuilt functions. These functions can be deployed easily on our existing OpenFaaS cluster.

The format of the OpenFaaS portal URL is **http://<openfaas-gateway-endpoint>/ui**. Let's use the following command to derive the OpenFaaS portal URL from the **$OPENFAAS_URL** environment variable that we set up previously:

```
echo $OPENFAAS_URL/ui/
```

The output should be as follows:

```
/serverless $ echo $OPENFAAS_URL/ui/
http://192.168.99.100:31112/ui/
/serverless $
```

Figure 9.32: Generating the OpenFaaS portal URL

Let's navigate to the output URL of **http://192.168.99.100:31112/ui/**.

You should be able to see a portal similar to the following, which we will use in the following steps to deploy and invoke OpenFaaS functions:

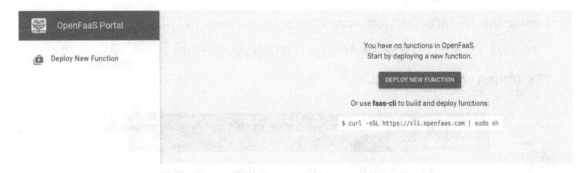

Figure 9.33: Navigating to the OpenFaaS portal URL

Deploying a Function from the Function Store

In this section, we will learn how to deploy a function from the function store. First, click on the **Deploy New Function** button in the OpenFaaS portal. This will prompt you with a dialog box that lists all the functions available in the function store. In this section, we are going to deploy the **Figlet** function, which can generate ASCII logos from the string input provided. Select **Figlet** from the function list and click on the **DEPLOY** button, as shown in the following figure:

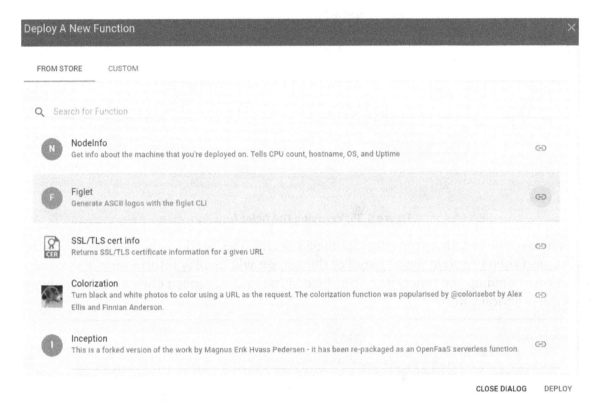

Figure 9.34: Deploying the figlet function

That's all you need to do! This will deploy the **Figlet** function into our existing OpenFaaS cluster. Now, you will be able to see a new function named **figlet** in the left-hand sidebar of the OpenFaaS portal, as shown in the following figure:

Figure 9.35: Verifying the figlet function

Let's invoke the function from the OpenFaaS portal. You need to click on the function name, and then the right-hand panel of the screen will display information about the function, including the function status, invocation count, replica count, function image, and the function URL:

Figure 9.36: Figlet function description

We can invoke this function by clicking on the **INVOKE** button available under the **Invoke function** section. If the function requires an input value, you can provide it under the **Request Body** section before invoking the function.

Let's invoke the **figlet** function by providing the **OpenFaaS** string as the request body, as shown in the following figure:

Figure 9.37: Invoking the figlet function

Now, you can see the expected output of the function. This will be the ASCII logo for the input value we provided when invoking the function. Additionally, the UI will provide you with the response status code and the execution duration for the function invocation.

Deploying a Custom Function

Now, let's deploy a custom function named **hello** using the Docker image that we built previously. Before deploying the functions from the OpenFaaS portal, we should have our functions written, and the Docker images built and pushed using the **faas-cli** command.

Click on the **Deploy New Function** button again, and, this time, select the **CUSTOM** tab from the dialog box. Now, we need to provide the Docker image name and function name as mandatory fields. Let's provide the `hello` Docker image we built previously (`<your-docker-id>/hello`) and provide `hello-portal` as the function name and click on the **DEPLOY** button:

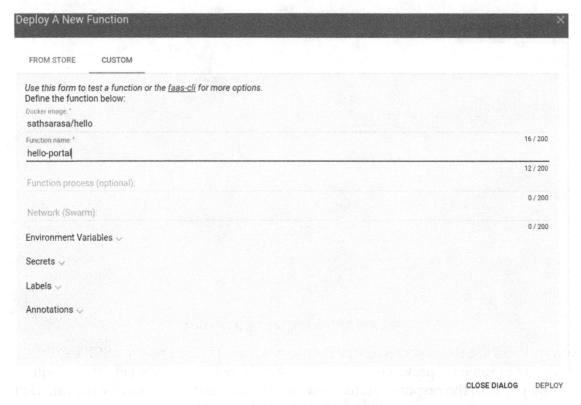

Figure 9.38: Deploying the hello-portal function

Then, you will see the **hello-portal** function added to the left-side menu of the OpenFaaS portal:

Figure 9.39: Verifying the hello-portal function

Now, you can follow similar steps to the ones that we discussed previously to invoke the **hello-portal** function.

OpenFaaS Functions with HTML Output

In this section, we are going to set up an OpenFaaS function to return HTML content. This allows us to create both static and dynamic websites using the OpenFaaS framework.

First, we will create the **html-output** function using the **php7** template, as shown in the following command:

```
$ faas-cli new html-output --lang=php7
```

The output should be as follows:

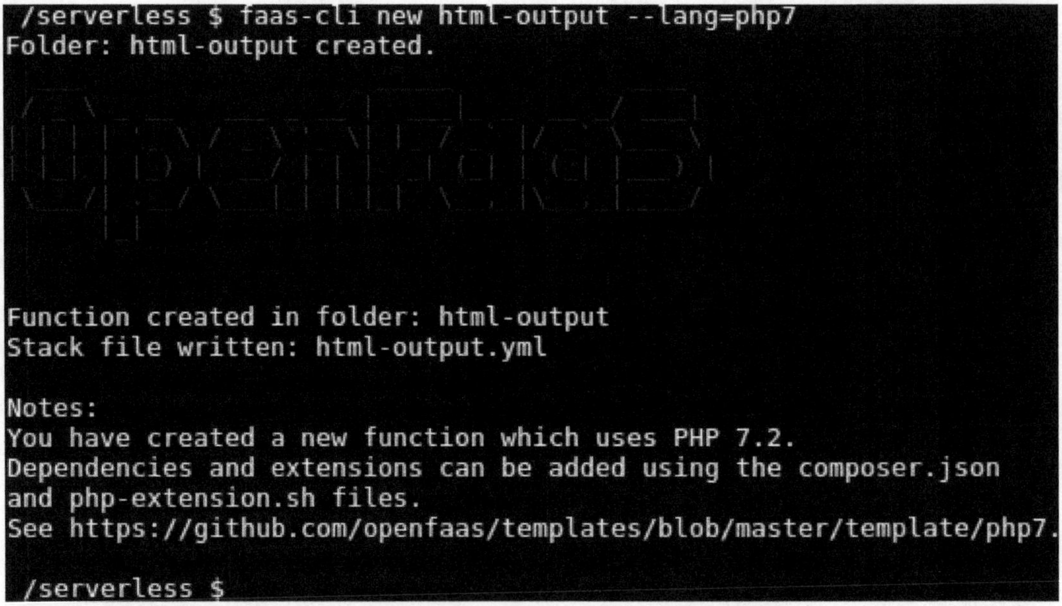

Figure 9.40: Creating the html-output function

Then, we will update the generated **Handler.php** file to return a hardcoded HTML string using the following command:

Open the **html-output/src/Handler.php** file using your favorite text editor. The following command will open this file with the **vi** editor:

```
$ vi html-output/src/Handler.php
```

Add the following content to the file. This is a simple PHP code that will return the text, **OpenFaaS HTML Output**, formatted as HTML header text:

```php
<?php

namespace App;

/**
 * Class Handler
 * @package App
 */
class Handler
{
```

```
/**
 * @param $data
 * @return
 */
public function handle($data) {
    $htmlOutput = "<html><h1>OpenFaaS HTML Output</h1></html>";
    return $htmlOutput;
}

}
```

Now, the PHP function is ready with the HTML output. The next step is to configure **Content-Type** of the function as **text/html**. This can be done by updating the **environment** section of the function definition file. Let's update the **html-output.yml** file with **content_type: text/html** inside the environment section, as shown in the following code:

```
$ vi html-output.yml

provider:
  name: faas
  gateway: http://192.168.99.100:31112

functions:
  html-output:
    lang: php7
    handler: ./html-output
    image: sathsarasa/html-output:latest
    environment:
      content_type: text/html
```

Now, let's build, push, and deploy the **html-output** function with the **faas-cli up** command:

```
$ faas-cli up -f html-output.yml
```

Once the preceding command is executed, we will receive an output similar to the following:

```
[0] > Building html-output.

Clearing temporary build folder: ./build/html-output/

Preparing ./html-output/ ./build/html-output//function

Building: sathsarasa/html-output:latest with php7 template. Please wait..

Sending build context to Docker daemon  13.31kB

...

Successfully built db79bcf55f33

Successfully tagged sathsarasa/html-output:latest

Image: sathsarasa/html-output:latest built.

[0] < Building html-output done.

[0] worker done.


[0] > Pushing html-output [sathsarasa/html-output:latest].

The push refers to repository [docker.io/sathsarasa/html-output]

b7fb7b7178f2: Pushed

06f1d60fbeaf: Pushed

b2f016541c01: Pushed

1eb73bc41394: Pushed

dc6f559fd649: Mounted from sathsarasa/php7

e50d92207970: Mounted from sathsarasa/php7

9bd686c066e4: Mounted from sathsarasa/php7

35b76def1bb4: Mounted from sathsarasa/php7

34986ef73af3: Mounted from sathsarasa/php7

334b08a7c2ef: Mounted from sathsarasa/php7

5833c19f1f2c: Mounted from sathsarasa/php7

98d2cfd0a4c9: Mounted from sathsarasa/php7

24291ffdb574: Mounted from sathsarasa/php7
```

```
eb2c5ec03df0: Pushed

3b051c6cbb79: Pushed

99abb9ea3d15: Mounted from sathsarasa/php7

be22007b8d1b: Mounted from sathsarasa/php7

83a68ffd9f11: Mounted from sathsarasa/php7

1bfeebd65323: Mounted from sathsarasa/php7

latest: digest:
sha256:ec5721288a325900252ce928f8c5f8726c6ab0186449d9414baa04e4fac4dfd0
size: 4296

[0] < Pushing html-output [sathsarasa/html-output:latest] done.

[0] worker done.


Deploying: html-output.

WARNING! Communication is not secure, please consider using HTTPS.

Letsencrypt.org offers free SSL/TLS certificates.


Deployed. 202 Accepted.

URL: http://192.168.99.100:31112/function/html-output
```

The function has now been deployed successfully. Now, we can visit the function URL at http://192.168.99.100:31112/function/html-output from a web browser to view the output, as shown in the following figure:

Figure 9.41: Invoking the html-output function

Exercise 31: Returning HTML Based on Path Parameters

In this exercise, we will create a function that can return one of the two static HTML files based on the path parameters of the function URL:

1. Create a new function named **serverless-website** based on the **php7** template:

   ```
   $ faas-cli new serverless-website --lang=php7
   ```

   The output should be as follows:

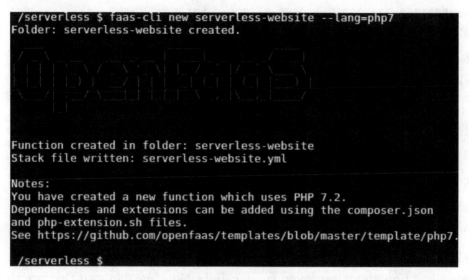

   Figure 9.42: Creating the serverless-website function

2. Create the HTML folder inside **serverless-website** to store all the HTML files:

   ```
   $ mkdir serverless-website/src/html
   ```

3. Create the first HTML file for the home page (**serverless-website/src/html/home.html**) with the following code. This HTML page will output the text, **Welcome to OpenFaaS Home Page**, as the page header, and **OpenFaaS Home** as the page title:

   ```
   <!DOCTYPE html>
   <html>
     <head>
       <title>OpenFaaS Home</title>
     </head>
     <body>
       <h1>Welcome to OpenFaaS Home Page</h1>
     </body>
   </html>
   ```

4. Create the second HTML file for the login page (**serverless-website/src/html/ login.html**). This HTML page will output a simple login form with two fields for **username** and **password** and a **Login** button to submit the form:

```
<!DOCTYPE html>
<html>
 <head>
    <title>OpenFaaS Login</title>
 </head>
 <body>
    <h1>OpenFaaS Login Page</h1>
    <form id="contact_us_form">
        <label for="username">Username:</label>
        <input type="text" name="username" required>
        <label for="password">Password:</label>
        <input type="text" name="password" required>
        <input type="submit" value="Login">
    </form>
 </body>
</html>
```

5. Update the handler file (**serverless-website/src/Handler.php**) to return the appropriate HTML file based on the path parameters of the function URL with the following code. This function will receive either **home** or **login** as the path parameter while invoking. It will then read the path parameter and set the HTML page name accordingly based on the path parameter provided. The next step is to open the HTML file, read the content of the file, and finally return the content of the file as the function response:

```
<?php

namespace App;

class Handler
{
    public function handle($data) {
            // Retrieve page name from path params
            $path_params = getenv('Http_Path');
            $path_params_array = explode('/',$path_params);
            $last_index = count($path_params_array);
            $page_name = $path_params_array[$last_index-1];

            // Set the page name
```

```
            $current_dir = __DIR__;
            $html_file_path = $current_dir . "/html/" . $page_name .
".html";

            // Read the file
            $html_file = fopen($html_file_path, "r") or die("Unable to open
HTML file!");
            $html_output = fread($html_file,filesize($html_file_path));
            fclose($html_file);

            // Return file content
            return $html_output;
    }
}
```

6. Set **content_type** as **text/html** in **serverless-website.yml**:

```
version: 1.0
provider:
  name: openfaas
  gateway: http://192.168.99.100:31112
functions:
  serverless-website:
    lang: php7
    handler: ./serverless-website
    image: sathsarasa/serverless-website:latest
    environment:
      content_type: text/html
```

7. Build, push, and deploy the **serverless-website** function using the following command:

```
$ faas-cli up -f serverless-website.yml
```

The following is the output of the preceding command:

```
[0] > Building serverless-website.
Clearing temporary build folder: ./build/serverless-website/
Preparing ./serverless-website/ ./build/serverless-website//function
Building: sathsarasa/serverless-website:latest with php7 template. Please
wait..
Sending build context to Docker daemon  16.38kB
...
```

```
Successfully built 24fd037ce0d0
Successfully tagged sathsarasa/serverless-website:latest
Image: sathsarasa/serverless-website:latest built.
[0] < Building serverless-website done.
[0] worker done.

[0] > Pushing serverless-website [sathsarasa/serverless-website:latest].
The push refers to repository [docker.io/sathsarasa/serverless-website]
...
latest: digest:
sha256:991c02fa7336113915acc60449dc1a7559585ca2fea3ca1326ecdb5fae96f2fc
size: 4298
[0] < Pushing serverless-website [sathsarasa/serverless-website:latest]
done.
[0] worker done.

Deploying: serverless-website.
WARNING! Communication is not secure, please consider using HTTPS.
Letsencrypt.org offers free SSL/TLS certificates.

Deployed. 202 Accepted.
URL: http://192.168.99.100:31112/function/serverless-website
```

8. Verify by invoking both the home page and login page on the following URLs:

http://192.168.99.100:31112/function/serverless-website/home

The home page should appear as follows:

Figure 9.43: Invoking the home page of the serverless website function

Next, run the following URL: **http://192.168.99.100:31112/function/serverless-website/login**.

The login page should look as follows:

Figure 9.44: Invoking the login page of the serverless website function

Thus, we have successfully parsed HTML based on the path parameters.

OpenFaaS Function Observability

Observability is a critical feature of every production system. This allows us to observe the health of the system and activities performed thereon. Once our applications are deployed and running in production, we need to make sure they are running as expected in terms of functionality and performance. Any service downtime can have a negative impact on the organization. So, it is very critical to observe the important application metrics, such as CPU usage, memory usage, request count, response duration over time, and then analyze for any anomalies.

OpenFaaS comes built-in with **Prometheus**, which can be used to collect function metrics. Prometheus contains a time series database, which can be used to store various metrics over time. The OpenFaaS API gateway collects metrics related to the function invocation and stores them in Prometheus. The following table shows the metrics exposed by the OpenFaaS API Gateway and stored with Prometheus:

Metric name	Description
`gateway_functions_seconds`	Function execution duration
`gateway_function_invocation_total`	Total number of function invocations
`gateway_service_count`	Number of function replicas
`http_request_duration_seconds`	Execution duration for HTTP requests
`http_requests_total`	Total number of HTTP requests

Figure 9.45: Function metrics with descriptions

We can use the **Prometheus** dashboard to visualize these metrics.

First, we need to expose the **Prometheus** deployment created during the installation. Execute the following command to expose Prometheus as a **NodePort** service:

```
$ kubectl expose deployment prometheus -n openfaas --type=NodePort
--name=prometheus-ui
```

This will expose the Prometheus deployment on a random port above **30,000**. Execute the following commands to get the URL of the **Prometheus** UI:

```
$ MINIKUBE_IP=$(minikube ip)
```

```
$ PROMETHEUS_PORT=$(kubectl get svc prometheus-ui -n openfaas -o jsonpath="{.
spec.ports[0].nodePort}")
```

```
$ PROMETHEUS_URL=http://$MINIKUBE_IP:$PROMETHEUS_PORT/graph
```

```
$ echo $PROMETHEUS_URL
```

The output should be as follows:

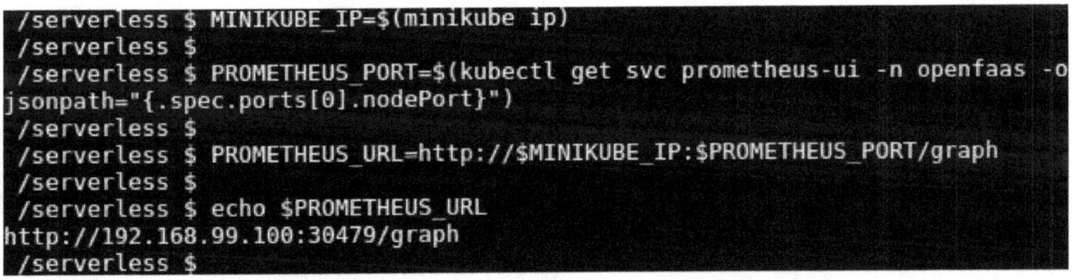

Figure 9.46: Generating the Prometheus URL

For me, the **PROMETHEUS_URL** output value is http://192.168.99.100:30479/graph. But the **<minikube-ip>** and **<node-port>** values may be different.

We can view the metrics exposed by Prometheus using the UI, as shown in the following figure:

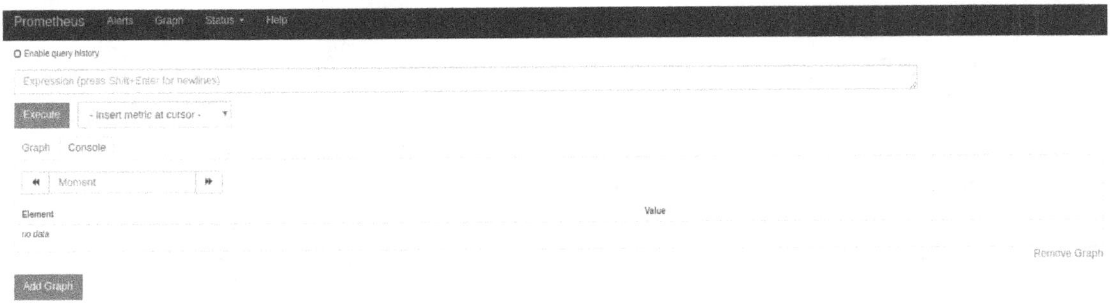

Figure 9.47: Prometheus UI

Type **gateway_function_invocation_total** in the **Expression** area and click on the **Execute** button. This will list the results under the **Console** tab. We can click on the **Graph** tab as we need to view the function invocation count in a line graph. Click on the **Add Graph** button available in the lower-left corner if you want to add this graph permanently to the Prometheus dashboard, as shown in the following figure:

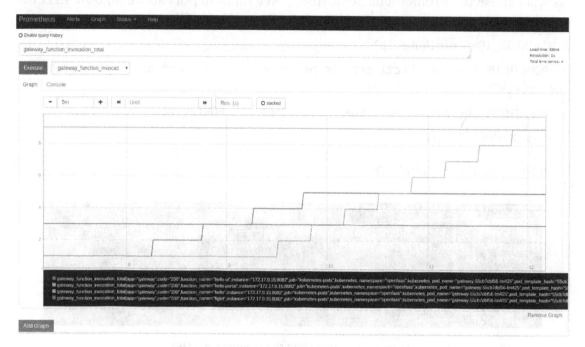

Figure 9.48: Prometheus graph for the gateway_function_invocation_total metric

> **Note**
>
> Invoke the available functions multiple times so that we can view the statistics of these invocations from the Prometheus dashboard.

In addition to the Prometheus dashboards that we discussed, we can also use **Grafana** to visualize the metrics stored in Prometheus. **Grafana** is an open source tool used to analyze and visualize metrics over a period of time. It can be integrated with multiple data sources such as **Prometheus**, **ElasticSearch**, **Influx DB**, or **MySQL**. In the next exercise, we are going to learn how to set up Grafana with OpenFaaS and create dashboards to monitor the metrics stored in the Prometheus data source.

Exercise 32: Installing an OpenFaaS Grafana Dashboard

In this exercise, we are going to install a Grafana dashboard to view the metrics from the **Prometheus** data source. Then, we will import another OpenFaaS dashboard into Grafana:

1. Create the **grafana** deployment in the **openfaas** namespace using the **stefanprodan/faas-grafana:4.6.3** Docker image:

```
kubectl run grafana -n openfaas \
    --image=stefanprodan/faas-grafana:4.6.3 \
    --port=3000
```

The output should be as follows:

```
/serverless $ kubectl run grafana -n openfaas \
> --image=stefanprodan/faas-grafana:4.6.3 \
> --port=3000
kubectl run --generator=deployment/apps.v1 is DEPRECATED and will be removed
in a future version. Use kubectl run --generator=run-pod/v1 or kubectl create
 instead.
deployment.apps/grafana created
 /serverless $
```

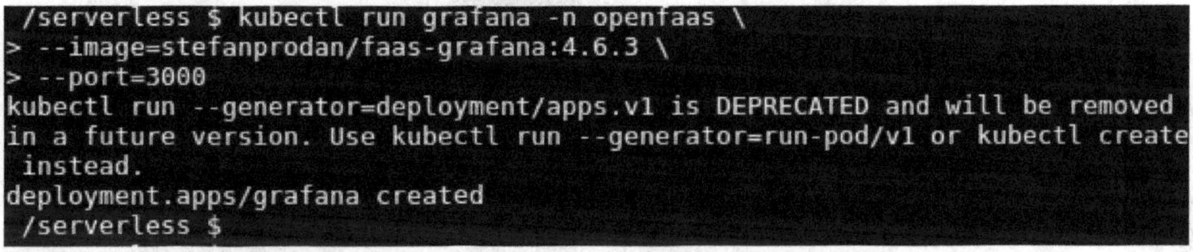

Figure 9.49: Creating the Grafana deployment

2. Expose the **grafana** deployment using the **NodePort** service:

```
kubectl expose deployment grafana -n openfaas  \
    --type=NodePort \
    --name=grafana
```

The output should be as follows:

```
/serverless $ kubectl expose deployment grafana -n openfaas  \
> --type=NodePort \
> --name=grafana
service/grafana exposed
 /serverless $
```

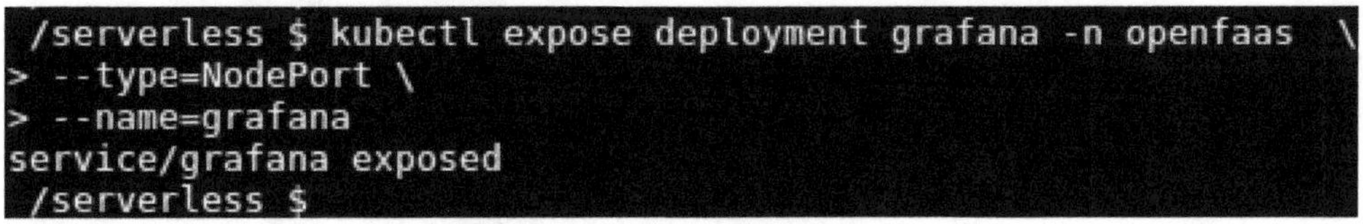

Figure 9.50: Exposing the grafana port

3. Find the URL of the **grafana** dashboard using the following commands:

```
$ MINIKUBE_IP=$(minikube ip)

$ GRAFANA_PORT=$(kubectl get svc grafana -n openfaas -o jsonpath="{.spec.ports[0].nodePort}")

$ GRAFANA_URL=http://$MINIKUBE_IP:$GRAFANA_PORT/dashboard/db/openfaas

$ echo $GRAFANA_URL
```

The output should be as follows:

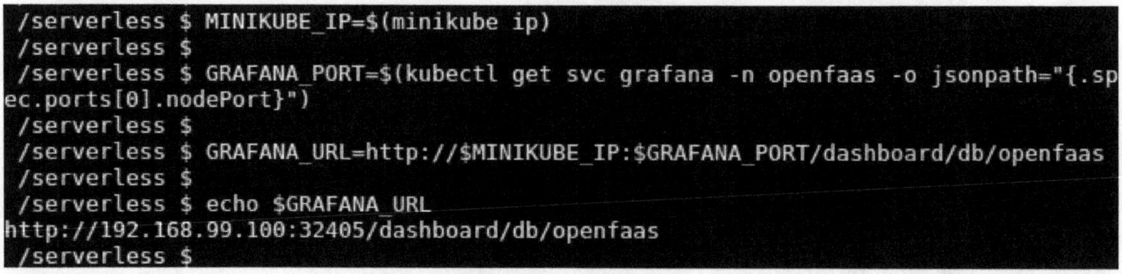

```
/serverless $ MINIKUBE_IP=$(minikube ip)
/serverless $
/serverless $ GRAFANA_PORT=$(kubectl get svc grafana -n openfaas -o jsonpath="{.sp
ec.ports[0].nodePort}")
/serverless $
/serverless $ GRAFANA_URL=http://$MINIKUBE_IP:$GRAFANA_PORT/dashboard/db/openfaas
/serverless $
/serverless $ echo $GRAFANA_URL
http://192.168.99.100:32405/dashboard/db/openfaas
/serverless $
```

Figure 9.51: Generating the grafana URL

4. Navigate to the **grafana** URL using the URL printed in the previous step:

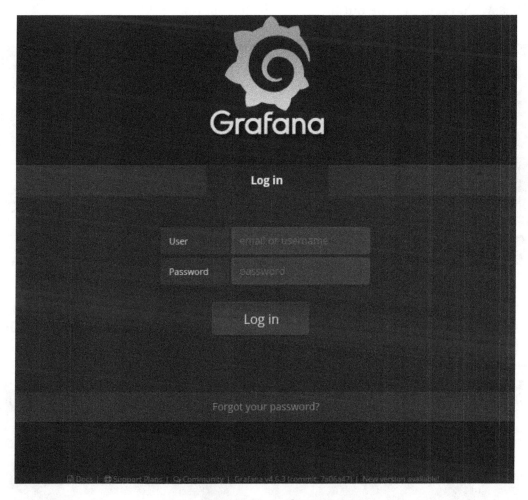

Figure 9.52: Grafana UI

5. Log in to **Grafana** using the default credentials (the username is **admin** and the

6. password is **admin**). The output should be as follows:

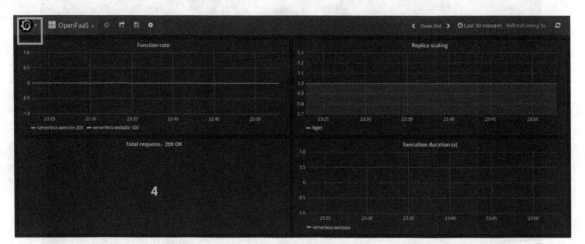

Figure 9.53: Grafana dashboards

From the **Grafana menu ()** in the top-left corner, as highlighted in *Figure* 9.53, select **Dashboards > Import**. Provide the ID of **3434** in the **Grafana.com Dashboard** input box and wait for a few seconds to load the dashboard data:

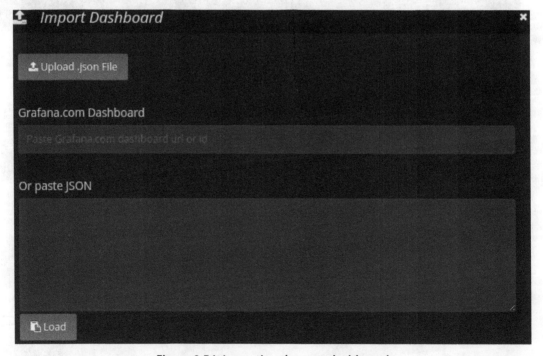

Figure 9.54: Importing the new dashboard

7. From this screen, select **faas** as the Prometheus data source and click on **Import**, as shown in the following figure:

Figure 9.55: Importing the new dashboard

8. Now you can see the metrics in the new dashboard:

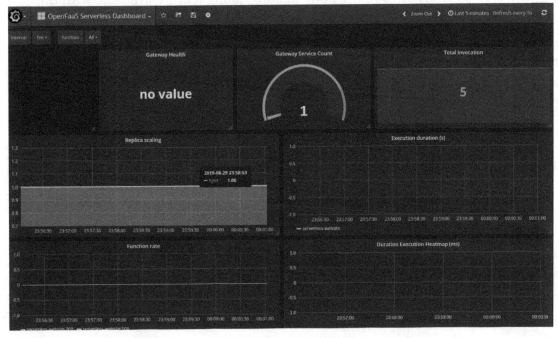

Figure 9.56: OpenFaaS serverless Grafana dashboard

Thus, we have successfully set up Grafana dashboards to visualize the metrics stored in Prometheus.

OpenFaaS Function Autoscaling

Autoscaling is a feature available in OpenFaaS that scales up or scales down function replicas based on demand. This feature was built using both **Prometheus** and the **Alert Manager** components available with the OpenFaaS framework. Alert Manager will fire alerts when the function invocation frequency exceeds the defined threshold.

While deploying the functions, the following labels are used to control the number of minimum replicas, maximum replicas, and the increase/decrease factor of the functions:

- `com.openfaas.scale.min` – This defines the initial number of replicas, which is 1 by default.

- `com.openfaas.scale.max` – This defines the maximum number of replicas.

- `com.openfaas.scale.factor` – This defines the percentage of pod replica increase (or decrease) when the Alert Manager fires the alerts. By default, this is set to **20%** and should have a value between **0** and **100**.

When OpenFaaS is deployed on Kubernetes, the Horizontal Pod Autoscaling feature from the Kubernetes framework can also be used to autoscale functions based on demand, as an alternative to the built-in autoscaling feature available with the OpenFaaS framework.

Let's now deploy the **figlet** function from the OpenFaaS function store to check the autoscaling feature in action:

```
faas-cli store deploy figlet \
    --label com.openfaas.scale.min=1 \
    --label com.openfaas.scale.max=5
```

The output should be as follows:

```
/serverless $ faas-cli store deploy figlet \
>    --label com.openfaas.scale.max=5 \
>    --label com.openfaas.scale.min=1
WARNING! Communication is not secure, please consider using HTTPS. Letsencrypt.org
offers free SSL/TLS certificates.

Deployed. 202 Accepted.
URL: http://192.168.99.100:31112/function/figlet

/serverless $
```

Figure 9.57: Deploying the figlet function

Now we can put a load on the **figlet** function by invoking it 1,000 times, as shown in the following code. The following script will invoke the **figlet** function 1,000 times by providing the **OpenFaaS** string as the input for the function and sleeps for 0.1 seconds in between each invocation:

```
for i in {1..1000}
do
    echo "Invocation $i"
    echo OpenFaaS | faas-cli invoke figlet
    sleep 0.1
done
```

Navigate to the **Grafana** portal and observe the increasing number of replicas for the **figlet** function. Once the load completes, the replica count will start scaling down and go back to the **com.openfaas.scale.min** count of 1 function replica.

The output should be as follows:

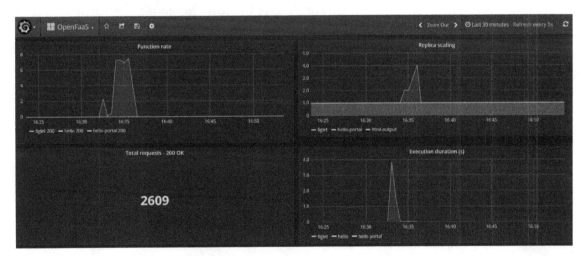

Figure 9.58: Verifying the autoscaling feature

In this section, we covered function autoscaling, we discussed what function autoscaling is, and the configuration we can use to set the minimum replica count, the maximum replica count, and the scale factor. Finally, we deployed a sample function, performed a load on the function, and observed the autoscaling functionality on a Grafana dashboard.

Activity 9: OpenFaaS Form Processor

In this activity, we will be creating a website for a brand that will have a contact form for potential customers to contact the brand personnel. We will be using **OpenFaas** extensively for this website.

Imagine that you are a freelancer and you want to create a website to increase your brand visibility. This website needs to have a "Contact Us" form that allows potential customers to contact you. You decided to create this website using serverless technologies and OpenFaaS was selected as the framework for this task.

Execute the following steps to complete this activity:

1. Create a SendGrid (https://sendgrid.com) account to send emails and save the API key.

2. Create the "Contact Us" form using HTML and return the HTML using an OpenFaaS function. The following is sample code that achieves the functionality of an HTML form with input fields for **name**, **email**, and **message** and a **submit** button; CSS to add styles to the HTML form; and a JavaScript function, which will be triggered when the user clicks on the **Submit** button and sends the form data as a **POST** request to the **form-processor** function:

```html
<!DOCTYPE html>
<html>
  <head>
    <meta charset="UTF-8">
    <title>OpenFaaS Contact Us  Form</title>
    <style>
      /** Page  background colour */
      body  {
        background-color: #f2f2f2;
      }
      /** Style the h1  headers */
      h1 {
        text-align: center;
        font-family: Arial;
      }

      /** CSS for the input box and textarea */
      input[type=text], input[type=email], textarea {
        width: 100%;
        margin-top: 10px;
        margin-bottom: 20px;
        padding: 12px;
        box-sizing: border-box;
```

```
          resize: vertical
        }
        /** Style the submit  button */
        input[type=submit] {
          color: white;
          background-color: #5a91e8;
          padding: 10px 20px;
          border: none;
          border-radius: 4px;
          cursor: pointer;
        }
        /** Change submit button  color for mouse hover */
        input[type=submit]:hover  {
          background-color: #2662bf;
        }
        /** Add padding around the form */
         container {
          padding: 20px;
          border-radius: 5px;
        }
       /** Bold font for response and add margin */
   #response {
     font-weight: bold;
margin-bottom: 20px;
   }
        </style>
      </head>
      <body>
        <h1>OpenFaaS Contact Form</h1>
        <div class="container">
              <!-- Placeholder for the response -->
          <div id='response'></div>
          <form id="contact_us_form">
            <label for="name">Name:</label>
            <input type="text" id="name" name="name" required>
            <label for="email">Email:</label>
            <input type="email" id="email" name="email" required>
            <label for="message">Message:</label>
            <textarea id="message" name="message" required></textarea>
            <input type="submit" value="Send Message">
            </form>
        </div>
```

```html
        <script src="http://code.jquery.com/jquery-3.4.1.min.js"></script>
        <script>
          $(document).ready(function(){
          $('#contact_us_form').on('submit', function(e){
            // prevent form from submitting.
              e.preventDefault();
$('#response').html('Sending message...');
              // retrieve values from the form field
              var name = $('#name').val();
              email = $('#email').val();
              var message = $('#message').val();
              var formData = {
                name: name,
                email: email,
                message: message
              };
              // send the ajax POST request
              $.ajax({
                type: "POST",
                url: './form-processor',
                data: JSON.stringify(formData)
              })
               done(function(data) {
                $('#response').html(data);
              })
               fail(function(data) {
                $('#response').html(data);
              });
            });
          });
        </script>
    </body>
</html>
```

3. Create the **form-processor** function, which takes the form values from the Contact Us form and sends an email to a specified email address with the information provided.

4. Invoke the **Contact Us** form function using a web browser and verify the email delivery.

The contact form should look as shown in the following figure:

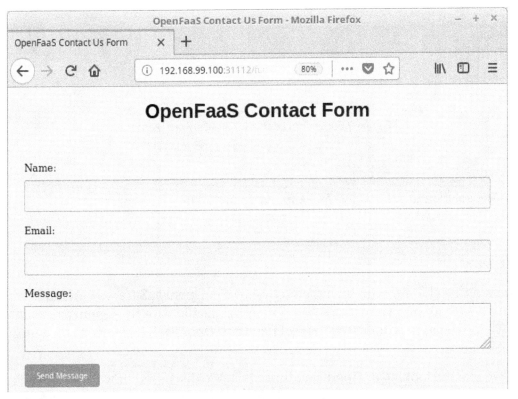

Figure 9.59: The Contact Us form

The email received from the contact form should look as shown in the following screenshot:

Figure 9.60: Email received from Contact Us form

> **Note**
>
> The solution to the activity can be found on page 444.

Summary

We started this chapter with an introduction to the OpenFaaS framework and continued with an overview of the components available with the OpenFaaS framework. Next, we looked at how to install **faas-cli** and the **OpenFaaS** framework on a local **Minikube** cluster.

Then, we started looking at **OpenFaaS** functions. We discussed how we can use **faas-cli** to create the function templates, build and push function Docker image, and deploy the function to the **OpenFaaS** framework. Then, we learned how to invoke the deployed functions with the **faas-cli** command and **curl** command. Next, we introduced the **OpenFaaS** portal, which is the built-in UI for the OpenFaaS framework.

We also learned how we can set up an **OpenFaaS** function to return HTML content and return different content based on provided parameters. We configured the **Prometheus** and **Grafana** dashboards to visualize the function metrics, including invocation count, invocation duration, and replica counts. Then, we discussed the function autoscaling feature, which scales up or scales down function replicas based on demand. We performed a load test on a function and observed autoscaling in action with Grafana dashboards.

Finally, in the activity, we built the frontend and backend of a Contact Us form of a website using the **OpenFaaS** framework.

Through the concepts and the various exercises and activities presented in this book, we have equipped you with all the skills you need to use serverless architectures and the state-of-art container management system, Kubernetes.

We are confident that you will be able to apply this knowledge toward building more robust and effective systems and host them on cloud providers such as **AWS Lambda**, **Google Cloud Function**, and more. You will also be able to use the highly effective features of best-in-class frameworks such as **OpenFaaS**, **OpenWhisk**, **Kubeless**, and more.

Appendix

About

This section is included to assist the students to perform the activities in the book.

It includes detailed steps that are to be performed by the students to achieve the objectives of the activities.

Chapter 01: Introduction to Serverless

Activity 1: Twitter Bot Backend for Bike Points in London

Solution:

Execute the following steps to complete this activity:

1. Create a `main.go` file for registering function handlers, as in *Exercise 1*.

   This code is the entry point of the application where functions are registered, and the main application is started:

   ```go
   package main

   import (
       "fmt"
       "net/http"
   )

   func main() {
       fmt.Println("Starting the 🚲 finder..")
       http.HandleFunc("/", FindBikes)
       fmt.Println("Function handlers are registered.")

       http.ListenAndServe(":8080", nil)
   }
   ```

2. Create a `function.go` file for the `FindBikes` function:

   ```go
   ...

   func FindBikes(w http.ResponseWriter, r *http.Request) {

       ...

       // Get bike points for the query
       bikePoints, err := httpClient.Get(fmt.Sprintf(TFL_API_URL + "BikePoint/Search?query=" + url2.QueryEscape(query)))

       ...
   ```

```
    // Get available number of bikes
    availableBikeResponse, err := httpClient.Get(TFL_API_URL + "BikePoint/"
+ bikePoint.ID)

...

        if bikeAmount == 0 {
            w.Write([]byte(fmt.Sprintf(RESPONSE_NO_AVAILABLE_BIKE,
bikePoint.CommonName, url)))
            return
        } else {
            w.Write([]byte(fmt.Sprintf(DEFAULT_RESPONSE, bikePoint.
CommonName, bikeAmount, url)))
            return
        }

...
```

> **Note**
>
> The files required for the activity can be found on the link: https://github.com/
> TrainingByPackt/Serverless-Architectures-with-Kubernetes/tree/master/Lesson01/
> Activity1.

In this file, the actual function and its helpers should be implemented. **FindBikes** is responsible for getting data from the **TFL Unified API** for the bike point locations and then the number of available bikes. According to the collected information, this function returns complete sentences to be used as Twitter responses.

3. Create a **Dockerfile** for building and packaging the function, as in *Exercise 2*:

```
FROM golang:1.12.5-alpine3.9 AS builder
ADD . .
RUN go build *.go

FROM alpine:3.9
RUN apk update && apk add ca-certificates && rm -rf /var/cache/apk/*
RUN update-ca-certificates
COPY --from=builder /go/function ./bikes
RUN chmod +x ./bikes
ENTRYPOINT ["./bikes"]
```

In this **Dockerfile**, the application is built in the first container and packaged in the second container for delivery.

4. Build the container image with Docker commands: `docker build . -t find-bikes`.

It should look something like this:

```
/serverless $
/serverless $ docker build . -t find-bikes
Sending build context to Docker daemon   7.68kB
Step 1/9 : FROM golang:1.12.5-alpine3.9 AS builder
 ---> c7330979841b
Step 2/9 : ADD . .
 ---> 069771304170
Step 3/9 : RUN go build *.go
 ---> Running in 5630dbcab26d
Removing intermediate container 5630dbcab26d
 ---> 27b54aa0a3d5
Step 4/9 : FROM alpine:3.9
 ---> cdf98d1859c1
Step 5/9 : RUN apk update && apk add ca-certificates && rm -rf /var/cache/apk/*
 ---> Using cache
 ---> b3204929e897
Step 6/9 : RUN update-ca-certificates
 ---> Using cache
 ---> d6871cb83a40
Step 7/9 : COPY --from=builder /go/function ./bikes
 ---> fe3350d50c19
Step 8/9 : RUN chmod +x ./bikes
 ---> Running in 22898565ff34
Removing intermediate container 22898565ff34
 ---> 2fc489795e9d
Step 9/9 : ENTRYPOINT ["./bikes"]
 ---> Running in a251820223e2
Removing intermediate container a251820223e2
 ---> 10713c14638a
Successfully built 10713c14638a
Successfully tagged find-bikes:latest
/serverless $
```

Figure 1.27: Building the Docker image

5. Run the container image as a Docker container and make the ports available on the host system: `docker run -it --rm -p 8080:8080 find-bikes`.

Things should look as shown in the following screenshot:

```
/serverless $ docker run -it --rm -p 8080:8080 find-bikes
Starting the finder..
Function handlers are registered.
```

Figure 1.28: Running the Docker container

6. Test the function's HTTP endpoint with different queries, such as **Oxford**, **Abbey**, or **Diagon Alley**.

    We expect to get real responses for London streets and failure responses for imaginary streets from literature:

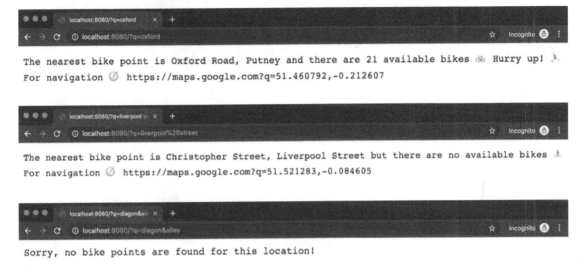

    The nearest bike point is Oxford Road, Putney and there are 21 available bikes 🚲 Hurry up! 🏃
    For navigation 🧭 https://maps.google.com?q=51.460792,-0.212607

    The nearest bike point is Christopher Street, Liverpool Street but there are no available bikes ⚠
    For navigation 🧭 https://maps.google.com?q=51.521283,-0.084605

    Sorry, no bike points are found for this location!

Figure 1.29: Function responses for different streets

7. Press *Ctrl* + C to exit the container:

```
/serverless $ docker run --it --rm -p 8080:8080 find-bikes
Starting the 🚲 finder..
Function handlers are registered.
^C /serverless $ █
```

Figure 1.30: Exiting the container

Chapter 02: Introduction to Serverless in the Cloud

Activity 2: Daily Stand-Up Meeting Reminder Function for Slack

Solution – Slack Setup:

1. In the **Slack** workspace, click on your username and select **Customize Slack**, as shown in the following screenshot:

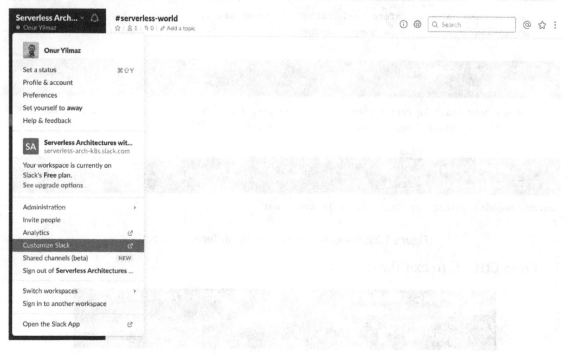

Figure 2.49: Slack menu

2. Click on **Configure apps** in the open window, as shown in the following screenshot:

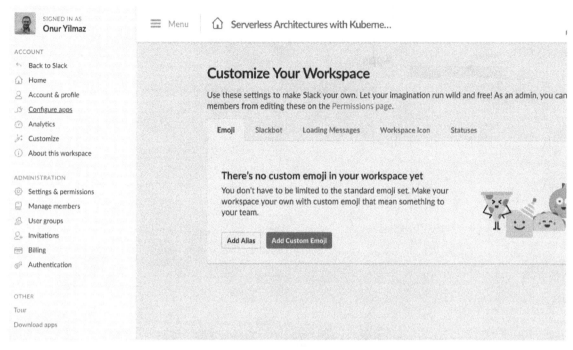

Fig 2.50: Slack configuration menu

3. Click on **Browse the App Directory** to add a new application from the directory, as shown in the following screenshot:

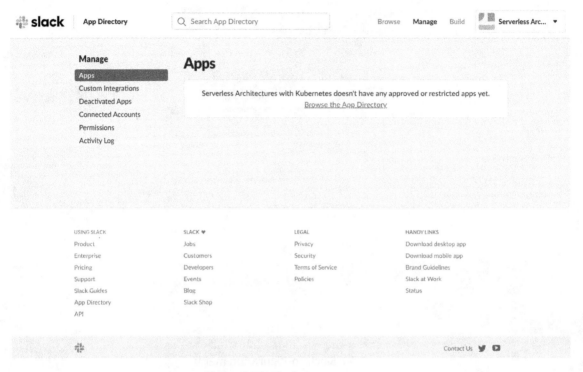

Figure 2.51: Slack management

4. Find **Incoming WebHooks** from the search box in **App Directory**, as shown in the following screenshot:

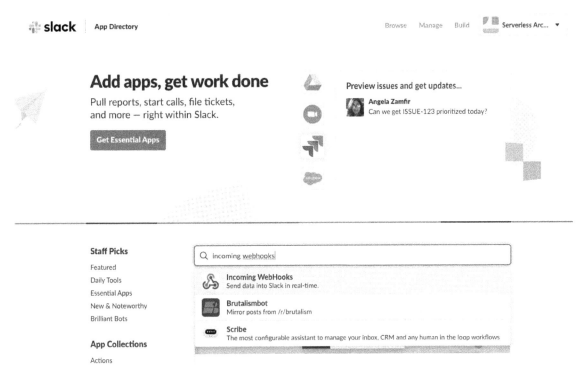

Figure 2.52: App Directory

5. Click on **Add Configuration** for the **Incoming WebHooks** application, as shown in the following screenshot:

Figure 2.53: Incoming Webhooks page

6. Fill in the configuration for the incoming webhook by specifying your specific channel name and icon, as shown in the following screenshot:

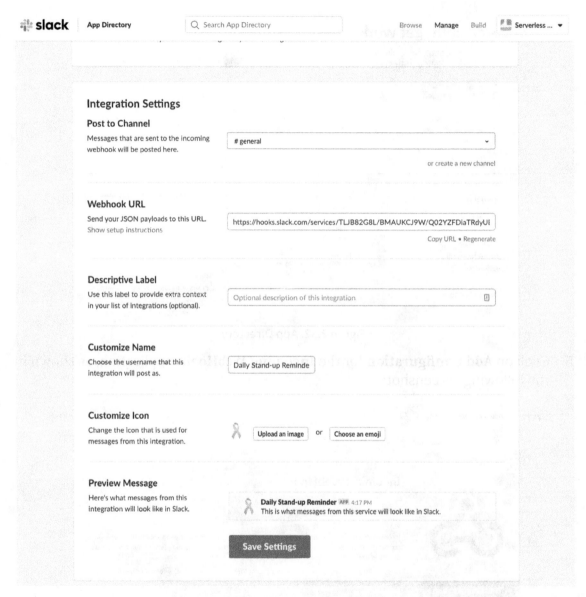

Figure 2.54: Incoming webhook configuration

Copy the **Webhook URL** and click **Save Settings**, as shown in the preceding screenshot.

7. Open the Slack workspace and channel we mentioned in step 6. You will see an integration message:

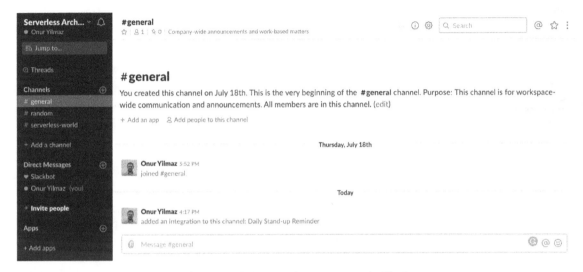

Figure 2.55: Integration message in Slack

Activity Solution

Execute the following steps to complete this activity:

1. Create a new function to call the Slack webhook when the function is invoked.

    In GCF, it can be defined with the name **StandupReminder**, 128 MB memory, and an HTTP trigger.

This function can be implemented in any supported language, such as **Go 1.11**, as shown in the following screenshot:

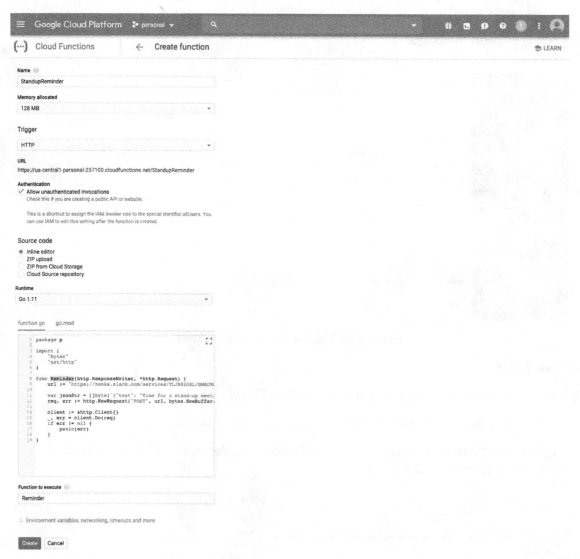

Figure 2.56: Cloud function in Google Cloud Platform

The code to be added is as follows:

```go
package p

import (
    "bytes"
    "net/http"
)

func Reminder(http.ResponseWriter, *http.Request) {
    url := "https://hooks.slack.com/services/TLJB82G8L/BMAUKCJ9W/
Q02YZFDiaTRdyUBTImE7MXn1"

    var jsonStr = []byte(`{"text": "Time for a stand-up meeting!"}`)
    req, err := http.NewRequest("POST", url, bytes.NewBuffer(jsonStr))

    client := &http.Client{}
    _, err = client.Do(req)
    if err != nil {
        panic(err)
    }
}
```

Note

Do not forget to change the **url** value with the Slack URL for the incoming web-hook configuration from step 6.

You can find the complete **function.go** file in the activity solutions of this book's GitHub repository: https://github.com/TrainingByPackt/Serverless-Architec-tures-with-Kubernetes/blob/master/Lesson02/Activity2/function.go.

2. Create a scheduler job with the trigger URL of the function and specify the schedule based on your stand-up meeting times.

   The scheduler can be defined in Google Cloud Scheduler with the name **StartupReminder** and the URL of the function, as shown in the following screenshot:

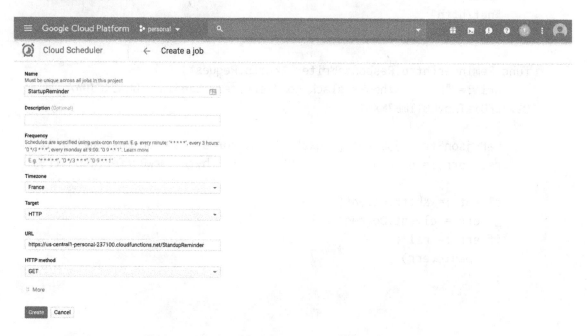

Figure 2.57: Cloud scheduler in Google Cloud Platform

With the schedule of 0 9 * * 1-5, the reminder will invoke the function at 09:00 on every day of the week from Monday through Friday.

3. Check the Slack channel when the time that was defined with the schedule has arrived for the reminder message.

   For the schedule of **0 9 * * 1-5**, you will see a message on your selected Slack channel at 09:00 on workdays, as shown in the following screenshot:

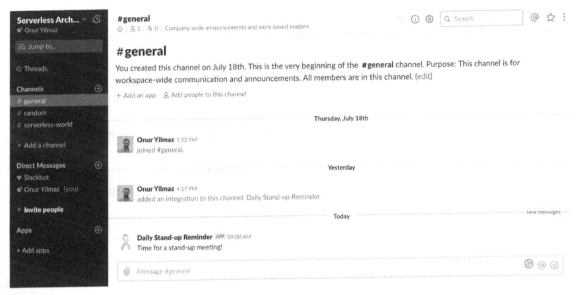

Figure 2.58: Slack reminder message

4. Delete the schedule job and function from the cloud provider, as shown in the following screenshot:

Figure 2.59: Deletion of the scheduler

The function can be deleted like so:

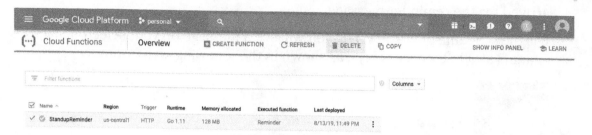

Figure 2.60: Deletion of the function

In this activity, we've built the backend of a Slack application using functions. We started by configuring Slack for incoming webhooks and then created a function to send data to the webhook. Since our function should be invoked at predefined times, we used the cloud scheduler services to invoke the function. With a successful reminder message in Slack, the integration of functions to other cloud services and external services was illustrated.

Chapter 03: Introduction to Serverless Frameworks

Activity 3: Daily Weather Status Function for Slack

Solution - Slack Setup

1. Execute the following steps to configure Slack:

2. In your Slack workspace, click on your username and select Customize Slack:

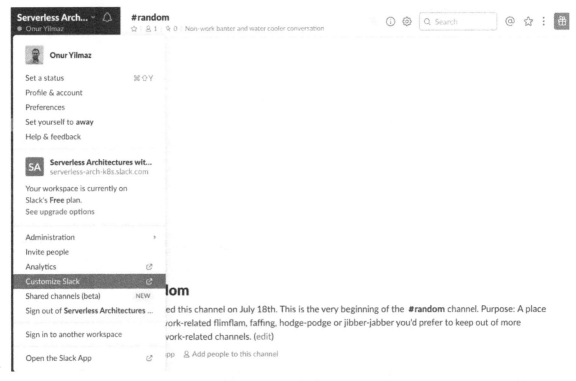

Figure 3.44: Slack menu

3. Click on Configure apps in the opened window:

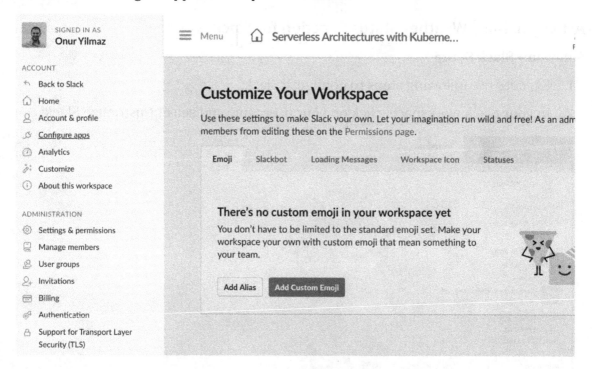

Figure 3.45: Slack configuration menu

4. Click on Browse the App Directory to add a new application from the directory:

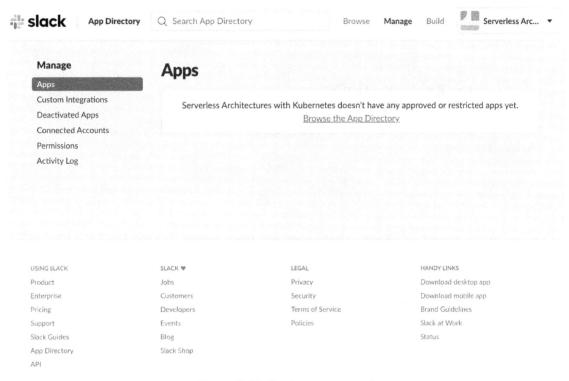

Figure 3.46: Slack management

5. Find Incoming WebHooks from the search box in App Directory:

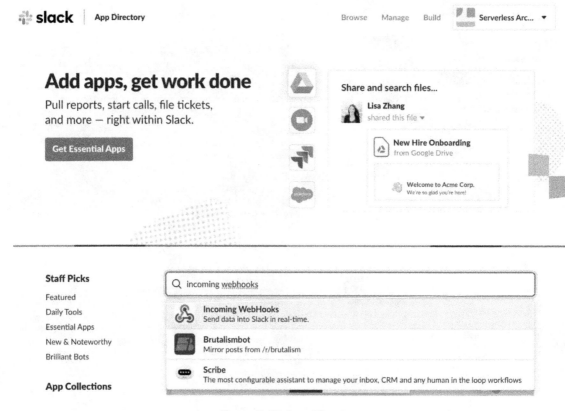

Figure 3.47: App Directory

6. Click on Set Up for the Incoming WebHooks application:

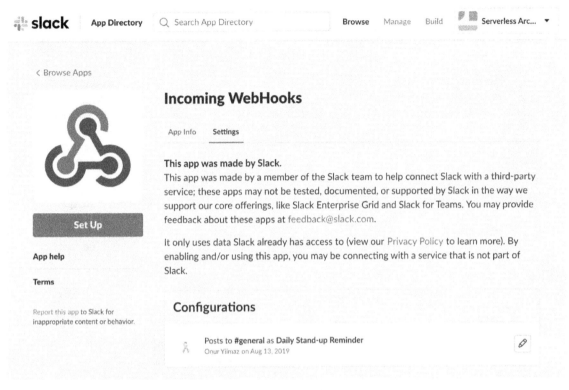

Figure 3.48: Incoming WebHooks page

7. Choose a channel for posting joke messages and click on the Add Incoming WebHooks integration:

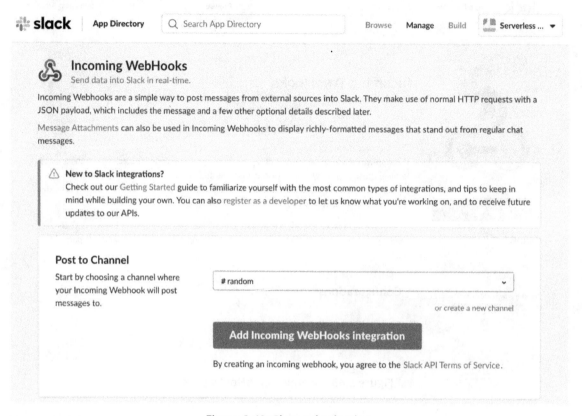

Figure 3.49: Channel selection

8. Fill in the configuration for the incoming webhook with your specific channel name and icon:

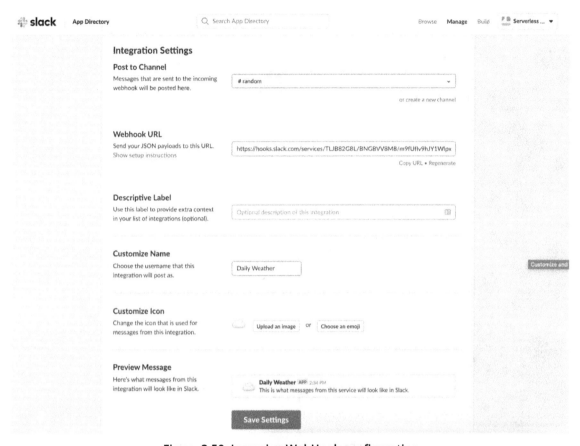

Figure 3.50: Incoming WebHook configuration

Copy the Webhook URL and click Save Settings.

9. Open your Slack workspace and the channel you configured in Step 6 to check the integration message:

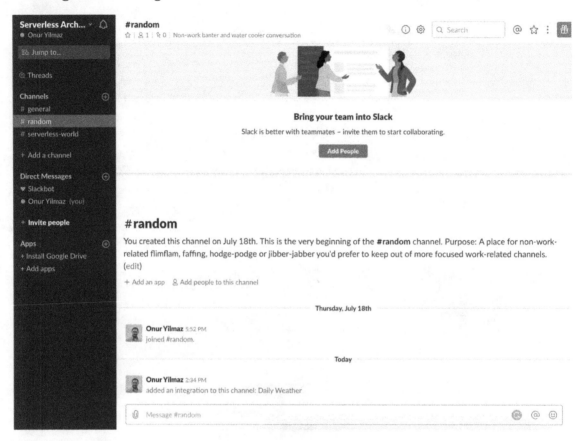

Figure 3.51: Integration message in Slack

Activity Solution

1. Execute the following steps to complete this activity:

2. In your Terminal, start the Serverless Framework development environment:

```
docker run -it --entrypoint=bash onuryilmaz/serverless
```

This command will start a Docker container in interactive mode. In the upcoming steps, actions will be taken inside this Docker container:

```
/serverless $ docker run -it --entrypoint=bash onuryilmaz/serverless
root@4299cc47ad83:/#
```

Figure 3.52: Starting a Docker container for serverless

3. In your Terminal, create a Serverless Framework application structure in a folder called daily-weather.

   Create a folder called daily-joker and change it into the following directory:

   ```
   mkdir daily-weather
   cd daily-weather
   ```

   > **Note**
   >
   > nano and vim are installed as text editors in the Serverless Framework development environment Docker container.

4. Create a serverless.yaml file with the following content and replace the value of SLACK_WEBHOOK_URL with the URL you copied from Step 6 of the Slack Setup. Furthermore, update the CITY environment variable with the current office location to get the correct weather information. In addition, you can change the schedule section, which is currently triggering the function every workday at 08:00:

   ```
   service: daily-weather

   provider:
     name: aws
     runtime: nodejs8.10

   functions:
     weather:
       handler: handler.weather
       events:
         - schedule: cron(0 8 ? * 1-5 *)
       environment:
         CITY: Berlin
         SLACK_WEBHOOK_URL: https://hooks.slack.com/services/.../.../...
   ```

   > **Note**
   >
   > serverless.yaml is available at https://github.com/TrainingByPackt/Serverless-Architectures-with-Kubernetes/blob/master/Lesson03/Activity3/serverless.yaml.

5. Create a package.json file to define the Node.js environment in the daily-weather folder.

    package.json defines the function and its dependencies:

```
{
  "name": "daily-weather",
  "description": "",
  "main": "handler.js",
    "dependencies": {
    "node-fetch": "^2.2.1",
    "slack-node": "0.1.8"
  }
}
```

> **Note**
>
> package.json is available at https://github.com/TrainingByPackt/Serverless-Architectures-with-Kubernetes/blob/master/Lesson03/Activity3/package.json.

6. Create a handler.js file to implement the actual functionality in the daily-weather folder.

    handler.js consists of the actual Node.js function:

```
const fetch = require('node-fetch');
const Slack = require('slack-node');

module.exports.weather = (event, context, callback) => {

    const webhookUri = process.env.SLACK_WEBHOOK_URL;
    const location = process.env.CITY;

    const slack = new Slack();
    slack.setWebhook(webhookUri);

    weatherURL = "http://wttr.in/" + encodeURIComponent(location) +
"?m&&format=1"

    console.log(weatherURL)

    fetch(weatherURL)
        .then(response => response.text())
```

```
                .then(data => {

                    console.log("======== WEATHER TEXT ========")
                    console.error(data);
                    console.log("======== WEATHER TEXT ========")

                    slack.webhook({
                        text: "Current weather status is " + data
                    }, function(err, response) {
                        console.log("======== SLACK SEND STATUS ========")
                        console.error(response.status);
                        return callback(null, {statusCode: 200, body: "ok" });
                        console.log("======== SLACK SEND STATUS ========")

                        if (err) {
                            console.log("======== ERROR ========")
                            console.error(error);
                            console.log("======== ERROR ========")
                            return callback(null, {statusCode: 500, body: JSON.
stringify({ error}) });
                        }
                    });

                }).catch((error) => {
                    console.log("======== ERROR ========")
                    console.error(error);
                    console.log("======== ERROR ========")
                     return callback(null, {statusCode: 500, body: JSON.
stringify({ error}) });
                });
};
```

Note

handler.js is available at https://github.com/TrainingByPackt/Serverless-Architec-
tures-with-Kubernetes/blob/master/Lesson03/Activity3/handler.js.

7. At the end of the file's creation, you will see the following file structure, with three files:

   ```
   ls -l
   ```

   The output should be as follows:

   Figure 3.53: Folder structure

8. Install the required Node.js dependencies for the serverless application. Run the following command to install the dependencies:

   ```
   npm install -i
   ```

   The output should be as follows:

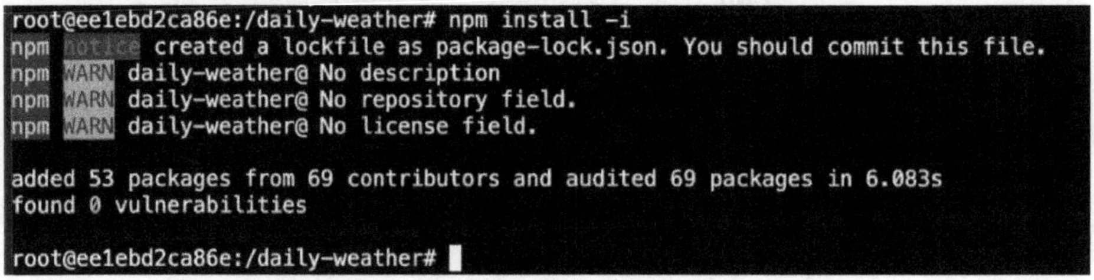

   Figure 3.54: Dependency installation

9. Export the AWS credentials as environment variables. Export the following environment variables and AWS credentials from Exercise xx:

   ```
   export AWS_ACCESS_KEY_ID=AKIASVTPHRZR33BS256U
   export AWS_SECRET_ACCESS_KEY=B***************************R
   ```

   The output should be as follows:

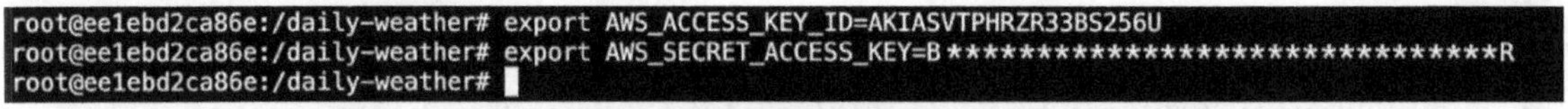

   Figure 3.55: AWS Credentials

10. Deploy the serverless application to AWS using the Serverless Framework. Run the following commands to deploy the function:

```
serverless deploy
```

These commands will make the Serverless Framework deploy the function into AWS. The output logs start by packaging the service and creating AWS resources for source code, artifacts, and functions. After all the resources have been created, the Service Information section provides a summary of the complete stack as you can see in the following figure:

```
root@ee1ebd2ca86e:/daily-weather# serverless deploy
Serverless: Packaging service...
Serverless: Excluding development dependencies...
Serverless: Uploading CloudFormation file to S3...
Serverless: Uploading artifacts...
Serverless: Uploading service daily-weather.zip file to S3 (2.46 MB)...
Serverless: Validating template...
Serverless: Updating Stack...
Serverless: Checking Stack update progress...
.....................
Serverless: Stack update finished...
Service Information
service: daily-weather
stage: dev
region: us-east-1
stack: daily-weather-dev
resources: 7
api keys:
  None
endpoints:
  None
functions:
  weather: daily-weather-dev-weather
layers:
  None
Serverless: Run the "serverless" command to setup monitoring, troubleshooting and testing.
root@ee1ebd2ca86e:/daily-weather# 
```

Figure 3.56: Serverless Framework deployment output

11. Check AWS Lambda for the deployed functions in the AWS Console as shown in the following figure:

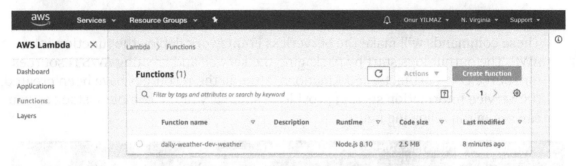

Figure 3.57: AWS Lambda in the AWS Console

12. Invoke the function with the Serverless Framework's client tools. Run the following command in your Terminal:

```
serverless invoke --function weather
```

This command invokes the deployed function and prints out the response as you can see in the following figure:

```
root@ee1ebd2ca86e:/daily-weather# serverless invoke --function weather
{
    "statusCode": 200,
    "body": "ok"
}
root@ee1ebd2ca86e:/daily-weather#
```

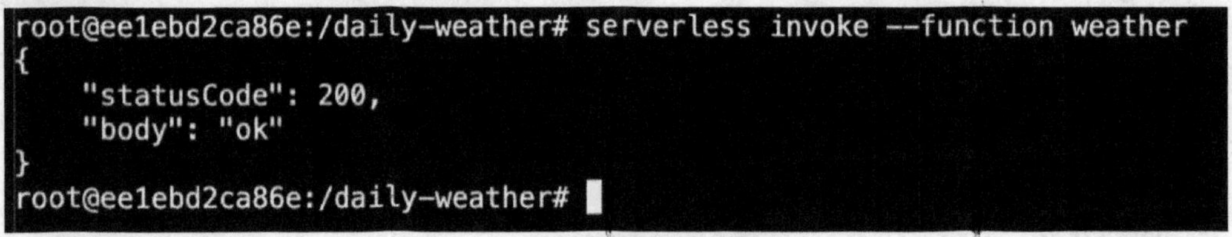

Figure 3.58: Function output

As we can see, statusCode is 200, and the body of the response also indicates that the function has responded successfully.

13. Check the Slack channel for the posted weather status:

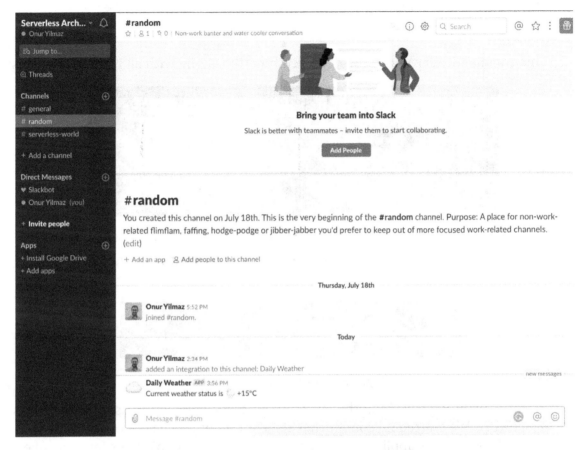

Figure 3.59: Slack message with weather status

14. Return to your Terminal and delete the function with the Serverless Framework. Run the following command in your Terminal:

```
serverless remove
```

This command will remove the deployed function, along with all its dependencies:

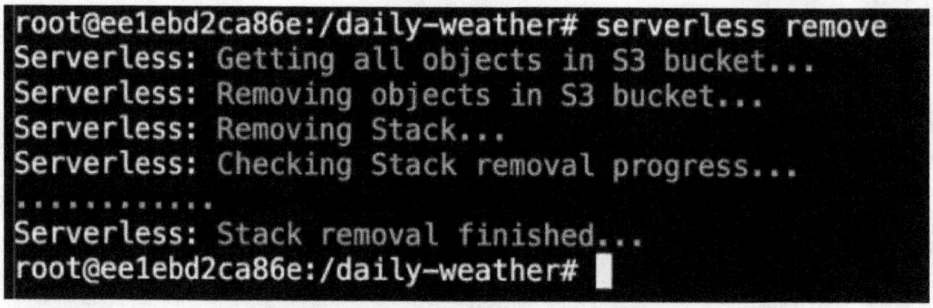

```
root@ee1ebd2ca86e:/daily-weather# serverless remove
Serverless: Getting all objects in S3 bucket...
Serverless: Removing objects in S3 bucket...
Serverless: Removing Stack...
Serverless: Checking Stack removal progress...
............
Serverless: Stack removal finished...
root@ee1ebd2ca86e:/daily-weather#
```

Figure 3.60: Removing the function

15. Exit the Serverless Framework development environment container. Run exit in your Terminal:

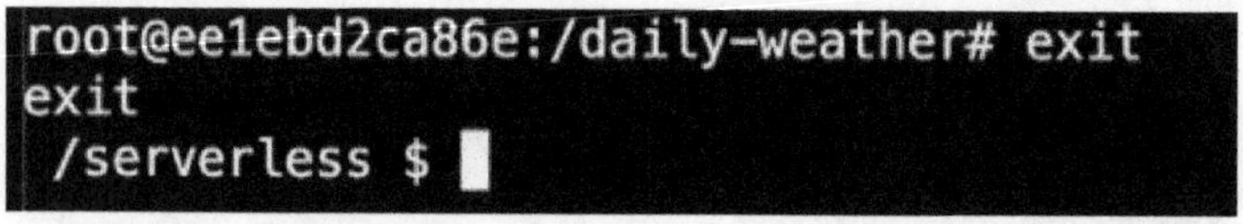

```
root@ee1ebd2ca86e:/daily-weather# exit
exit
/serverless $
```

Figure 3.61: Exiting the container

In this activity, we have built the backend of a Slack application using a serverless framework. We started by configuring Slack for incoming webhooks and then created a serverless application to send data to the webhook. In order to invoke the function at predefined times, the configuration of the serverless framework was utilized instead of cloud-specific schedulers. Since serverless frameworks create an abstraction for the cloud providers, the serverless application that we developed in this activity is suitable for multi-cloud deployments.

Chapter 04: Kubernetes Deep Dive

Activity 4: Collect Gold Prices in a MySQL Database in Kubernetes

Solution:

Execute the following steps to complete this activity:

1. Create an application to retrieve the gold price from **CurrencyLayer** and insert it into the MySQL database.

   It is possible to implement this function in Go with the following main.go file:

   ```
   . . .

   func main() {

       db, err := sql.Open("mysql",  ...
       . . .
       r, err := http.Get(fmt.Sprintf(„http://apilayer.net/api/...
       . . .
       stmt, err := db.Prepare("INSERT INTO GoldPrices(price) VALUES(?)")
       . . .
       _, err = stmt.Exec(target.Quotes.USDXAU)
       . . .
       log.Printf("Successfully inserted the price: %v", target.Quotes.
   USDXAU)
       . . .
   }
   ```

The main function starts with database connection, followed by price retrieval from **CurrencyLayer**. Then it continues with creating a SQL statement and executing on the database connection.

> **Note**
>
> main.go is available at https://github.com/TrainingByPackt/Serverless-Architectures-with-Kubernetes/blob/master/Lesson04/Activity4/main.go.

2. Build the application as a Docker container. It is possible to build the application from Step 1 with the following Dockerfile:

```
FROM golang:1.12.5-alpine3.9 AS builder
RUN apk add --no-cache git

ADD main.go /go/src/gold-price-to-mysql/main.go
WORKDIR /go/src/gold-price-to-mysql/
RUN go get -v
RUN go build .
FROM alpine:3.9
COPY --from=builder /go/src/gold-price-to-mysql/gold-price-to-mysql ./
gold-price-to-mysql
RUN chmod +x ./gold-price-to-mysql
ENTRYPOINT ["./gold-price-to-mysql"]
```

> **Note**
>
> Dockerfile is available at https://github.com/TrainingByPackt/Serverless-Architectures-with-Kubernetes/blob/master/Lesson04/Activity4/Dockerfile.

3. Run the following command in your Terminal:

```
docker build -t <USERNAME>/gold-price-to-mysql .
```

This command builds the application as a Docker container, as shown in the following figure:

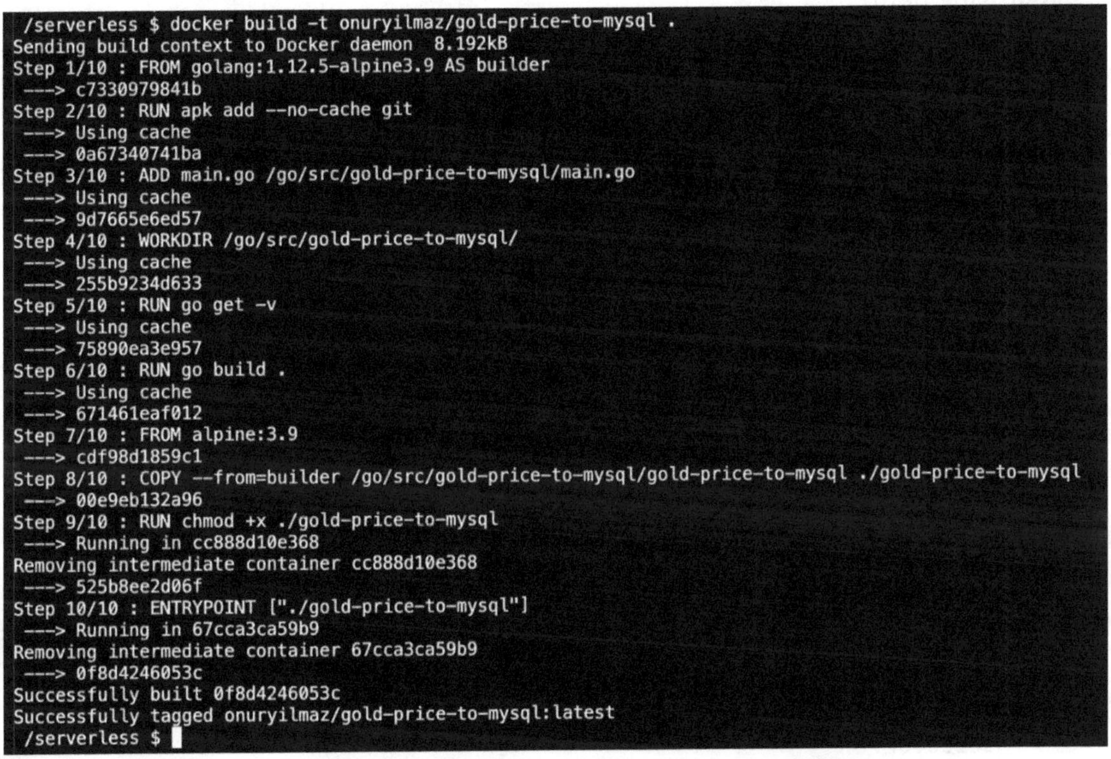

```
/serverless $ docker build -t onuryilmaz/gold-price-to-mysql .
Sending build context to Docker daemon  8.192kB
Step 1/10 : FROM golang:1.12.5-alpine3.9 AS builder
 ---> c7330979841b
Step 2/10 : RUN apk add --no-cache git
 ---> Using cache
 ---> 0a67340741ba
Step 3/10 : ADD main.go /go/src/gold-price-to-mysql/main.go
 ---> Using cache
 ---> 9d7665e6ed57
Step 4/10 : WORKDIR /go/src/gold-price-to-mysql/
 ---> Using cache
 ---> 255b9234d633
Step 5/10 : RUN go get -v
 ---> Using cache
 ---> 75890ea3e957
Step 6/10 : RUN go build .
 ---> Using cache
 ---> 671461eaf012
Step 7/10 : FROM alpine:3.9
 ---> cdf98d1859c1
Step 8/10 : COPY --from=builder /go/src/gold-price-to-mysql/gold-price-to-mysql ./gold-price-to-mysql
 ---> 00e9eb132a96
Step 9/10 : RUN chmod +x ./gold-price-to-mysql
 ---> Running in cc888d10e368
Removing intermediate container cc888d10e368
 ---> 525b8ee2d06f
Step 10/10 : ENTRYPOINT ["./gold-price-to-mysql"]
 ---> Running in 67cca3ca59b9
Removing intermediate container 67cca3ca59b9
 ---> 0f8d4246053c
Successfully built 0f8d4246053c
Successfully tagged onuryilmaz/gold-price-to-mysql:latest
/serverless $
```

Figure 4.26: Docker build

> **Note**
>
> Do not forget to change **<USERNAME>** to your Docker Hub username.

4. Push the Docker container to the Docker registry. Run the following command in your Terminal:

    ```
    docker push <USERNAME>/gold-price-to-mysql
    ```

    This command uploads the container image to the Docker Hub, as shown in the following figure:

    ```
    /serverless $ docker push onuryilmaz/gold-price-to-mysql
    The push refers to repository [docker.io/onuryilmaz/gold-price-to-mysql]
    beb2ceda744b: Layer already exists
    a464c54f93a9: Layer already exists
    latest: digest: sha256:15b722f865963ab8f186935ab7a04626d034ed83ffc081168ff92b7119b379ff size: 950
    /serverless $
    ```

    Figure 4.27: Docker push

    > **Note**
    >
    > Do not forget to change **<USERNAME>** to your Docker Hub username.

5. Deploy the MySQL database into the Kubernetes cluster. Create a mysql.yaml file with the MySQL StatefulSet definition:

    ```
    apiVersion: apps/v1
    kind: StatefulSet
    metadata:
      name: mysql
    spec:
      selector:
        matchLabels:
          app: mysql
      serviceName: mysql
      replicas: 1
      template:
        metadata:
          labels:
            app: mysql
        spec:
          containers:
          - name: mysql
            image: mysql:5.7
            env:
            - name: MYSQL_ROOT_PASSWORD
    ```

```
            value: "root"
          - name: MYSQL_DATABASE
            value: "db"
          - name: MYSQL_USER
            value: "user"
          - name: MYSQL_PASSWORD
            value: "password"
          ports:
          - name: mysql
            containerPort: 3306
          volumeMounts:
          - name: data
            mountPath: /var/lib/mysql
            subPath: mysql
  volumeClaimTemplates:
  - metadata:
      name: data
    spec:
      accessModes: ["ReadWriteOnce"]
      resources:
        requests:
          storage: 1Gi
```

> **Note**
>
> mysql.yaml is available at https://github.com/TrainingByPackt/Serverless-Architec-
> tures-with-Kubernetes/blob/master/Lesson04/Activity4/mysql.yaml.

6. Deploy the StatefulSet with the following command in your Terminal:

   ```
   kubectl apply -f mysql.yaml
   ```

   This command submits the file to Kubernetes and creates the mysql StatefulSet, as shown in the following figure:

   Figure 4.28: StatefulSet creation

7. Deploy a Kubernetes service to expose MySQL database. Create a service.yaml file with the following Kubernetes Service definition:

```
apiVersion: v1
kind: Service
metadata:
  name: gold-price-db
spec:
  selector:
    app: mysql
  ports:
    - protocol: TCP
      port: 3306
      targetPort: 3306
```

> **Note**
>
> service.yaml is available at https://github.com/TrainingByPackt/Serverless-Architectures-with-Kubernetes/blob/master/Lesson04/Activity4/service.yaml.

8. Deploy the service with the following command in your Terminal:

```
kubectl apply -f service.yaml
```

This command submits the file to Kubernetes and creates the gold-price-db service, as shown in the following figure:

```
/serverless $ kubectl apply -f service.yaml
service/gold-price-db created
/serverless $ █
```

Figure 4.29: Service creation

9. Deploy a CronJob to run every minute. Create an insert-gold-price.yaml file with the following Kubernetes CronJob definition:

```
apiVersion: batch/v1beta1
kind: CronJob
metadata:
  name: gold-price-to-mysql
spec:
  schedule: "* * * * *"
```

```
      jobTemplate:
        spec:
          template:
            spec:
              restartPolicy: OnFailure
              containers:
              - name: insert
                image: <USERNAME>/gold-price-to-mysql
                env:
                - name: MYSQL_ADDRESS
                  value: "gold-price-db:3306"
                - name: MYSQL_DATABASE
                  value: "db"
                - name: MYSQL_USER
                  value: "user"
                - name: MYSQL_PASSWORD
                  value: "password"
                - name: API_KEY
                  value: "<API-KEY>"
```

Note

insert-gold-price.yaml is available at https://github.com/TrainingByPackt/Server-less-Architectures-with-Kubernetes/blob/master/Lesson04/Activity4/insert-gold-price.yaml.

Do not forget to change **<USERNAME>** to your Docker Hub username and **<API-KEY>** to your CurrencyLayer API key.

10. Deploy the CronJob with the following command in your Terminal:

```
kubectl apply -f insert-gold-price.yaml
```

This command submits the file to Kubernetes and creates the gold-price-to-mysql CronJob, as shown in the following figure:

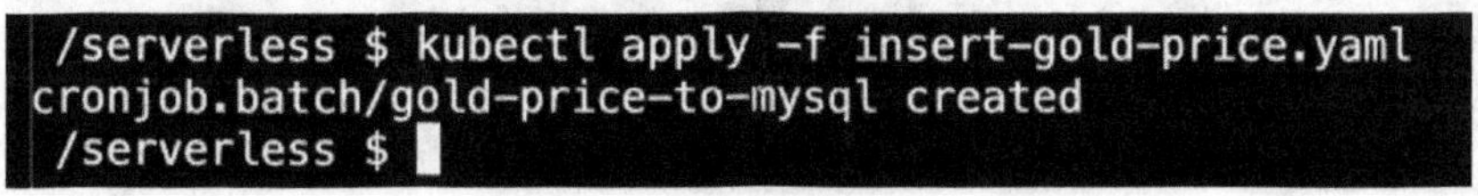

```
/serverless $ kubectl apply -f insert-gold-price.yaml
cronjob.batch/gold-price-to-mysql created
/serverless $
```

Figure 4.30: CronJob creation

11. Wait for a couple of minutes and check the instances of CronJob. Check the running pods with the following command in your Terminal:

```
kubectl get pods
```

This command lists the pods, and you should see a couple of instances whose names start with gold-price-to-mysql and with a STATUS of Completed, as shown in the following figure:

```
/serverless $ kubectl get pods
NAME                                      READY   STATUS      RESTARTS   AGE
gold-price-to-mysql-1568864100-gcmh6      0/1     Completed   0          2m
gold-price-to-mysql-1568864160-zd8ms      0/1     Completed   0          1m
gold-price-to-mysql-1568864220-2sxtd      0/1     Completed   0          42s
mysql-0                                   1/1     Running     0          12m
/serverless $
```

Figure 4.31: Pod listing

12. Connect to the database and check for the entries:

```
kubectl run mysql-client --image=mysql:5.7 -i -t --rm --restart=Never \
-- mysql -h gold-price-db -u user -ppassword  db -e "SELECT * FROM
GoldPrices;"
```

This command runs a temporary instance of the mysql:5.7 image and runs the SELECT * FROM GoldPrices command, as shown in the following figure:

```
/serverless $ kubectl run mysql-client --image=mysql:5.7 -i -t --rm --restart=Never \
> -- mysql -h gold-price-db -u user -ppassword  db -e "SELECT * FROM GoldPrices;"
mysql: [Warning] Using a password on the command line interface can be insecure.
+---------------------+----------+
| timestamp           | price    |
+---------------------+----------+
| 2019-09-18 00:39:06 | 0.000665 |
| 2019-09-18 00:39:29 | 0.000665 |
| 2019-09-19 03:30:06 | 0.000663 |
| 2019-09-19 03:31:06 | 0.000663 |
| 2019-09-19 03:32:05 | 0.000663 |
| 2019-09-19 03:33:05 | 0.000663 |
| 2019-09-19 03:34:05 | 0.000663 |
| 2019-09-19 03:35:05 | 0.000663 |
| 2019-09-19 03:36:06 | 0.000663 |
| 2019-09-19 03:37:06 | 0.000663 |
| 2019-09-19 03:38:06 | 0.000663 |
| 2019-09-19 03:39:06 | 0.000663 |
+---------------------+----------+
pod "mysql-client" deleted
/serverless $
```

Figure 4.32: Table listing

In the GoldPrices MySQL table, there is price data collected every minute. It shows that MySQL StatefulSet is up and running the database successfully. In addition, the CronJob has been creating the pods every minute and is running successfully.

13. Clean the database and automated tasks from Kubernetes. Clean the resources with the following command in your Terminal:

```
kubectl delete -f insert-gold-price.yaml,service.yaml,mysql.yaml
```

You should see the output shown in the following figure:

```
/serverless $ kubectl delete -f insert-gold-price.yaml,service.yaml,mysql.yaml
cronjob.batch "gold-price-to-mysql" deleted
service "gold-price-db" deleted
statefulset.apps "mysql" deleted
/serverless $
```

Figure 4.33: Resource deletion

In this activity, we have created a MySQL database as a StatefulSet in Kubernetes. Kubernetes has created the required volume resource and attached to the MySQL containers. Following that, we have created and packaged our serverless function. The function is deployed to the Kubernetes cluster as a CronJob. Kubernetes ensures that the function is scheduled and running every minute. Running functions in Kubernetes provides two essential advantages. The first one is the reuse of Kubernetes clusters and resources. In other words, we are not using any extra cloud resources to run our serverless workloads. The second advantage is the proximity to the data. Since our microservices are already running on Kubernetes, it is recommended to have our databases in Kubernetes. When the serverless applications are also running in the same cluster, it is easier to operate, manage, and troubleshoot the applications.

Chapter 05: Production-Ready Kubernetes Clusters

Activity 5: Minimizing the Costs of Serverless Functions in a GKE Cluster

Solution

1. Create a new node pool with preemptible servers.

    Run the following and upcoming functions in your GCP cloud shell:

    ```
    gcloud beta container node-pools create preemptible --preemptible \
    --min-nodes 1 --max-nodes 10  --enable-autoscaling  \
    --cluster serverless --zone us-central1-a
    ```

    > **Note**
    >
    > Change the **zone** parameter if your cluster is running in another zone.

    This function creates a new node pool named **preemptible** with an automatically scaled minimum of 1 node and a maximum of 10 nodes, as shown in the following figure:

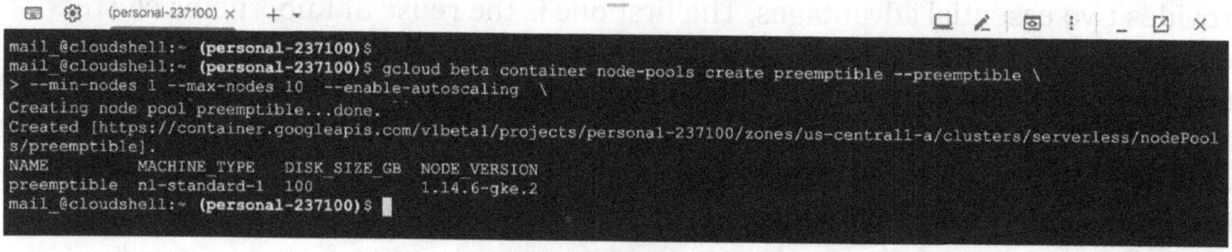

    Figure 5.29: Node pool creation

2. Taint the preemptible servers to run only serverless functions:

```
kubectl taint node -l cloud.google.com/gke-nodepool=preemptible    \
preemptible="true":NoSchedule
```

This command will apply taints to all nodes with the label **cloud.google.com/node-pool = preemptible**. The taint key will be **preemptible**, and the value is **true**. The action of this limit is **NoSchedule**, which means only the pods with the matching toleration will be scheduled to these nodes, as shown in the following figure:

Figure 5.30: Tainting the nodes

3. Create a Kubernetes service to reach backend pods:

```
kubectl expose deployment backend --port 80 --target-port=80
```

This command creates a service for the deployment backend on port **80**, as shown in the following figure:

Figure 5.31: Exposing the deployment

4. Create a **CronJob** to connect to the backend service every minute. The CronJob definition should have tolerations to run on preemptible servers.

Create a **CronJob** definition with the following content inside a file named **cronjob.yaml**:

```
apiVersion: batch/v1beta1
kind: CronJob
metadata:
  name: backend-checker
spec:
  schedule: "*/1 * * * *"
  jobTemplate:
    spec:
      template:
        spec:
```

```
          containers:
          - name: checker
            image: appropriate/curl
            args:
            - curl
            - -I
            - backend
          nodeSelector:
            cloud.google.com/gke-nodepool: "preemptible"
          tolerations:
          - key: preemptible
            operator: Equal
            value: "true"
            effect: NoSchedule
          restartPolicy: OnFailure
```

The file has a **CronJob** definition for running the **curl -I backend** function every minute. **nodeSelector** indicates that the scheduler will choose to run on the nodes with the label key **cloud.google.com/gke-nodepool** and a value of **preemptible**. However, since there are taints on the preemptible nodes, tolerations are also added.

> **Note**
>
> **cronjob.yaml** is available on GitHub: https://github.com/TrainingByPackt/Server-less-Architectures-with-Kubernetes/blob/master/Lesson05/Activity5/cronjob.yaml.

5. Deploy the CronJob with the following command:

```
kubectl apply -f cronjob.yaml
```

The output should be as follows:

Figure 5.32: CronJob creation

6. Check the node assignments of the **CronJob** functions:

```
kubectl get pods -o wide
```

This command lists the pod with their corresponding nodes. As expected, there are exactly 10 instances of backend running on **high-memory** nodes. In addition, there are 3 instances of the CronJob function running on **preemptible** nodes, as shown in the following figure:

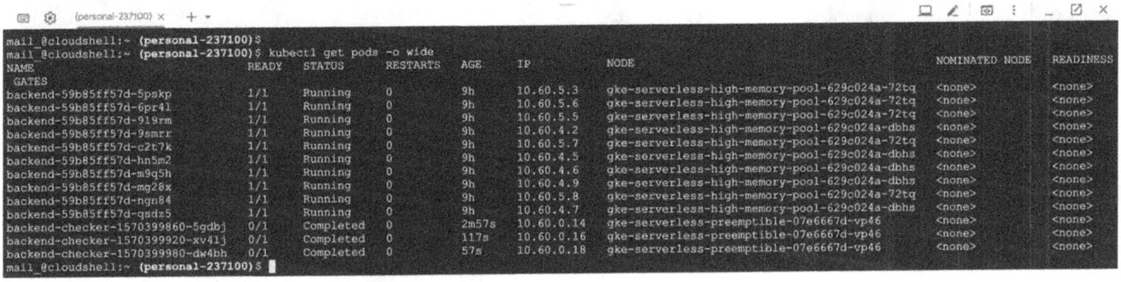

```
mail_@cloudshell:~ (personal-237100)$
mail_@cloudshell:~ (personal-237100)$ kubectl get pods -o wide
NAME                              READY   STATUS      RESTARTS   AGE     IP           NODE                                             NOMINATED NODE   READINESS
 GATES
backend-59b85ff57d-5pskp          1/1     Running     0          9h      10.60.5.3    gke-serverless-high-memory-pool-629c024a-72tq    <none>           <none>
backend-59b85ff57d-6pr4l          1/1     Running     0          9h      10.60.5.6    gke-serverless-high-memory-pool-629c024a-72tq    <none>           <none>
backend-59b85ff57d-919rm          1/1     Running     0          9h      10.60.5.5    gke-serverless-high-memory-pool-629c024a-72tq    <none>           <none>
backend-59b85ff57d-9smrr          1/1     Running     0          9h      10.60.4.2    gke-serverless-high-memory-pool-629c024a-dbhs    <none>           <none>
backend-59b85ff57d-c2t7k          1/1     Running     0          9h      10.60.5.7    gke-serverless-high-memory-pool-629c024a-72tq    <none>           <none>
backend-59b85ff57d-hn5m2          1/1     Running     0          9h      10.60.4.5    gke-serverless-high-memory-pool-629c024a-dbhs    <none>           <none>
backend-59b85ff57d-m9q5h          1/1     Running     0          9h      10.60.4.6    gke-serverless-high-memory-pool-629c024a-dbhs    <none>           <none>
backend-59b85ff57d-mg28x          1/1     Running     0          9h      10.60.4.9    gke-serverless-high-memory-pool-629c024a-dbhs    <none>           <none>
backend-59b85ff57d-ngn84          1/1     Running     0          9h      10.60.5.8    gke-serverless-high-memory-pool-629c024a-72tq    <none>           <none>
backend-59b85ff57d-qsdz5          1/1     Running     0          9h      10.60.4.7    gke-serverless-high-memory-pool-629c024a-dbhs    <none>           <none>
backend-checker-1570399860-5gdbj  0/1     Completed   0          2m57s   10.60.0.14   gke-serverless-preemptible-07e6667d-vp46         <none>           <none>
backend-checker-1570399920-xv41j  0/1     Completed   0          117s    10.60.0.16   gke-serverless-preemptible-07e6667d-vp46         <none>           <none>
backend-checker-1570399980-dw4bh  0/1     Completed   0          57s     10.60.0.18   gke-serverless-preemptible-07e6667d-vp46         <none>           <none>
mail_@cloudshell:~ (personal-237100)$
```

Figure 5.33: Pod listing

7. Check the logs of **CronJob** function instances:

```
kubectl logs brand-checker-<ID>
```

> **Note**
>
> Replace **<ID>** with a pod name from *Step 5*.

The output of the function shows the trail of **curl** connecting to the **nginx** instance, as shown in the following figure:

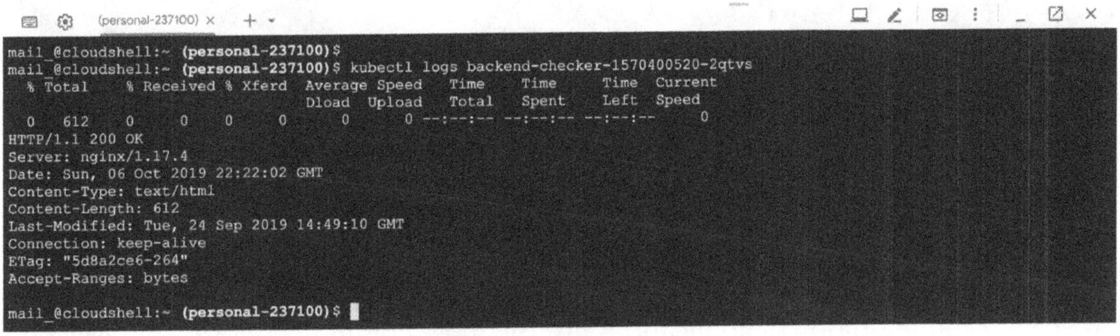

```
mail_@cloudshell:~ (personal-237100)$
mail_@cloudshell:~ (personal-237100)$ kubectl logs backend-checker-1570400520-2qtvs
  % Total    % Received % Xferd  Average Speed   Time    Time     Time  Current
                                 Dload  Upload   Total   Spent    Left  Speed

  0   612    0     0    0     0      0      0 --:--:-- --:--:-- --:--:--     0
HTTP/1.1 200 OK
Server: nginx/1.17.4
Date: Sun, 06 Oct 2019 22:22:02 GMT
Content-Type: text/html
Content-Length: 612
Last-Modified: Tue, 24 Sep 2019 14:49:10 GMT
Connection: keep-alive
ETag: "5d8a2ce6-264"
Accept-Ranges: bytes

mail_@cloudshell:~ (personal-237100)$
```

Figure 5.34: curl output

8. Clean the backend deployment and serverless functions:

```
kubectl delete deployment/backend cronjob/backend-checker
```

This command deletes the **backend** deployment and **backend-checker** CronJob, as shown in the following figure:

```
mail_@cloudshell:~ (personal-237100)$
mail_@cloudshell:~ (personal-237100)$ kubectl delete deployment/backend cronjob/backend-checker
deployment.extensions "backend" deleted
cronjob.batch "backend-checker" deleted
mail_@cloudshell:~ (personal-237100)$
```

Figure 5.35: Cleanup

9. Remove the Kubernetes cluster if you do not need it anymore:

```
gcloud container clusters delete serverless --zone us-central1-a
```

> **Note**
>
> Change the **zone** parameter in the command if your cluster is running in another zone.

This command deletes the cluster from GKE, as shown in the following figure:

```
mail_@cloudshell:~ (personal-237100)$
mail_@cloudshell:~ (personal-237100)$ gcloud container clusters delete serverless --zone us-central1-a
The following clusters will be deleted.
 - [serverless] in [us-central1-a]

Do you want to continue (Y/n)?  Y

Deleting cluster serverless...done.
Deleted [https://container.googleapis.com/v1/projects/personal-237100/zones/us-central1-a/clusters/serverless].
mail_@cloudshell:~ (personal-237100)$
```

Figure 5.36: Cluster removal

In this activity, we have undertaken administrative tasks on a live production cluster. Creating different types of nodes and running a heterogeneous set of nodes in a Kubernetes cluster helps to decrease the cost of the complete cluster. Besides, autoscaling is enabled to meet user demand automatically without human interaction.

Autoscaling and migration of applications are the most common operational tasks on production clusters. These tasks enable better performance with minimal downtime and costs. However, the selected Kubernetes platform for your production environment should also meet such requirements of your daily operations. The capabilities of Kubernetes and cloud providers are essential to install, monitor, and operate applications running in the cloud.

Chapter 06: Upcoming Serverless Features in Kubernetes

Activity 6: Deploy a Containerized Application in a Serverless Environment

Solution

1. First, create a new directory to store the files for this activity and change directory to the newly created directory:

    ```
    $ mkdir chapter-06-activity
    $ cd chapter-06-activity
    ```

2. Create an application that can return the current date and time for the given timezone. We will be using PHP to write this function, but you can choose any language that you're comfortable with. Create an index.php file with the content given in step 1.

    Now we need to create the Docker image according to the container runtime contract (https://cloud.google.com/run/docs/reference/container-contract) for Google Cloud Run. Create a new file named Dockerfile with the content in step 2.

3. Once the Dockerfile is ready, we can build the Docker image. Replace **<your-gcp-project-name>** with the ID of your GCP project. Next, use the docker build command to build the Docker image. The **--tag** flag is used to tag the Docker image as per the **[HOSTNAME]/[GCP-PROJECT-ID]/[IMAGE-NAME]:[TAG]** format, as we will be pushing this to **Google Container Registry (GCR)** in the next step:

    ```
    $ export GCP_PROJECT=<your-gcp-project-name>
    $ docker build . --tag gcr.io/${GCP_PROJECT}/clock:v1.0
    ```

    The output should be as follows:

```
/serverless $ export GCP_PROJECT=serverless-kubernetes-project
/serverless $ docker build . --tag gcr.io/${GCP_PROJECT}/clock:v1.0
Sending build context to Docker daemon  3.584kB
Step 1/4 : FROM php:7.3-apache
 ---> 6f7c5e29a126
Step 2/4 : COPY index.php /var/www/html/
 ---> Using cache
 ---> ecaa45609563
Step 3/4 : RUN sed -i 's/80/${PORT}/g' /etc/apache2/sites-available/000-default.conf
/etc/apache2/ports.conf
 ---> Using cache
 ---> c406d8f22fa1
Step 4/4 : RUN mv "$PHP_INI_DIR/php.ini-production" "$PHP_INI_DIR/php.ini"
 ---> Using cache
 ---> 3bbdc9c21116
Successfully built 3bbdc9c21116
Successfully tagged gcr.io/serverless-kubernetes-project/clock:v1.0
/serverless $
```

Figure 6.57: Building the Docker image

4. Next, we can push the docker image to GCR:

   ```
   $ docker push gcr.io/${GCP_PROJECT}/clock:v1.0
   ```

   The output should be as follows:

```
/serverless $ docker push gcr.io/${GCP_PROJECT}/clock:v1.0
The push refers to repository [gcr.io/serverless-kubernetes-project/clock]
943dc76d6122: Pushed
a9ef1ddb1f7c: Pushed
45d48c0c8acf: Pushed
56c9c67e0364: Layer already exists
4c45321cfae8: Layer already exists
f75094174745: Layer already exists
d5b9ecc3be66: Layer already exists
ad110a9c838c: Layer already exists
24a659abd14a: Layer already exists
f096caea8774: Layer already exists
e0269f37dcfa: Layer already exists
3e6f95434588: Layer already exists
c08a9d858420: Layer already exists
1a53f90adf8d: Layer already exists
11f457f4618a: Layer already exists
7e59cbad3af2: Layer already exists
2db44bce66cd: Layer already exists
v1.0: digest: sha256:487c58cde22ee34ce246a116a646836a9455745e7f63175bda4310ef8953975
1 size: 3866
/serverless $
```

Figure 6.58: Pushing the Docker image

5. Now we have a Docker image created and pushed to the registry. Now navigate to the GCP console and open the Cloud Run page. Click on the **CREATE SERVICE** button to create a new service with the following information:

   Container Image URL: `gcr.io/<your-gcp-project-id>/clock:v1.0`

   Deployment platform: Cloud Run (fully managed)

   Location: Select any region you prefer from the available options

   Service name: clock

   Authentication: **Allow unauthenticated invocations**

The page would look as follows:

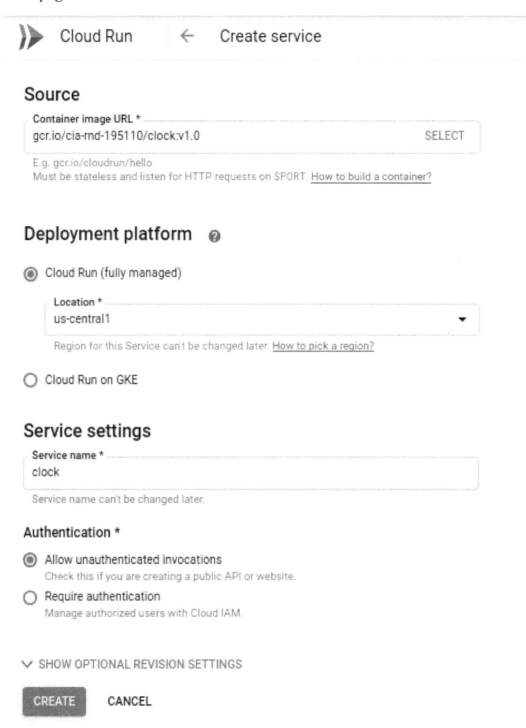

Figure 6.59: Creating a service

6. Click on the **CREATE** button and you will be navigated to the Service details page:

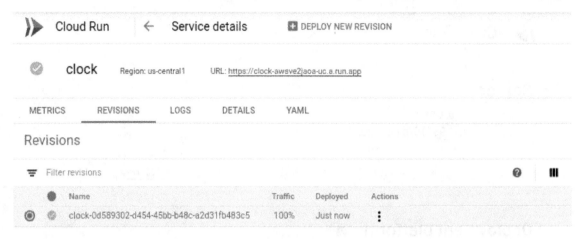

Figure 6.60: Service details

7. Open the provided URL from the Service details page. For me, this URL is **https:// clock-awsve2jaoa-uc.a.run.app/**, but your URL will be different:

Figure 6.61: Timezone error

8. We are receiving this error as we have not provided the timezone parameter.

9. Let's invoke the URL again with the timezone parameter, `https://clock-awsve-2jaoa-uc.a.run.app/?timezone=Europe/London`

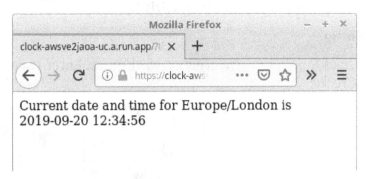

Figure 6.62: Output with timezone

In this activity, we have successfully deployed a containerized application on Google Cloud Run that can output the current date and time based on a provided `timezone` value.

Chapter 07: Kubernetes Serverless with Kubeless

Activity 7: Publishing Messages to Slack with Kubeless

Solution - Slack Setup

1. Visit https://slack.com/create to create a workspace. Enter your email address and click on Create:

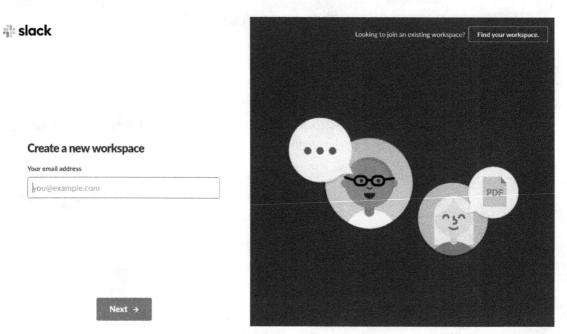

Figure 7.77: Creating a new workspace

2. Now, you will receive a six-digit confirmation code to the email that you entered on the previous page. Enter the received code on the following page:

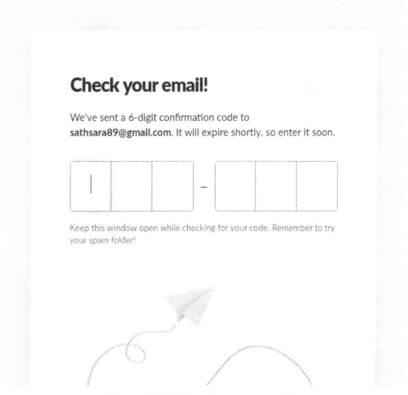

Figure 7.78: Checking your email

3. Add a suitable name here. This will be your workspace name:

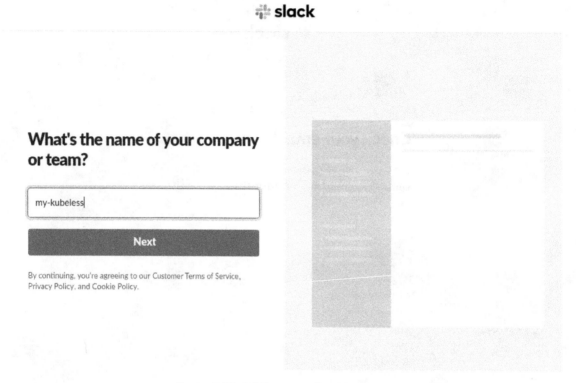

Figure 7.79: Adding a workspace name

4. Add a suitable name here. This will be your Slack channel name:

Figure 7.80: Adding a Slack channel name

You can skip the following section if you wish to:

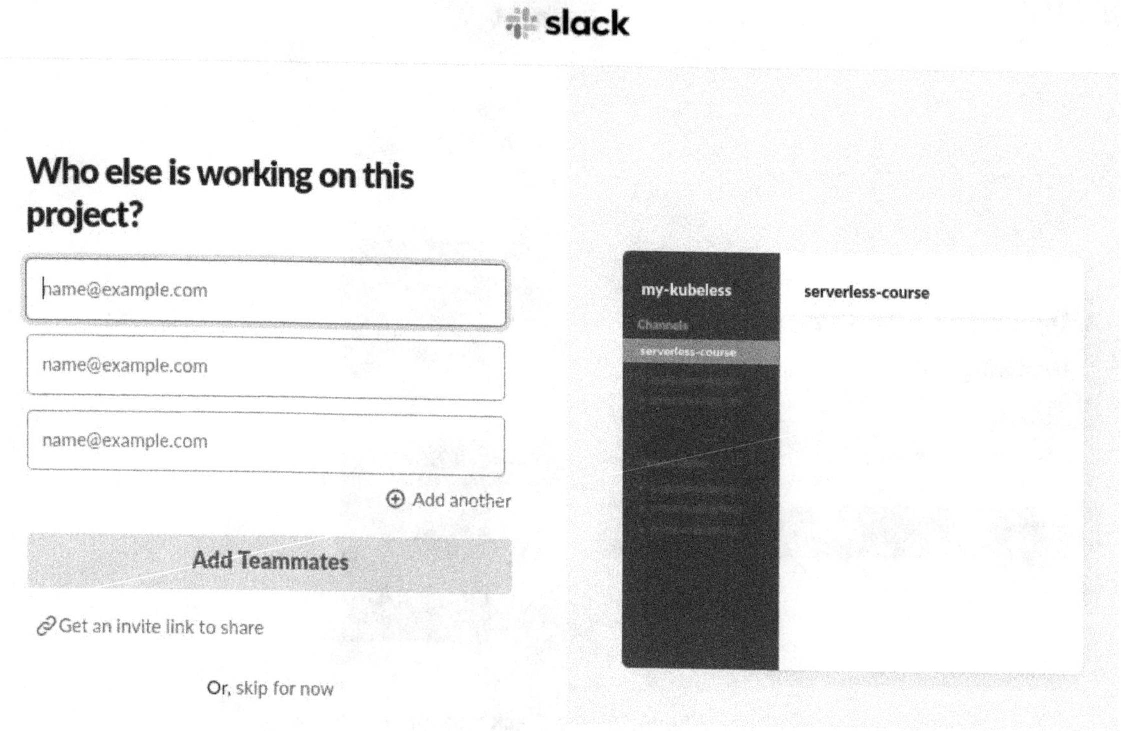

Figure 7.81: Filling in further details or choosing to skip

5. Now your Slack channel is ready. Click on **See Your Channel in Slack**, as shown in the following screenshot:

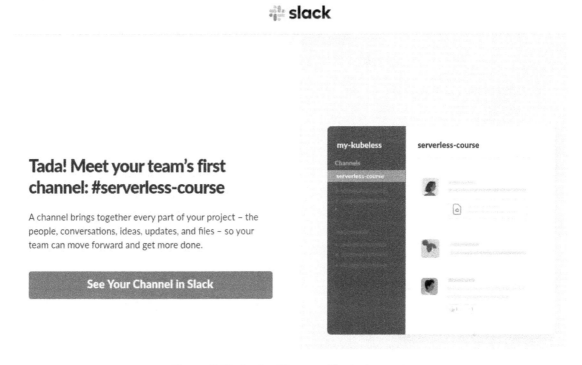

Figure 7.82: Seeing the new Slack channel

Once clicked, we should see our channel as follows:

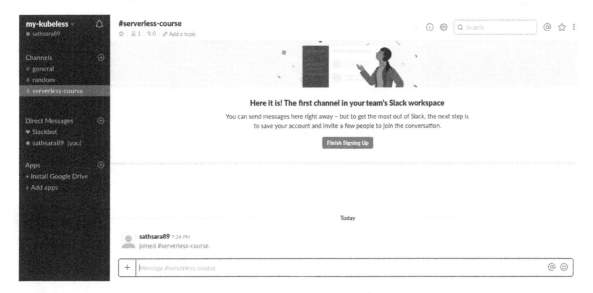

Figure 7.83: Your new Slack channel

6. Now we are going to add an Incoming Webhook app to our slack. From the left menu, select Add apps under the Apps section:

Figure 7.84: Adding apps under the Apps section

7. Enter `Incoming Webhooks` in the search field and click on **Install** for the Incoming Webhook app:

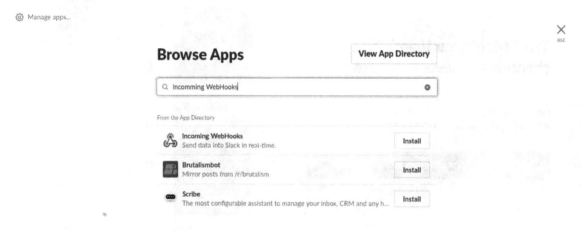

Figure 7.85: Browsing apps

8. Click on **Add Configuration**:

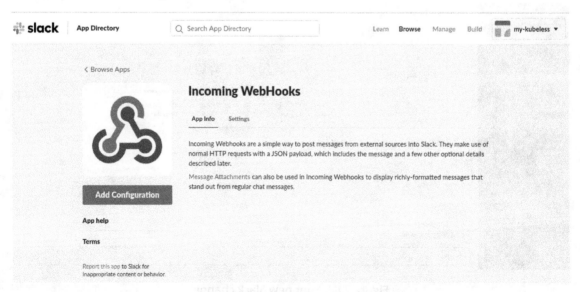

Figure 7.86: Adding configuration

9. Click on **Add Incoming WebHooks Integration**:

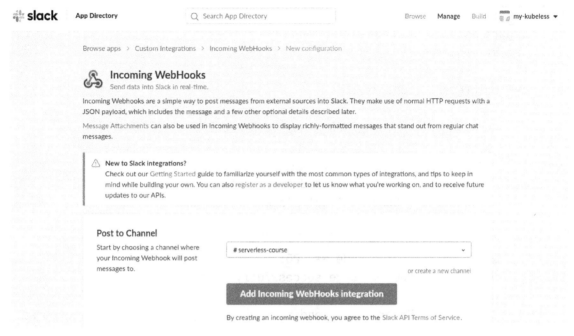

Figure 7.87: Adding incoming webhooks

10. Save the webhook URL. We will need this when we are writing the Kubeless function.

11. Now, let's create the function and deploy it. First, we need to create the requirements.txt file, which specifies the dependencies we need to install for the function's runtime. These are the additional modules we need in order to run our function successfully. We will be using the requests package to send the HTTP POST request to the Slack webhook endpoint:

```
Requests==2.22.0
```

Activity Solution

1. Create the function as follows.

```python
import json
import requests

def main(event, context):

    webhook_url = 'YOUR_INCOMMING_WEBHOOK_URL'

    response = requests.post(
        webhook_url, data=json.dumps(event['data']),
        headers={'Content-Type': 'application/json'}
    )

    if response.status_code == 200:
        return "Your message successfully sent to Slack"
    else:
        return "Error while sending your message to Slack: " + response.
get('error')
```

2. Deploy the function:

```
$ kubeless function deploy slack --runtime python3.6 \
                                 --from-file slack.py \
                                 --handler slack.main \
                                 --dependencies requirements.txt
```

Deploying the function will yield the following output:

```
/serverless $ kubeless function deploy slack \
> --runtime python3.6 \
> --from-file slack.py \
> --handler slack.main \
> --dependencies requirements.txt
INFO[0001] Deploying function...
INFO[0001] Function slack submitted for deployment
INFO[0001] Check the deployment status executing 'kubeless function ls slack'
/serverless $
```

Figure 7.88: Deploying the function

We are passing the requirements.txt file that we created in the previous step as a dependency while deploying the slack function. This will ensure that the Kubeless runtime contains the required Python packages for function execution.

3. Invoke the kubeless function:

```
$ kubeless function call slack --data '{"username": "kubeless-bot",
"text": "Welcome to Serverless Architectures with Kubeless !!!"}'
```

This yields the following output:

```
/serverless $ kubeless function call slack --data '{"username": "kubeless-bot",
"text": "Welcome to Serverless Architectures with Kubeless !!!"}'
Your message successfully sent to Slack
/serverless $
```

Figure 7.89: Invoking the function

4. Go to your Slack workspace and verify that the message was successfully posted to the Slack channel:

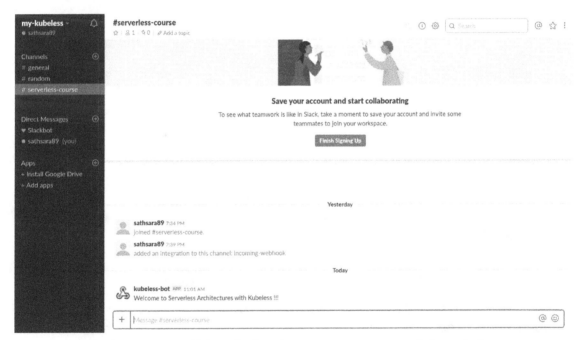

Figure 7.90: Verifying whether the message was successfully posted

In this activity, we created a Slack space and created an incoming webhook. Next, we created and deployed a Kubeless function that can post messages to the Slack channel.

Chapter 08: Introduction to Apache OpenWhisk

Activity 8: Receive Daily Weather Updates via Email

Steps to create an OpenWeather and SendGrid account:

1. Create an **OpenWeather** account at https://home.openweathermap.org/users/sign_up:

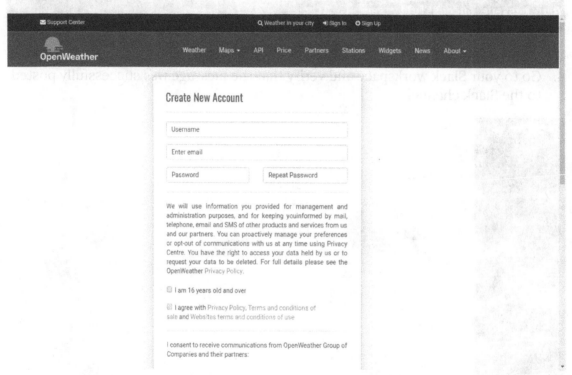

Figure 8.72: Creating an OpenWeather account

2. Once you have signed up to **OpenWeather**, an API key will be generated automatically for you. Go to the **API keys** tab (https://home.openweathermap.org/api_keys) and save the API key because this key is required to fetch the data from OpenWeather API:

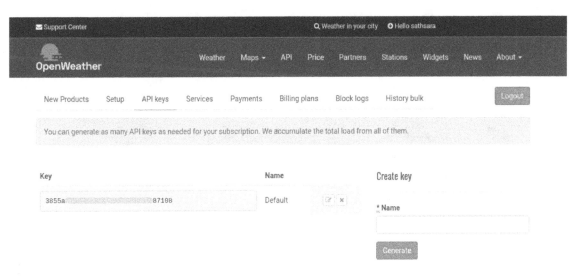

Figure 8.73: OpenWeather API key

3. Test the **OpenWeather** API using `https://api.openweathermap.org/data/2.5/weath-er?q=London&appid=<YOUR-API-KEY>` in a web browser. Please note that you need to replace `<YOUR-API-KEY>` with your API Key from step 2:

> **Note**
>
> It may take a few minutes to get your API key activated. Wait for a few minutes and retry if you receive **Invalid API key**. Please see http://openweathermap.org/faq#error401 for more info. error while invoking the URL.

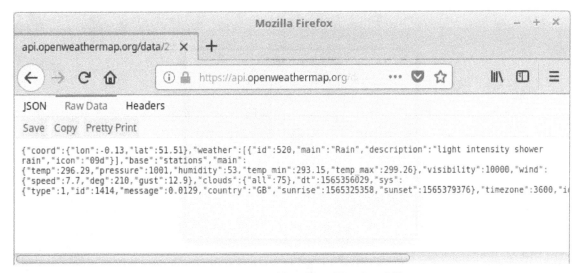

Figure 8.74: Invoking OpenWeather API

4. Create a **SendGrid** account at https://signup.sendgrid.com/.
   It should look as follows:

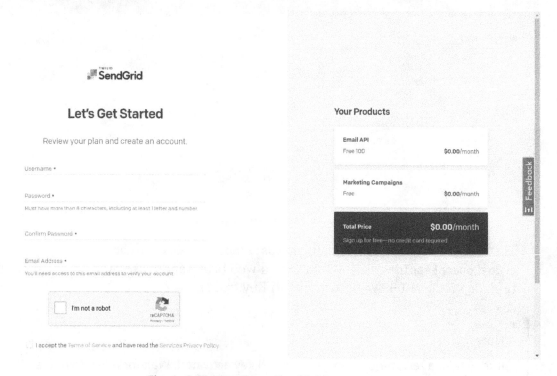

Figure 8.75: Creating a SendGrid account

5. Go to **Settings** > **API Keys** and click on the **Create API Key** button:

Figure 8.76: API key page in SendGrid

6. Provide a name in the **API Key Name** field, select the **Full Access** radio button, and click on the **Create & View** button to create an API key with full access:

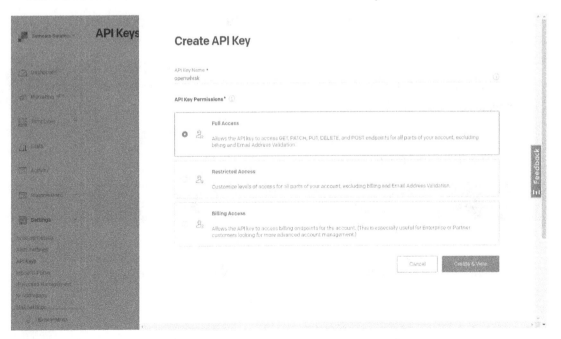

Figure 8.77: Generating an API key in SendGrid

7. Once the key is generated, copy the API key and save it somewhere safe because you will see this key only once:

Figure 8.78: Generated API key in SendGrid

Activity Solution

1. Create the **get-weather.js** function with the function code provided in *step* 3. Replace **<OPEN_WEATHER_API_KEY>** with the API key saved in *step* 1.

2. Create the action named **getWeather** with the **get-weather.js** function created in the preceding step and provide the default value of the **cityName** parameter as **London**:

```
$ wsk action create getWeather get-weather.js --param cityName London
```

The output should be as follows:

```
/serverless $ wsk action create getWeather get-weather.js --param cityName London
ok: created action getWeather
/serverless $
```

Figure 8.79: Creating the getWeather action

3. Verify that the action is working as expected by invoking the action:

```
$ wsk action invoke getWeather --result
```

```
{
    "weatherData": {
        "base": "stations",
        "clouds": {
            "all": 75
        },
        "cod": 200,
        "coord": {
            "lat": 51.51,
            "lon": -0.13
        },
        "dt": 1565357630,
        "id": 2643743,
        "main": {
            "humidity": 53,
            "pressure": 1001,
            "temp": 22.8,
            "temp_max": 26.11,
            "temp_min": 19.44
        },
        "name": "London",
        "sys": {
            "country": "GB",
            "id": 1414,
            "message": 0.0126,
            "sunrise": 1565325358,
            "sunset": 1565379376,
            "type": 1
        },
        "timezone": 3600,
        "visibility": 10000,
        "weather": [
            {
                "description": "shower rain",
                "icon": "09d",
                "id": 521,
                "main": "Rain"
            }
        ],
        "wind": {
            "deg": 210,
            "gust": 12.9,
            "speed": 7.7
        }
    }
}
```

Figure 8.80: Invoking the getWeather action

4. Now we can create the action to send emails (we will be using the API key generated with SendGrid). We will be using the **sendgrid** module for this function. First, we need to create a directory to store the function code and the dependencies:

```
$ mkdir send-email
$ cd send-email
```

The output should be as follows:

```
/serverless $ mkdir send-email
/serverless $ cd send-email
/serverless $
```

Figure 8.81: Creating the send-mail directory

5. Run the **npm init** command by accepting the default parameters:

```
$ npm init
```

The output should be as follows:

```
/serverless $ npm init
This utility will walk you through creating a package.json file.
It only covers the most common items, and tries to guess sensible defaults.

See `npm help json` for definitive documentation on these fields
and exactly what they do.

Use `npm install <pkg>` afterwards to install a package and
save it as a dependency in the package.json file.

Press ^C at any time to quit.
package name: (send-email)
version: (1.0.0)
description:
entry point: (index.js)
test command:
git repository:
keywords:
author:
license: (ISC)
About to write to /home/sathsara/packt/chapter-8-openwhisk/send-email/package.json:

{
  "name": "send-email",
  "version": "1.0.0",
  "description": "",
  "main": "index.js",
  "scripts": {
    "test": "echo \"Error: no test specified\" && exit 1"
  },
  "author": "",
  "license": "ISC"
}


Is this OK? (yes) yes
/serverless $
```

Figure 8.82: npm init

6. Install the **sendgrid npm** package, which is required for the function:

```
$ npm install sendgrid -save
```

The output should be as follows:

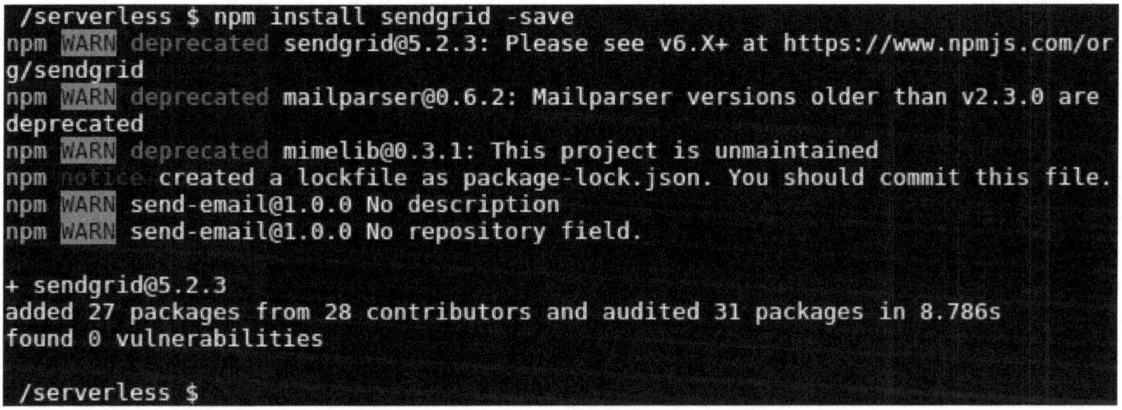

```
/serverless $ npm install sendgrid -save
npm WARN deprecated sendgrid@5.2.3: Please see v6.X+ at https://www.npmjs.com/or
g/sendgrid
npm WARN deprecated mailparser@0.6.2: Mailparser versions older than v2.3.0 are
deprecated
npm WARN deprecated mimelib@0.3.1: This project is unmaintained
npm notice created a lockfile as package-lock.json. You should commit this file.
npm WARN send-email@1.0.0 No description
npm WARN send-email@1.0.0 No repository field.

+ sendgrid@5.2.3
added 27 packages from 28 contributors and audited 31 packages in 8.786s
found 0 vulnerabilities

/serverless $
```

Figure 8.83: Adding the sendgrid dependency package

7. Create the **index.js** file with the function code provided in *step* 4. Replace **<SEND_GRID_API_KEY>** with the key, which was saved when creating the SendGrid account. Similarly, replace **<TO_EMAIL>** to receive weather data and **<FROM_EMAIL>** to send weather data with your email address.

8. Compress the code with all the dependencies:

```
$ zip -r send-email.zip *
```

9. Now we can create an action named **sendEmail** using **send-email.zip**:

```
$ wsk action create sendEmail send-email.zip --kind nodejs:default
```

The output should be as follows:

```
/serverless $ wsk action create sendEmail send-email.zip --kind nodejs:default
ok: created action sendEmail
/serverless $
```

Figure 8.84: Creating the sendEmail action

10. Verify that the **sendEmail** action is working as expected:

> **Note**
>
> Make sure to check your spam folder because the email client might have catego-
> rized this as a spam email.

```
$ wsk action invoke sendEmail --param message "Test Message" -result
```

The output should be as follows:

```
/serverless $ wsk action invoke sendEmail --param message "Test Message" --result
{
    "msg": "Message sent!"
}
/serverless $
```

Figure 8.85: Invoking the sendEmail action

11. Create the **format-weather-data.js** function with the function code provided in *step* 5.

12. Create the action named **formatWeatherData** with the **format-weather-data.js** function created in the preceding step:

```
$ wsk action create formatWeatherData format-weather-data.js
```

The output should be as follows:

```
/serverless $ wsk action create formatWeatherData format-weather-data.js
ok: created action formatWeatherData
/serverless $
```

Figure 8.86: Creating the formatWeatherData action

13. Create a sequence named **weatherMailSender** by combining the **getWeather**, **format-
WeatherData**, and **sendEmail** actions:

```
$ wsk action create weatherMailSender --sequence
getWeather,formatWeatherData,sendEmail
```

The output should be as follows:

```
/serverless $ wsk action create weatherMailSender --sequence getWeather,
formatWeatherData,sendEmail
ok: created action weatherMailSender
/serverless $
```

Figure 8.87: Creating the weatherMailSender action sequence

14. Invoke the **weatherMailSender** sequence:

    ```
    $ wsk action invoke weatherMailSender --result
    ```

    The output should be as follows:

    ```
    /serverless $ wsk action invoke weatherMailSender --result
    {
        "msg": "Message sent!"
    }
    /serverless $
    ```

    Figure 8.88: Invoking the weatherMailSender action sequence

15. Check the mail account that you added as **<TO_EMAIL>** (check the spam folder). Check the status of email delivery at https://app.sendgrid.com/email_activity.

    The output should be as follows:

    to me ▾

    It's 21.58 degrees celsius in London

    ◀ Reply   ➡ Forward

    Figure 8.89: Received email from the weatherMailSender action sequence

16. Finally, we need to create the trigger and rule to invoke the sequence every day at 8 AM. First, we will create **weatherMailSenderCronTrigger**, which will be triggered daily at 8.00 AM:

    ```
    $ wsk trigger create weatherMailSenderCronTrigger \
                         --feed /whisk.system/alarms/alarm \
                         --param cron "0 8 * * *"
    ok: invoked /whisk.system/alarms/alarm with id
    cf1af9989a7a46a29af9989a7ad6a28c
    {
        "activationId": "cf1af9989a7a46a29af9989a7ad6a28c",
        "annotations": [
            {
                "key": "path",
                "value": "whisk.system/alarms/alarm"
            },
            {
    ```

```
                "key": "waitTime",
                "value": 66
            },
            {
                "key": "kind",
                "value": "nodejs:10"
            },
            {
                "key": "timeout",
                "value": false
            },
            {
                "key": "limits",
                "value": {
                    "concurrency": 1,
                    "logs": 10,
                    "memory": 256,
                    "timeout": 60000
                }
            }
        ],
        "duration": 162,
        "end": 1565457634929,
        "logs": [],
        "name": "alarm",
        "namespace": "sathsara89@gmail.com_dev",
        "publish": false,
        "response": {
            "result": {
                "status": "success"
            },
            "status": "success",
            "success": true
        },
        "start": 1565457634767,
        "subject": "sathsara89@gmail.com",
        "version": "0.0.152"
    }
ok: created trigger weatherMailSenderCronTrigger
```

17. Then, we will create a rule named **weatherMailSenderCronRule** to connect the trigger (**weatherMailSenderCronTrigger**) and action (**weatherMailSender**):

    ```
    $ wsk rule create weatherMailSenderCronRule weatherMailSenderCronTrigger
    weatherMailSender
    ```

    The output should be as follows:

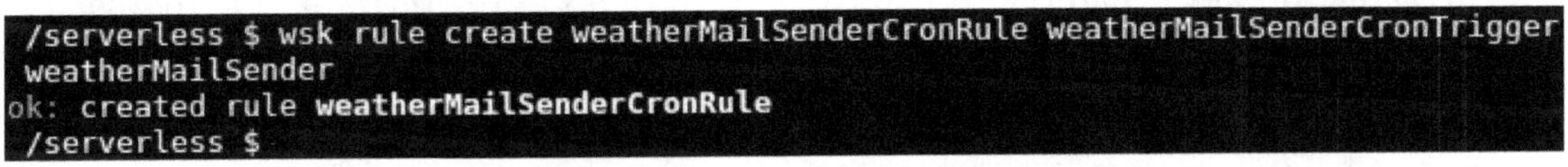

    ```
    /serverless $ wsk rule create weatherMailSenderCronRule weatherMailSenderCronTrigger
    weatherMailSender
    ok: created rule weatherMailSenderCronRule
    /serverless $
    ```

    Figure 8.90: Creating weatherMailSenderCronRule

Once the preceding steps are completed, you should receive an email daily at 8.00 AM to the specified email address with the weather data for the requested city.

Chapter 09: Going Serverless with OpenFaaS

Activity 9: OpenFaaS Form Processor

Solution

1. First, you need to create a SendGrid account and generate an API key. You can use the same API key created in the activity from *Chapter 08, Introduction to Apache OpenWhisk*. Refer to steps 4-7 in the activity of *Chapter 08, Introduction to Apache OpenWhisk* on how to create a SendGrid account and generate an API key.

2. Create an OpenFaaS function named contact-form using the python3 template. This will be the frontend of the contact form:

   ```
   $ faas-cli new contact-form --lang=python3
   ```

   The output should be as follows:

   ```
   /serverless $ faas-cli new contact-form --lang=python3
   Folder: contact-form created.




   Function created in folder: contact-form
   Stack file written: contact-form.yml
   /serverless $
   ```

   Figure 9.59: Creating the contact-form function

3. Create a new directory named html inside the contact-form directory to store the HTML files:

   ```
   $ mkdir contact-form/html
   ```

   The output should be as follows:

   ```
   /serverless $ mkdir contact-form/html
   /serverless $
   ```

   Figure 9.60: Creating the HTML folder

4. Create the contact-us.html file inside the contact-form/html folder with the code provided in step 2.

5. Update the **handler.py** Python file inside the contact-form folder. This Python function will read the content of the **contact-us.html** file and return it as the function response:

```python
import os

def handle(req):

    current_directory = os.path.dirname(__file__)
    html_file_path = os.path.join(current_directory, 'html', 'contact-us.
html')

    with(open(html_file_path, 'r')) as html_file:
        html = html_file.read()

    return html
```

6. Update the function definition (**contact-form.yml**) file to specify content_type as **text/html**, as explained in the following code:

```yaml
version: 1.0
provider:
  name: openfaas
  gateway: http://192.168.99.100:31112
functions:
  contact-form:
    lang: python3
    handler: ./contact-form
    image: sathsarasa/contact-form:latest
    environment:
      content_type: text/html
```

7. Build, push, and deploy the contact-form function:

```
$ faas-cli up -f contact-form.yml
```

The output of the command should be as follows:

```
[0] > Building contact-form.
Clearing temporary build folder: ./build/contact-form/
Preparing ./contact-form/ ./build/contact-form//function
Building: sathsarasa/contact-form:latest with python3 template. Please
wait..
Sending build context to Docker daemon  14.34kB

...
```

```
Successfully built 6c008c91f0bb
Successfully tagged sathsarasa/contact-form:latest
Image: sathsarasa/contact-form:latest built.
[0] < Building contact-form done.
[0] worker done.

[0] > Pushing contact-form [sathsarasa/contact-form:latest].
The push refers to repository [docker.io/sathsarasa/contact-form]
...
latest: digest:
sha256:b4f0a4f474af0755b53acb6a1c0ce26e0f91a9a893bb8bfc78501cab267d823e
size: 4282
[0] < Pushing contact-form [sathsarasa/contact-form:latest] done.
[0] worker done.

Deploying: contact-form.
WARNING! Communication is not secure, please consider using HTTPS.
Letsencrypt.org offers free SSL/TLS certificates.

Deployed. 202 Accepted.
URL: http://192.168.99.100:31112/function/contact-form
```

8. Create the second OpenFaaS function named form-processor using the python3 template. This will be the backend of the contact form:

```
$ faas-cli new form-processor --lang=python3
```

The output should be as follows:

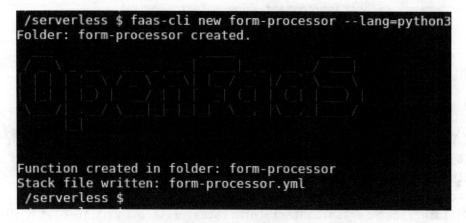

Figure 9.61: Creating the form-processor function

9. Update the **handler.py** Python file inside the form-processor folder. This Python function performs receives the email, name, and message parameters entered into the Contact Us form, formats the email body to be sent, sends the email using SendGrid, and returns the email sending status as the function response.

10. Replace <SEND_GRID_API_KEY> with the SendGrid API key saved in step 1, and <TO_EMAIL> with the email address to receive the Contact Us form data:

```python
import json
from sendgrid import SendGridAPIClient
from sendgrid.helpers.mail import Mail

def handle(req):

    SENDGRID_API_KEY = '<SEND_GRID_API_KEY>'
    TO_EMAIL = '<TO_EMAIL>'
    EMAIL_SUBJECT = 'New Message from OpenFaaS Contact Form'

    json_req = json.loads(req)
    email = json_req["email"]
    name = json_req["name"]
    message = json_req["message"]
    email_body = '<strong>Name: </strong>' + name + '<br><br>
<strong>Email: </strong>' + email + '<br><br> <strong>Message: </strong>'
+ message

    email_object = Mail(
        from_email= email,
        to_emails=TO_EMAIL,
        subject=EMAIL_SUBJECT,
        html_content=email_body)

    try:
        sg = SendGridAPIClient(SENDGRID_API_KEY)
        response = sg.send(email_object)
        sendingStatus = "Message sent successfully"
    except Exception as e:
        sendingStatus = "Message sending failed"

    return sendingStatus
```

11. Add the sendgrid module as a dependency in form-processor/requirements.txt of the form-processor function:

```
sendgrid
```

12. Increase the timeout (read_timeout, write_timeout, and exec_timeout) values in form-processor.yml, as shown in the following code:

```
version: 1.0
provider:
  name: openfaas
  gateway: http://192.168.99.100:31112
functions:
  form-processor:
    lang: python3
    handler: ./form-processor
    image: sathsarasa/form-processor:latest
    environment:
      read_timeout: 20
      write_timeout: 20
      exec_timeout: 20
```

13. Build, deploy, and push the form-processor function:

```
$ faas-cli up -f form-processor.yml
```

The output of the command should be as follows:

```
[0] > Building form-processor.
Clearing temporary build folder: ./build/form-processor/
Preparing ./form-processor/ ./build/form-processor//function
Building: sathsarasa/form-processor:latest with python3 template. Please
wait..
Sending build context to Docker daemon  10.24kB
...
Successfully built 128245656019
Successfully tagged sathsarasa/form-processor:latest
Image: sathsarasa/form-processor:latest built.
[0] < Building form-processor done.
[0] worker done.

[0] > Pushing form-processor [sathsarasa/form-processor:latest].
The push refers to repository [docker.io/sathsarasa/form-processor]
...
latest: digest:
```

```
sha256:c700592a3a7f16875c2895dbfa41bd269631780d9195290141c245bec93a2257
size: 4286
[0] < Pushing form-processor [sathsarasa/form-processor:latest] done.
[0] worker done.

Deploying: form-processor.
WARNING! Communication is not secure, please consider using HTTPS.
Letsencrypt.org offers free SSL/TLS certificates.

Deployed. 202 Accepted.
URL: http://192.168.99.100:31112/function/form-processor
```

14. Open the **Contact Us** form by opening the URL in a web browser:

    http://192.168.99.100:31112/function/contact-form

    The contact form should appear as follows:

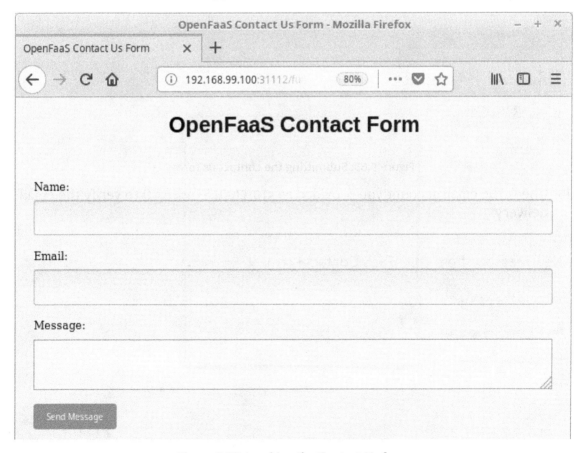

Figure 9.62: Invoking the Contact Us form

15. Fill in the form and then submit the form, as shown in the following figure:

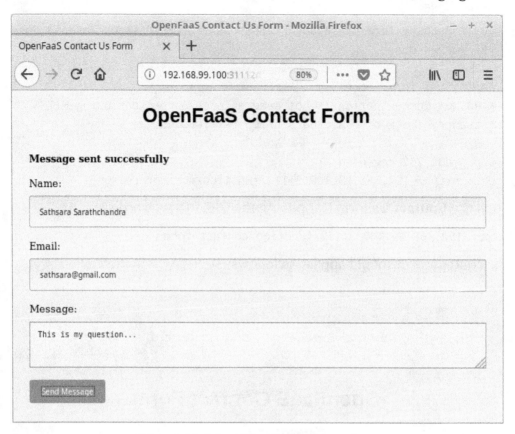

Figure 9.63: Submitting the contact us form

16. Check the email account you provided as `<TO_EMAIL>` in step 9 to verify the email delivery:

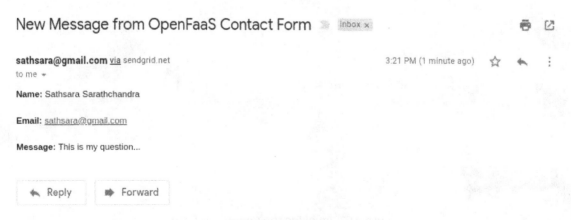

Figure 9.64: Verifying email delivery

Index

About

All major keywords used in this book are captured alphabetically in this section. Each one is accompanied by the page number of where they appear.

www.ingramcontent.com/pod-product-compliance
Lightning Source LLC
Chambersburg PA
CBHW060643060326
40690CB00020B/4503

9 781838 983277